The Political Logic of the US–China Trade War

The Political Logic of the US–China Trade War

Edited by Shiping Hua

LEXINGTON BOOKS
Lanham • Boulder • New York • London

Published by Lexington Books
An imprint of The Rowman & Littlefield Publishing Group, Inc.
4501 Forbes Boulevard, Suite 200, Lanham, Maryland 20706
www.rowman.com

86-90 Paul Street, London EC2A 4NE

British Library Cataloguing in Publication Information Available

Library of Congress Cataloging-in-Publication Data

Names: Hua, Shiping, 1956- editor.
Title: The political logic of the US-China trade war / edited by Shiping
   Hua.
Other titles: Political logic of the United States-China trade war
Description: Lanham, Maryland : Lexington Books, [2022] | Includes
   bibliographical references and index.
Identifiers: LCCN 2021051622 (print) | LCCN 2021051623 (ebook) | ISBN
   9781793624987 (Cloth) | ISBN 9781793625007 (Paper) |
   ISBN 9781793624994 (eBook)
Subjects: LCSH: United States—Commerce—China—History—21st century. |
   China—Commerce—United States—History—21st century. | United
   States—Politics and government—2017- | China—Politics and
   government—21st century.
Classification: LCC HF3128 .P65 2022 (print) | LCC HF3128 (ebook) | DDC
   382.0973051—dc23/eng/20211220
LC record available at https://lccn.loc.gov/2021051622
LC ebook record available at https://lccn.loc.gov/2021051623

Contents

v

Introduction

The Global Context and Personality Politics of the Trade War

Shiping Hua

This book attempts to serve as a forum to discuss the political logic of the US–China trade war that started in March 2018 and reached the first major agreement on January 15, 2020. It deals with the theories that may help explain the trade war, the global context from which the trade war has emerged, and the domestic factors that contributed to the trade war.

In scope, this project is not only narrow enough to have a focus (i.e., the trade war), but also broad enough to give meanings to the event. An alternative title would be *US–China Relations Amidst the Trade War*. Since this project is not interested in the details of the trade war, such as how many soybeans China has purchased from the United States, all the authors invited are political scientists, not economists.

I have been teaching US–China relations for more than two decades on American campuses. The textbooks that I used for this course have never become outdated as fast as they did in the last few years, since the events in the US–China relations have evolved so fast during the time period.

For instance, although Thomas Christenson's *The China Challenge: Shaping the Choice of a Rising Power* is a great book, I found myself constantly making modifications for the students when teaching the course. Lots of the remarks in the book that were considered by most scholars in the field as accurate a few years ago now need modifications.

The bilateral relationship was viewed as essentially constructive by most scholars as well as the two governments throughout the last four decades and a drastic change did not occur until Donald Trump became president of the United States.

I started to look for more updated teaching materials for this course, only to be disappointed. For instance, for the current US–China trade war, a topic that can't be avoided in teaching the course, the half dozen published books

1

were written by either journalists or economists. A book-length study that deals with the political logic of the trade war written by a political scientist or those who focus on the political logic of it does not exist.

The lack of academic research on the subject looks more acute considering that the Trump administration relied more on strategists than China specialists to guide the country's policy towards China. With the inauguration of President Joe Biden, changes in the US–China policy are expected.

THEORIES AND THE GLOBAL CONTEXT

The book is divided into three parts. The first part discusses some influential theories related to the current US–China relations and the global context in which the trade war has emerged. As a tool to explain history, the Thucydides Trap theory has received much attention among scholars and practitioners in the last few years. In *The History of the Peloponnesian War,* the Greek historian's metaphor describes a rising power rivaling a ruling power—as Athens challenged Sparta in ancient Greece. The rise of Athens caused fears in Sparta, the dominant power that subsequently started to arm itself for war. Sparta eventually won the war but at a tremendous cost.

For some, the United States is in the position of Sparta, while China resembles Athens. In modern history, the United States was successful in dealing with a global power that was in a comparable position: the United States successfully replaced the United Kingdom as the global superpower in the early twentieth century; together with the Allies, it defeated Nazi Germany during World War II; it defeated the former Soviet Union, the other superpower after World War II; it successfully undercut the growth of Japan since the 1980s to such an extent that most observers no longer view Japan as a challenging power of the United States now.

There might be a parallel between the current US–China trade war and the one in the 1980s between the United States and Japan. Many American leaders believed that the United States helped Japan to recover from the disasters of World War II, in an attempt to keep Japan from falling into the Soviet bloc. But many Japanese both in the elites and the public believed that it was the quality of the Japanese people that made the miracle after World War II happen (Hayes, 2009).

Following this logic, some leading scholars insisted that China's rise will challenge the global dominant position of the United States (Mearsheimer, 2014). Such line of logic is consistent with the American philosophical understanding of human nature. Human beings by nature have the tendency for domination (Magstadt, 2012).

In an attempt to explain China's more assertive foreign policy in recent years, some Chinese scholars tried to develop their own international relations theories. To discredit the Western concept of "nation-state," they have coined the term *"ren lei ingy un gong tong ti,"* or the common welfare of mankind that shares a common dynasty.

The Chinese IR theory has been used to explain such initiatives of the "one belt one road" to the effect that while many Western strategists view it as China's attempt for global competition with the United States, the Chinese scholars tried to describe the initiative as for the benefits of those countries involved, not necessarily for the national interest of China.

However, the premodern Chinese military thinker Sun Tzu would disagree with this theory. Sun believed that domestic politics may rely on law and morality; foreign policy, however, is for opportunism (Sun, 1971). On human nature, the Chinese philosopher Sun Tzu's belief is not that different from Machiavelli. Much of the court politics embodied in the ancient Chinese classic *The Twenty-Four Histories* (Sima, 2011) is similar to that in *The Prince* (Machiavelli, 2015). In line with this argument, some western observers regard the present-day China as an empire, just like the United States (Kaplan, 2019).

Hopefully China and the United States won't fall into the Thucydides Trap, not because of good will on either side, but because of nuclear weapons and the globalization process in which the interests of the two countries are so interconnected that a zero-sum game is something of the past.

The trade war emerged against the background that the international environment has changed drastically in the last four decades. Such countries like Taiwan and South Korea started their democratization process shortly after they reached a higher level of industrialization in the late 1980s (Huntington, 1993). The United States was looked upon as a "shining city upon a hill" as described by Ronald Reagan in January 1989.

There comes the belief that there is a strong connection between economic development and democratization, because industrialization produces a large middle class that demands not only economic prosperity, but also democracy. Following this logic, the US governments in the last four decades tried to help China to get modernized (Christenson, 2015).

But recent developments did not seem to follow this logic. In spite of rapid economic development in recent decades, democratization did not occur in China. Instead, Xi's regime pushed back the pluralization started by Deng Xiaoping (1904–1997) and continued under the Jiang Zemin and Hu Jintao regimes (Zhao, 2016).

The recent Chinese authoritarian tendency is consistent with the fact that for more than a decade, democratization globally has been in decline

(Freedom House, 2019). In 2019, about one third of the world's population live in countries that are undergoing autocratization.[1]

"China, Russia and Vietnam have revived and prolonged authoritarianism precisely by adapting capitalism to their own designs. Turkey and Egypt have created new forms of sultanism. . . . And in east-central Europe, Hungary and Poland—once bright spots of the 1989 revolutions—are once again embracing one-party rule in all but name. Germany, once the standard-bearer for Eastern Europe, now also finds itself bedeviled by right-wing populism" (Asian Survey Editor, 2018).

This situation may be connected with the two major events that greatly weakened Western democracies in general and the United States in particular. The September 11, 2011, terrorist attack on the Twin Towers in New York City compelled the United States to divert considerable resources to fight the terrorism, spending as much as $5.9 trillion during the process (DePatris, 2019). The 2008 economic crisis further weakened the United States's global dominant position, costing as much as $22 trillion (Melendez, 2013). The U.S. annual GDP is only about $20 trillion. Michael Fowler in this book has more detailed discussions on the evolvement of the international order after World War II.

The authors in the volume not only tried to look at the trade war from the theoretical and global perspectives, but also the empirical and historical angles.

To begin with, the uniqueness of Xi and his counterpart Trump certainly had an impact on the historical events unleased under their leadership. This chapter briefly outlines the personal backgrounds of the two leaders in the following.

But the inner workings of individual leaders are hard to know empirically. Therefore, most of the authors in this volume have chosen to analyze the empirical evidence and historical events that have occurred amidst the trade war. That is to say, instead of viewing the two leaders as history makers, they are viewed largely as reflections of historical events that are beyond individual leaders' control. For the authors, history has chosen Tramp and Xi, not the other way around.

Sure enough, the problems related to the trade war had existed long before Trump or Xi came to power. For instance, in 2002, Chinese ownership of American treasury securities was worth slightly more than $100 billion. By 2010 China owned over $1 trillion's worth (Morrison, 2011). In the realm of trademark violations, China accounted for around 70 percent of global counterfeit items between 2008 and 2010 (Brander et al., 2017) before Xi came to power in 2012.

XI JINPING AND THE TRADE WAR

The second part of the book discusses the domestic politics of China related to the trade war including Xi's personal role in shaping the political process. Xi distinguishes himself from his two predecessors of Jiang Zemin (1926–) and Hu Jintao (1942–) in terms of the backgrounds in family, profession, education, and geographical origins. Xi belongs to the group of Chinese leaders that were called "princelings," in that his father Xi Zhongxun (1912–2002) was a veteran revolutionary who eventually became a vice premier. Jiang and Hu on the other hand came from common-folk families. Obviously, Xi is more likely to link his own career to the early days of the Communist Revolution.

Under the Xi regime, the party organized the government officials to visit places like Jing Gang Shan in Jiangxi Province and Yan'an in Shaanxi Province, the bases of the communist forces in the 1920s and during World War II. The Xi regime wants the cadres *"bu wang chu hong"* (not to forget about the origins of the Communist Revolution) (i.e., the Chinese Communist Pary [CCP] is a party of the common folks such as poor peasants, not a party of the elites). At Jing Gang Shan, these cadres often wear the uniforms of the Red Army, use the name of the communist forces in the early times, and take short courses there as well. In the eyes of those "princelings," Jiang Zemin and Hu Jintao were "temporary managers" of the country, not committed to the ideologies of the CCP, while Xi is the real inheritor of the communist cause.

The likelihood of those "princelings" to stick to the communist cause was also reflected in the case of Xi's arch enemy Bo Xilai (1949–), whose father was Bo Yibo (1908–2007), another revolutionary veteran. Bo Xilai adopted similar policies as that by Xi Jinping in the mega city of Chongqing when he was the party secretary. Bo's *"Chang hong, da hei"* or chanting the revolutionary songs and punishing the organized crime, looked like a nostalgia for the Mao era (Anderlini, 2012).

In terms of education background, Xi's PhD is in Marxist theory, while that of Jiang Zemin and Hu Jintao were in engineering. This is not accidental: In the late 1980s, half of China's cabinet ministers were engineers who were viewed as less interested in ideologies (Lee, 1990). Xi got his PhD in the School of Marxism of Tsinghua University. The public have no access to the contents of his dissertation. Although these kinds of on-the-job postgraduate degrees were criticized by scholars as not academically rigorous, Xi looks more committed to ideology than his predecessors.

Xi's growth path was also different from the Hu generation. When the Cultural Revolution broke out in 1966, Xi was thirteen, just ready to understand this world. His father Xi Zhongxun was in jail for political reasons for many years. Xi Jinping was then sent down to Northern Shaanxi, a poor area, " to be re-educated by the peasants." He had seen the brutality of real-world politics in China. With this background, some Western observers called him a modern "Machiavellian" (Hilhorst & Zonneveld, 2018).

In contrast, his predecessor Hu Jintao's world outlook was shaped in the 1950s when the party enjoyed higher prestige and the Chinese youths were taught to be "obedient tools" of the party, not rebels as was the case during the Cultural Revolution. The Hu regime was known to advocate the notion of the so-called Harmonious Society.

The geographic location where the leaders were born probably also played a role in shaping their political views. Many first-generation leaders such as Mao Zedong (1893–1976), Liu Shaoqi (1898–1969), Li Biao (1907–1971) and Peng Dehuai (1898–1974) come from Hunan, Sichuan, and Hubei, the places that used to be within the territory of Chu during the Spring Autumn Period (771 to 476 BC). At that time, many in Central China (i.e., present-day Shandong, Shanxi, Shaanxi, Hebei, and Henan) considered those in Chu less civilized. In modern times, many people from the Chu area flourished when there was social turmoil, such as civil wars or the Cultural Revolution.

China's situation during the post-Mao era was different. In the 1990s, with the collapse of the Soviet bloc, the most urgent item on the CCP agenda was to develop the country's economy, not to advocate communist ideology. So many top leaders came from the well-developed coastal areas of Zhejiang Province and Jiangsu Province, especially Shanghai, the most modern city in China. Two hundred years ago, Shanghai was a small village. So those pro-Western gestures of Jiang Zemin, such as the remembering of the Gettysburg Address and singing American songs, were probably not just for show, but a sincere admiration of Western life style. Jiang is from Jiangsu and worked in Shanghai for many years.

The current situation of China is different from that under Jiang and Hu. As will be discussed later, the new situation calls for a new type of leader. For instance, the largest number of members of the Central Party Committee of the 19th National Party Congress in 2018 are from Shandong Province, with thirty, and Hebei Province, with twenty-five.[2] The people in Central China (*hong yuan*) (i.e., Shandong, Hebei, Henan, Shanxi, and Shaanxi) are supposed to better represent the mainstream Chinese political culture, Confucianism. Confucius was born in Shandong.

Xi is from Shaanxi with the provincial capital of Xi'an, the capital site of more dynasties in premodern China than any other cities. In contrast to Shanghai, which symbolizes modernity, people in Shaanxi are supposed to be more conservative. Shaanxi writer Chen Zhongshi's nationally acclaimed novel *Bai Lu Yuan (White Deer Plain)* is an epoch that describes the sophistication of traditional Chinese politics in a small village (Zhongshi, 2008).

Historically, China always gives people less freedom, compared with Russia and Japan (Hua, 2019). This tradition can be traced to Qin (221–207 BCE). The agreement between the ruler and the people was that the people gave up part of their freedom, and in return, the ruler provided them with security and a decent living. This tradition has continued to this day.

This looks worrisome to many people in the West. The worship of the state and autocracy at the expense of the individual freedom are shared by the Chinese tradition and fascist ideology. A parliamentary member from Australia called China "fascist" and he was denied visa to China for saying that.[3]

Three decades of rapid developments have produced lots of wealth for China. But at the same time, government corruption and the income gap between the rich and poor had also reached to a dangerously high level. Stability could no longer be achieved by high growth alone. Social justice has become more and more important. In 2012 when Xi came to power, Western observers believed that China was on the verge of a revolution (Platt, 2012).

In the popular TV series *"Renmin de mingy,"* or *"In the Name of the People,"* released in 2017 using the word of a character in the TV program, "In the past, the people did not believe that the government would do bad things; now the people do not believe that the government would do good things" (Zeng, 2017).

Xi's anticorruption campaign relied on the party police, the Central Disciplinary Commission, not the legal system that is underdeveloped. This was conveniently borrowed from the legal system of Qin (221–207 BCE), which could better be described by the term "rule by law," not "rule of law" (Hua, 2019). Incidentally, much of Qin's territory is in today's Shaanxi Province, the hometown of Xi.

For the Chinese leaders, the Western rule of law was unable to solve China's income gap problem: "Rule of law" can't even solve the income gap problem of the United States, how can China rely on it to resolve its own problem of the unequal distribution of wealth that is dangerously high? China's income gap is larger than that of the United States. This is an irony for a country that claims to be communist.

At the 19th National People's Congress in early 2018, the constitution amendment emphasizes the role of personality, ideology, and centralization of power (Lardy, 2019; Chen, 2016). Lots of policies under Xi resembled those before the start of the 1978 reform.

Accordingly, Fudan University recently changed its charter: It removed the clause of "endorsement of free ideas." It also added the clause that the university serves the purpose of the CCP. In addition, the university president reports to the party committee of the university. Other leading universities took similar steps. This may reflect the worry by the party that the Chinese intelligentsia had been exposed too much to Western ideas in the last four decades and the situation needs to be corrected. The control of society under Xi is so thorough that even the appearance of stores has to look the same (Jiangsusheng, 2019).

China's foreign policy has become a lot more assertive in recent years. This is consistent with the rapid growth of the Chinese economy (e.g., in 1978 when China started to open up to the outside world, the country's GDP was 4 percent of that of the United States; now, it is about 65 percent). In addition, China no longer depends on foreign trade for its economic growth as it used to. In 2008, about 70 percent of China's GDP was generated through foreign trade. Now it is 38 percent.

For some, China is not only trying to be independent from the liberal international order ideologically and politically, but also economically. Recently, China has stopped using the international academic standard of "SCI" to judge the Chinese scientists' achievements (Qing, 2019). It also banned the sale of the Bible online (Johnson, 2018). There is even the request recently to eliminate the test of English for middle school students—a practice that has been in place since the 1980s. Some influential China watchers started to believe that China under Xi wants to export its model (Economy, 2019).

Xi's assertive foreign policy is in sharp contrast to that prior to his administration. For instance, from 1978 through 1997 China as a permanent member of the UN Security Council used veto power only once; the United States used it sixty times. All other permanent members used it more than ten times during the time period. With China's rapid growth in the last three decades, it is inconceivable that China under Xi would continue the low-profile foreign policy posture of the past.

Is Xi a Maoist? While it is true lots of Xi's policies look similar to those in the prereform era, the answer is unclear, because there was much counter evidence. Xi's policies in the first year or two looked oriented towards law and market. That's why the West showed some initial enthusiasm towards him (Hua, 2013). His father, Xi Zhongxun, though a veteran revolutionary, was believed to be one of the reformers, not those left-wing ideologues like Hu Qiaomu (1912–1992) or Deng Liqun (1915–2015) (Fan, 2012). Xi's regime cracked down on dissent not only from the right, but also that from the left (Dui Hua Foundation, 2020).

An interpretation is that Xi's policies were pragmatic in nature (Weiss, 2019). The CCP is known to have this kind of pragmatic attitude. In 1946 when the CCP participated in drafting a new constitution, working with the KMT and other smaller parties, the CCP advocated a constitution similar to that of the United States instead of that of the former Soviet Union. This is because a constitution similar to the US one would give the smaller party of CCP more power, while the Soviet type of constitution would give more power to the then dominant KMT (Hua, 2019).

The policy adjustments under Xi may be viewed as part of the pendulum effect of the country's policy making that is described as "*fang* (loosening control)" and "*shou* (tightening control)." Either policy orientation produces undesirable results: "*yi fang jiu luan* (the loosening of control will produce chaos)"; "*yi shou jiu si* (tightening control will suffocate society)". The Jiang and Hu regimes were more in the direction of "*fang*," the Xi regime moved in the direction of "*shou*."

"I think a lot of Chinese policy is driven by fear," Klaus Mühlhahn, a professor of Chinese history at the Free University of Berlin. "This fear of losing power, of a development similar to what happened in the Soviet Union, shapes much of the policy and thinking" (Fifield, 2019).

The policy orientation under Xi contributed to the worsening of US–China relations. As a demonstration, in the recent congressional legislation in support of the Hong Kong demonstrations, all but one Congress member voted in favor of the legislation. The consensus among the American leadership against China is unprecedented in US history.

In the past, the tradition of the China field in the United States was typified by John King Fairbank in that they viewed the Chinese Communist Revolution more positively (Fairbank, 1983). This time, however, even the well-known letter to advise the US government not to treat China as an enemy signed by over a hundred China specialists made it clear that they disagreed with what the Xi regime had done in the last few years (Qing et al., 2019).

In 2018, for the first time in five years, the number of wealthy Chinese had decreased. More and more rich people escaped abroad (Hess, 2016). In a speech delivered at Central Party School in 2019, Xi used the term "struggle" 58 times—a sense of crisis (Nakazawa, 2019). Chinese economy has experienced downward growth for the last seven years since Xi came to power.

In spite of the worsening situation, the regime still enjoys the tolerance of people from a wide spectrum of social sectors (Yan, 2018). For instance, Chinese citizens seem to be more tolerant to digital social engineering than many would expect (Wang, 2019). During the Tiananmen Massacre three decades ago, most of the Chinese students studying in the United States went to the street protesting against the communist regime. This year, few Chinese students studying in the United States went public to support the Hong Kong demonstrators. In spite of the tightening of social control in recent years, with the exception of some super rich, most Chinese don't want to leave the country. In 2018, over 130 million Chinese traveled overseas, and most came back (Wang, 2018).

DONALD TRUMP AND THE TRADE WAR

Trump is the only American president who is a businessman by background, whereas the majority of US national leaders are lawyers. In addition, he is heavily involved in the entertainment business such as boxing and pageant, the areas where most American political leaders try to avoid. Not surprisingly, he focused on the economic dimension of US–China relations, often at the expense of the US global commitment for democracy. He is the only American president that did not raise the issue of human rights when visiting China.

Trump came to power when America is faced with considerable challenges abroad and domestically. In a well-known article in 1989, "The End of History," Francis Fukuyama optimistically announced that liberal democracy is a perfect political system that can't be improved (Fukuyama, 1989). Three decades later, he was no longer that optimistic (Fukuyama, 2017).

The US international status was weakened considerably as a result of the war against terror and the 2008 economic crisis (Tooze, 2018). Domestically, America is in trouble, marked by inefficient bureaucracy, the deadlock in the government caused by fierce competition between the two parties.

The larger picture is globalization. In general, globalization is profitable to those countries involved, including the United States. The current U.S. GDP per capita, with over $60,000 USD, is the highest among major industrialized countries. The few countries that have higher GDP per capita are all small ones whose wealth comes from accidental sources such as gambling with Macau, oil with Qatar, or geographic location such as Singapore.

However, not every American benefited equally from the globalization process. Those who have benefited the most are people along the two coasts, the better educated, those connected with Wall Street and Silicon Valley (Craig, 2019–2020). This has contributed to the already large income gap between the rich and poor.

As a country of immigrants, a socialist agenda is not acceptable to many Americans because the foundation of the United States is based on freedom, not equality (de Tocqueville, 2000). It also does not seem to serve the long-term national prosperity of the United States. Based on the classical liberalism theory, capitalism is not only free but also rich. The logic is that to increase tax for the rich will decrease productivity, because the rich can invest, while the poor can only consume (Friedman, 1979). Although a socialist option may be useful in easing social tension in the short run, it may not be able to keep the high growth of the United States in the long term.

Obviously, in addressing the problems that America is faced with, Trump is not particularly targeted against China. His policies are based on a combination of conservativism and populism that include those measures on the border with Mexico, the correction of Obama's welfare program, and the pressure on the allies of the United States in western Europe, Japan, and South Korea to contribute more to defense.

But the China issue is probably the most important in Trump's foreign policy. Many believe that the United States has helped China in its modernization drive for decades. The decisive event is that the United States allowed China to enter WTO in 2001. China's economy had grown more rapidly than before. However, China's compliancy to WTO regulations was always in dispute (Lu & Yu, 2015).

To confront China as a national policy was endorsed by American leaders overwhelmingly. In fact, this is probably the only important issue that was supported by almost all members of Congress.

In terms of leadership style, Trump is perhaps one of the few US presidents who treat diplomacy personally. Although he has probably hurt China badly since coming to office, he claims to love China. To demonstrate his sincere love for China, he brought his own granddaughter along to play the game by singing in Chinese (Denyer, 2017). He claims to be a good friend of Xi. As a demonstration, he has never said anything negative about Xi in public.

He is supposed to like Sun Tzu, the premodern Chinese military strategist. His way of waging this trade war resembles lots of principles in Sun Tzu (Cunningham, 2017). He wrote in his Twitter on July 17th, 2012, on Sun Tzu: "The Supreme Art of war is to subdue the enemy without fighting."[4] Using the strategy of this "indirectness," he blamed his predecessors more than China for the trade problems.

Trump does not seem to care about how other people feel about him. This is consistent with Sun Tzu, who believes that the supreme commander should not have too much pride. Nothing is more important than to win the war, and the commander should do anything to ensure that even at the expense of his own dignity. Trump may very well draw some inspiration from the ancient Chinese classic.

After almost two years, the phase one treaty of the trade war has been signed. Who is the winner? The Chinese government claimed both are winners. The Trump administration believed that the United States is the winner, pointing at those things like that the stocks are at an all-time high and the unemployment rate is very low, while China's growth has been in decline in seven years since Xi came to power. The authors of this volume will answer these and other important questions related to the trade war.

NOTES

1. https://www.v-dem.net/en/news/democracy-facing-global-challenges-v-dem-annual-democracy-report-2019/
2. http://news.ifeng.com/mainland/special/sbjszqh/zywyjg.shtml
3. https://www.dw.com/en/australian-lawmaker-likens-china-threat-to-nazi-germany/a-49939059
4. July 17, 2012. https://twitter.com/realdonaldtrump/status/225244643837751296

REFERENCES

Anderlini, J. (2012). "Bo Xilai: Power, Death and Politics," *Financial Times,* July 20, 2012. Available at: https://www.ft.com/content/d67b90f0-d140-11e1-8957-00144feabdc0 (accessed January 13, 2021).

Asian Survey Editor (January/February 2018). "Asia in 2017: Return of the Strongman," *Asian Survey* 58(1).

"Australian Lawmaker Likens China Threat to Nazi Germany" (August 8, 2019). *Deutsche Welle.* Available at: https://www.dw.com/en/australian-lawmaker-likens-china-threat-to-nazi-germany/a-49939059 (accessed January 13, 2021).

Brander, J. A., Cui, V., & Vertinsky, I. (2017). "China and Intellectual Property Rights: A Challenge to the Rule of Law," *Journal of International Business Studies* 48(7): 908–921.

Chen, C. (2016). *The Return of Ideology: The Search for Regime Identities in Post-communist Russia and China.* Ann Abor: University of Michigan Press.

"Clip of President Jiang Interview" (September 4, 2000). *C-Span.* Available at: https://www.c-span.org/video/?c4813522/user-clip-jiang-zemin-gettysburg-address (accessed January 13, 2021).

Christenson, T. (2015). *The China Challenge: Shaping the Choice of a Rising Power.* Oxford, UK: Oxford University Press.

Craig, D. J. (Winter 2019–2020). "Why the US–China Trade War Is Unwise and Unwinnable," *Columbia Magazine.* Available at: https://magazine.columbia.edu/article/why-us-china-trade-war-unwise-and-unwinnable (accessed January 18, 2021).

Cunningham, J. (March 1, 2017). "Sun Tzu and the Trump Doctrine," *Thunderbird School of Global Management: Knowledge Network.* Available at: https://thunderbird.asu.edu/knowledge-network/suntzu-trump-doctrine (accessed January 18, 2021).

Denyer, S. (November 9, 2017). "Trump's Granddaughter Gets Praise and Sympathy for Singing for Chinese President," *Washington Post.* Available at: https://www.washingtonpost.com/news/worldviews/wp/2017/11/09/trumps-granddaughter-gets-praise-and-sympathy-for-singing-for-chinese-president/ (accessed January 18, 2021).

DePetris, D. (January 12, 2019). "The War on Terror's Total Cost: $5,900,000,000,000," *The National Interest.* Available at: https://nationalinterest.org/blog/skeptics/war-terrors-total-cost-5900000000000-41307 (accessed January 11, 2021).

Dittmer, L. (2018). "Asia in 2017: Return of the Strongman," *Asian Survey* (58)1.

Dui Hua Foundation (2020). "Leftist Dissent under Xi: The Young Leftists Part I, Who Are the Young Leftists?" *Human Rights Journal*. Available at: https://www.duihuahrjournal.org/2020/01/leftist-dissent-under-xi-young-leftists.html (accessed January 27, 2021).

Economy, E. C. (December 11, 2019). "Yes, Virginia, China Is Exporting Its Model," *Council on Foreign Relations*. Available at: https://www.cfr.org/blog/yes-virginia-china-exporting-its-model (accessed January 14, 2021).

Fairbank, J. (1983). *The United States and China*. Cambridge, MA: Harvard University Press.

Fan, J. (February 23, 2012). "Dreams from Xi Jinping's Father," *New Yorker*. Available at: https://www.newyorker.com/news/news-desk/dreams-from-xi-jinpings-father (accessed January 14, 2021).

Fifield, A. (September 29, 2019). "China's Communist Party Has One More Reason to Celebrate — A Year Longer in Power than the U.S.S.R," *Washington Post*. Available at: https://www.washingtonpost.com/world/asia_pacific/chinas-communist-party-has-one-more-reason-to-celebrate--a-year-longer-in-power-than-the-soviet-union/2019/09/28/993bb832-dfc0-11e9-be7f-4cc85017c36f_story.html (accessed January 14, 2021).

Freedom House (2019). Democracy in Retreat. Available at: https://freedomhouse.org/report/freedom-world/freedom-world-2019/democracy-in-retreat (accessed January 11, 2021).

Friedman, M. (1979). *Free to Choose*. New York: Harcourt Brace and Company.

Fukuyama, F. (1989). "The End of History?" *The National Interest* (16): 3–18.

Fukuyama, F. (2014). *Political Order and Political Decay: From the Industrial Revolution to the Globalization of Democracy*. New York: Farrar, Straus and Giroux.

Fukuyama, F. (December 13, 2016). "America: The Failed State," *Prospect*. Available at: https://www.prospectmagazine.co.uk/magazine/america-the-failed-state-donald-trump (accessed January 14, 2021).

Hayes, L. (2009). *Introduction to Japanese Politics*. Armonk, NY: M.E. Sharpe.

Hess, S. (July/August 2016). "The Flight of the Affluent in Contemporary China Exit, Voice, Loyalty, and the Problem of Wealth Drain," *Asian Survey* (56) 4: 629–650.

Hilhorst, P., & Zonneveld, M. (March 19, 2018). "Machiavelli: Xi Jinping Is the New World Prince," *The Great Dead Thinkers*. Available at: https://medium.com/thegreatdeadthinkers/machiavelli-xi-jinping-is-the-new-world-prince-bb90ba4b0ee (accessed January 13, 2021).

"H.R.3289—Hong Kong Human Rights and Democracy Act of 2019" (2019). Available at: https://www.congress.gov/bill/116th-congress/house-bill/3289 (accessed January 18, 2021).

Hua, S. (May 2013). "Xi Jinping Will Emphasize Rule of Law/Rule by Law," *People's Tribune* (402): 34–35.

Hua, S. (2019). *Chinese Legal Culture and Constitutional Order*. London: Routledge.

Huntington, S. (1993). *Third Wave: Democratization in the Late 20th Century*. Norman: University of Oklahoma Press.

Jiangsusheng pinpaixuehui (December 12, 2019) 被统一的中国店面招牌，丑得整整齐齐https://mp.weixin.qq.com/s/0GjzXRtAKNTDjUCEdcsDIA.

Johnson, I. (April 5, 2018). "China Bans Online Bible Sales as It Tightens Religious Controls," *New York Times*. Available at: https://www.nytimes.com/2018/04/05/world/asia/china-bans-bible-sales.html (accessed January 14, 2021).

Kaplan, R. (June 17, 2019). "America Must Prepare for the Coming Chinese Empire," *The National Interest*. Available at: https://nationalinterest.org/feature/america -must-prepare-coming-chinese-empire-63102 (accessed January 11, 2021).

Lardy, N. R., ed. (2019). *The State Strikes Back: The End of Economic Reform in China.* Washington, DC: Peterson Institute for International Economics.

Lee, H. Y. (1990). From Revolutionary Cadres to Technocrats in Socialist China. (Berkley: University of California Press).

"List of Countries by GDP (nominal) Per Capita" (2021). Wikipedia. Available at: https://en.wikipedia.org/wiki/List_of_countries_by_GDP_(nominal)_per_capita (accessed January 14, 2021).

Lu, Y., & Yu, L. (2015). "Trade Liberalization and Markup Dispersion: Evidence from China's WTO Accession," *American Economic Journal: Applied Economics* 7(4): 221–253. Retrieved from www.jstor.org/stable/24739065 (accessed January 18, 2021).

Machiavelli, N. (2015). *The Prince.* CreateSpace Independent Publishing Platform.

Magstadt, T. (2012). *Understanding Politics: Ideas, Institutions, Issues.* Belmont, CA: Wadsworth Publishing.

Maqian, S., et al. (2011). *Dian xiao Ben ershisi shi (Annotated 24 Histories).* Beijing: Zhonghua shuju.

Mearsheimer, J. (October 25, 2014). "Can China Rise Peacefully?" *The National Interest*. Available at: https://nationalinterest.org/commentary/can-china-rise-peace fully-10204 (accessed January 11, 2021).

Melendez, E. (February 14, 2013). "Financial Crisis Cost Tops $22 Trillion, GAO Says," *Huffington Post*. Available at: https://www.huffpost.com/entry/financial -crisis-cost-gao_n_2687553 (accessed January 11, 2021).

Morrison, W. M. (2011). *China–U.S. Trade Issues.* Washington, DC: Congressional Research Service.

Nakazawa, K. (September 12, 2019). "With Whiffs of Cultural Revolution, Xi Calls for Struggle 50 Times," *Nikkie Asia*. Available at: https://asia.nikkei.com/Editor-s -Picks/China-up-close/With-whiffs-of-Cultural-Revolution-Xi-calls-for-struggle -50-times (accessed January 14, 2021).

Palumbo D., & Nicolaci da Costa, A. (May 10, 2019). "Trade War: US–China Trade Battle in Charts," *BBC News*. Available at: https://www.bbc.com/news/business -48196495 (accessed January 11, 2021).

Platt, S. R. (February 9, 2012). "Is China Ripe for a Revolution?" *New York Times*. Available at: https://www.nytimes.com/2012/02/12/opinion/sunday/is-china-ripe -for-a-revolution.html? (accessed January 13, 2021).

Qing Ta (November 29, 2019). 国家科技奖重磅改革：取消SCI他引次数，取消期刊影响因子，鼓励国内期刊论文为代表作！ *Keji Ribao*. https://mp.weixin .qq.com/s/DVUoTwmwdtmUigZr8lFMjA (accessed January 27, 2021).

Qing, Ying, et al. (2019). "Update: 'China is Not an Enemy,' Says Open Letter Signed by American China Experts," *Caixin Globa.* Available at: https://www .caixinglobal.com/2019-07-04/china-is-not-an-enemy-says-open-letter-signed-by -american-china-experts-101435672.html (accessed January 2021).

"The Rich Escape: More and More People Are Preparing to Move Family and Capital" (August 20, 2019). *Lesperance Associates.* Available at: https://lesperance associates.com/2019/08/the-rich-escape-more-and-more-people-are-preparing-to -move-family-and-capital/ (accessed January 14, 2021).

Sun Tzu (1971). *The Art of War.* Cambridge, UK: Oxford University Press.

Tharor, I. (November 8, 2019). "The Berlin Wall's Chinese Shadow," *Washington Post.* Available at: https://www.washingtonpost.com/world/2019/11/08/berlin -walls-chinese-shadow/ (accessed January 11, 2021).

de Tocqueville, A. (2000). *Democracy in America.* New York: Bantam Classics.

Tooze, A. (2018). *Crashed: How a Decade of Financial Crises Changed the World.* New York: Viking.

"Trade (% of GDP)" (2019). World Bank National Accounts Data. Available at: https://data.worldbank.org/indicator/NE.TRD.GNFS.ZS (accessed January 14, 2021).

"US Senate Unanimously Passes Hong Kong Rights Bill, Sending Legislation to House" (November 19, 2019). CNBC. Available at: https://www.cnbc .com/2019/11/20/us-senate-passes-hong-kong-rights-bill-sending-legislation-to -house.html (accessed January 14, 2021).

V-Dem. (2019). "Democracy Facing Global Challenges" — V-Dem Annual Democracy Report. Available at: https://www.v-dem.net/en/news/democracy-facing -global-challenges-v-dem-annual-democracy-report-2019/ (accessed January 11, 2021).

Wang, Hailin (March 5, 2018). "A record high of 13 million Chinese tourists travel abroad in 2017: Report," *People's Daily.* Available at: http://en.people.cn/ n3/2018/0305/c90000-9433076.html (accessed January 2021).

Wang, X. (December 19, 2019). "Hundreds of Chinese citizens feel just fine about the controversial social credit system," *The World.* Available at: https://www.pri .org/stories/2019-12-19/hundreds-chinese-citizens-feel-just-fine-about-controver sial-social-credit-system (accessed January 14, 2021).

Weiss, J. C. (June 11, 2019). "A World Safe for Autocracy? China's Rise and the Future of Global Politics," *Foreign Affairs.*

Xu, Zi, & Hutton, E. (trans.) (2012). *Xun Zi: The Complete Text.* Princeton, NJ: Princeton University Press.

Yan, A. (August 22, 2018). "Chinese tourist numbers surge as overseas travel becomes easier," *South China Morning Post.* Available at: https://www.scmp .com/news/china/society/article/2160906/chinese-tourist-numbers-surge-overseas -travel-becomes-easier (accessed January 14, 2021).

Ying, Q., Qiuyu, R., & Wei, H. (2019). "Update: 'China is Not an Enemy,' Says Open Letter Signed by American China Experts." Available at: https://www .caixinglobal.com/2019-07-04/china-is-not-an-enemy-says-open-letter-signed-by -american-china-experts-101435672.html (accessed January 14, 2021).

Shiping Hua

Zeng, Y. (May 4, 2017). "In the Name of the People: China's new political thriller is no House of Cards," ABC News. Available at: https://www.abc.net.au/news/2017 -05-05/chinas-new-political-drama-is-no-house-of-cards/8499648 (accessed January 13, 2021).

Zhao, S. (2016). "Xi Jinping's Maoist Revival," *Journal of Democracy* (accessed January 13, 2021).

Zhongshi, C. (2008). *Bai Lu Yuan*. Beijing: October Literature & Art Publishing House.

Part I

THEORIES AND
THE GLOBAL CONTEXT

Chapter One

The Logic of Power Politics

The Thucydides Trap and the US–China Trade War

Gregory J. Moore

What is the rationale for the US trade war against China? Is it A, power politics, which is to say the United States is simply trying to keep China down because of China's rising power, with Washington using the trade war to slow China's growth and thereby weaken China in the game of great power competition? In other words, the Thucydides Trap is at work here, to be explained below. Or is it B, that the United States has legitimate concerns about China's trade practices, cyber espionage, and intellectual property theft, and these are the primary reasons for the United States launching a trade war against China? One might debate about whether the trade war is an effective tool for either A keeping China down, or B punishing China and/or deterring China's bad trade practices or not, but what was the Trump administration trying to accomplish here, what was its motives? Addressing that question is the task at hand.

Methodologically, the approach here is straightforward. If A, we'd expect to see X. If B, we'd expect to see Y. More specifically, if A, the trade war is explained by great power politics, the Thucydides Trap, and the US desire to thwart China's rise; we would expect to see the United States push back more and more on China as China's power increases, and we'd expect China's specific actions to be more or less irrelevant. In other words, even if China was on the best of behavior the United States would be bent on preventing, even containing, China's rise. On the other hand, if B, that the trade war is explained by China's misbehavior and the scale and nature thereof, we'd see the US response directed/targeted at specific actions of China, and we'd expect the US response to rise and fall with the nature and ferocity of specific instances of Chinese misbehavior. The study will entail looking at comparative measurements of US and Chinese economic strength (GDP, GDP/capita,

PPP, etc.), population, technological power, defense spending, numbers of active duty military personnel, number of Navy battle force ships, as well as US interests, Chinese behavior, and the timing of the US trade war versus China's material capabilities data above (in other words, as China's capabilities rise, the intensity of the US trade war as a weapon against China rises as well).

The hypothesis offered here is that B explains the US trade war launched by Donald Trump against China. In other words, China's fast growth and its rise vis-à-vis the United States is not, in and of itself, the key to understanding the trade war. Rather, it is what China is doing that has provoked the United States and led American leaders to believe a trade war was a fit response to and remedy for China's actions.

BACKGROUND: THE SINO-AMERICAN TRADE WAR

The Sino-American Trade War began in 2018 and continues to the present day. It follows a long history of American complaints about illiberal Chinese trade practices. The American charges range from Chinese manipulation of its currency, the renminbi, over the years, to intellectual property rights (IPR) violations, to Chinese government subsidies of Chinese state owned enterprises to push exports, to dumping of Chinese products in the United States at costs below cost so as to attain a hold on certain markets, to an array of nontariff barriers to US goods going into China, and others. These US charges began to appear in the 1980s, but became big issues in the bilateral relationship in the 1990s and 2000s, accelerating in quantity, quality, and scope over the years. An important underlying issue is the difference in the two countries' political economic systems, with the US government and its philosophical commitment to a freer market economic system giving it a much smaller role in economics and trade than China's, with its one-party state system of "socialism with Chinese characteristics," giving the state a major role in almost every aspect of major economic activity in China.

Table 1.1 depicts the evolution and key dates of the China–US trade war to date. The tensions involved did not start with the arrival of Donald Trump in the White House in Washington, but his arrival and in particular the presence of arch trade hawk and trade advisor to the president Peter Navarro (Rappeport & Swanson, 2019) made a much more confrontational approach to China all but assured. Trump and Navarro arrived in Washington convinced that China had been fleecing the United States for years and were determined to put an end to it, as part of a Trump's stated policy of "making America great again." Though Trump's trade policy was controversial in the United States

(Walters & Smith, 2012) as well as in China, Trump found many supporters in Washington on both sides of the political aisle for a more confrontational approach to China on trade, IPR violations, and China's ongoing and illegal state-led hacking campaign against American companies, aimed at gaining the fruits of American ingenuity.

Trump's protectionist turn began in earnest in early 2018 and ran in earnest until early 2020, when he forged Phase 1 of a trade deal with China prior to the outbreak of COVID-19 worldwide. His first two salvos were fired broadly at all US trading partners, not China alone. They focused first on solar panels and washing machines, then steel and aluminum. As he began to work out deals with a number of America's more liberal trading partners, he lowered his sights more squarely on China and in July 2018 opened fire in his broader trade war with China, starting with 25 percent tariffs on $50 billion of Chinese products in two phases. As China responded tit for tat with like retaliations against American products and producers, starting with Trump's initial broad salvos in early 2018, and making no moves to address any of the issues the Trump administration had highlighted, Trump turned up the heat with a massive wave of tariffs on an additional $200 billion in Chinese goods. China followed with another wave of tariffs of its own on $60 billion of American goods. In December 2018 Beijing and Washington announced a truce in the trade war, but in May 2019, having made no progress in talks with China, the United States announced it would raise a series of 10 percent tariffs on Chinese goods to 25 percent, followed by China raising some of its tariffs in kind. Finally, in January 2020, Chinese negotiators met US negotiators in Washington and a Phase 1 trade deal was announced with China agreeing to purchase some $200 billion of US goods and to abide by a series of new agreements on intellectual property (US Trade Representative, 2020). In Table 1.1 is a detailed account of the history and content of the trade war from early 2018 to time of writing (February 2021).

While the onset of the global COVID-19 pandemic has hampered economies around the world and arguably slowed China's purchase of US goods agreed to in the trade deal, the provisions of the deal are still in effect at time of writing. With the arrival of a new presidential administration in Washington in January 2021, it is not yet clear what approach the Biden team will ultimately take to the trade war with China. Joe Biden told *New York Times* columnist Tom Friedman in December 2020 that he would not immediately remove the tariffs the Trump administration imposed on China but would undertake a review of the trade war policies of his predecessor and announce his position later in 2021 (Friedman, 2020).

Table 1.1. A China-US Trade War Timeline

Part 1: Trump's First General Salvo
— 1/22/2018 Trump tariffs on 8.5$ of solar panels and washing machines (not China specific)
— China retaliates with tariffs (same day) of 178.6% of US sorghum

Part 2: Trump's Second General Salvo
— 3/01/2018 Trump tariffs of 25% on steel and 10% on aluminum imports (not China specific)
— exemptions announced over following week for Can, Mex, S. Kor, EU, Bra, Arg, Aus
— China retaliates with $2.4bn of tariffs on US fruits, nuts, pork, etc.
— 6/01/2018 Trump removes exemptions for all except Aus. Deals cut by S. Kor, Bra, Arg to avoid tariffs
— 5/17/2019 Trump lifts tariffs on Can and Mex

Part 3: Full-on Trade War, China-US Tariffs
— 7/06/2018 Mutual China-US tariffs of 25%, US on $34bn of Chinese intermediate inputs and capital equipment, and China retaliates on $34bn of US agricultural and food products
— 8/23/2018 Mutual China-US tariffs of 25%, US on $16bn of Chinese products, China retaliates on $16bn of US products
— 9/24/2018 Mutual China-US tariffs on $200bn of Chi imports to US, Chi retaliates on $60bn imports of US products
— 12/01/2018 Truce announced between China and US
— 5/10/2-19 US raises tariffs on Chinese goods that were 10% to 25%, China retaliates in kind on US goods hit in 9/2018
— 1/15/2020 Phase 1 Trade Deal signed between China and US (China agrees to buy $200bn more US goods, though most issues not addressed and US doesn't agree to remove extant tariffs)
— 12/31/2020 It is clear that China has fallen far short of promises, Covid impact being a factor

Part 4: Telecoms
— 3/17/2016 US (Obama Admin.) sanctions telecom equipment manufacturer ZTE, adds ZTE to "entity list" so US tech companies can't sell to ZTE without license.
— 3/17/2017 US settles with ZTE, fines ZTE $1.9bn for selling tech to N. Kor and Iran in violation of US sanctions on those two countries
— 4/16/2018 US punishes ZTE for violating 3/2017 settlement, bans all US sales to ZTE
— 7/13/2018 Trump ends US sales ban to ZTE
— 1/28/2019 US Dep. of Commerce indicts Huawei on fraud and money laundering charges, etc.
— 4/27/2019 US further limits US tech exports to Chi/Rus/Ven that could be used in military applications
— 5/15/2019 and 8/19/2019 US adds Huawei and affiliates to "entity list" so license required for US companies to sell to them
— 12/18/2020 SMIC (only major Chinese semiconductor company besides Huawei) added to "entity list"

Source: Author drawing from Bown and Kolb 2000.

SCENARIO A: POWER POLITICS AND THE
THUCYDIDES TRAP—WHAT WE'D EXPECT TO SEE

Having laid out a basic introduction to the Sino-American trade war, it is now time to turn to the first of the two hypotheses that might explain its rise. The argument that China's leadership makes, and that one might expect if one were working in the tradition of what in the international relations literature is known as "power transition theory," and more recently has been articulated as "The Thucydides Trap," is that it is American fear of and prejudice toward China's growing power that has led American policy makers to try to contain China's rise, to hold back China's economic growth. They argue that for these reasons US leaders have launched a trade war against China, and that by doing so the United States hopes to inhibit China's growth and delay if not stop its rise. In other words, it has nothing to do with the nature of China's conduct itself, such that a more innocuous portfolio of Chinese policies on intellectual property, currency, telecommunications/5G, government subsidies of Chinese companies working abroad, policies toward foreign companies in China, and the like, would have led to a less harsh US policy toward China in recent years. Let us consider that proposition.

Overview of Power Transition Theory and the Thucydides Trap Argument

An important theory in international relations studies is "power transition theory," a subset of Realist theory and most closely associated with its progenitor, A. F. K. Organski (1958). Jack Levy also writes in this tradition and puts it this way: "A key proposition of power transition theory is that war is most likely when a dissatisfied challenger increases in strength and begins to overtake the dominant power" (Levy, 2015, 13). China appears to be a dissatisfied challenger according to an anonymous author in the recent and impactful "Longer Telegram" from a US official apparently working in China (Anonymous, 2021), a rising power with global ambitions including helping spread its socialist system to other countries according to Xi Jinping himself (Xi, 2017, 10). The key notion in the world of power transition theory is the notion of parity in the domain of power. Is China yet at the place where it has achieved parity with the United States, or in Levy's words, the place where "the dissatisfied challenger increases in strength and begins to overtake the dominant power"? This will be considered in detail below. Before doing that, however, a more recent articulation of power transition theory has come by way of Graham Allison.

Graham Allison and colleagues at Harvard's Belfer Center conducted a study of five hundred years of diplomatic/war history and concluded that war between China and the United States "is more likely than not" (Allison, 2015, 2). In his own words, Allison says this:

> The defining question about global order for this generation is whether China and the United States can escape Thucydides's Trap. The Greek historian's metaphor reminds us of the attendant dangers when a rising power rivals a ruling power—as Athens challenged Sparta in ancient Greece, or as Germany did Britain a century ago. Most such contests have ended badly, often for both nations, a team of mine at the Harvard Belfer Center for Science and International Affairs has concluded after analyzing the historical record. In 12 of 16 cases over the past 500 years, the result was war.

Allison's argument is consistent with power transition theory. Rooted in materialist understandings of power, it concludes that war "is more likely than not" because of the material reality of China's rise and the challenge to America's relative hegemony in the international system this leads to in most cases. The veracity of the results of the study of Allison et al., while rooted in material-driven power transition theory calculations, is actually based on the historical cases assembled for the study, the notion that "in 12 of 16 cases over the past 500 years, the result was war." This is a powerful argument, rooted in empirical and historical analysis.

Moving from power transition theory to the Thucydides Trap now to the question of parity in China–US relations, where are China and the United States in terms of power parity? Are they in danger of falling into the Thucydides Trap, or is it still too early to say? In other words, has China's power thus far risen to the level that it is at or near parity with that of the United States, thus making more likely the possibility that China and the United States will fall into the Thucydides Trap? To address this question, we will consider respective measurements of their power. Power can be measured in many different ways, so more than one indicator thereof will be necessary. Below we will consider several indicators of power in the context of China and the United States, including several different measurements of economic strength, population, technological power, defense spending, numbers of active duty military personnel, and number of Navy battle force ships.

Based on the data in Table 1.2, China has superior numbers in economic growth rates and purchasing power parity (PPP) indicators of GDP, but in terms of GDP and GDP/capita the United States is still ahead of China. As the data here indicates, economic power parity between the United States and China has not been reached unless one uses PPP to compare the two. Using PPP has pros and cons (Callen, 2007). Given how integrated into the

Table 1.2. Four Key Economic Indicators Comparing China and the US, Using 2019 Data

GDP, 2019 (IMF, USD)
USA: $21.4 Trillion
China: $14.3 Trillion

PPP, 2019 (World Bank, USD for US, adjusted USD for China)
China: $23.5 Trillion
USA: $21.4 Trillion

Growth Rates, 2019 (IMF, USD)
China: 6.1%
USA: 2.2%

GDP/CAPITA, 2019 (World Bank, USD)
USA: $65,298 (US population in 2019 was 328 million, World Bank)
China: $10,262 (China's population in 2019 was 1.4 billion, World Bank)

Source: Author, drawing from IMF and World Bank data.

international trading system China is, and the fact that much of that trade is denominated in dollars, it is not unreasonable to compare the two in dollar-denominated GDP, though PPP catches local costs more accurately in most cases. Whether using PPP or dollar-denominated GDP, factoring in per capita numbers also adds a different perspective, as the data above shows, giving the United States an advantage in terms of spreading a larger GDP across a smaller population. Consequently, while there may be an argument that China and the United States are comparable in terms of size of economy (by using PPP), per capita numbers make the comparison more difficult to sustain, especially when one considers the aging of China's population, that its elderly/retired population is so large, compared to its more youthful, employed, more productive population.

Population itself might be another way to compare the two. As the data above indicate, China has a greater population base than the United States, with 1.4 billion people as opposed to a US population of 328 million using 2019 numbers from the World Bank. One might conclude that China can, therefore, field more soldiers and workers, as well as more researchers and others who can contribute to national power. True as that might be, population is also a liability in times of war/crisis, given that China would have four times as many mouths to feed. While GDP/capita does capture that aspect of China's large population, it does not capture the productive potential of China's larger population. Consequently, again giving the graying of China's population demography, it is not clear whether its large population is more an asset or a liability in the end.

Related to economic power is technological power. If one factors in technological advantages, by most metrics the United States is ahead as well. For example, a Center for Strategic and International Studies report comparing China and the United States on three key indicators (5G, AI/semiconductors, and web services) puts China in front on 5G technology and roll-out, but the United States leads in AI/semiconductors and web services (Ortega, 2020). The United States leads on most every dimension of technology as it regards those employed by the two countries' military industrial complexes as well. Economic, demographic, and technological data/sectors are not the only important indicators of power, however.

Ascertaining the material power capabilities of a nation must also, of course, factor in its military strength. While there are different ways to do this, two of the most widely used means of comparing national military power are defense spending and the number of active duty military personnel. While it is well known that China's defense budgeting is calculated differently than that to of the United States (China's military doesn't include pensions, R&D, etc., in its military budget, whereas the United States does), it is still a good indicator of defense spending and changes therein over time. Table 1.3 presents a comparison of Chinese and American defense spending

Table 1.3.   China-US Defense Spending Compared

2012 data (measured in billions of US dollars):
  US=645.7; China=102.4; so China is 15.8% of US
2013 data (measured in billions of US dollars):
  US=600.4; China=112.2; so China is 18.7% of US
2014 data (measured in billions of US dollars):
  US=581.0; China=129.4; so China is 22.2% of US
2015 data (measured in billions of US dollars):
  US=597.5; China=145.8; so China is 24.4% of US
2016 data (measured in billions of US dollars):
  US=604.5; China= 145.0; so China is 24.0% of US
2017 data (measured in billions of US dollars):
  US=602.8; China=150.5; so China is 25.0% of US
2018 data (measured in billions of US dollars):
  US=643.3; China=168.2; so China is 26.1% of US
2019 data (measured in billions of US dollars):
  US=684.6; China=181.1; so China is 26.5% of US

Conclusions:
1. Over 2012-2019, US defense spending was up 6%.
2. Over 2012-2019, China's defense spending was up 77%.
3. China's defense spending was 15.8% of the US in 2012, but 26.5% in 2019.

Source: Author calculations based on International Institute of Strategic Studies numbers1
1. International Institute of Strategic Studies, *The Military Balance 2013-2020*, "Top Defence Budgets" and "Defence Spending: Top 15" (https://www.iiss.org/-/media/images/publications/military-balance/2020/mb2020-defence-spending.jpg).

from 2012 to 2019. As the numbers clearly show, China's defense spending is rising at a much faster rate than America's, with the United States raising its defense spending across that time period by 6 percent, and China raising its own by 77 percent across the same time period. The gap between them is still immense, however, with China's defense spending accounting for only 26.5 percent of US defense spending in the most recent time frame (2019). It should be noted that that is a marked rise from 2012, when China's defense spending accounted for only 15.8 percent of US defense spending. While the United States is ahead, this is not to say it has the advantage in every domain, for surely as it regards the East China Sea and the South China Sea areas, for example, were the two to face off it would be more likely that China would have the immediate advantage in terms of forces at hand, its ability to project power. In more absolute terms, however, from a military spending perspective the two sides are nowhere near parity, the United States being out in front by a large margin.

As it regards active duty military personnel, China has superiority in raw numbers, fielding the largest armed forces in the world. Given its population is four times the size of that of the United States, the difference between the two should not come as a surprise. In 2020, China had 2,035,000 (IISS, 2020, 259) active duty military personnel, whereas the United States had 1,379,800 (IISS, 2020, 46). On a per capita basis, the United States actually has a higher proportion of citizens in uniform than China (the United States with approximately .4 percent of its population in uniform, and China with approximately .07 percent). Those numbers have not changed dramatically over the past decade, though there has been a shift in forces within the Chinese services, with a decrease in the Army and increases in the Air Force and Navy. One area where China's military (both hardware and personnel) has increased markedly is in its blue water naval forces. Based on 2020 data, China has 239 "battle force ships" as opposed to 297 for the US Navy, including carriers, submarines, amphibious ships and other ships (Erickson, 2020). Quantity is not the same as quality, but the rapid growth in China's navy is something the United States and China's neighbors have paid close attention to.

Summing up China's power and capabilities, a few conclusions can be drawn. China is a formidable power, however one cuts it. Yet whether in military, economic, or technological terms, the United States still reigns at the top across most dimensions. That is to say, based on the data presented here, the parity or near parity that those who study power transition focus on has not yet been achieved by China. So while China's growth and its gains across all the indicators discussed here is impressive and parity with the United States is likely if not inevitable in the not-too-distant future, we are not there yet. Consequently, it does not appear that the conditions are yet ripe for Allison's

Thucydides Trap to have been activated yet, and the predicted danger of great power conflict between the two is not yet imminent. It is still just too soon to know if the United States and China will fall, or avoid falling, into the trap. Consequently, I conclude that it seems unlikely that this hypothesis has the explanatory power to explain the US decision to prosecute a trade war against China. China has not yet reached parity with the United States in most dimensions of national power and so Washington was not under any acute pressure in early 2018 that would provide a rationale for launching a trade war against China so as to keep it down.

SCENARIO B: CHINESE MISBEHAVIOR IN TRADE, IPR, SECURITY—WHAT WE'D EXPECT TO SEE

What, then, would we expect to see if the US prosecution of a trade war against China was motivated by what it saw as China's misconduct in the areas of trade and technology acquisition? We'd expect to see a growing scale and scope of (from Washington's perspective) misconduct from Chinese companies and Chinese government actors such that the United States increasingly comes to see China as a menace to its economic interests. The hypothesis presented here is that China's material power is *not* the key to understanding the onset of the trade war, but that it is China's actions which have driven the United States under President Donald Trump to press a trade war against China after many, many years of negotiating with China, even as China continued its economic malpractice, and that these [mal]practices are what drove US trade policy under Trump, first and foremost.

Given that the argument presented here is about the Trump administration's trade policies toward China and its decisions to pursue a trade war, let's look at what one might reasonably argue is the key statement of the Trump administration's national security priorities: the National Security Strategy the White House put out in December 2017. Below is a list of statements about the Trump team's views of China's economic and technology acquisition practices.

China and Russia challenge American power, influence, and interests, attempting to erode American security and prosperity. They are determined to make economies less free and less fair, to grow their militaries, and to control information and data to repress their societies and expand their influence. (NSS, 2)

Every year, competitors such as China steal U.S. intellectual property valued at hundreds of billions of dollars. Stealing proprietary technology and early-stage ideas allows competitors to unfairly tap into the innovation of free societies. (NSS, 21)

China gathers and exploits data on an unrivaled scale and spreads features of its authoritarian system, including corruption and the use of surveillance. (NSS, 25)

China is gaining a strategic foothold in Europe by expanding its unfair trade practices and investing in key industries, sensitive technologies, and infrastructure. (NSS, 47)

China is expanding its economic and military presence in Africa, growing from a small investor in the continent two decades ago into Africa's largest trading partner today. Some Chinese practices undermine Africa's long-term development by corrupting elites, dominating extractive industries, and locking countries into unsustainable and opaque debts and commitments. (NSS, 52)

These statements were made in Trump's first year in office, 2017. The situation between China and the United States only worsened in subsequent years, on almost any dimension of Sino–US relations, but culminating in a broad-based trade war launched by the United States against China, with China matching every move with tariffs and other countermeasures of its own.

Let us discuss some of the issues the US government has been observing in recent years, leading up to the Trump administration's decision to launch a trade war against China in 2018. First, rather than a liberalizing trend, under Xi Jinping economic trends were for greater centralization in the central government for economic decision-making, the favoring of state-owned companies, and increasing discrimination by the government against private companies in China. Nicholas Lardy noted that up to 2012, China's economy had been liberalizing apace, with private firms accounting for 70 percent of the GDP of China by 2012, when Xi took over as China's core leader (Lardy, 2019).

Since 2012, however, this picture of private, market-driven growth has given way to a resurgence of the role of the state in resource allocation and a shrinking role for the market and private firms. Increasingly ambitious state industrial policies carried out by bureaucrats and party officials have been directing investment decisions, most notably in the program proclaimed by President Xi Jinping known as "Made in China 2025." (Lardy, 2019)

Made in China 2025 has been seen by American observers as a celebration of Chinese protectionism and discrimination against foreign companies at home, coupled with state subsidization of Chinese companies exporting abroad, a neomercantilist policy that is at heart profoundly illiberal.

Included in US criticisms of China's economic and trade policies are also charges of Chinese "dumping" of products in the United States and other markets, state subsidies of exports, and currency manipulation, and arbitrary use of nontariff barriers and other forms of protectionism at home. Dumping entails charges of state subsidization of Chinese companies such that they can afford to sell mass quantities of product into foreign markets at below-cost prices so as to drive out competitors and achieve market dominance in a given sector. The United States charged Chinese sales of solar panels in the United States as dumping, and so it imposed tariffs on Chinese solar panels in January 2018.[1] Along with this has been long-standing charges that the Chinese government manipulates the renminbi in international currency markets to keep its price artificially low so as to benefit Chinese exporters over and against foreign competition abroad. As Fred Bergsten put it,

> China was the champion currency manipulator of all time from 2003 through 2014. During this "decade of manipulation," China bought more than $300 billion annually to resist upward movement of its currency by artificially keeping the exchange rate of the dollar strong and the renminbi's exchange rate weak. China's competitive position was thus strengthened by as much as 30 to 40 percent at the peak of the intervention. Currency manipulation explained most of China's large trade surpluses, which reached a staggering 10 percent of its entire GDP in 2007. (Bergsten, 2016)

Most American experts would agree with Bergsten in saying that China stopped its currency manipulation at some point after 2014 (there are debates on this, of course). However, in 2019, following a sudden and steep devaluation of the renminbi, the US Department of the Treasury officially deemed China a currency manipulator once again (US Department of the Treasury, 2019). Moreover, the Chinese government has long used nontariff barriers of various and sundry kinds, wrapped in cloaks of intransparency, to inhibit foreign competition and favor local companies in China. Its recent (2020) policies vis-à-vis Australia have been cases in point, with its blockage of Australian wine and beef imports coming as punishments for the Australian government's demand for transparency and cooperation regarding the outbreak of COVID-19 in early 2020. One longstanding American charge against China has been that the Chinese government makes it very difficult, if not impossible, for foreign companies to gain access to the enormous Chinese market unless they are willing to turn over key technologies to their Chinese partners.

The final and perhaps most contentious issues between China and the United States as it regards trade/economics/technology have been China's practice of stealing American intellectual property and related to this, and often the means by which it does so, its cyberattacks against American companies for commercial and technological advantage. As Elizabeth Economy put it,

> A 2013 report, published by a consortium made up of several governments and businesses, found that of 120 incidents of government-directed cyber-espionage of intellectual property, 96% came from China.[2] (Economy, 2019, 141)

China has been a world leader, in fact *the* world leader, in cyberattacks and IPR violations, many of them focused on the United States. James Griffiths and Jason Fritz have independently documented the threat to global commerce and cherished notions of privacy and free speech the Chinese Communist Party increasingly poses to all, inside and increasingly outside of China as well (Griffiths, 2019; Fritz, 2017). Since President Obama confronted President Xi about these attacks in 2015 at their Sunnyland summit, while Chinese attacks (mostly state-sponsored) subsided for a season, they were back in force within a year and have now reached new levels, the highlight being the Equifax breach of 2017, one of the largest cyberattacks in history (Barret, 2020). What is most frustrating from an American perspective is perhaps the fact that most of the successful attacks and IPR thefts have come from Chinese state actors, whether the People's Liberation Army (*New York Times*, 2013) or Chinese state-owned enterprises or other national champions like Huawei, despite US pleas to the Chinese state to cease and desist (Moore, 2021).

In concluding this section, it appears that there are many reasons to believe the Trump administration's strong response to China's trade and technology acquisition practices in the past few years have been driven by China's increasingly bold and brazen cyberattacks, IPR violations, and neomercantilist trade practices, among others. More and more China experts in Washington, including those advising the Trump administration during Trump's term as president, came to see the then-current policy of the continuation of the longstanding status quo policy of engagement with China as unsustainable. China had changed under Xi Jinping, and the scope of many old problems in China–US trade relations had reached a scale that was just beyond acceptability for American policy makers. With the arrival of Trump and Navarro in the White House in 2017 and the continued growth of China's infractions, a showdown over trade and technology was all but inevitable. It came to a head with Trump's trade war beginning in 2018.

CONCLUSIONS: WHAT WE SEE

What conclusions might be drawn from this study, seeking to explain the motivation for the Trump administration to launch a trade war against China? One factor perhaps not considered deeply enough here is the role of agents, in this case Donald Trump and his China trade advisor Peter Navarro. A good case could be made that if Donald Trump had not won the election in 2016, a Hillary Clinton administration would have handled trade relations with China very differently. This certainly matters, but what is at stake here is not a counterfactual about different characters winning in the 2016 US presidential election, but what drove the winner of that election, Donald Trump (and his China trade advisors, led by Peter Navarro), to levy a trade war against China.

The data presented here leads to one conclusion. While the material rise of China certainly matters to US policy makers, it was not primarily that which drove the Trump administration to wage a trade war against Beijing. As a number of indicators presented in Scenario A above shows, there was not a significant change in China's material power from 2017 to 2018, or from 2016 to 2017. If one looks at China's defense spending between 2012 and 2019, one sees a slow, incremental increase in spending, year on year, not a sudden increase that would have provoked the United States. In terms of China's economy, there too we see a slow, incremental increase in the size of China's economy. One might even note that China's growth rate has slowed in recent years, and this is even true prior to the onset of COVID-19. So too with China's population—it is growing, but very slowly, nothing that would provoke fear in the United States, and in fact China's demographics show a greying population, an upside-down population triangle, not a right-side up triangle that would spawn Malthusian fears of a population bubble–inspired conflict between China and the United States. America's GDP/capita is still four to five times that of China as well and there has been no sudden change in those numbers. Even if one looks at the growth of China's economy in purchasing power parity terms over the past decade, the changes there are not sudden or surprising. China's economy surpassed that of the United States in 2013 in PPP terms, so the slow growth of China's PPP numbers likewise do not seem of such a kind that they would lead to a desire to suppress China's economic growth in Washington by way of a trade war. In conclusion, there was no dramatic change in any of these dimensions in 2017 or in 2018, the year the trade war was launched, that would lead one to believe that these were the reasons that trade war was launched at that time. Moreover, as argued above, China has not reached parity with the United States on almost any of the indicators considered in this study.

We must note here that while I have argued that the trade war is not primarily about the Thucydides Trap, at least at this point in time, China's size and the scope of its activities does matter. A mouse chewing a hole in a bag of granola in one's pantry is a different matter than a hacker making off with $500,000 from one's bank account. This point can be seen more clearly by noting that China has been absconding with US intellectual property for many years, and the changing threat perception the United States has had there about. In the 1980s, for example, the nature, scale, and strategic implications of such theft were not as alarming to the United States as it has been in the last few years, as any number of reliable studies indicate.[3]

What we have seen in recent years under Xi Jinping is an increasingly assertive China across all fronts of political endeavor, domestic and international. Xi rose to power in 2012, but it was the 19th Party Congress in October 2017 where Xi had consolidated his rule and had made it clear that he was taking China down a more assertive road, a road wherein he said that he saw China's model as something worthy of export (Xi), a model that could benefit many other nations. The Chinese Communist Party was once again becoming evangelical. Moreover, in March 2018 the Chinese Communist Party announced an end to term limits for Xi Jinping, clearing the way for him to rule China indefinitely. Both of these things were deeply concerning to US policy makers. Again, these are things China did/enacted, not simply a change in China's material capabilities. Xi was the leader who lied to President Obama at Sunnylands in 2015 about bringing an end to China's IPR violations and hacking, and about his pledge not to militarize China's maritime claims in the South China Sea. He did not keep either pledge. With the consolidation and apparent prolongation of his rule in Beijing, it became increasingly clear to US policy makers that he would be leading China's foreign policy for many years to come. It also became increasingly clear to the Trump administration that the United States would have to begin to push back harder on many fronts, which did much to pave the way for the more aggressive trade policies of Peter Navarro and those who thought like him, to gain sway with the Trump administration.

Scenario B, the hypothesis that Trump's move to start a trade war with China was motivated primarily by what he and his advisors say was an increasingly brazen, increasingly aggressive Chinese set of trade and technology acquisition policies, seems most persuasive as it regards understanding those decisions. China's neomercantilism, it's IPR violations, its state-led cyberattacks for commercial gain, its nontariff barriers at home and its subsidies of Chinese companies abroad, its currency manipulation, its dumping, and the general trend of centralization of economic decision making power in Beijing rather than decentralizing and marketization of the Chinese economy, led the Trump team to conclude that painful as it would be, a trade war that might bring change to the relationship was better than continuation of the status quo, which they felt was increasingly disadvantageous to US national interests. While a new president, Joe Biden, has taken control of US policy in Washington recently, there is no indication that US interests are viewed much differently in the present period than was the case by the previous administration. Until or unless the Chinese government makes significant alterations to its trade and technology acquisition policies, the dysfunction now inherent in China–US trade relations seems likely to continue.

NOTES

1. The US tariffs were not targeted solely at China, but China was viewed as the chief offender as it regarded solar panels.

2. She cites Craig Timberg, "Vast Majority of Global Cyber-Espionage Emanates from China, Report Finds," *Washington Post* (April 22, 2013).

3. For example, see Larry Diamond, and Orville Schell, eds., *China's Influence and American Interests: Promoting Constructive Vigilance* (Stanford, CA: Hoover Institution Press, 2019).

REFERENCES

Allison, G. (September 24, 2015). "The Thucydides Trap: Are the US and China Headed for War?" *Atlantic Monthly*. Available at: http://www.theatlantic.com/inter national/archive/2015/09/united-states-china-war-thucydides-trap/406756/ (accessed February 15, 2021).

Anonymous (February 2021). *The Longer Telegram: Toward a New American China Strategy*. Washington, DC: Atlantic Council.

Barret, B. (February 10, 2020). "How 4 Chinese Hackers Allegedly Took Down Equifax," *Wired*. Available at: https://www.wired.com/story/equifax-hack-china/ (accessed February 15, 2021).

Bergsten, F. (November 18, 2016). "China Is No Longer Manipulating Its Currency," Peterson Institute of International Economics. Available at: https://www.piie.com/ blogs/trade-investment-policy-watch/china-no-longer-manipulating-its-currency? gclid=Cj0KCQiA1KiBBhCcARIsAPWqoSpk6u3_JbDjmOBn6x8ziw83W3hCX 5BJRQs0qtO6mpV7kOgx4FkroxYaAiwCEALw_wcB (accessed February 15, 2021).

Bown, C., and Kolb, M. (2020). Trump's Trade War Timeline: An Up-to-Date Guide. Washington, DC: Peterson Institute for International Economics (last updated on December 18, 2020).

Callen, T. (2007). "PPP vs the Market: Which Weight Matters?" *Finance & Development* 44 (1). Available at: https://www.imf.org/external/pubs/ft/fandd/2007/03/ basics.htm (accessed February 13, 2021).

Diamond, L., and O. Schell, eds. (2019). *China's Influence and American Interests: Promoting Constructive Vigilance*. Stanford, CA: Hoover Institution Press.

Economy, E. (2019). *The Third Revolution: Xi Jinping and the New Chinese State*. Oxford and New York: Oxford University Press.

Erickson, A. (2020). "China Navy Ship Numbers through 2040—Unique U.S. Navy Projections." Washington: Congressional Research Service, December 10. Available at: https://www.andrewerickson.com/2020/12/china-navy-ship-num bers-through-2040-unique-u-s-navy-projections-published-only-by-crs-china-na val-modernization-implications-for-u-s-navy-capabilities/ (accessed February 12, 2021).

Friedman, T. (December 2, 2020). "Biden Made Sure 'Trump Is Not Going to Be President for Four More Years,'" *New York Times*. Available at: https://www.nytimes.com/2020/12/02/opinion/biden-interview-mcconnell-china-iran.html (accessed, December 2, 2020).

Fritz, J. R. (2017). *China's Cyber Warfare: The Evolution of Strategic Doctrine*. Lanham, MaA: Lexington Books.

Griffiths, J. (2019). *The Great Firewall of China: How to Build and Control an Alternative Version of the Internet*. London: Zed Books.

International Institute for Strategic Studies (2019). *The Military Balance 2019*. London: Routledge.

International Institute of Strategic Studies (2020). "Top Defence Budgets" and "Defence Spending: Top 15," *The Military Balance 2013–2020*. Available at: https://www.iiss.org/-/media/images/publications/military-balance/2020/mb2020-defence-spending.jpg (accessed February 8, 2021).

Lardy, N. (2019). *The State Strikes Back: The End of Economic Reform in China?* Washington, DC: Peterson Institute of International Economics.

Levy, J. (2015). "Power Transition Theory and the Rise of China." In Robert Ross and Feng Zhu, *China's Ascent: Power, Security and the Future of International Politics*. Ithaca, NY: Cornell University Press.

Moore, G. J. (2017). "Avoiding a Thucydides Trap in Sino-American Relations (. . . and 7 Reasons Why That Might be Difficult)," *Asian Security* 13 (2): 98–115.

Moore, G. J. (2020). "The True Origins of the Sino-American Thucydides Trap." In Bart Gaens and Ville Sinkkonen (eds.), *The US and China: Rising Rivalry*, FIIA Report. Helsinki: Finnish Institute of International Affairs, September.

Moore, G. J. (2021). "Huawei, Cyber-Sovereignty and Liberal Norms: China's Challenge to the West/Democracies," unpublished manuscript, February.

National Security Strategy of the United States or America (December 2017). Washington, DC: The White House.

New York Times (February 18, 2013). "Industries Targeted by the Hackers." Available at: http://www.nytimes.com/interactive/2013/02/18/business/Industries-Targeted-by-the-Hackers.html?ref=technology (accessed February 15, 2021).

Organski, A. F. K. (1958). *World Politics*. New York: Knopf.

Ortega, A. (2020). "The U.S.–China Race and the Fate of Transatlantic Relations: Part 1—Tech, Values and Competition." Center for Strategic and International Studies, January. Available at: https://csis-website-prod.s3.amazonaws.com/s3fs-public/publication/200113_USChinaTranstlanticRelations.pdf?wAP_dixs27EiM wZ0E76aP5amt2AVlpAJ (accessed February 5, 2021).

Rappeport, A., and A. Swanson (December 26, 2019). "Peter Navarro, Trump's Trade Warrior, Has Not Made His Peace With China," *New York Times*. Available at: https://www.nytimes.com/2019/12/26/us/politics/peter-navarro-china-trade.html (accessed February 13, 2021).

Timberg, C. (April 22, 2013). "Vast Majority of Global Cyber-Espionage Emanates from China, Report Finds," *Washington Post*.

US Department of the Treasury (August 5, 2019). "Treasury Designates China as a Currency Manipulator." Available at: https://home.treasury.gov/news/press-releases/sm751 (accessed February 15, 2021).

US Trade Representative (January 2020). "United States-China Phase One Trade Agreement." Available at: https://ustr.gov/phase-one (accessed February 15, 2021).

The White House, National Security Strategy of the United States of America (Washington, D.C.: December 2017). https://trumpwhitehouse.archives.gov/

Walters, R., and T. K. Smith (May 12, 2020). "Eliminating Tariffs Would Free Up to $6 Billion a Month for Americans." Heritage Foundation Issue Brief No. 5071. Available at: http://report.heritage.org/ib5071 (accessed February 13, 2021).

Xi, J. (2017). "Secure a Decisive Victory in Building a Moderately Prosperous Society in All Respects and Strive for the Great Success of Socialism with Chinese Characteristics for a New Era," Delivered at the 19th National Congress of the Communist Party of China (Beijing: October 18).

Chapter Two

IR Theory with Chinese Characteristics

Interpreting Global Politics Through a
Chinese Exceptionalism Lens

Benjamin Tze Ern Ho

The idea that theory is always for someone and for some purpose is a dictum that is often more quoted than believed, especially among political scientists (Cox 1981, p. 128). For various reasons, the pursuit of universal laws to govern political behavior in the theatre of international politics has always been some kind of holy grail quest for IR scholars. After all, being able to offer up universal explanations for social sciences phenomena is a way to stamp one's mark on one's professional discipline. Much as Albert Einstein was synonymous with the theory of general relativity or Charles Darwin with the theory of evolution, scholars who develop theories that are able to proffer universal explanations are almost certain to be conferred a distinguished position in the pantheon of intellectual giants. At the same time, there is a growing discontent among IR scholars—both within and outside the West—that IR theory is inherently Western-centric and is too focused on developments within the Anglo-American world and does not quite speak to broader concerns and issues in the non-Western world. To this end, the rise of China in global affairs since the early 2000s has witnessed a growing interest among Chinese scholars in theorizing the conduct of international politics and infusing mainstream IR frameworks with Chinese insights and perspectives. This attempt to shift the discourse from a Western- (or American-) centric worldview to one that takes seriously Chinese ideas and contributions reflects to some extent the political logic of the current (and ongoing) tensions between the United States and China and consequently frames the manner in which both countries understand their global role.

In this chapter, I will examine specifically "Chinese ways" of thinking about international relations, taking into account traditional Chinese ideas and incorporating them into mainstream IR scholarship. More broadly, I will analyze how China's political worldview and IR—as an academic discipline—is being understood among Chinese intelligentsia. I will argue Chinese IR thinking is deeply shaded by a strong sense of exceptionalism, one that is closely—though not entirely—associated with state power and the political worldview of the Chinese Communist Party (CCP). Why is this important? For one, the study of international relations in China is not a neutral activity that is pursued for purely academic endeavor and for the generation of new forms of inquiry. It is, however, highly politicized and subjected to broader political objectives, in particular the preservation of Communist Party rule, as we will subsequently discuss. As such, we might surmise that the study of IR in China reflects not only the thinking of Chinese IR scholars about international affairs, but also to some extent incorporates features of Chinese political culture and its political life, insofar as these are being embedded within scholarly perception and practice of international politics.

Given this, I argue that China's prominence in international relations has emboldened Chinese IR scholars in recent years in suggesting a "Chinese way" of thinking about international relations, and to take into account traditional Chinese ideas and incorporating them into mainstream IR scholarship, which is seen to be privileging a Western-centric reading of international affairs. As this chapter will show, within the Chinese political worldview, there is a deep sense of superiority and difference vis-à-vis the West and the discipline of international relations ought to reflect these attributes. In a study of the development of Chinese IR theory, Qin Yaqing, also the president of the China Foreign Affairs University, observes that efforts to develop Chinese IR theory have gathered momentum since the start of the twenty-first century given China's economic strength and international influence (Qin 2009a). While these concepts have yet to obtain universal traction and are still largely in an embryonic stage, the ability to theorize, as Qin puts it, "is a sign of intellectual maturity" (Qin 2009a, p. 198), and Chinese scholars are increasingly using Chinese indigenous resources in attempting to articulate what they view as a unique Chinese contribution to the wider IR discipline.

In the following, I will examine the ideas promulgated by two prominent Chinese scholars, namely Yan Xuetong and Qin Yaqing, whose engagement of international relations theory through the use of so-called Chinese indigenous ideas provide a useful vantage point of comparison with existing mainstream IR theories. Both men are well known for their theorizing work on Chinese international politics as we shall see. To be certain, the ideas of both men do not exhaust the permutations of scholarly debates that characterize the study of international relations thinking in China (Li 2020), but given the prominence of their ideas to Chinese IR scholarly discourse as well as their contribution to global debates on international politics, discussing their ideas would be a good starting point. As such, what I hope to do in this essay is examine the theoretical paradigms offered by both men in their study of international relations and consequently what they tell us about the Chinese worldview and more broadly about Chinese thinking on international relations. As I will later show, what their ideas have in common is a strong belief that *existing IR paradigms derived from Western experiences are insufficient to account for Chinese international relations and the Chinese political worldview.* More than that, these ideas also seek to challenge the universal insights claimed by Western IR paradigms while attempting to emphasize even universalizing the insights proffered by Chinese IR thought. To understand Chinese thinking about international relations, they argue for the need to take into account traditional Chinese culture and experiences gathered from Chinese history. In addition, they also contest the universal validity of Western IR theories in explaining state behavior, in particular the importance of power, and attempt to conceptualize China's approach to international relations with reference to other considerations, such as patterns of relationality, emotional affectivity, and moral conduct. While these scholars do not aim to entirely supplant Western IR theories with Chinese alternatives, their arguments—to a large extent—call into question the relevance of Western thinking and worldview, and consequently, seek to relativize the conclusions arrived at.

This chapter will proceed as follows. I will first provide a brief overview of the development of international relations theory in China, and in particular on scholarly discussions emerging from China in the 2000s, a period which China's global rise become more pronounced, and where debate over Chinese IR insights became more prevalent. I will then go on to analyze in turn the ideas put forth by Yan and Qin, whose ideas represent different conceptualizations of Chinese IR thought. In the process, I will attempt to draw similarities and differences between these ideas and existing IR schools of thought (realism and constructivism) and to examine the extent to which Chinese traditional ideas can be said to be unique or distinct.[1] I argue that while it is possible to incorporate Chinese traditional ideas into our understanding of Chinese state behavior, China's political system and political culture impose limits to the degree these ideas can be properly termed as an IR theory, and that it lacks generalizability.

IR THEORY WITH CHINESE CHARACTERISTICS

The importance of articulating a Chinese approach to international relations theory can be said to be motivated in part by the need to establish and present Chinese national interests to the international community. In a study of the relationship between China's global ascendancy and its international relations, Hung-jen Wang identifies three main features of Chinese IR scholarship as "identity, appropriation, and adaptation" (Wang 2013b, p. 2). In the first phase of scholarship, the identities of Chinese IR scholars were being shaped by China's political systems, cultural values, and historical experiences. Such work began in the late 1980s and early 1990s following China's reintegration into the international system. Following that, Chinese scholars began to appropriate Western IR theories and applied them with the Chinese principle of *ti-yong* ("substance-function")—that is, combining Chinese concerns with the learning of foreign knowledge. The third feature saw Chinese scholars adapt concepts of Western IR scholarship (such as "balance of power" and "nation-state") to analyze events in China. To this end, Wang observed that "repeated cycles of learning and appropriation may ultimately relativize the universal values of those and other concepts found in Western IR theories so as to transform their original Western meanings" (Wang 2013a, p. 4).

Similarly, Qin Yaqing in his survey of the development of international relations theory in China argued that the development of IR as an academic discipline in China has moved from pre-theory to a theory-learning (or theory-deepening) stage. The "theory-innovation phase," whereby "scholars will seek to explain reality and understand social phenomena from a distinctly Chinese perspective," had yet to materialize, although Chinese scholars have increasingly emphasized the need to incorporate Chinese traditional thinking in responding to global issues. One central feature of this theory-deepening stage is a fascination with constructivism (following Alexander Wendt) and the saliency of constructivist ideas towards Chinese IR. In addition, given the debate on China's peaceful rise, the issue of Chinese identity became a central concern among Chinese scholars. Hence, constructivist ideas dovetailed well with the Chinese philosophy of *I Ching* (Change), which advocated that identity and behavior are changeable (Qin 2009, p. 191). This constructivist turn in Chinese IR theory, I argue, reflects a broader debate about what it means to be Chinese in the twenty-first century, and the role and contribution of China to the rest of the world. Beyond the quest for scholarly enquiry, the emergence of Chinese perspectives to the study of international relations can also be said to be a reaction to the 2008–2009 US financial crisis, which had consequently called into question the ongoing legitimacy of a Western-led international system. As such, the possibility for non-Western alternatives, and in China's case, for Chinese thinking to take root and permeate the structure of the international order became more pronounced (Zhong 2017; Zheng & Lim 2017; Sun 2016).

From the above, we see that the study of Chinese IR should be viewed within a larger framework of perceived Chinese self-identity, and in this case, seen to be in tension, if not in opposition, to Western conception of self, society, and statehood. Why is this so? One reason, according to Robert Cox, lies in the difference in how the past and future is being understood by the Chinese, as opposed to Western thinking. While Western thinkers are wont to read change as a "movement towards an ultimate preordained unity of thought and organized life" (i.e., the inevitable triumph of liberal democracy), in the Chinese mentality, the meaning of change has been a "movement to and fro, rise and fall, alternation in a cyclical pattern with a continuing moral injunction to achieve some degree of harmony among conflicting forces " (Cox 2010, pp. 6–7). Likewise, Fei Xiaotong has also explicated on organizational patterns that are deeply entrenched in Chinese society that stand in contrast with those derived in the West (Fei 1992). While the merits and limitations of these arguments are beyond the scope of this essay to discuss, any analysis of Chinese IR must necessarily include some aspects of Chinese self-identity and its relevance to the study of international relations.

In my subsequent discussion, I will examine the thinking of the said Chinese IR scholars and uncover aspects of Chinese self-identity within their theoretical framework. I will attempt to critically assess these elements of self-identity with respect to realism and constructivism and to highlight differences and similarities between these existing schools and those conceptualized by Chinese IR scholars. This is not to say that other factors, such as the structure of international system, material capabilities, or ideology are not relevant. However, I argue that these factors matter less insofar as the study of Chinese self-identity is concerned as much of this is a matter of perception. To this end, the arguments made below reflect an attempt by Chinese IR scholars to distinguish Chinese ideas concerning international relations from existing paradigms.

YAN XUETONG: A CHINESE REALIST CONFRONTS REALISM

Due to Yan's scholarly prominence both within and outside China, a number of critical assessments of his political ideas have been undertaken, following the publication of his 2011 book, *Ancient Chinese Thought, Modern Chinese Power*, which provided an account of Chinese political thought and its implications for contemporary Chinese international relations (Yan 2011). Yan identifies himself outright as a realist scholar, noting that "realist logic is clear, simple, and easy to understand . . . [unlike] dialectic method . . . by which any form of explanation is possible" (Yan 2011, pp. 240–241). A central theme in Yan's overall analysis is the need to incorporate morality into the practice of international politics. In his 2016 book *The Transition*

of World Power: Political Leadership and Strategic Competition, Yan proposes a framework of moral realism (daoyi xianshizhuyi 道义现实主义) as
a foundational premise for the conduct of international politics (Yan 2015).
Yan prefaces his study by rejecting the claim made by John Mearsheimer that
countries with a moralistic approach are more dangerous in international affairs; instead he argues that a proper understanding of morality is necessary:
states ought not to confuse their own moral concepts with universal moral
standards. Yan adds that the concepts of moral realism that he puts forth are
not restricted to China only, but universally applicable. Yan also tells us that
the Confucian concept of "welcoming without exception, but not to teach"
（laierbuju buwangjiaozhi来而不拒,不往教之) is sharply contrasted with
the Christian tradition of "asking others to convert" (*curen guiyi*促人皈依),
and that China adopts a nonconfrontational foreign policy. This is in contrast
to the United States in which Yan argues, that in the process of implementing
its own moral standards have resulted in countless conflict (Yan 2015, p. 7).
In addition, Yan contends that in Western thinking, power and "elements of
power" are often used interchangeably and thus confused whereas the Chinese language distinguishes clearly between "might/power" (*quanli* 权力)
and "capability/strength" (*shili* 实力). Yan also emphasizes that the ability of
a country to sustain its leading role in the international system is premised
upon its preservation of its moral foundations, in addition to having a "strategic reputation" (*zhanlue xinyu*战略信誉) (Yan 2015, p. 8).

Yan also seeks to distinguish moral realism from Chinese theories of international relations, arguing that a universal theory of international relations
is not confined to national boundaries. Yan proposes that the goal of moral
realism is to achieve a universal theory and that moral realism best explains
the transition of world power between a leading power and a rising power
(Yan 2015, p. 105). Yan also argues that moral realism is a scientific method
of inquiry and thus ought to be viewed as logical, verifiable, and having
predictive properties. In this respect, moral realism—as an IR theory—in
accounting for patterns of behavior in Chinese history, can also be applied to
contemporary international relations given its foundations in human nature
which is unchanging (Yan 2015, p. 113). Yan further contends that moral
realism—due to its emphasis on moral leadership—coheres well with the
Chinese Communist Party (CCP) tenets and is thus being accepted. Yan also
notes that moral realism does not mean that leading countries ought to practice "self-constraint" (*ziwo yueshu*自我约束) on purely moral considerations,
but include other factors such as their own "strategic interests" (*zhanlue liyi*
战略利益) (Yan 2015, pp. 126–127).

Yan concludes his analysis by proposing for the need to establish China's
credentials as a "humane authority" (*wangquan*王权) as opposed to a "hege-

monic power" (*baquan*霸权). Yan criticizes the present US-led international system as a hegemonic one and argues that a humane authority would be superior to the existing arrangement (Yan 2015, p. 216). Furthermore, the litmus test of whether China is able to fulfil its role of a humane authority is whether other countries view China as a model for emulation. In this respect, Yan perceives the intensification of anti-corruption efforts since 2013 by the Chinese government as a positive force for attracting others to follow (Yan 2015, p. 217). On the relationship between China and the United States, Yan argues that the strategic competition between both countries was not just about material capabilities but also involves the values that both countries hold. Hence for China to achieve national rejuvenation, it would not only have to provide the world with a set of values, but these values would have to be of a higher standard than those promoted by the United States. To this end, Yan contends that values like "fairness" (*gongping*公平), "righteousness" (*zhengyi*正义), and "civilization" (*wenming*文明) were more important than "equality" (*pingdeng*平等), "democracy" (*minzu*民主), and "freedom (*ziyou*自由). Yan adds that it was natural for countries to emulate those who are more powerful, richer, and more prosperous and in the process of doing so, also subconsciously absorb the values upon which these successes were built upon. This will consequently result in new international norms and global order (Yan 2015, pp. 217–218).

Given the above brief summary of Yan's arguments, how should we approach the ideas of moral realism, and to what extent does Yan's exposition reflect a unique Chinese way of perceiving and ordering the international system? To be certain, the issue of morality is not solely particular to Chinese IR thinking, many Western IR thinkers—realist scholars or otherwise—have long debated the relationship between morality and power politics (Williams 2004; Lebow 2003). The difference, however, lies in how IR theory relates to practical realities. In the case of Western IR scholarship, theory is seen as descriptive (what is), whereas Chinese IR theory purports also to be propagative (what ought to be). While the saying that "theory is always for someone and for some purpose" (Cox 1981, p. 128) can be applied equally to both Western and Chinese IR theories, Chinese IR scholars operate under a domestic environment that is far more restrictive and inhibitive of academic freedom than is the case in the West. [2] Hence scholarly writings are not purely academic exercises for the pursuit and dissemination of knowledge, but also reflect individual and institutional positions vis-à-vis the Chinese government, and in some cases, function as political gambles to be on the right side of those in power. In the case of Yan, he makes clear that he sees his role as both a scholar and a policy advisor, and consequently to be able to contribute to China's success on the global stage (Yan 2011, pp. 229–251). By mixing together both his scholarly and patriotic positions, it is difficult to take Yan's arguments on moral realism as having sufficiently universal reach. Rather it can be said that Yan's prescriptions are largely framed with *only* China's national interests at heart, and are not framed with the interests of other states in mind, notwithstanding the rhetoric of China's inclusive diplomacy (Lai 2018).

Finally, Yan's formulation of moral realism is also highly contentious: by conceiving moral realism in a law-like manner, Yan does not leave room for any debate as to the role of morality in international politics. Indeed, Yan writes of moral realism as if it is an established scientific law (like the law of gravity) that states and statesmen ought to follow. In the *Transition of World Power*, Yan frequently prefaces his arguments by the phrase "moral realism contends" (*daode xianshizhuyi renwei*道义现实主义认为), thus essentially taking moral realism as unproblematic and as a given fact (or law). To this end, one might pose the question: can one be always moral in the pursuit of one's interests? As it were, a true realist (in a Machiavellian manner) would privilege interests over morality, the latter acting as a support only where it is expedient to do so. Yan is thus unclear as to where he stands on this matter. Does he perceive morality as necessary to the exercise of power politics and consistent with realist principles, or does he treat morality as being ultimately subjected to political objectives, therein seen as useful but not necessary. Indeed, the possibility that morality is used as an instrumental veil for political goals is not factored into Yan's analysis. Given Yan's reputation as a realist scholar, the absence of a critical perspective towards the issue of morality somewhat undermines the strength of Yan's arguments and challenging the validity of his conclusions.

QIN YAQING: FROM CONSTRUCTIVISM TO RELATIONALITY

In the case of Qin Yaqing, the influence of constructivism is evident in his scholarly musings and his proposal of a relational paradigm in order to understand contemporary Chinese international politics. To be certain, this relational paradigm is neither new nor a unique Chinese contribution; rather it is located within a wider epistemological and methodological debate in IR that seeks to problematize the notion of how states ought to be understood. Instead of perceiving states as a "substance" or an autonomous entity, this line of scholarship seeks to advance the position that states are best conceived as processes and that relations possess ontological significance (Ashley 1988). Indeed, in his analysis of China's IR theories, Qin attempts to build upon the insights made by Western scholars such as Alexander Wendt as well as

Jackson and Nexon in their respective analysis, whereby social identities and social relations are being privileged in the analysis of state behavior (Wendt 1999; Jackson & Nexon 1999).

In his 2009 article "Relationality and Processual Construction: Bringing Chinese Ideas into International Relations Theory," which was published by the *Social Sciences in China* journal, Qin makes the central claim that relations possess ontological quality, and are not merely peripheral to the conduct of international politics (Qin 2009b).[3] In Qin's view, the biggest weakness of mainstream Western IR theory is the focus on the systemic (state) level but fails to sufficiently account for social interactive processes as well as social relations that are involved. To be fair, such a line of critique is not unwarranted as constructivist IR scholars over the years have attempted to articulate a variety of ways to bring into sharper focus and to emphasize the social aspect of human existence. In this view, structures are not a given, but are "constantly produced, reproduced, and altered by discursive practices of agents" (Guzzini & Leander 2006, p. 3). Where Qin attempts to distinguish his ideas from mainstream constructivist scholars are his assumptions concerning relationality, and which—in his view—are uniquely borne out within Chinese sociocultural experience. They are: relationality has ontological significance, relations define identity, and relations generate power (Qin 2009b, p. 14).

In arguing for the ontological significance of relationality, Qin maintains that one of the basic features of Chinese society is its relational orientation, and that relations are the most significant content of social life and social activity. According to Qin, "The political philosophy of Confucianism starts with relations and defines social classes and political order in terms of relationships. Social and political stability first and foremost relies on the management of relations" (Qin 2009b, p. 14). In addition, Qin also posits a sharp cleavage between Western and Chinese ways of thinking, the former is inclined to thinking in a "logic of causation" (i.e., if A>B, and B>C, then A>C) while in the Chinese way of thinking, "Relationality is to be found in the relational web as a whole [. . .] things or variables change along with the change of their relations; individuals in the web are subject to change in the relational web as a whole; and similarly the interaction among individuals can have an impact on the web" (Qin 2009b, p. 15).

The idea of "relational identity" is also posited by Qin as a way of thinking about individual human beings. Qin argues that social actors "exist only in social relations [r]ather than being independent and discrete natural units" and that "individuals per se have no identities" (Qin 2009b, p. 15). Qin also postulates that within Chinese thought, one's identity can be "multifold, interactive, and changeable along with practice" hence "truth" and "falsehood" are not mutually exclusive categories, that is, something is either true or false and cannot be both true or false. In Qin's words, "There is truth in falsehood and falsehood in truth, and true can become false and vice versa." Qin would go on to suggest that relationship processes would ultimately influence the behavior of individual actors and that changes in one's relational web would also lead to "identity-reshaping" and "behavior-transforming of an actor in relations" (Qin 2009b, p. 16).

Qin's last assumption concerns the use of power, which the study of IR is most intimately concerned with. According to Qin, "Relations generate power" in that for power to be exercised, a relational platform would be required. For instance, Qin argues that China possesses greater influential power than the United States in determining the outcome of the North Korean nuclear issue, as it springs from the "relational web it is in, and from the operation and coordination of the web involving all the parties involved in the crisis" (Qin 2009b, p. 17). Also, relations can enlarge power or constrain the exercise of power. To illustrate this, Qin contends that in China's patriarchal society, "a father's power over his son was absolute and supreme" by virtue of the power that a patriarchal society accords towards father–son relations. Paralleling this, according to Qin, is China's relations with ASEAN states (where China wields considerably more power than each of the respective states). Nevertheless, Qin argues that China has constrained itself in its exercise of coercive powers and in some cases, was restrained in maintaining and developing these relations. Consequently, Qin argues that relations in and of themselves are power and that these relational webs ought to be viewed as important power resources (Qin 2009b, p. 17).

RELATIONALISM MEETS POWER POLITICS

If we take the above arguments by Qin as reflective of the thinking among Chinese IR scholars who subscribe to relationalism, then what kind of behavior are we to expect from China in its international relations? Based on relational scholarship, the conclusion is that other states will accept China's hierarchy over them over them and will willingly submit themselves as vassal states to China. But that begs the more fundamental question: upon what basis will these states do so? Is it on the basis of China's superior conduct and thus being held as a model for emulation, or is it due to China's coercive behavior? But this line of argument poses several problems: one, it assumes Chinese moral standards as being normative and universally applicable; two, it fails to sufficiently take into account the structural constraints of the existing international system; and three, it is premised on a highly optimistic view of human nature which runs contrary to many of the core assumptions behind IR scholarship. Given that the first two points have been previously discussed at length by other scholars (Wang 2013a; Clark 2014), I will focus my attention on the third point, which I argue also represents the biggest flaw in relational scholarship.

Indeed, one blind spot of relational scholarship lies in its optimistic view of human nature and that it ignores the coercive character of social life as played out in international politics. For instance, a core strand of Qin's relational scholarship lies in the assumption that Chinese leaders are wont to use power resources in a proper manner, and that abuses of power are best checked, not through an external system of checks and balance, but by arrogation of power to a centralized authority (be it in the form of a strongman leader or a collective group of top decision makers). For instance, the establishment of the National Security Commission of the Communist Party of China is said to be not only for more effective coordination of China's security policies, but also as a means of centralizing party control and strengthening President Xi Jinping's grip on the Chinese state apparatus (You 2015). Hence, relational scholarship provides a strong theoretical justification for political control. As Qin puts it, "The political philosophy of Confucianism starts with relations and defines social classes and political order in terms of relationships. Social and political stability first and foremost relies on the management of relations. Social norms are mostly the norms of relation-management and social harmony is characterized by the domination of morality and mediation of disagreements" (Qin 2009, p. 14). To this end, we might argue that relationality scholarship is ultimately premised upon a socially conservative approach to politics whereby the maintenance of relations is primary and social disruption is frowned upon, regardless of the consequences that are resulted.[4] Furthermore, one might also locate the seeds of corruption within such a system of rule: in the absence of external checks or scrutiny (which may require disrupting familial relationships), there exists the propensity for internal decay which if unchecked can result in devastating consequences. Indeed, a glance at China's history suggests that this insistence on social and political stability at *all costs* can result in catastrophic consequences if individuals are not given sufficient rein to express their own personal misgivings. A case in point can be seen in Yang Jisheng's work *Tombstone: The Great Chinese Famine*, a study of the ill-fated Great Leap Forward policies enacted by Chairman Mao between 1958 and 1962 in which more than thirty-six million Chinese died (Yang 2012). Notwithstanding Chairman Mao's erroneous judgments in the matter, it was evident that the Chinese political structure was equally culpable. As Yang wrote:

> In the face of a rigid political system, individual power was all but nonexistent. The system was like a casting mold; no matter how hard the metal, once it was

melted and poured into that mold, it came out the same shape as everything else. Regardless of what kind of person went into the totalitarian system, all came out as conjoined twins facing in opposite directions: either despot or slave, depending on their position in respect of those above or below them. Mao Zedong was a creator of this mold . . . and he himself was to some extent a creature of this same mold. Within the framework of this system, Mao's own actions were conscious but to a certain extent also beyond his control. No one had the power to resist such a system, not even Mao. . . . In accordance with the logic of that time and under the prevailing framework, things that now appear patently absurd at that time seemed reasonable and a matter of course. (Yang 2010, p. 775)

In sum, Qin's relational scholarship—I argue—remains largely limited to accounting for China's domestic situation (which is to maintain the CCP's monopoly of power and to manage intra-China relations). It is also overly optimistic towards the CCP in making the *right* decisions for China (without taking into account the fallibility of even its highest leaders) while largely dismissive of individual ability to make meaningful change or contribution to social life.

CONCLUSION

In this chapter, I discussed recent developments in Chinese international relations thinking and how they provide us with important clues to the Chinese worldview concerning China's international relations thinking and its claims to exceptionalism. As shown, what is strikingly common about the ideas in both schools is that they seek to present China's approach to international politics as being unique and also superior to Western thinking. Indeed their proponents seek to differentiate these ideas from existing scholarship and more importantly, attempt to infuse them with concepts and motifs taken from Chinese traditional culture. Part of the reason for doing so, apart from a dissatisfaction with existing IR scholarship in accounting for Chinese political behavior, is the more deeply seated belief that China's international relations must be interpreted on Chinese terms which include taking its culture and history seriously, which are important elements of the Chinese worldview. Furthermore, Chinese IR thinking also harbor a deep mistrust of the existing IR theory frameworks, believing them to be serving the vested interests of the United States and the West. As such, Chinese IR scholarship attempts to include the elements of morality and relationality in their theoretical exposition, believing that these added aspects are necessary to remedy Western-centric IR theory, so as to allow a more equitable distribution of international voices to global issues.

That said, Chinese IR scholarship, as shown, presents problems of its own: one, it remains largely Sino-centric in nature; two, it is mostly anti-Western and anti-American; three, it assumes benevolence in Chinese leaders; and lastly, it is premised on an essentialized view of the East and West. Taken together, these themes provide the basis of Chinese exceptionalism and represent the main themes in discussions of China's international relations. I argue that Chinese IR theories, in attempting to distinguish China from the West, seek to justify their relevancy in reference to so-called Chinese conditions (or Chinese characteristics) without critically examining whether these conditions are indeed unique to the Chinese experience. To this end, the question "When is a Chinese condition a Chinese condition?" needs to be posed. To be certain, I am sympathetic to the view of these scholars in arguing for the need to take into account Chinese history and cultural traditions in understanding the Chinese worldview. Yet at the same time, to speak of Chinese culture and history as something given and unproblematic is to also ignore the highly politicized nature of Chinese social life and to take for granted the legitimacy of these narratives as part of the Chinese worldview. Also, these theories assume a priori the legitimacy and uncontested character of Communist Party rule and ultimately can be said to be preserving the status quo as far as Chinese domestic governance is concerned. Furthermore, the issue of power—as a central piece in politics—is largely understated in Chinese IR thinking, unlike Chinese domestic politics where the discussion of power remains primary. All these raise further skepticism as to the ultimate objective(s) of Chinese IR thinking. In my view, Chinese IR thinking lends itself mostly to support the policy decisions and political objectives of the Chinese state and thus presents—at its core—a highly Sino-centric perspective of the world. Issues of academic freedom in China further problematize the work of Chinese IR scholarship. Indeed, the body of ideas of high-profile Chinese scholars like Yan Xuetong and Qin Yaqing cannot be divorced from their affiliations with the Chinese government and hence can be said to be broadly sympathetic of the positions and political goals of the CCP, and not for sole purposes of academic inquiry. The need then to "speak truth to power" remains the Achilles heel of Chinese IR scholars, without which IR theorizing in China would be inherently limited.

NOTES

1. Given the limitation of this essay, I have only focused on realism and constructivism. For a discussion of liberalism and Chinese interpretations of it, see Wu 2018.

2. In China, academic think tanks are usually required to provide policy positions that *support political objectives* and have less autonomy to conduct purely academic research.

3. Qin's work is further elaborated in the most recent 2018 book *A Relational Theory of World Politics* (Cambridge: Cambridge University Press). For purposes of this chapter, I will engage with his 2009 work, which sketches most of his major ideas that his latter work is based upon. For a more in-depth analysis of Qin's book by the author, see Ho 2019.

4. This is most vividly illustrated in the COVID-19 outbreak in which early whistleblowers were being harassed by the Chinese authorities for attempting to disrupt social harmony.

REFERENCES

Ashley, R. (1988). "Untying the Sovereign State: A Double Reading of the Anarchy Problematique," *Millennium* 17 (2): 227–262.

Campbell, D. (1988). *Writing Security: United States Foreign Policy and the Politics of Identity*. Manchester: Manchester University Press.

Clark, I. (2014). "International Society and China: The Power of Norms and the Norms of Power," *Chinese Journal of International Politics* 7(3): 315–340.

Cox, R. (1981). "Social Forces, States and World Orders: Beyond International Relations Theory," *Millennium* 10 (2): 126–155.

Cox, R. (2010). "Historicity and International Relations," in Yongnian Zheng, ed., *China and International Relations: The Chinese View and the Contribution of Wang Gungwu*. New York: Routledge, pp. 3–17.

Fei, X. (1992). *From the Soil: The Foundations of Chinese Society*. Berkeley: University of California Press.

Guzzini, S., & Leander, A. (2006). *Constructivism and International Relations: Alexander Wendt and His Critics*. New York: Routledge.

Ho, B. (2019). "The Relational-Turn in International Relations Theory: Bringing Chinese Ideas into Mainstream International Relations Scholarship," *American Journal of Chinese Studies* 26 (2): 91–106.

Jackson, P., & Nexon, D. (1999). "Relations Before States: Substance, Process and the Study of World Politics," *European Journal of International Relations* 5(3): 291–332.

Lai, C. (2018). "Acting One Way and Talking Another: China's Coercive Economic Diplomacy in East Asia and Beyond," *Pacific Review* 31(2): 169–187.

Lebow, R. (2003). *The Tragic Vision of Politics: Ethics, Interests, and Orders*. Cambridge: Cambridge University Press.

Li, K. (2020). *Zhongguo Guoji Guanxi Xuepai de Zhishi Shehuixue Fenxi* [A Sociological Knowledge Analysis of China's International Relations Schools]. *Yun Meng Xue Kang* [*Journal of Yunmeng*] (4): 9–20.

Qin, Y. (2009a). "Development of International Relations Theory in China," *International Studies* 46(1/2): 185–201.

Qin, Y. (2009b). "Relationality and Processual Construction: Bringing Chinese Ideas into International Relations Theory," *Social Sciences in China* 30(4): 5–20.

Qin, Y. (2018). *A Relational Theory of World Politics*. Cambridge: Cambridge University Press.

Sun, J. (2016). "Sunjianguo: Wei Yinlingshijie Hepingfazhan Hezuo Gongying Gongxian Zhongguo Zhihui" [Sunjianguo: To Lead the Peaceful Development of the World and Win-win Cooperation Contribution of China's wisdom], April 18. Available at: http://www.71.cn/2016/0418/884939.shtml (accessed December 24, 2020).

Wang, H. (2013a). "Being Uniquely Universal: Building Chinese International Relations Theory," *Journal of Contemporary China* 22 (81): 518–534.

Wang, H. (2013b.) *The Rise of China and Chinese International Relations Scholarship*. Plymouth, UK: Lexington Books.

Wendt, A. (1999). *Social Theory of International Politics*. Cambridge: Cambridge University Press.

Williams, M. (2004). "Why Ideas Matter in International Relations: Hans Morgenthau, Classical Realism, and the Moral Construction of Power Politics," *International Organization* 58(4): 633–665.

Wu, X. (2018). "China in Search of a Liberal Partnership International Order," *International Affairs* 94 (5): 995–1018.

Yan, X. (2011). *Ancient Chinese Thought, Modern Chinese Power*. Princeton, NJ: Princeton University Press.

Yan, X. (2015). *Shijie Quanli de Zhuanyi: Zhengzhi Lingdao yu Zhanlue Jingzhen [The Transition of World Power: Political Leadership and Strategic Competition]*. Beijing: Peking University Press.

Yang, J. (2010). "The Fatal Politics of the PRC's Great Leap Famine: The Preface to Tombstone," *Journal of Contemporary China* 19 (66): 755–776.

Yang, J. (2012). *Tombstone: The Great Chinese Famine, 1958–1962*. New York: Farrar, Straus and Giroux.

You, J. (2015). "China's National Security Commission: Theory, Evolution and Operations," *Journal of Contemporary China* 25 (98): 178–196.

Zheng, Y., & Lim, W. (2017). "The Changing Geopolitical Landscape, China and the World Order in the 21st Century," *China: An International Journal*, Vol. 15 (1): 4–23.

Zhong, F. (2017). *Fazhanxing Anquan: Zhongguo Jueqi yu Zhixu Chonggou* [Developmental Security: China's Rise and the Construction of Order]. Beijing: China Academy of Social Sciences Press.

Chapter Three

The Liberal International Order After World War II

Michael Fowler

Economic dissatisfaction is a continuing refrain in modern international relations, whether criticisms are levied at trade, development, or foreign investment. Such unhappiness provides a potent tool in domestic politics and underlies much heated discourse on the world stage. Clashing economic interests, a complex system, and marked differences in diagnoses of problems and proposed solutions, all make substantial reform challenging.

A volume on US–Chinese economic relations, highlighting the political logic of trade wars, ought to reconsider the liberal international order established after World War II, now experiencing notable stresses and strains. Here, the Bretton Woods Conference of 1944 charted a theoretical path that established a new regime. The key Bretton Woods institutions never functioned precisely as their creators had anticipated; instead they evolved, in some cases dramatically, over the decades. This chapter will thus address the following questions:

- What were the antecedents of postwar international economic liberalism?
- What key institutions defined the postwar economic order?
- What successes, failures, and problems resulted?
- With respect to the current trade war, what future developments might occur?

ANTECEDENTS: PRE–WORLD WAR II ECONOMICS

Traditionally, problems in getting products to foreign markets greatly limited economic growth. By the mid-nineteenth century, although bilateral economic transactions among nearby countries had long occurred, Western states dominated more far-flung trade. Capable and sizeable merchant fleets, plus supporting navies, were prerequisites for increasing exports and imports from distant places. Here, Great Britain and the United States boasted advanced industrial and maritime strength, as did Germany, France, and the Netherlands.

By the 1870s Great Britain, the country that "ruled the seas," controlled 40 percent of all manufacturing and about a fifth of all global trade (Luard 1983, 64). Much nineteenth-century trade involved Western empires and their colonies or former colonies. Although some regional trade was occurring in Asia, Africa, the Middle East, and Latin America, its scale was paltry. Before World War I India was the only developing country with a substantial export trade (Luard, 1983, 64), an export-oriented economy having developed during colonialism.

"In liberal economic theory," one source noted, "trade is the engine of economic growth" (Karns, Mingst, & Stiles 2015, 396). America's founders had seen enhancing trade as the best route to developing economic power. Thereafter, many influential American politicians favored free trade. For example, Daniel Webster, senator and secretary of state, believed that, if "national markets and the great highways of commerce could be kept open to the vessels of all nations on a most-favored-nation basis, . . . Americans could 'command the ocean, both oceans, all oceans'" (Shewmaker 1985, 329).

As the twentieth century approached, with growing American economic influence, US foreign policy was no longer confined to Western hemisphere affairs. With respect to China, in 1899 Secretary of State John Hay proposed the Open Door policy, calling for "an open market for all the world's commerce" in China and for Chinese tariffs to be applied equally to merchandise "no matter to what nationality it may belong" (Brockway 1968, 48). Such principles resonated with Americans, with variations soon applied in other circumstances.

World War I then devastated the British, French, and German economies. This had dire rippling repercussions for many primary producers, which had depended on selling raw materials and foodstuffs to Europe. Currency difficulties soon arose. Since a commodity highly valued in many societies could lubricate commercial transactions, by the late nineteenth century, all major European states had "adopted gold as their exclusive standard" (Latham 1997, 22). During World War I, however, European states set aside some gold on national security grounds and used other gold reserves to help finance the fighting. Much flowed into the United States, as Americans supplied the Allied side. Before long, a precarious gold standard further threatened international commerce.

Most broadly, the first World War shifted the global distribution of power. The unprecedented destruction, including catastrophic numbers of killings, greatly sapped national strength. Further, one aspect of total war involved stirring up unhappy national minorities across the empires of enemy states. The Great War seriously weakened the Russian, German, Ottoman, and Austro-Hungarian empires, and neither Britain nor France would again reach the heights of imperial power enjoyed beforehand.

The United States stood as the cardinal exception. World War I had raged across many countries, but not that new great power—America. The United States had rapidly mobilized millions of soldiers, then had suffered the fewest casualties among the strongest countries. America also emerged vastly strengthened economically. Before America's entry in the fighting, US exports, mostly to Britain and France, had brought the country booms in steel, weapons, and agriculture. All told, the war transformed the Unites States from a debtor to a creditor country. When fighting broke out in 1914, the United States owed Europe about $3 billion. By conflict's end, Europeans owed Americans about $13 billion, with New York replacing London as the leading global financial center (Paterson et al. 2010, 105).

Furthermore, World War I intervention signaled American resolve to take international leadership. Woodrow Wilson espoused free-trade principles, and in July 1917, with America busily supplying the Allied side, the president wrote to his confidant, Colonel Edward House: "When the war is over, we can force them to our way of thinking, because by that time they will, among other things, be financially in our hands" (US Senate, 86).

While US support for a liberal post–World War II economic order is sometimes pictured as an abrupt break from preceding isolationist views, closer inspection reveals many common threads from the 1920s through the 1940s (Hogan 2004, 50). In 1919 Wilson had linked growing interdependence with political and economic disorder, declaring: "The world is all now one single whispering gallery. All the impulses . . . reach to the ends of the earth; . . . with the tongue of the wireless and the tongue of the telegraph, all the suggestions of disorder are spread" (Paterson et al. 2010, 106).

After the Versailles Treaty, Republican administrations focused on the growing interdependence of European and American economies (Leffler 2004, 130). They saw economic rivalries threatening peace and worried about converting currencies, settling war debts, and assisting with European reconstruction (Hogan 2004, 44). In the late 1920s, when crises struck German and central European financial systems, the Hoover administration responded with debt-settlement initiatives (Braeman 2000, 103). During the New Deal, Congress passed the Reciprocal Trade Agreements Act of 1934, aimed at reducing high American tariffs to help free trade.

However, American economic policy in this interwar "era of nascent hegemony" (McCormick 2004, 155) was also deeply flawed, as the United States "played its international economic role haltingly and irresponsibly" (Block 1977, 18). Bipartisan consensus was elusive, and, too often, the United States failed to engage abroad or did so too little or late. In the 1920s a laissez-faire ideology interfered and rampant speculation eventually occurred, with Congress more attuned to protecting the home market than to expanding markets abroad (McCormick 2004, 155). Even before the global economy could fully recover from the first World War, the crash of the US stock market, followed by world depression, flattened it again.

Between 1929 and 1932, as unemployment climbed and living standards declined, global trade in raw materials fell by 25 percent and in manufactured goods by 40 percent (Luard 1983, 66). States responded to the Great Depression with protectionist measures that made matters worse. Governments concerned with high unemployment introduced quotas and heightened tariffs to try to safeguard jobs. "Import quotas were more rigid barriers to trade than tariffs; a tariff was a tax that increased the price for the consumer, whereas a quota permitted only a fixed number of imports, regardless of consumer demand" (Ziring, Riggs, & Plano 2000, 392). To stimulate national economic activity, states reduced their imports, subsidized their producers, and depreciated their currencies. America's Smoot-Hawley tariff of 1930 formed "the most protectionist law of the century" (Spero & Hart, 2010, 72), provoking thirty-one states into retaliatory measures (Casey 2001, 8).

Interwar commercial relations were complex and confused, as scores of governments entered into different bilateral deals, resulting in a "patchwork quilt" of economic treaties. Then, escalating government restrictions encouraged retaliation, bringing on spiraling instances of economic nationalism, sometimes shorthanded as "beggar-thy-neighbor polices" aimed at improving one state's position at the expense of others (Ziring, Riggs, & Plano 2000, 386). As international commerce collapsed, down two-thirds between 1930 and 1936 (Ziring, Riggs, & Plano 2000, 389), political relations seemed expendable. Rival trading blocs emerged, and these posed the danger of turning into rival alliances.

Thus, in the 1920s and 1930s international economic problems threatened world order. As fascism flourished, Adolf Hitler's economic nationalism attracted many Germans, with his vow to return Germany to strength and wealth. Indeed, the interwar era witnessed state after state moving to dictatorial regimes with a large military role. This occurred in Japan, Italy, and various Latin American and Eastern and Central European countries.

After the worst years of the Great Depression, domestic production finally began to rise. In part, this resulted from enhanced government spending, not least via rearmament, as governments girded their militaries anticipating future conflict. Overall, however, international trade and investment continued to lag: "Relative to GDP [Gross Domestic Product] . . . , the foreign trade of most industrial countries fell to about two-thirds of the level prevailing before 1914; international investment largely disappeared in the 1930s" (Schwartz 2000, 181).

Then, with World War II, international economics suffered another shattering blow. Once again, the fighting devastated Europe and the primary producers, though not the United States, as European countries increasingly depended on American imports. As the fighting concluded in 1945, the global economic outlook has been summarized as follows (Karns, Mingst, & Stiles 2015, 382). The roughly fifty sovereign states were not yet extensively interdependent: economies were organized nationally, where elites set national policies. Few international economic organizations had been created. Barriers to trade obstructed commerce. Capital did not readily cross borders, and converting currencies was problematic. The United States led a handful of liberal market states, but mercantile thinking predominated elsewhere. The economic system of European empires featured imperial preferences established with colonies, while the Soviet model of socialist, command economies rested on central planning and state ownership. Neither developing countries nor more advanced governments mired in economic difficulties could call on effective outside assistance.

Under these precarious circumstances, revising international economics stood as an exciting possibility. With memories fresh of two tremendously destructive world wars within three decades, Western leaders hoped to encourage flourishing liberal democracies. Prosperity might forestall a third World War. Governments, as well as businesses and their employees, would not be eager to march off to war if people were busily cooperating to raise standards of living. The old system, in which countries had simply assessed their own self-interest and created unilateral policies, had proved disastrous. A different approach seemed in order: formulate a new economic system—stable, multilateral, and forward-thinking—that might promise vastly expanded opportunities.

POST–WORLD WAR II
INNOVATIONS AND INSTITUTION BUILDING

British economist John Maynard Keynes popularized theories of economic reform. He emphasized "utilizing the fiscal and monetary policies of government to guide and direct a free enterprise economy. . . . Government institutions must play a major role in guiding and directing international as well as domestic activity" (Ziring, Riggs, & Plano 2000, 387). With the rising popularity of Keynesian economics, a move toward a new liberal international order rapidly gained momentum: "a type of political economic system marked by the open movement of goods and capital between a plurality of states and societies. Generally, such a system emerges under the leadership of a liberal hegemon, which can shape the institutions and influence the policies of states in a fashion that creates and maintains openness" (Latham 1997, 33).

The new order, led by the United States, would feature multilateral negotiations, with a strong role for privately owned entities in determining the movement of goods in international commerce (Krasner 1985, 61). Secretary of State Cordell Hull had a deep-rooted faith in free trade delivering economic prosperity. During the war "his argument for a more open system was translated . . . into American foreign policy" (Spero 1981, 75).

One specific issue also helped deliver a reformed postwar order. During and immediately after World War II, major Allied leaders, peering into the future, fixated on the potential for Germany, once again, to wreck the peace. The overriding question was what ought to be done to minimize chances for future German aggression? Would world order be advanced by allowing Germany to rebuild or "denuding it" of its industrial base?

An Anglo-American government consensus on how to handle the German threat slowly coalesced. During the fighting Franklin Roosevelt had mused about the Allies prohibiting a postwar German air force, and Treasury Secretary Henry Morgenthau had produced a 1943 plan to turn Germany into a pastoral country, stripped of industrial might. Although Winston Churchill initially agreed with this prescription, once the Germans had surrendered he reversed field, declaring in 1949: "You must forget the past. . . . You must regard the reentry of Germany into the family of European nations as an event which the Western world must desire, and must, if possible, achieve" (Fowler 1985, 45–46).

Some top US officials also lobbied to include Germany in postwar international economic plans. Dean Acheson, Averell Harriman, Robert Lovett, and John McCloy drew on extensive backgrounds in law, business, military, and diplomatic affairs, including considerable experience in foreign commercial ventures. To them, destroying German industry "would remove the 'spark plug' . . . of the European economy. With its capacity to export manufactured goods and import raw materials, Germany could play a critical role in a system of world trade." Walter Isaacson and Evan Thomas continued:

> The leading American advocates of a revived Germany were Wall Streeters, men firmly committed to Europe, internationalism, and free trade. Their private careers had been spent making foreign deals, and a multilateral system of commerce was integral to their philosophy of world order. This ideal was as old as John Hay's "Open Door" and had found its twentieth-century expression as the

third of Woodrow Wilson's Fourteen Points: "the removal, so far as possible, of all economic barriers." Trade restrictions, it was believed, would lead to gluts in domestic markets, unemployment, and possibly the rise of totalitarian sentiments. (Isaacson & Thomas 1986, 234–35)

Such views were exceedingly important since the postwar United States had hegemonic intentions with "unrivaled military power" and "a preponderant position across the leading commercial, financial, and industrial sectors of the age: most importantly petroleum, but also automobiles, steel, chemicals, aerospace, international banking, pharmaceuticals, and electronics" (Simpson 2016, 60).

The destruction of World War II had shaken international affairs in unprecedented ways, yet the fighting had also brought much international collaboration. Allied states, joined by governments-in-exile and resistance groups, had worked together to contend with the formidable forces of Germany, Japan, and Italy. The western Allied governments, led by the United States, wanted to extend this cooperation into peacetime, while drawing on new initiatives in international organization to overhaul the global economic system.

This appeared especially beneficial to America. US officials foresaw the need for additional raw materials; they wanted to encourage American investment abroad and anticipated that enhanced production would produce postwar surpluses. Furthermore, as Kevin Casey observed, "An open multilateral economy, free of restrictions on international investment, trade, and payments would help foreign countries earn and attract the dollars they needed to buy American goods" (Casey 2001, 8). Western Europeans and others also needed dollars to finance US loans. Note, however, from early in the Cold War, America's ideological rivals—the Soviet Union and other Marxist states—existed largely outside this liberal order. They came to focus much commerce on one another, with the Soviet bloc utilizing the Council for Mutual Economic Assistance (COMECON) to promote its trade.

Post–World War II US officials were now inspired to recast venerable free-trade ideas, such as the Open Door, in a multilateral guise (Hogan 2004, 145–146). The United States advanced or supported an array of initiatives somehow affecting the global economy. The Organization for Economic Cooperation and Development (OECD) and the US Export-Import Bank and development banks deserve a mention, as does the United Nations Relief and Rehabilitation Administration. Bilateral loans, especially that to Britain, played a notable role, and the European Recovery Act, or Marshall Plan, was supremely important in bringing about economic recovery, reconstruction, and integration across Western Europe.

Among the institutions of the new liberal economic order that particularly stand out, US officials helped establish the World Bank and International

Monetary Fund in 1944–1945 and the General Agreement on Tariffs and Trade in 1947. Each formed part of the "three-legged stool" Keynes foresaw for the new system.

Banking and Finance

In 1944 the United States hosted an international conference at Bretton Woods, a New Hampshire ski resort, focused especially on discussions of a new monetary and banking system. The endeavor directed attention away from punishing the Axis states and imperial Japan and toward rebuilding the global economy. Top officials hoped to gain a consensus that favored establishing permanent multilateral institutions to help governments to collaborate in international economic affairs. In 1941–1942, US Treasury official Harry Dexter White had created the first blueprints for the new system, with alterations thereafter hammered out with the British Treasury, led by Keynes (Casey 2001, 12, 19–32).

Perhaps on account of the extensive preliminary spadework, the conference was not especially contentious. The United Kingdom and the United State—the former economic hegemon and the emerging one—dominated discussions and decision making with "little disagreement on the features of a desired system" (Spero 1981, 77). Although delegates from forty-four countries attended, John Maynard Keynes held the center of attention. "The Bretton Woods Conference was not a conference among nations," John Kenneth Galbraith later wrote. "It was a conference of nations with Keynes. His only rival was Harry D. White, his friend and disciple at the US Treasury" (Galbraith 1977, 224).

A first Bretton Woods institution, established in 1946, was the International Bank of Reconstruction and Development (IBRD). To found a World Bank for states to draw on was highly innovative, with the potential to assist trade, raise productivity, create new or enhanced markets, and forestall recession or depression. While member states were to supply the bank with its initial funding, the IBRD aimed to finance an increasing proportion of its activities just as other banks did—utilizing money repaid from past loans, including interest payments.

The early IBRD emphasis was on lending to governments very likely to repay the borrowed funds, while helping to rebuild their economies. As the bank considered financing projects, it appraised whether the proposals would turn into sound economic decisions. But, where initially much World Bank financing involved heavy industry and large public projects like dams, over time, the projects diversified, encompassing efforts to develop agriculture, improve education, install water and sewer systems, and expand energy output and telecommunications.

The bank soon began to help poorer countries, a complementary undertaking in that it might enhance the exports and imports of established economies and developing ones alike. By the twenty-first century the bank had reached out even to quite fragile countries, where longstanding poverty and meager economic opportunities might increase risks—terrorism, disease, and violent conflict—that could spill across borders. Through the Cold War, the organization grew into the World Bank Group, as the International Finance Corporation (IFC), the International Development Association (IDA), and the Multilateral Investment Guarantee Agency (MIGA) joined the IBRD.

Where the IBRD had traditionally assisted governments in financing public projects, the IFC focused on private-sector loans, helping companies improve operations, in projects likely to stimulate national economic growth. The bank also recognized that governments with very limited resources would find conventional loans to impose exorbitant debt burdens. The IDA task was thus to provide long-term loans, at exceptionally low interest rates, to the very poorest states. Via favorable repayment terms, the IDA helped developing states to provide better basic human services in education, sanitation, health care, and water resources. Finally, to draw more investors into poorer states, MIGA encouraged investment in the developing world by offering guarantees against potential losses from noncommercial risks, including political disturbances.

Over time, the scope of World Bank Group activities increased spectacularly. By the twenty-first century it was providing more than "$30 billion annually to 100 countries for more than 300 projects" (Karns, Mingst, & Stiles 2015, 433). And, the numbers have continued to climb. In 2019 the World Bank Group loaned $59.5 billion, a figure that rose during the pandemic to $74.1 billion in 2020 (World Bank 2020).

As for the International Monetary Fund, the Bretton Woods representatives approved its role in managing the new monetary system. With the member states again contributing the initial funds, the IMF could assist with currency-exchange and balance-of-payments problems and make loans to countries running low on reserves. In the ensuing decades, however, the IMF dramatically expanded its operations to become a "lender of last resort," providing "financial assistance to otherwise uncreditworthy states" (Weiss et al. 2010, 298). Michael Barnett and Martha Finnemore observed that the fund "has become intimately involved in members' domestic economies in ways specifically rejected by its founders." They wrote, "The Fund now intervenes in members' monetary, fiscal, income, labor, industrial, and environmental policies. It has become active in reconfiguring domestic political and business institutions of all kinds, advising countries on appropriate configurations or everything from their social spending to their stock markets and banking sectors" (Barnett & Finnemore 2004, 45). Another source noted: "The World Bank and . . . IMF . . . were endowed with capacities that enabled them to penetrate the national sovereignties of those states that they assisted, often to the extent that the national macroeconomic policies of Third World clients were devised and prescribed at [their] . . . headquarters" (Puchala, Laatikainen, & Coate 2007,160).

Continuing controversies thus accompanied these extensive IMF and World Bank operations. In voting, the financially stronger states carried far more weight than the weaker ones. In a sense this is a familiar feature of all banking: banks are run by those with wealth and influence in their societies. The majority of the board of directors of the World Bank Group have always come from the most highly developed states in Europe, North America, and Asia.

By the 1990s people were referring to "the Washington Consensus": "fiscal discipline, privatization of industry; liberalization of trade and foreign direct investment; government deregulation in favor of open competition; and tax reform. . . . [This] became the dominant approach undergirding almost all international development lending and IMF aid to countries experiencing financial and debt crises" (Karns, Mingst, & Stiles 2015, 384).

International borrowing, like any other bank loans, comes with strings attached: the money is lent with particular terms and conditions the borrower must respect. However, the gulf in thinking between those making the loans and those receiving the funds has led critics to charge that World Bank and IMF officials do not always understand the development needs and perspectives of developing countries. Louis Pérez observed: "The capacity of international lending agencies . . . to exact austerity measures as condition of loans often leads to calamitous internal consequences" (Pérez 2004, 171).

Another longstanding complaint is that some World Bank projects have caused "collateral damage." Economic goals may have been met, but with negative consequences for other aspects of society, including the environment. Both the IBRD and IMF have attempted to respond to such criticisms by creating procedures and internal institutions designed to enhance accountability and social responsibility. For instance, the bank created an independent inspection panel that invites and attends to objections by stakeholders. Here, community members who fear the adverse effect of a potential project can ensure that their voices are heard. The panel has stopped some projects and altered the profile of others (Brown Weiss, Lallas, & Herken 2009 271–302). Nevertheless, the criticisms have shaken public support for these key Bretton Woods institutions in many countries.

Trade

The postwar liberal economic consensus was that international trade should be freed from government restrictions, with existing protectionist barriers diminished and future ones discouraged. In 1947 representatives of twenty-three governments met in Geneva, looking to reduce trade barriers; simultaneously, American officials proposed that a new economic organization be created to apply principles of fair business dealings to trade.

Direct reform of international trade, however, was always a dicey proposition. Joan Edelman Spero observed: "The international monetary policy of various nations has been left largely to their respective central bankers, finance ministers, and a handful of cognescenti who can fathom the intricacies of exchange rate management, Special Drawing Rights (SDRs), and Eurodollar markets. Trade policy, however, is the stuff of domestic politics." She continued: "Tariffs, quotas, and non-tariff barriers are familiar issues for a broad range of economic groups. . . . The intricacies of trade policy are . . . the subject of frequent and often highly charged domestic political conflict for the simple reason that trade policy often determines prosperity or depression, profits or bankruptcy, survival or death for many industries" (Spero 1981, 74).

Although the Havana Conference of 1947–1948 did approve the International Trade Organization (ITO), domestic political problems stopped it from coming into existence. The British insisted on carving out exceptions for their Imperial Preference System. Other countries were concerned with issues ranging from economic development to balance-of-payments problems. After noting that "the Havana Charter was a complex compromise that embodied in some way the wishes of everyone, but in the end satisfied no one," Spero and Jeffrey Hart observed of American attitudes: "The traditionally high tariff policy of the Republican party; the opposition of both the protectionists, who felt that the charter went too far, and the liberals, who felt that it did not go far enough toward free trade; and the opposition of business groups that opposed compromises on open trade and at the same time feared increased government involvement in trade management coalesced in a majority against the United States' own charter" (Spero & Hart 2010, 77). By 1950 the Truman administration realized the ITO would not gain congressional approval. It withdrew, and the concept was shelved.

Back at Geneva, however, the participants had considered fifty thousand items of commerce, agreeing to reduce many tariffs (Ziring, Riggs, & Plano 2000, 390). These "tariff concessions" became part of a General Agreement on Tariffs and Trade (GATT). The GATT came into operation in 1948, and in the next decades it stood alone as the framework for regulating international trade. However, it was always a highly unusual economic organization, lacking much of a permanent administrative structure, with only a modest staff. And then, the GATT "contracting parties" neither met continuously nor voted constantly on resolutions.

Instead, the essence of the General Agreement was a set of basic principles, aligned with the new liberal economic order. In practice, each became subject to exceptions, qualifications, and elaborations, and sometimes principles were breached. (Finlayson & Zacher 1981, 566, 570, 576). Yet the vision retained real importance. One overarching principle was that all protectionist measures—all arrangements inhibiting or obstructing the free flow of goods in international commerce—ought to be minimized. Quotas were to be eliminated, and tariffs in effect when a country joined the GATT had to be changed, if at all, toward freeing trade.

Another fundamental principle was that the welter of 1930s bilateral deals ought to be replaced by a more rational and systematic regime of international commerce. Hence, trade agreements should be discussed in multilateral fora: states would periodically meet, looking to come to group decisions. GATT members thus held, notably, the Dillon Round of trade talks (1959–1962), the Kennedy Round (1964–1967), the Tokyo Round (1973–1979), and the Uruguay Round (1986–1994). These attempted to free trade in increments and sometimes in new ways.

Another key principle involved nondiscrimination: all the contracting parties had to agree that all GATT members would have equal trading rights. Governments were not to provide more favorable treatment to products made at home than those manufactured abroad. Here, for generations a staple of economic treaties had been a most-favored-nation (MFN) clause, which stated, in effect, "Whatever trade benefits you give to the most favored of your trading partners, you must also give to me." Each government that signed on to the GATT had to extend MFN status to all other contracting parties. Tariffs thus had to be the same for all GATT members.

Scores of detailed provisions put such broad principles into operation. One fundamental rule was that GATT members were not supposed to subsidize their exports, which could happen should a government fund or provide other breaks to its own companies. If a GATT member did aid a particular national industry, and another GATT party felt the subsidy harmed its competing industries, then the damaged state could institute penalties via fines ("anti-dumping levies") and "countervailing duties" that could be imposed on imports of the product being subsidized. Dispute-settlement procedures worked to resolve differences, but such penalties could be imposed until the government straying from GATT principles returned to being an upstanding trade partner.

The GATT never enjoyed great public attention, remaining, for decades, a temporary, provisional step toward a "full-blown organization . . . for policing mutual trade agreements." However, as Rosemary Righter argued, "the record of this small secretariat in bringing real prosperity to millions far outshone that of most UN agencies; its championing and refereeing of an open trading system underpinned a long and mutually enriching postwar global boom" (Righter 1995, 366).

PROGRESS AND PROBLEMS

Indeed, the postwar international economic order, with its progressive liberalization and its innovations in banking, finance, and trade, helped bring on an economic rebound and a surge in trade that was furthered by falling transportation costs and the communications revolution.

In the decades after World War II, trade grew more rapidly than ever before: doubling in the 1950s, and more than doubling again in the 1960s (Luard 1983, 67). From 1955 to 1970 the percentage of exports to gross national product rose substantially in major countries: from 4.4 percent to 6.8 percent in the United States, from 8.1 percent to 14.1 percent in Japan, from 7.6 percent to 24 percent in Italy, from 38.6 percent to 63.1 percent in the Netherlands (Spero 1981, 82). The newly industrializing countries (NICs)—led by such "Little Tigers of Asia" as Malaysia, Taiwan, Singapore, and South Korea—managed to attract much foreign investment, while developing manufacturing capacity and a healthy export trade.

As the Cold War ended and the post–Cold War era commenced, trade was far more plentiful and much freer than ever before. GATT membership had grown from the original 23 contracting parties to fully 125 states, representing about 85 percent of world trade, and tariffs for most products "averaged only 2–5 percent of the imported article's value" (Ziring, Riggs, & Plano 2000, 392–393). Joan Edelman Spero and Jeffrey Hart calculated, "From 1960 to 2006, the percentage of GDP derived from trade (exports plus imports) went from 9.6 to 28.2 percent in the United States, from 35.5 percent to 84.7 percent in Germany, and from 14.5 percent to 55.1 percent in France" (Spero & Hart 2010, 80).

More broadly, longstanding divisions in international affairs were dissipating. With the Soviet collapse, capitalism took hold in Russia and Eastern Europe, while the remaining Marxist systems pivoted toward more market-oriented policies. Some midrange countries experienced a takeoff, particularly in regional trade, and India and China were starting to add the great weight of their sizeable populations and economies to global trade numbers.

Yet, while one might have expected a rosy outlook for twenty-first-century international economics, serious problems abounded—exceptions, constraints, qualifications, and unresolved issues. Most important, the tremendous growth in trade had been heavily concentrated in more developed states. And, the variety of trade that was soaring spectacularly higher was not trade in raw materials or agricultural commodities; instead, trade climbed in basic manufactured goods, then in other consumer products, like cars and aircraft, and then in machinery, chemicals, and other capital goods. Eventually, trade in high-technology items grew rapidly, too, by the 1980s reaching microchips and computers.

All of these, however, were specialties of industries in developed countries, whose trade grew much faster than that of the developing world. Indeed, exports from developing states, standing at 30 percent of total world exports in 1950, had dropped to 17 percent by 1975 (Luard 1983, 68). In 1973, after major oil-producing countries formed the Organization of Petroleum Exporting Countries (OPEC), using the cartel to coordinate oil exports, the price of oil rose dramatically. If one excludes oil shipments from these wealthy Third World states, the percentage of exports from developing countries drops to 12 percent (Luard 1983, 68). By the mid-1970s, then, the poor countries, representing four-fifths of the world population, accounted for only one-eighth of total trade (Luard 1983, 68).

In addition, between 1947 and 1992 the international economic system suffered seven recessions, triggering trade disputes, proliferating nontariff trade barriers, and bitter rhetoric over unfair trade practices. Cracks appeared in the American consensus favoring the postwar economic order, as politicians attributed layoffs in particular industries to unfair global trade. And, while American lawyers prevailed in many trade cases, both the GATT and WTO did issue some rulings adverse to US interests.

Furthermore, the least developed countries (LDCs) experienced tremendous difficulties in enhancing trade and national incomes. Often plagued by problems of longstanding poverty, illiteracy, and overpopulation, the LDCs had stagnant economies and low growth rates and offered few attractive prospects for foreign investors. Their governments, especially during crises, found themselves relying on charity, with international and nongovernmental organizations directing and managing incoming resources.

Then, various governments were circumventing the letter or spirit of the GATT. Many developed states were not eager to extend free-trade principles to agriculture and other politically sensitive sectors, while tariffs helped developing states to protect domestic industries that were not as efficient as foreign competitors. Moreover, a range of governments, sometimes subtly, seemed to be promoting their own consumers to buy domestic products. For instance, the United States claimed the Japanese economy remained closed to many American imports because of nontariff barriers. Examples would be government procurement policies or rules concerning licensing, or special standards in health or labeling that Japanese businesses could meet more readily than foreign businesses could.

By the 1980s some governments had started to manage trade with each other, weakening the resolve to further free-trade principles. Americans were buying much more from Japanese businesses than Japanese were from US companies, resulting in a lopsided balance of payments. Under pressure to address the problem, Japan agreed simply to reduce Japanese exports to America. Such "voluntary restraint agreements" were designed to improve the balance-of-payments problem the United States had raised, but without liberalizing trade.

Despite all of these threats to the post–World War II liberal economic order, GATT members were able to forge a new commitment to free trade principles during the Uruguay Round. Most important, they established the World Trade Organization (WTO) to further promote, oversee, and regulate international trade. Not only did the GATT contracting parties become new WTO members in 1995, but 14 additional governments signed up, bringing the roster to 146 members by 2000.

The fundamental principles of the GATT, tempered by evolutionary changes, amendments, and embellishments, continued to underpin the workings of the WTO. But, the organization could do more to police trade, including sanctioning offenders, reviewing nontariff barriers and government policies, and issuing binding decisions on cases brought before it. And, the WTO focus expanded to agriculture, intellectual property, and service industries.

A leading goal of the architects of the postwar liberal economic regime had been to bring the vast majority of countries into a multilateral trade regime. That objective has now been met, as the original 23 members of the GATT have turned into 164 WTO members, covering about 98 percent of world trade (World Trade Organization 2020). New members are supposed to change their trade practices over time to come into accord with WTO trade rules and practices. However, the issue of just how conscientiously this commitment is being carried out has repeatedly engendered controversy. After many years of negotiations, China joined the WTO in 2001, as did Russia in 2012. However, Chinese compliance with its trade commitments has been legitimately questioned, while being used to justify launching a trade war.

CONCLUSION: PROBLEMS IN THEORY AND PRACTICE

In 2011 Georg Sørenson argued that two strains of liberalism tend to clash. A "liberalism of imposition" sees liberal values as universally valid and does not shy from employing power to secure expansion of liberal principles. However, a "liberalism of restraint" emphasizes "pluralism, nonintervention, respect for others, moderation, and peaceful cooperation on equal terms." He concluded that "imposition is too much and restraint is too little: that is the liberal dilemma" (Sørenson 2011, 1–2). An important theoretical issue involves how this dilemma will play out with respect to international trade. Will the liberal economic order, whose basic pillars were constructed during and after World War II, continue to provide the essential framework for global commerce? Or, are trade wars signals that wholesale changes to international economics, in general, and to the trade regime, in particular, are impending?

In 2016 Donald Trump entered office with a more benevolent view of protectionist policies than any other modern American president. Indeed, he had espoused protectionism as a cure for US economic ills ever since publicly attacking the Reagan administration and suggesting that renewed protectionism, and the raising of tariff barriers, was the proper solution for American trade deficits with Japan (Gillespie 2016). Then, in campaigning and in office, Trump regularly criticized US trade agreements, at one point calling them "disgusting, the absolute worst ever negotiated by any country in the world" (Rampell 2016), claiming that his administration could negotiate far more favorable bilateral deals than the multilateral agreements in place. Most important, the Trump administration proved eager to trigger trade conflicts, stating, "Who the hell cares if there's a trade war?" (Rampell 2016). In short, despite the prospect of other countries raising counterbarriers to American products, a dynamic repeatedly carried out in the Trump years, the president believed that the US economy could ride out such trade storms and emerge in better shape.

And yet, the clash of what might be called "two super-heavyweight economies" threatens major repercussions. The World Bank recently calculated that the US and Chinese economies "constitute almost two-fifths of global GDP" (Plummer 2019, 195). By 2018 the US–Chinese trade frictions were being called "unprecedented since the establishment of the World Trade Organization," representing "the largest 'tariff war' in economic history to date" (Tu, Du, Lu, & Lou 2020, 200).

Now, with the election of 2020 having turned Donald Trump out of office, if narrowly, a key question is how international trade is likely to evolve. Will the US government continue to edge away from the multilateral economic regime in favor of bilateral or regional approaches? Or, will the Bretton Woods order adapt itself further to the world of the twenty-first century?

In trying to look into the future, one might first note that, to date, the US–China trade war has failed to resolve the underlying economic disputes between the two countries. Allegations concerning unfair Chinese trading practices, forced technology transfers, other intellectual property and trade secrets disputes, and Chinese government subsidies and other intervention in its economy continue to be viewed as highly problematic in both the United States and Europe (Plummer 2019, 195). Tensions are likely to remain high, an ongoing characteristic of US–Chinese relations well past Trump's departure from office.

One might also note that the pandemic of 2020–2021 has exacerbated the problems of the current international economic regime. Global economic woes caused demand to drop precipitately, causing a considerable subsequent decline in trade. What, to many, over the last decades may have seemed an inexorable process of increasing globalization suddenly stalled and then rapidly shifted to deglobalization, with travel restrictions and fragmented or strained supply chains particularly afflicting global commerce. With widespread economic distress and unemployment suddenly cardinal problems in many countries, the allure of economic nationalism has surged forward again. This strengthens the populist policy prescriptions that feature calls to roll back multilateral economic initiatives in favor of unilateral or bilateral deals.

Incoming president Joe Biden's rhetoric as well as his proposed cabinet selections suggest that more mainstream international economic policies may be in the offing. However, in politics one can rarely simply turn back the clock to some prior status quo. In a deeply and evenly divided US polity, appealing to workers by criticizing the liberal postwar economic order will likely attract politicians for years to come.

And yet, resolving costly trade conflicts may come to win votes, too. Over time, the extent to which tariffs heighten costs for consumers may become increasingly apparent, and the US economy has long been unusually consumer-driven. Large subsidies to farmers and other interest groups harmed by the trade war may be difficult to maintain in a period of post-pandemic belt-tightening. Furthermore, an extended trade war between two economic powerhouses like China and the United States will bring other countries to look to seize new economic opportunities, benefitting their economies. Such trade diversion may provide a real impetus to settle differences, sooner rather than later.

As for the current system of international trade, with the World Trade Organization as its centerpiece, neither scrapping it nor reforming it will be readily accomplished. Given the weight of the US economy, bringing about substantial changes must involve overcoming political divisions and gaining an American consensus. Identifying a potent threat can stimulate change—as it did with the threat of Germany after World War II—but, more often, the international economic regime undergoes incremental alterations, not abrupt and sweeping ones.

My sense is that it is more likely than not that the essence of the postwar liberal economic order will prove to have additional staying power. For all of its shortcomings, its accomplishments over the past seventy years continue to stand out. In various regards it has proven to be flexible and adaptable before, and may reveal those qualities again. Furthermore, while we have seen how America took and maintained a leadership role in the system, throughout the post–World War II period the US government has been preeminent in multilateral institutions, but not wholly dominant in them (Schwartz 2000, 183). Other governments had real voices in the system and retain them today. This offers hope for negotiated reforms in years to come. And yet, how to do that in a period of bitterly divided and deadlocked US government poses a very difficult question indeed.

REFERENCES

Barnett, Michael, and Martha Finnemore. 2004. *Rules for the World: International Organizations in Global Politics*. Ithaca: Cornell University Press.

Block, Fred. 1977. *The Origins of International Economic Disorder*. Berkeley: University of California Press.

Braeman, John. 2000. "Powerful, Secure and Involved: What More Should the United States Have Done?" In *Major Problems in American Foreign Relations: Vol. II Since 1914*, 5th ed., edited by Dennis Merrill and Thomas Paterson, 96–104. Boston: Houghton Mifflin.

Brockway, Thomas. 1968. *Basic Documents in United States Foreign Policy*, rev. ed. New York: Van Nostrand Reinhold.

Brown Weiss, Edith, Peter Lallas, and Anna Herken. 2009. "The World Bank Inspection Panel." In *Envisioning Reform: Enhancing UN Accountability in the Twenty-first Century*, edited by Sumihiro Kuyama and Michael Fowler, 271–302. New York: United Nations University Press.

Casey, Kevin. 2001. *Saving International Capitalism During the Early Truman Presidency*. New York: Routledge.

Finlayson, Jock, and Mark Zacher. 1981. "The GATT and the Regulation of Trade Barriers," *International Organization* 35, no. 4 (Autumn): 561–602.

Fowler, Michael. 1985. *Winston S. Churchill: Philosopher and Statesman*. Lanham, MD: University Press of America.

Galbraith, John Kenneth. 1977. *The Age of Uncertainty*. Boston: Houghton Mifflin.

Gillespie, Patrick. 2016. "Trump praises Reagan on Trade — but saw it differently in 1989." *CNN Business*, October 19, 2016, https://money.cnn.com/2016/10/19/news/economy/trump-reagan-japan-trade-1989/index.html.

Hogan, Michael. 2004. "Corporatism." In *Explaining the History of American Foreign Relations*, 2nd ed., 137–148. New York: Cambridge University Press.

Isaacson, Walter, and Evan Thomas. 1986. *The Wise Men: Six Friends and the World They Made*. New York: Touchstone.

Karns, Margaret, Karen Mingst, and Kendall Stiles. 2015. *International Organization*. Boulder, CO: Lynne Rienner.

Krasner, Stephen. 1985. *Structural Conflict: The Third World Against Global Liberalism*. Berkeley: University of California Press.

Latham, Robert. 1997. *The Liberal Moment: Modernity, Security, and the Making of Postwar International Order*. New York: Columbia University Press.

Leffler, Melvyn. 2004. "National Security." In *Explaining the History of American Foreign Relations*, 2nd ed., 123–136. New York: Cambridge University Press.

Luard, Evan. 1983. *Management of the World Economy*. New York: St. Martin's Press.

McCormick, Thomas. 2004. "World Systems." In *Explaining the History of American Foreign Relations*, 2nd ed., 149–161. New York: Cambridge University Press.

Paterson, Thomas, Garry Clifford, Shane Maddock, Deborah Kisatsky, and Kenneth Hagan. 2010. *American Foreign Relations: A History Since 1895*, 7th ed. Boston: Wadsworth Cengage Learning.

Pérez, Louis, Jr. 2004. "Dependency." In *Explaining the History of American Foreign Relations*, 2nd ed., 162–175. New York: Cambridge University Press.

Plummer, Michael. 2019. "The US–China Trade War and Its Implications for Europe," *Intereconomics* 54, 3 (May 2019): 195–196.

Puchala, Donald, Katie Verlin Laatikainen, and Roger Coate. 2007. *United Nations Politics: International Organization in a Divided World*. Upper Saddle River, NJ: Pearson Prentice Hall.

Rampell, Catherine. 2016. "Donald Trump's trade policies are dangerous." *Washington Post*, December 5, 2016, https://www.washingtonpost.com/opinions/the-dangers-of-a-trade-war/2016/05/23/ac977b.

Righter, Rosemary. 1995. *Utopia Lost: The United Nations and World Order*. New York: Twentieth Century Fund.

Schwartz, Herman. 2000. *States versus Markets*, 2nd ed. New York: St. Martin's Press.

Shewmaker, Kenneth. 1985. "Forging the 'Great Chain': Daniel Webster and the Origin of American Foreign Policy Toward East Asia and the Pacific, 1841–1852," *Proceedings of the American Philosophical Society* 129, no. 3 (September): 225–259.

Simpson, Brad. 2016. "Explaining Political Economy." In *Explaining the History of American Foreign Relations*, edited by Frank Costigliola and Michael J. Hogan, 3rd ed., 58–73. New York: Cambridge University Press.

Sørenson, Georg. 2011. *A Liberal World Order in Crisis*. Ithaca, NY: Cornell University Press.

Spero, Joan Edelman. 1981. *The Politics of International Economic Relations*, 2nd ed. New York: St. Martin's Press.

Spero, Joan Edelman, and Jeffrey Hart. 2010. *The Politics of International Economic Relations*, 7th ed. Belmont: Wadsworth, Cengage Learning.

Tu, Xinquan, Yingxin Du, Yue Lu, and Chengrong Lou. 2020. "US–China Trade War: Is Winter Coming for Global Trade?" *Journal of Chinese Political Science* 25 (2020) 199–240.

US Senate. 1936. Special Committee on Investigations of the Munitions Industry. *Munitions Industry Report*. 74th Cong., 2d sess., 1936. S Rpt. 944.

Weiss, Thomas, David Forsythe, Roger Coate, and Kelly-Kate Pease. 2010. *The United Nations and Changing World Politics*, 6th ed. Boulder, CO: Westview Press.

World Bank. 2020. "Amid Multiple Crises, World Bank Refocuses Programs and Increases Financing to $74 Billion in Fiscal Year 2020." https://www.worldbank.org/en/news/press-release/2020/07/10/amid-multiple-crises-world-bank-group-re-focuses-programs-and-increases-financing-to-74-billion-in-fiscal-year-2020.

World Trade Organization. 2020. "The WTO." https://www.wto.org/english/thewto_e/thewto_e.htm

Ziring, Lawrence, Robert Riggs, and Jack Plano. 2000. *The United Nations: International Organization and World Politics*, 3rd ed. New York: Harcourt College Publishers.

Part II

DOMESTIC FACTORS IN CHINA

Chapter Four

Institutional Adaptation and Regime Resilience under Xi Jinping

Steve Hess

INTRODUCTION

Over the last decade, China's leadership has increasingly grappled with the country's conflicting sense of identity in the international system—it is a both country that is realizing its newfound status as an assertive and confident global power and also a developing nation struggling to address significant underlying domestic fragilities and vulnerabilities. In the wake of the 2008 financial crisis, while the United States struggled with a sluggish economic recovery, Beijing applied a large stimulus package and monetary expansion to generate continued economic growth in the face of a sudden drop in global demand for Chinese exports. During this period, China's robust growth propelled it past Japan to secure the position of the world's second largest economy. For many leading officials and thinkers in China, this experience was profound. It indicated that America's relative decline was more imminent than previously assumed and that China had "emerged as a leading global power with new interests and responsibilities" (Liao 2016, 819). The number of references to "U.S. decline" in Chinese academic articles surged in 2008 and 2009 (Liao 2016, 829). Political leaders and intellectuals spoke more frequently of the "Beijing consensus" (Ramo 2004) or the "China model" as an alternative to the western mode of development. As noted by David Shambaugh (2011), the country's domestic discourse had shifted; traditionally, many Chinese elites had debated *whether* China was great power, the way to becoming one, "the discourse in recent years ha[d] shifted to what kind of major power should China be" (Shambaugh 2011, 8). This suggested that China's foreign policy posture might be shifting away from Deng Xiaoping's mantra to "hide one's capabilities and bide one's time" [*taoguang yanghui*]) to a more confident and assertive posture more in line with the country's new strength and stature. Such a shift was confirmed with the ascension of Xi Jinping to power in 2012, who has since made the attainment of the "Chinese dream," defined as "achieving the great revival of the Chinese nation," the central ideological objective of his administration (Li 2012).

Despite China's emerging status as a global power, the CCP's fifth generation of leaders continue to be heavily focused on addressing domestic sources of vulnerability. While China has emerged as a stronger and more confident player in its foreign policy, its leadership nevertheless has continued to have a "deep sense of domestic insecurity" and has been "concerned first and foremost with [its] own political survival" (Shirk 2007, 6). This concern for survival and the preservation of the Communist Party would always be the "number one priority" in shaping its foreign policy (Shirk 2007, 8). The chapter discusses a range of serious structural challenges that have confronted the Xi Jinping administration since its inception, including a rapidly graying population, slowing productivity, overcapacity, inefficient state-owned enterprises (SOEs), and official corruption—all of which are compounded by growing competition and trade confrontations with the status quo economic power, the United States. Facing the endemic inertia of the Leninist Chinese Communist Party-state and the resistance of entrenched vested interests, Xi Jinping has worked to overcome these barriers through sweeping institutional reforms of the regime, overturning decades-long efforts to institutionalize, routinize and decentralize the Party-state to personalize and recentralize the state. Such institutional reforms heavily concentrate power in Xi's hands, giving him a degree of power that has not been seen in a Chinese leader since Deng Xiaoping, if not Mao Zedong. To the present, it remains unclear whether these reforms will enable the kind of deeper, more meaningful economic reforms needed to guarantee China's continued development or whether they will ultimately undermine the hard-fought stability and dynamism of China over the last four decades, leading to regime decay or possible collapse.

SOURCES OF VULNERABILITY

The regime inherited by Xi Jinping in 2012–2013 has faced and continues to face a number of serious structural challenges that threaten China's march toward the "Chinese dream"—the attainment of becoming a fully developed country by 2049. Heading forward, China's economy is increasingly burdened by demographic challenges. Shifts in population policies and the ultimate imposition of the one-child policy in the 1980s have led to a serious gender imbalance and a rapidly decline in the national fertility rate—from a peak of 6.36 average births per woman in 1965 to 1.68 in 2017 (World Bank

Indicators 2020). A positive improvement, the increased average life expectancy at birth, up from 43.7 years in 1960 to 66.8 years in 1980 and 76.5 years in 2017 (World Bank Indicators 2020), has contributed to China's rapidly aging population. Unfortunately, it has also led to an increasing higher old-age dependency rate—the number of those aged above 65 years (currently defined as old age) as a share of those working age individuals between 15 to 64 years. In the coming decades, the working-age population will face a growing burden to support elderly dependents, cutting into the country's overall economic growth (Eggleston et al. 2013, 928–952; Hsu et al. 2018, 928–952).

Aside from demographic challenges, the Chinese economy has many additional underlying structural weaknesses. Behind the robust GDP economic growth rates witnessed after the global financial crisis, productivity growth has dropped steadily since 2008, with total factor productivity (TFP) growth occurring at a rate about half that of the decade prior to the global financial crisis. Increasingly, China's economy is shifting from a "catch up" phase of high productivity growth to a phase of slower productivity growth as it approaches the world productivity frontier—a point at which productivity gains are much harder to realize. Moreover, China's financial stimulus package in the wake of the crisis steered large volumes of funds into less productive state-owned enterprises (SOEs) (West 2019). This compounded an existing problem—with diminishing gains in productivity, China's economy has become increasingly dependent on high volumes of investment to maintain its overall growth, and continues to see policies and lending practices that favor less-productive and less-profitable SOEs over private and foreign-owned firms (West 2019). Related to these challenges, the economy has been plagued by the problem of overcapacity in sectors such as manufacturing, coal, steel, cement, gas, and aluminum, and also by the abundance of unproductive "zombie firms"—enterprises "that are unable to cover debt servicing costs from current profits over an extended period" (Banerjee & Hofmann 2018, 67). During the post-2008 stimulus, national officials pressed state banks to extend credit to subnational governments so they might invest heavily in local infrastructure projects. Local governments spent aggressively, even borrowing additional funds through the use of "local government financing vehicles," resulting in short-term stimulus, but also contributing to the country's ongoing creating a massive volume of debt amounting to $1.7 trillion USD (Naughton 2014, 21). Of great concern, many of these were low- or nonperforming investments that were unlikely to generate the income needed to service these mounting debts (Naughton 2014, 21). Additionally, since the 1990s, China has increasingly struggled with the problem of corruption. Scholars have noted that problem is pervasive and involves an array of practices, including embezzlement, graft, bribe-taking, and statistics falsification;

the theft of public resources; the protection of organized crime networks; and the buying and selling of offices (*maiguan maiguan*) (Pei 2016, 1–22). Corruption has come with serious economic costs, including capital flight (Gunter 2017, 105–117); the loss of public expenditures on education, research and development, and public health; a reduction in inbound foreign direct investment (FDI) (Dong & Torgler 2010, 18–31); and losses in the productivity of Chinese firms (Cai, Fang, & Xu 2011, 55–78). Corruption, in short, has become "predatory, pervasive and entrenched" within the CCP party-state (Pei 2016, 2), and has come to threaten the country's growth and stability.

Upon his ascension to power in 2012, Xi Jinping in many ways inherited the leadership of China at a time of great economic success and achievement. The country's GDP growth had reached an annual growth rate of 10.4 percent from 2003 to 2012, in spite of the global financial crisis in 2007–2008. However, many Chinese elites realized that the preceding Hu Jintao–Wen Jiabao administration had done relatively little to address many of the larger challenges facing the economy and the party, characterizing this as a "lost decade" in terms of meaningful economic reform (Naughton 2014, 15). Hu and Wen had spent heavily in defense, education and healthcare; cut burdensome rural taxes; and initiated the basis for a national pension and healthcare system. However, the Hu–Wen administration had not pushed the kind of deeper structural reforms to the economy that might require confronting powerful "vested interests" in Chinese society (Naughton 2014, 15). As a consequence, in December 2012, just one month after assuming the position of general secretary, Xi Jinping conducted an inspection tour of Shenzhen and Guangzhou. The symbolism of the visit was clear; in a replication Deng Xiaoping's 1992 southern tour, Xi was signaling his commitment to deepening market reforms. At a December 9 seminar with cadres in Guangzhou, Xi stated: "We must implement the strategy of using innovation to drive development, and push forward structural changes in economic development. . . . The reforms will not stop and the pace of opening up will not slacken" (Lam 2012, 3). At the Third Plenary Session of CCP Central Committee in November 2013, Xi advanced a sixty-point "Decision on Major Issues Concerning Comprehensively Deepening Reforms." The decision stated that the market should play "a decisive role in the allocation of resources" and that the CCP "must actively and steadily advance market-oriented reforms in breadth and depth, greatly reduce the government's direct allocation of resources, and promote resource allocation in accordance with market rules, market prices, and market competition to maximize efficiency and optimize efficiency" (Central Committee of the Communist Party of China 2013). However, like those of his predecessors, Xi's bold calls for deepened reforms faced serious obstacles both within and outside the party. The "vested interests" that had helped stall reforms in the Hu–Wen era remained (Naughton 2014). This resistance to reform was deeply entrenched within the party itself, constituting a *quanguitizhi* (system of special privilege). According to Tsinghua sociologist Sun Liping in spring 2014, "The reality of so many years has told us that the *quanguitizhi* is a wall that blocks up everything; up against this wall, China can't go anywhere" (Sun 2015, xv). As noted by Naughton (2014), the party, as it underwent heavy institutionalization in the preceding decades, had become an organization where cadres had stable and predictable pathways for advancement in the party-state. And advancement in the party-state meant accessing "abundant and increasing opportunities to earn outside income" (Naughton 2014, 16). In other words, many of the same institutionalizing reforms of the preceding decades that had added predictability, professionalism, and stability to the party-state had also helped entrench vested interests that worked against the kind of additional structural reforms needed to further develop the country and attain the "China dream" sought by President Xi.

As a consequence, the early Xi administration faced a dilemma. On one hand, the Chinese economy faced serious economic headwinds—declining productivity, overcapacity in many sectors, pervasive corruption among the party cadres, capital flight, and with a quickly graying society, a rising dependency ratio. An economic slowdown, moreover, raised the risk of destabilizing social unrest (Campante et al. 2019, 1–2). On the other hand, addressing the deeper structural hurdles that might prevent Xi Jinping from achieving his overarching "Chinese dream"—the rejuvenation of the Chinese nation, required shaking up and disrupting a system that had helped to stabilize the party-state over the last several decades. In pursuit of this goal, Xi has worked to consolidate power under the central leadership, has led a sweeping anticorruption campaign, has attacked and marginalized factional rivals at the top of the party, and has acted assertively to root out and eliminate rival ideologies and foreign values in Chinese society and the party cadre and cultivate a compelling and unifying national ideology. In Xi's view, such methods have been necessary to overcome the party's own resistance to change, strengthen the party and sustain its grip on power, and ultimately implement the deeper economic reforms needed for China to continue on its current growth trajectory and realize the Chinese dream.

However, after initiating this process early in his first term in office, Xi's efforts have faced increasing complications—first associated with an escalating US–China trade war and later with the 2020 COVID-19 outbreak. Accusing China of unfair trade practices, the United States raised import tariffs on steel and aluminum in March 2018. China immediately retaliated with tariffs on U.S. meat, fruit, wine and aluminum. The United States thereafter imposed additional 25 percent tariffs on $50 billion USD of Chinese imports in July and August, and China retaliated with its own 25 percent tariffs on $50 billion USD of American imports. This process of escalation and retaliation, continued on throughout 2019, ultimately resulted in the United States placing tariffs on a grand total of $550 billion USD in Chinese goods, and China imposing tariffs on $185 billion USD of American imports (Itakura 2020, 77–78; Wong & Koty 2020). The ongoing trade war has contributed to "volatility in the stock market, greater uncertainty and declining levels of consumer confidence" (Economy 2019, 50). China's slowing rate of economic growth, which expanded at an annual rate of 6.1 percent in 2019—its slowest growth rate in twenty-nine years (Reuters 2020). However, as noted by Andrew Polk (2019), "China's current economic slump is overwhelmingly, indeed almost entirely due to domestic economic challenges and policy choices . . . [and] while trade tensions over the past year have had a significant effect on financial markets, individual companies and specific geographies, in aggregate, the direct effect on the Chinese economy has been minimal" (Polk 2019, 26). The economy was also negatively impacted by the COVID-19 outbreak, which slowed annual GDP growth to 1.9 percent in 2020. However, by the fall of the 2020, early International Monetary Fund forecasts indicated that China was likely to experience a faster than expected recovery in the forthcoming year, reaching a rate of 8.2 percent growth that far outpaced other major economies and would contribute greatly to pulling up global economic numbers (International Monetary Fund 2020, 1–9). And while the ongoing trade war and impact of the 2020 COVID-19 pandemic has added additional headwinds to a slowing Chinese economy, Xi Jinping's grip on power has remained very secure. As noted by Victor Shih (2019), "Xi Jinping remains the undisputed leader of China. It would take a truly massive economic shock to threaten his power" (Shih 2019, 18).

MULTILATERAL THREAT MANAGEMENT

Even for Xi Jinping, firmly entrenched atop the CCP party-state, the political elite of nondemocratic regimes lack the kind of procedural legitimacy enjoyed by democracies. Leaders are not selected by the population through regular, competitive elections and political decisions are not made through an open, deliberative process. Consequently, authoritarian regimes always have a relatively tenuous grip on power and must rely on a combination of performance, cooptation, and repression to sustain themselves (Frantz & Stein 2012, 295). Threats to an authoritarian regime's survival can emerge from two directions: "horizontal threats" posed by regime insiders and "vertical threats" presented by popular challengers. Maintaining the survival of the regime requires developing and maintaining a system of "multilateral threat management" (Schedler 2009, 326). In China, scholars have identified a number of institutional adaptations that the Chinese Communist Party (CCP) has applied to address horizontal and vertical threats and maintain the survival of the regime.

In terms of horizontal threats, the CCP has over the last three decades established a pattern of norm-bound leadership successions and merit-based criteria for cadre appointments and promotions. This shift has helped to normalize and institutionalize the selection of leaders and minimize the threat posed by factionalism (Nathan 2003, 7–11). As noted by Montinola, Qian, and Weingast (1995), Beijing has established a system that can be described as "market-conforming federalism." Under this system, local cadres are granted a high degree of autonomy over economic decision making within their own territories. Operating under hard budgetary constraints, local officials have a strong incentive to compete with one another to best foster local economic activity and attract outside investment. This can be accomplished by minimizing rent-seeking behavior and through the effective provision of public goods, such as infrastructure and effective property protections (Montinola et al. 1995, 55–59). The personnel management system adopted by the post-Mao CCP leadership has also embraced economic growth as one of several criteria used by central authorities to score and rank the performance of cadres. Chen, Li, and Zhou (2005) and Chen et al. (2017) have found that a cadre's record of economic growth has been a strong predictor of his/her likelihood of being promoted to higher office (Chen et al. 2005, 422–424; Chen et al. 2017, 341–359). In addition to economic growth, cadres were also scored according to other "hard targets," such as fiscal collection and stability maintenance, and less important "soft targets," such as propaganda work and recruiting party members (Edin 2003, 39–40). Some recent research has begun to challenge the notion that advancement in the party is a largely merit-based process. Using a biographical data set, Shih, Adolph, and Liu (2012) found no evidence that party officials with strong economic growth were more likely to be rewarded with promotions. Instead, other factors, including provincial revenue collection, educational credentials and importantly, factional ties to leading officials, were the strongest predictors for advancement into higher office (Shih et al. 2012, 166).

This pattern of normalized and institutionalized rule has also been premised upon the principle of collective leadership, emphasized since the leadership of Deng Xiaoping since the beginning of the 1980s. In August 1980, Deng warned, the "over-concentration of power is liable to give rise to arbitrary rule by individuals at the expense of collective leadership" (Deng 1980). To avoid the arbitrary excesses associated with over-concentrated power under a single leader, namely the Great Leap Forward and Cultural Revolution, the party would eventually adopt term limits for the top leadership, establish a mandated retirement age, hold regular meetings, and delegate more power from the party to state institutions and agencies (Shirk 2018, 22–23). Through these changes, power was transferred away from the paramount leader to other members of the ruling elite as he "delegate[d] control to the access-to-power positions" to a privileged political organization, the Chinese Communist Party (Magaloni 2008, 716). With this "credible power-sharing" agreement, even factional rivals of the leader could realize the benefits of sustained loyalty to regime and come to believe that their long-term interests are best served by investing in the regime's institutions rather than forming "subversive coalitions" aimed at undermining these institutions (Magaloni 2008, 715). Such a shift from the personalist rule of the Mao period to a form of "institutionalized collective leadership" helped minimize the threat of divisive factionalism within the CCP and ultimately stabilize the party's grip on power (Shirk 2018, 23).

In managing vertical threats, the CCP also made important institutional adaptations. It established "input institutions" to improve regime responsiveness and popular legitimacy. This included formal petitioning and complaints systems, public opinion polling, public hearings or online commenting on draft legislation, more autonomous and active people's congresses and people's political consultative conferences, village-level elections, and a more autonomous and market-driven media landscape (Nathan 2003, 13–15; Dimitrov 2015, 50–72; He & Warren 2011, 269–289). Additionally, the state has decentralized, delegating more power and autonomy to subnational officials and making these authorities more responsible for addressing outbreak of social unrest. This has created a structure wherein the central authorities avoided blame for the use of repression, limited the number of incidents of unrest the center needed to directly address and encouraged citizens to engage in localized campaigns of contention in isolation rather than linking up with claimants in other localities to form nationally coordinated (and regime-destabilizing) movements. Moreover, such protests tended to be focused on material and parochial issues, targeted at local rather than national officials (Cai 2008, 415–420; Hess 2017, 21–24), and embrace regime-affirming slogans and framing, constituting a form of contention that Kevin O'Brien (1996) identified as "rightful resistance" (O'Brien 1996, 31–55). The CCP has also continually worked to improve its repressive capacity. Since the 1989 Tiananmen Square incident, the party has developed an increasingly sophisticated system of "stability maintenance" (*weiwen*) designed to maintain social and political stability. Preserving stability within one's jurisdiction was established as an important criterion for promotion among local cadres, and the number of petitions delivered to national or provincial authorities as well as the number of recorded "mass incidents" in a locality were established as performance measures (Yang 2017, 35–53; Wang & Minzer 2015, 349). Seeking to improve their assessed performance in social stability maintenance, cadres across the country developed "an expansive, well-funded, extra-legal *weiwen* apparatus" (Wang & Minzer 2015, 352), utilizing local Ministry of Public Security (MPS) and People's Armed Police Force (PAPF) personnel as well as hired thugs to suppress protests and intercepts petitioner (Wang & Minzer 2015, 352; Hess 2017, 22–23). Methods of repression have also become more sophisticated in recent years, as many local officials have adopted grid-style or net management (*wangge hua guanli*) systems. Under this approach, localities are subdivided into small grids. Within each grid, a designated official would gather and receive information about the grievances and activities of residents, reporting on criminal activities and potential sources of social discontent (Cai 2019, 483–485). Scholars have found that the party utilizes an extensive toolkit to "find, evaluate and censor" objectionable content online, using "the Great Firewall" to block entire websites, "keyword blocking" to automatically detect and remove banned words and phrases, and an army of human censors and informants to manually delete unwanted posts (King et al. 2013, 326–343). Recently, the CCP has deployed new technologies, including artificial intelligence (AI), advanced biometrics, and facial recognition software, to further deepen its ability to maintain social control over the general population. Incredible volumes of data stripped from online, records of card swipes and photos taken at security checkpoints, live feeds from a growing number of public cameras (often equipped with facial recognition software), and increasingly DNA samples collected from citizens, feed into national databases. Algorithms are then generated that allow officials to sift through this data to surveil citizens, track the movements of suspected criminals and political dissidents, and even identify those individuals most likely to participate in criminal or politically subversive activities (Feldstein 2019, 40–45). Through a combination of decentralization and institutionalization, as well as improvements to the repressive capacity of the state, the CCP party-state has remained resilient through turbulence of the reform period, effectively managing both vertical and horizontal threats to the stability of the system.

PERSONALIZATION AND RECENTRALIZATION UNDER XI

Through the dual processes of institutionalization and decentralization, Xi's predecessors proved capable of both managing vertical and horizontal threats *and* generating decades of sustained economic growth. But for Xi, these processes had also empowered vested interests resistant to change need to address deeper structural challenges—declining productivity, overcapacity, growing debt, and systemic corruption that threatened China's long-term development and the attainment of the dream of China's "great revival of the Chinese nation" (Li 2012). As a result, Xi broke with many of the patterns of leadership put in place by his predecessors, concentrated power under his person, recentralized state power, and acted to bolster the supremacy of the CCP over both the Chinese state and society. Upon assuming office, Xi worked to consolidate personal power, acting to forcefully drive potential rivals from power, namely Zhou Yongkang, Bo Xilai, Xu Caihou, Ling Jihua, and Su Rong and accusing them of "seriously violat[ing] party discipline and law" and engaging in "anti-party activity" (Fewsmith & Nathan 2020, 173–174; Shirk 2018, 24–25). Fewsmith notes that Xi pushed much further and faster than either Jiang or Hu in reshaping China's political elite. He compelled three Politburo members—Liu Qibao, Zhang Chunxian, and Li Yuanchao—to step down before reaching their retirement age during the 19th Party Congress (2017), forced high-ranking officers in the People's Liberation Army (PLA) into retirement, and breaking with perceived norms of "collective leadership" or "intraparty democracy," overwhelmingly packed the leadership of the party-state and military with close allies, granting little space for rival factions or powerbrokers (Fewsmith & Nathan 2020, 175). In contrast, under Hu, leading party officials had been given significant autonomy to oversee their own policy domains and build up their own patronage networks. Under the cover of a wide-ranging campaign against corruption led by the Central Commission for Discipline Inspection (CCDI), Xi worked to systematically deconstruct patronage networks connected to other senior party leaders (Shirk 2018, 24).

Xi has also used formal mechanisms of ideological control to ensure loyalty towards the party and his person. Worried that the loss of "ideals and convictions" among party members might lead the CCP to Soviet-style collapse (Fewsmith & Nathan 2020, 174), Xi has mandated that party officials, including those at senior levels, participate in the Mao-era practice of *biaotai* or "declaring where one stands," by engaging in public self-criticism and pledges of loyalty to the party, its leadership, and its official ideology (Shirk 2018, 25; Shambaugh 2015). In October 2015, the CCP issued new disciplinary regulations that forbade cadres from engaging in "improper discussion" (*wangyi*) or more specifically, the "discussion of the fundamental policies of the Central Party authorities, causing damage to the centralism and unity of the Party," for which violators would be subject to party discipline (Bandurski 2015). In April 2013, the central leadership circulated a communique throughout the party membership, now known as "Document 9," which warned against seven "perils": constitutionalism, universal values, civil society, neoliberalism, freedom of the press, reassessments of the history of Communist China, and the "questioning of Reform and Opening Up and the socialist nature of socialism with Chinese characteristics" (Lubman 2013; *China File* 2013). Document 9 also exhorted party officials to prioritize ideological work in their everyday operations, ensure strong adherence to "true" over "false theory" among the party cadre to "uphold strict and clear discipline, maintaining a high-level unity with the Party Central Committee under the leadership of General Secretary Xi Jinping in thought, political stance, and action," strengthen the party's control over the media, and enhance propaganda work so that the party might better guide public opinion (*China File* 2013). Around the same time, the Ministry of Education issued instructions to universities calling for "enhancing the role of the ideology in universities," which were later extended in 2015 into mandated reviews of textbooks for potential advocacy of Western values, requiring interviews of all new university hires for "political correctness"—their adherence to the party ideology (Economy 2018, 38–39). The release of Document 9 in 2013 was immediately followed by a crackdown on media outlets and civil society actors that featured several well-known cases—the censorship of an editorial titled "The Chinese Dream is the Dream of Constitutionalism" in Guangzhou-based *Southern Weekend;* the banning of Zhang Xuezhong, a professor at the East China College of Politics and Law from teaching duties after his alleged advocacy of constitutionalism; and the arrest of activist Xu Zhiyong, known for his call for greater government transparency and associated with the "new citizens movement" (Lubman 2013; Xu 2013). On July 9, 2015, the Ministry of Public Security (MPS) initiated a coordinated nationwide campaign against 236 lawyers, legal assistants, and activists across 24 provinces associated with the *weiquan*/human rights lawyering movement (Fu 2018, 554–558). After extended detentions, several leading human rights attorneys detained in the so-called 709 Incident, Wang Quanzhang and Yu Wensheng were separately tried and convicted of "inciting subversion of state power" and given jail sentences of four years or longer (Schwartz 2019; Yu 2020). While applying pressure on party members and Chinese society to adhere to the party's official ideology, Xi worked to establish himself and his ideology at the center of the party. In 2014, the State Council Information Office published Xi's *Governance of China*, a book-length collection of speeches, interviews, and photos that would later be expanded to a three-volume set with additional volumes published in 2017 and 2020. The first volume elaborated Xi's political philosophy and applied it to governance, economic development, and foreign policy (Peters 2017, 1301). In October 2016, the

Communique of the Sixth Plenum of the 18th Central Committee of the CCP referred Xi Jinping as the *hexin lingdao* or "core leader" of the party (Buckley 2016). Later, at the 19th CCP National Congress in October 2017, "Xi Jinping Thought on Socialism with Chinese Characteristics for a New Era" or "Xi Jinping Thought" was formally added to the Constitution of the Communist Party of China. This change added Xi Jinping Thought to the official party cannon, effectively elevating Xi to a position of power and leadership previously accorded only to Mao Zedong (Economy 2018, 18). With these actions, Xi has both cemented his position at the core of the Party's ideology and mission and also dramatically tightened the party's commitment to and capability of enforcing ideological adherence and discipline within its ranks and in larger Chinese society.

During the mid-1980s, the CCP leadership made efforts, spearheaded by Zhao Ziyang, to bring about the "separation of Party and government" and the "separation of Party and enterprise" (Nathan 2003, 11). As noted by Nathan (2003), after Zhao's post-Tiananmen collapse from power in 1989, these ideas were formally abandoned. However, in practice, the following two decades unleashed a process of institutional differentiation within the party-state. Some specialists in the party center oversaw ideology and propaganda, while specialists in the State Council handled economic policy (Nathan 2003, 12). Provincial and local officials were issued "mandates" from the center on what targets and priorities to pursue but also granted extensive autonomy over their everyday operations, allowing them the flexibility to determine how to achieve those mandates (Birney 2013, 55–56). Additionally, more state-owned enterprises were released from state management and allowed to pursue profits, legislative bodies such as the National People's Congress took a more prominent role in developing and advancing legislation, a norm of judicial independence was emerging in courts in criminal and economic cases, and the military was becoming more professional, less political, and more exclusively focused on national defense (Nathan 2003, 12). Under Xi, many of these patterns associated with institutionalization and decentralization have reversed—or as suggested by Fewsmith (2020), were "considerably overstated" to begin with (Fewsmith & Nathan 2020, 174). Soon after ascending to power, Xi earned the nickname "chairman of everything," as he took direct leadership of an array of leading small groups (LSGs) and commissions, including the Central National Security Commission (CNSC) and Central Comprehensively Deepening Reforms Commission (CCDRC) (originally the Central Leading Group for Comprehensively Deepening Reforms), both established after the Third Plenum of the Party's 18th Central Committee in November 2013. He also serves as chair of LSGs on cybersecurity, Taiwan affairs, military reform, foreign affairs, and economic policy (Miller

2014, 6; Shirk 2018, 23–24). These small groups each have their own devoted staff that is independent from the larger state bureaucracy and have broad, overarching mandates that allow Xi to personally oversee and direct critically important policy areas (Economy 2018, 23). The CCDRC in particular quickly emerged as a "shadow State Council," meeting on a monthly basis and issuing hundreds of policy documents providing guidance on policy areas as wide-ranging as public security, legal affairs, the environment, economic policy, public administration, discipline and party building, SOE reform, and culture and sports (Johnson, Kennedy, & Qiu 2017).

Xi has also overseen a deeper and more comprehensive reform of China's institutions at all levels of the party and state that has culminated in the personalization and recentralization of state power. After initially commissioning a feasibility study on national institutional reform in 2015, a sweeping reform amounting to an "institutional revolution" ostensibly in the interest of greater efficiency and improved governance was announced at the Third Plenum of the 19th CCP Central Committee in February 2018 and the subsequent National People's Congress (NPC) in March 2018 (Guo 2020, 816). Article 1 of the PRC Constitution, which stated "The socialist system is the basic system of the People's Republic of China," was amended to add the subsequent phrase: "The defining feature of socialism with Chinese characteristics is the leadership of the Communist Party of China" (Lawrence 2018). Combined with an earlier declaration at the 19th CCP National Congress in 2017 that "Party, government, military, civilian, and academic; East, West, South, North, and center, the Party leads everything," these reforms forcefully terminated any notion that party and state functions were to be separated and clearly asserted the supremacy of the CCP over all other institutions (Tiezzi 2019). In addition, an amendment to the PRC Constitution removed the two-term limit on the presidency, enabling Xi to serve beyond the expiration of his second term of office in 2023. Paired with the aforementioned amendment that added Xi Jinping Thought to the preamble of the Constitution, this greatly enhanced the personal power of Xi over the party-state (Lawrence 2018). With these reforms, the CCP's leadership over China's state, economy, and society was enhanced and Xi's position as the core leader of the party and developer of its guiding ideology was firmly established. Additionally, a sweeping institutional reorganization of the party-state only further cemented these positions. The 2018 NPC also created a new organization, the National Supervision Commission, designed to both complement and expand the reach of the CCP Central Discipline Commission, which was responsible for cracking down on corruption and indiscipline with the party. The new National Supervision Commission's mandate extended to "all public employees who exercise public power," regardless of whether or not they were CCP party members, including officials in the party, state bureaucracy, courts, legislatures, and administrators in "public education, scientific research, culture, health care, sports, and other such units" (Lawrence 2018). This meant academics, doctors, and employees of state-owned enterprises could fall under its purview (Shirk 2018, 24–25). The commission also has expanded enforcement powers, including the power to "interrogate and detain suspects, impose travel bans, freeze assets, conduct searches, seize property, and employ 'technical investigative measures,' all before turning cases over to the regular justice system" (Lawrence 2018). Additional institutional reforms shifted significant authority from the State Council to the party leadership. Four SLGs, including the powerful leading group on Comprehensively Deepening Reforms led personally by Xi, were upgraded to full-fledged commissions. The party's Propaganda Department acquired control over "news media, publishing and the film industry" from the State Council; the party's United Front absorbed authority over the regulation of ethnic affairs, religious affairs, and relations with overseas Chinese from the State Council; and building upon a 2017 reform, the powerful internal security force, the People's Armed Police (PAP) was removed from the joint supervision of the State Council's Ministry of Public Security, now reporting only to the Party's Central Military Commission, chaired by Xi (Lawrence 2018). Through these reforms, the party center has strengthened the power vertical within China. Xi's administration has reversed the deconcentration of power from the central leadership to specialized and professionalized state ministries, subnational authorities, the military, courts, and state-owned enterprises that had occurred over the last several decades. Instead, the nascent separation of party and state has quickly eroded, replaced instead by a rejuvenated supremacy of the party and its ideology over all other state and societal actors.

IMPLICATIONS

With recentralization, personalization, and an effective sweep of his factional rivals, Xi has established a position of power within the Chinese party-state that has not existed in the regime for decades—stretching back to Deng Xiaoping if not Mao Zedong. This development presents both great opportunity and risk. Xi's administration faces serious structural challenges—a quickly aging society and rising dependency ratio, slowing economic productivity, the persistence of inefficient state-owned enterprises and zombie firms, rising debt, deeply entrenched corruption, well-established vested interests resistant to reform, and increasingly problematic international environment—exemplified not only by trade wars with the United States but also in increasingly negative views of Beijing in countries as diverse as Australia, the United Kingdom, Germany, Canada, South Korea, and Japan (Silver, Devlin, & Huang 2020). In dealing with these structural challenges in a difficult environment, Xi's recentralization of power gives him the opportunity to leverage his control over the party-state to fundamentally reshape China's economy in order to help it achieve the "Chinese dream" of the "great rejuvenation of the Chinese people"—attaining the Two Centenary Goals of becoming a "moderately well off society" by 2021, the 100th anniversary of the CCP and a "completely developed country" by 2049, the 100-year anniversary of the People's Republic of China (Omoruyi 2018). Analysts suggest that China's economy is in serious need of financial reforms, such as relaxing constraints on the operation of foreign financial institutions in the Chinese market to allow them to compete with China's four big but inefficient state-owned banks, reforming capital markets to increase flexibility in China's interest rates, loosening up controls over capital inflows and outflows to better integrate into the global financial system, reforming the tax system, improving the social safety net, reforming (or completely eliminating) the *hukou* system, improving property rights protections, and deregulating state controls over land and energy resources (Dollar 2020, 6–9; Kroeber 2013). Many such goals align with the ambitious economic agenda proposed early in the Xi administration at the Third Plenary Session of the 18th Central Committee of the Communist Party of China in November 2013 (CCP Central Committee 2014). If Xi seeks to pursue meaningful reform, his formidable power may be necessary to overcome the resistance of powerful vested interests and the heavy inertia of a bureaucratic state lacking in transparency and accountability. Centralization, however, also poses substantial risk. As noted by Fewsmith (2020), Xi's reforms to the system seem incompatible with the type of dynamic economy he seeks to create: "The centralization of power, the renewed emphasis on the role of the party, and the tightening of ideology all seem inconsistent with an increasingly diverse and contentious society, the close integration of the Chinese and global economies, and the need for innovation and embedded in global production chains" (176). Minzer (2018) warns that many of Xi's actions have effectively ended a dynamic period of reform in post-Maoist China, where "tentative efforts at political institutionalization," which enabled "political stability, ideological openness, and rapid economic growth" have become undermined, leading to a new age—the "counter-reform era" (Minzer 2018, 26–34). Hopes that China might gradually evolve into a liberal and representative country have faded, and sustained authoritarianism, likely of a more repressive and hardline nature than in the recent past, seems to be the country's most likely future (Minzer 2018, 161–166). For Shambaugh (2016), this hardening of authoritarianism, demonstrated by growing "coercion, control and bureaucratization," increased demands for "feigned compliance with the regime's propaganda," and the flight of affluent citizens and their capital abroad is symptomatic of a system in "a state of atrophy and inexorable decline" (125–129).

REFERENCES

Bandurski, David. 2015. "Improper Readings of Improper Discussion." *Medium: China Media Project,* November 29, 2015. https://medium.com/china-media-project/improper-readings-of-improper-discussion-80a99a0f0eda

Banerjee, Ryan, and Boris Hofmann. 2018. "The Rise of Zombie Firms: Causes and Consequences." *BIS Quarterly Review* (September): 67–78. https://www.bis.org/publ/qtrpdf/r_qt1809g.pdf

Bin Dong and Benno Torgler. 2010. "The Consequences of Corruption: Evidences from China," Fondazione Eni Enrico Mattei (FEEM) Working Paper, No. 73: 1–39.

Birney, Mayling. 2013. "Decentralization and Veiled Corruption under China's 'Rule of Mandates.'" *World Development* 53: 55–67.

Buckley, Chris. 2016. "Xi Jinping Is China's 'Core' Leader." *New York Times,* October 30, 2016. https://www.nytimes.com/2016/10/31/world/asia/china-xi-jinping-communist-party.html

Cai Hongbin, Hanming Fang, and Lixin Colin Xu. 2011. "Eat, Drink, Firms, Government: An Investigation of Corruption from the Entertainment and Travel Costs of Chinese Firms." *Journal of Law and Economics* 54, No. 1: 55–78.

Cai Yongshun. 2008. "Power Structure and Regime Resilience: Contentious Politics in China." *British Journal of Political Science* 38, No. 3 (July): 411–432.

Cai Yongshun. 2019. "Information as a Source of Pressure: Local Government and Information Management in China." *Interdisciplinary Political Studies* 5, No. 2: 477–509.

Campante, Filipe R., Davin Chor, and Bingjing Li. 2019. "The Political Economy Consequences of China's Export Slowdown." National Bureau of Economic Research Working Paper w25925 (December): 1–2.

Central Committee of the Communist Party of China. 2013. "Decision of the Central Committee of the Communist Party of China on Several Important Issues Concerning Comprehensively Deepening the Reform." Third Plenary Session of the 18th Central Committee of the Communist Party of China. November 12, 2013. http://www.gov.cn/jrzg/2013-11/15/content_2528179.htm.

Central Committee of the Communist Party of China. 2014. Decision of the Central Committee of the Communist Party of China on Some Major Issues Concerning Comprehensively Deepening the Reform. January 16, 2014. http://www.china.org.cn/china/third_plenary_session/2014-01/16/content_31212602.htm

Chen Jie, Danglun Luo, Guoman She, and Qianwei Ying. 2017. "Incentive or Selection? A New Investigation of Local Leaders' Political Turnover in China." *Social Science Quarterly* 98, No. 1 (2017): 341–359.

Chen Ye, Hongbin Li, and Li-An Zhou. 2005. "Relative Performance Evaluation and the Turnover of Provincial Leaders in China." *Economics Letters* 88, No. 3 (2005): 421–425.

China File. 2013. "Document 9: A ChinaFile Translation." November 8, 2013. https://www.chinafile.com/document-9-chinafile-translation

Deng Xiaoping. 1980. "On the Reform of the System of Party and State Leadership." *The Selected Works of Deng Xiaoping,* August 18, 1980. https://dengxiaopingworks.wordpress.com/2013/02/25/on-the-reform-of-the-system-of-party-and-state-leadership/.

Dimitrov, Martin. 2015. "Internal Government Assessments of the Quality of Governance in China." *Studies in Comparative International Development* 50, no. 1: 50–72.

Dollar, David. 2020. "China's Economy Bounces Back, But to Which Growth Path?" *China Leadership Monitor* 65 (Fall): 1–11. https://www.prcleader.org/dollar

Economy, Elizabeth. 2018. *The Third Revolution: Xi Jinping and the New Chinese State*. Oxford, UK: Oxford University Press.

Economy, Elizabeth. 2019. Testimony before Hearing on "U.S.–China Relations in 2019," *U.S.–China Economic and Security Review Commission.* September 4, 2019. https://www.uscc.gov/hearings/us-china-relations-2019-year-review.

Edin, Maria. 2003. "State Capacity and Local Agent Control in China: CCP Cadre Management from a Township Perspective." *China Quarterly* 173: 35–52.

Eggleston, Karen, Jean C. Oi, Scott Rozelle, Ang Sun, Andrew Walder, and Xueguang Zhou. 2013. "Will Demographic Change Slow China's Rise?" *Journal of Asian Studies* 72, no. 3: 505–518.

Feldstein, Steven. 2019. "The Road to Digital Unfreedom: How Artificial Intelligence is Reshaping Repression." *Journal of Democracy* 30, no. 1: 40–52.

Fewsmith, Joseph, and Andrew Nathan. 2020. "Authoritarian Resilience Revisited: Joseph Fewsmith with Response from Andrew J. Nathan." *Journal of Contemporary China* 28, no. 216: 167–179.

Frantz, Erica, and Elizabeth A. Stein. 2012. "Comparative Leadership in Non-Democracies." *Comparative Political Leadership,* edited by Ludger Helms: 292–314. New York: Springer.

Fu Hualing. 2018. "The July 9th (709) Crackdown on Human Rights Lawyers: Legal Advocacy in an Authoritarian State." *Journal of Contemporary China* 27, no. 112: 554–568.

Gunter, Frank R. 2017. "Corruption, Costs, and Family: Chinese Capital Flight, 1984–2014." *China Economic Review* 43: 105–117.

Guo Baogang. 2020. "A Partocracy with Chinese Characteristics: Governance System Reform under Xi Jinping." *Journal of Contemporary China* 29, no. 126: 809–823.

He Baogang and Mark E. Warren. 2011. "Authoritarian Deliberation: The Deliberative Turn in Chinese Political Development." *Perspectives on Politics* 9, no. 2: 269–289.

Hess, Steve. 2017. "Decentralized Meritocracy: Resilience, Decay, and Adaptation in the CCP's Threat-Management System." *Problems of Post-Communism* 64, no. 1: 21–24.

Hsu Minchung, Pei–Ju Liao, and Min Zhao. 2018. "Demographic Change and Long–Term Growth in China: Past Developments and the Future Challenge of Aging." *Review of Development Economics* 22, no. 3: 928–952.

International Monetary Fund. 2020. "World Economic Outlook, October 2020: A Long and Difficult Ascent." *World Economic Outlook* (October 2020). https://www.imf.org/en/Publications/WEO/Issues/2020/09/30/world-economic-outlook-october-2020

Itakura, Ken. 2020. "Evaluating the Impact of the US–China Trade War." *Asian Economic Policy Review* 15, no. 1: 77–93.

Johnson, Christopher, Scott Kennedy, and Mingda Qiu. 2017. "Xi's Signature Governance Innovation: The Rise of Leading Small Groups." Center for Strategic and International Studies, October 17, 2017. https://www.csis.org/analysis/xis-signature-governance-innovation-rise-leading-small-groups

King, Gary, Jennifer Pan, and Margaret E. Roberts. 2013. "How Censorship in China Allows Government Criticism but Silences Collective Expression." *American Political Science Review* 107, no. 2: 326–343.

Kroeber, Arthur. 2013. "Xi Jinping's Ambitious Agenda for Economic Reform in China." Brookings Institution, November 17, 2013. https://www.brookings.edu/opinions/xi-jinpings-ambitious-agenda-for-economic-reform-in-china/

Lam, Willy. 2012. "Xi Jinping's 'Southern Tour' Reignites Promises of Reform." *China Brief* 12, no. 24, December 14, 2012. https://jamestown.org/program/xi-jinpings-southern-tour-reignites-promises-of-reform/

Lawrence, Susan. 2018. "China's Communist Party Absorbs More of the State," Congressional Research Service, March 23, 2018. https://crsreports.congress.gov/product/pdf/IF/IF10854/2

Li, Ellen. 2012. "Chasing the China Dream." *The Atlantic,* December 13, 2012. https://www.theatlantic.com/international/archive/2012/12/chasing-the-chinese-dream/266236/.

Liao Nien-chung Chang. 2016. "The Sources of China's Assertiveness: The System, Domestic Politics or Leadership Preferences?" *International Affairs* 92, no. 4: 817–833.

Lubman, Stanley. 2013. "Document No. 9: The Party Attacks Western Democratic Ideals." *Wall Street Journal,* August 27, 2013. https://www.wsj.com/articles/BL-CJB-18646

Magaloni, Beatriz. 2008. "Credible Power-Sharing and the Longevity of Authoritarian Rule." *Comparative Political Studies* 41, nos. 4–5: 715–741.

Miller, Alice. 2014. "More Already on the Central Committee's Leading Small Groups," *China Leadership Monitor* 44 (Summer): 1–8. https://www.hoover.org/research/more-already-central-committees-leading-small-groups

Minzer, Carl. 2018. *An End of an Era: How China's Authoritarian Revival is Undermining Its Rise.* Oxford, UK: Oxford University Press.

Montinola, Gabriella, Yingyi Qian, and Barry R. Weingast. 1995. "Federalism, Chinese Style: the Political Basis for Economic Success in China." *World Politics* 48, no. 1: 50–81.

Nathan, Andrew. 2003. "China's Changing of the Guard: Authoritarian Resilience." *Journal of Democracy* 14, no.1 (January): 86–99.

Naughton, Barry. 2014. "China's Economy: Complacency, Crisis, and the Challenge of Reform." *Daedalus* 143, No. 2: 14–25.

O'Brien, Kevin J. 1996. "Rightful Resistance." *World Politics* 49, no. 1: 31–55.

Omoruyi, Ehizuelen Michael Mitchell. 2018. "China's March towards a Moderately Well-off Society," *China Daily,* March 16, 2018. http://www.chinadaily.com. cn/a/201803/16/WS5aab21d6a3106e7dcc142020.html

Pei Minxin. 2016. *China's Crony Capitalism: The Dynamics of Regime Decay.* Cambridge, MA: Harvard University Press.

Peters, Michael. 2017. "The Chinese Dream: Xi Jinping Thought on Socialism with Chinese Characteristics For a New Era." *Educational Philosophy and Theory* 49, no. 14: 1299–1304.

Polk, Andrew. 2019. Testimony before Hearing on "U.S.–China Relations in 2019." *U.S.–China Economic and Security Review Commission,* September 4, 2019. https://www.uscc.gov/hearings/us-china-relations-2019-year-review

Ramo, Joshua Cooper. 2004. "The Beijing Consensus." The Foreign Policy Center. http://www.chinaelections.org/uploadfile/200909/20090918021638239.pdf

Reuters. 2020. "China's Economic Growth Slows to 6.1% in 2019, Near 30-Year Low." January 16, 2020. https://www.reuters.com/article/us-china-economy-gdp -instantview/instant-view-chinas-economic-growth-slows-to-6-1-in-2019-near -30-year-low-idUSKBN1ZG092

Schedler, Andreas. 2009. "The New Institutionalism in the Study of Authoritarian Regimes." *Totalitarianism and Democracy* 6, no. 2: 323–340.

Schwartz, Matthew. 2019. "Chinese Human Rights Lawyer Sentenced To More Than 4 Years in Prison." *NPR News,* January 29, 2019. https://www.npr.org/ 2019/01/28/689238095/chinese-human-rights-lawyer-sentenced-to-more-than -4-years-in-prison

Shambaugh, David. 2011. "Coping with a Conflicted China." *Washington Quarterly* 34, no. 1 (Winter): 7–27.

Shambaugh, David. 2015. "The Coming Chinese Crackup." *Wall Street Journal,* March 5, 2015. https://www.wsj.com/articles/the-coming-chinese-crack-up-1425659198

Shambaugh, David. 2016. *China's Future.* Cambridge, UK: Polity Press.

Shih, Victor. 2019. Testimony before Hearing on "U.S.–China Relations in 2019." *U.S.–China Economic and Security Review Commission,* September 4, 2019. https://www.uscc.gov/hearings/us-china-relations-2019-year-review

Shih, Victor, Christopher Adolph, and Mingxing Liu. 2012. "Getting Ahead in the Communist Party: Explaining the Advancement of Central Committee Members in China." *American Political Science Review* 106, no. 1: 166–187.

Shirk, Susan. 2007. *China: Fragile Superpower.* Oxford, UK: Oxford University Press.

Shirk, Susan. 2018. "The Return to Personalistic Rule." *Journal of Democracy* 29, no. 2 (April): 22–36.

Silver, Laura, Kat Devlin, and Christine Huang. 2020. "Unfavorable Views of China Reach Historic Highs in Many Countries," Pew Research Center, October

6, 2020. https://www.pewresearch.org/global/2020/10/06/unfavorable-views-of
-china-reach-historic-highs-in-many-countries/

Sun Liping. 2015. Quoted in Willy Lam, *Chinese Politics in the Era of Xi Jinping*. New York: Routledge.

Tiezzi, Shannon. 2019. "Xi Jinping Continues His Quest for Absolute Party Control," *The Diplomat*, July 10, 2019. https://thediplomat.com/2019/07/xi-jinping-contin ues-his-quest-for-absolute-party-control/

Wang Yuhua and Carl Minzner. 2015. "The Rise of the Chinese Security State." *The China Quarterly* 222: 339–359.

West, John. 2019. "China, a Low Productivity Superpower." *The Interpreter*, October 31, 2019, https://www.lowyinstitute.org/the-interpreter/china-low-productivity-super power

Wong, Dorcas, and Alexander Chipman Koty. 2020. "The US-China Trade War: A Timeline." *China Briefing*, January 16, 2020. https://www.china-briefing.com/ news/the-us-china-trade-war-a-timeline/

World Bank Indicators. 2020. https://data.worldbank.org/

Xu Zhiyong. 2013. "New Citizens' Movement." *Chinese Law and Government* 46, nos. 5–6: 148–154.

Yang, Dali L. 2017. "China's Troubled Quest for Order: Leadership, Organization and the Contradictions of the Stability Maintenance Regime." *Journal of Contemporary China* 26, no. 103: 35–53.

Yu, Verna. 2020. "Chinese Human Rights Lawyer Jailed for Four Years, Says His Wife." *The Guardian*, June 18, 2020. https://www.theguardian.com/world/2020/ jun/18/chinese-human-rights-lawyer-yu-wensheng-jailed-for-four-years-says-wife

Chapter Five

Great Power Diplomacy with Chinese Characteristics and the US–China Trade War

Ngeow Chow Bing

The US–China trade war erupted in 2018 under the Trump administration. It has since morphed into a more comprehensive, intense, dangerous and across-the-board strategic rivalry between the two most powerful countries in the world. More than just trade and economic issues, the US–China rivalry now encompasses many spheres, including technology, cyber-security, military, diplomacy, media, higher education and scientific research, human rights, and political ideology and values. The term "New Cold War" or "Cold War 2.0" has now registered increasing currency. Tensions between the United States and China had already steadily built up in the later years of the Obama administration. However, it was the Trump administration's determination to confront China over trade issues that precipitated the downward spiral of the bilateral relationship, which was further accelerated by the outbreak of the COVID-19 pandemic in late 2019. Barring a major turn of events, and despite a new Joe Biden presidency in place since 2021, US–China relations will unlikely recover in the immediate and near future.

As documented in the other chapters of this edited volume, the complex interplay of political, economic, and technological factors, domestic and international factors, and structural and immediate factors accounted for the outbreak of the US–China trade war, and for the overall deterioration of the US–China bilateral relationship. This chapter will add on to this analysis, through examining the idea of great power diplomacy with Chinese characteristics (*Zhongguo tese de daguo waijiao* 中国特色的大国外交, abbreviated as GPDCC in this chapter), which has become the mainstream diplomatic conception, discourse, and practice under Xi Jinping. Understanding GPDCC is crucial in understanding how the Chinese leadership see China's place in the world and its relations with the United States. When confronted with the US–China trade war, GPDCC was the lens through which the Chinese leadership interpreted the trade war's origins and development, prepared themselves, mobilized domestic and international support, and counteracted.

RISE OF THE GREAT POWER NATIONAL IDENTITY IN CHINA

In the Chinese official translation, the term *daguo* is often translated as "major country" and *daguo waijiao* as "major country diplomacy." The English term "great power" has some negative connotations in China, as it is sometimes also understood (or misunderstood) as referring to *baquan* 霸权 (hegemonic power). Still, by all accounts, China is definitely a great power.

China did not always see itself as a great power. Deng Xiaoping's famous dictum of "keeping a low profile" (*taoguang yanghui* 韬光养晦) was based on the premise of China being a relatively weak power. However, since the 2000s, the conception of China as a great power has steadily emerged in Chinese official, scholarly, and popular discourses. China had already experienced two decades of continuous high growth so far (and would experience more rapid growth in the years to come), and its growing importance was acknowledged, with approval, by then US deputy secretary of state, Robert Zoellick, who urged China to undertake the role of a responsible stakeholder. The responsible stakeholder concept, whatever the intention from the United States and its policy implications, was clearly an endorsement of China as a rising areat power from the United States. China also had then its own conception of peaceful rise (*heping jueqi* 和平崛起), articulated by the influential Chinese theorist Zheng Bijian. Peaceful rise, of course, suggested China was on ascendance to a great power status, but Zheng argued that China would pursue such ascendance with peaceful means and would not be a disruptor to the international order, nor would China be a challenger to the established status of the United States (Zheng 2005).

While the theoretical and intellectual discussions of China as a Great Power were active in think tank, academic, and media circles, the official side of China was still cautious to embrace such a conception. However, this began to change after the global financial crisis in 2008. Jeffrey Bader, an official of the first Obama administration specializing in East Asian affairs, wrote in his memoir about the "emergence of a somewhat different China" between 2008 and 2010 "from the one the United States had been dealing with for several decades" before. "One could detect a changed quality in the writing of Chinese security analysts and Chinese official statements, and in some respects in Chinese behavior" (Bader 2012, 79–80; see also Christensen 2015, 242–243). The more assertive China since 2008 was a manifestation of an incipient great power national identity (Ngeow 2017; Hoo 2018). When the identity changed, the behavior changed too.

With the cautious style of leadership under Hu Jintao and Wen Jiabao, China was still perhaps unsure whether it was too early to drop *taoguang yanghui*. China was still thought to be not fully ready to embark on a more proactive, confident, and assertive foreign policy. The ascendance of Xi Jinping to the top leadership position of China in November 2012, however, dispensed the cautious attitude of his predecessors, and accelerated the momentum towards the full assumption of the great power identity by China. As a great power, China would behave the way a great power behaves. China's foreign policy and diplomacy would be different since then, encapsulated in the concept of great power diplomacy with Chinese characteristics (GPDCC).

GREAT POWER DIPLOMACY WITH CHINESE CHARACTERISTICS: RECLAIMING CHINA'S LEADERSHIP ROLE IN THE WORLD

Since coming into power, Xi Jinping has unveiled many concepts and terms that have significantly enriched the diplomatic discourses coming out of China. Compared to his predecessor, Hu Jintao, whose two notable diplomatic concepts were peaceful development (*heping fazhan* 和平发展, modified from peaceful rise) and harmonious world (*hexie shijie* 和谐世界), Xi introduced many more terms and concepts into the lexicon of Chinese diplomats. Each of these concepts stands on its own right and is also a constitutive component of the GPDCC discourse.

Xi convened his first Central Conference on the Work Related to Foreign Affairs in November 2014, in which for the first time he coined the phrase GPDCC, and articulated its ideas and vision. Xi followed up with his second Central Conference on the Work Related to Foreign Affairs in June 2018, which reaffirmed GPDCC and further introduced new concepts. (Again, the diplomatic activism of Xi can be clearly contrasted with that of his predecessor, Hu Jintao, whose ten-year tenure only saw the Central Conference on the Work Related to Foreign Affairs convened once, in August 2006.)

In the 2014 conference, Xi outlined what GPDCC was meant to accomplish: to continue and enrich the path of peaceful development, to build a community of shared future (*mingyun gongtongti* 命运共同体), to build a new type of great power relations (*xinxing daguo guanxi* 新型大国关系), to propose and implement a correct view on morality and interest (*zhengque yili guan* 正确义利观), to advocate for a "common, comprehensive, cooperative, and sustainable" new security concept (*xin Yazhou anquanguan* 新亚洲

安全观), to practice amity, sincerity, mutual benefit and inclusiveness in its relations with neighboring countries (*qincheng huirong de zhoubian waijiao* 亲诚惠容的周边外交), and to practice a policy towards Africa based on truthfulness and sincerity. Xi took note that the trends towards multi-polarity, globalization, peace and development, changes in the international system, and overall prosperity in the Asia-Pacific region had not changed. The world had been undergoing profound changes with the simultaneous appearance of many opportunities and challenges, but the overall trend was toward the direction of peace and development. Hence, China must make correct strategic judgment based on understanding of historical laws, and not be confused by immediate events. At this historic juncture, he urged that China must now further enrich and develop its diplomatic work ideas, and to have distinctive "Chinese style, Chinese manner and Chinese attitude" in its diplomacy (Xi 2018, 198–201).

His 2018 speech reiterated the main points laid out in 2014, but added some new emphases, which together were summarized as the ten main aspects of the diplomatic thought of GPDCC. Compared to the 2014 speech, Xi added phrases such as "baseline thinking" and (*dixian siwei* 底线思维) and "risk consciousness" (*fengxian yishi* 风险意识) in his 2018 speech, an indication of the more severe international environment China was facing, and a marked reminder to both domestic and foreign audiences that China would resolutely and assertively react to any perceived infringement on its core national interests. In addition, he restated the crucial need to base decisions on a correct understanding of historical law (*lishiguan* 历史观), and added also that such correct understanding be extended to the macro situation (*dajuguan* 大局观) and proper place of China's role in the world (*jiaoseguan* 角色观).

The concept of China's proper role in the world is interesting. As Xi expounded it, Chinese diplomats and policy makers not only have to calmly analyze the world situation, they have to insert the proper role of China into the multiple relations in the world, have a clear understanding of such a role, and formulate proper foreign policies. Xi went on to assert that China was facing the best developmental period in modern time, and at the same time the world has also been experiencing profound systemic changes that only occur once in centuries (Xi 2018, 538–539). The implication was clear. China's proper role is that it is a rising great power, facing the opportunities and risks coming from the systemic changes in the international system. As scholar Jianwei Wang commented, Xi's GPDCC discourses effectively have placed China at the central stage of the world (Wang 2018, 18–19). China could no longer be a passive actor, but must act proactively and assertively, to carve out its own destiny and shape the future trajectory.

Arguably Xi himself has been the driving force in projecting a qualitatively different sort of Chinese foreign policy and diplomacy. Observers outside of mainland China termed Xi Jinping a "transformational leader" with wide implications for China's relations with the world (Hu 2018). His foreign policy ideas and initiatives effectively constitute a "paradigm shift" (Wang 2018). Inside China, many Chinese scholars echo and provide the intellectual support to Xi's ambitions by elucidating further the meaning and implications of GPDCC. A group of scholars associated with the Central Party School (CPS), for example, suggested that GPDCC is the third generation of the foreign policy and diplomacy of the People's Republic of China (PRC). In their periodization scheme, the first generation refers to the first thirty years of the PRC, under Mao Zedong's rule, as "sovereignty protection" (*zhuquan weihuxing* 主权维护型) diplomacy, while the second generation refers to the next thirty years, beginning with Deng Xiaoping's leadership, as "development driven" (*fazhan zhudaoxing* 发展主导型) diplomacy. GPDCC is the third generation, defined as "great power responsibility" (*daguo zerenxing* 大国责任型), which essentially is about how to bear and deliver more responsibilities not only to the people of China but also to the international community (Luo et al. 2016, 28–30).

According to these CPS scholars, this third generation of Chinese diplomacy will be defined by the better abilities of China to protect and advance its national interests (including defending core interests, protecting expanding overseas interests, and expanding China's discourse power and soft power in the international scene), the proactive engagements by China to improve the international order and global governance system, and the carrying out of the international responsibilities of China as a great power. GPDCC can be further analyzed at three levels (concept, strategy, responsibility). At the conceptual level, GPDCC calls for China to innovate on diplomatic concepts, to explain to the world what are China's visions and answers to the major questions facing the international community. Concepts such as peaceful development, new security concept, neighborhood diplomacy based on amity, sincerity, mutual benefit and inclusiveness, and so forth, are essentially meant to convince the world how acceptable China's visions and answers are (Luo et al. 2016, 40–129).

At the strategy level, there are several components. China has elevated the importance of its neighborhood regions to a much higher level, encapsulated in the notion of "big neighborhood" (*dazhoubian* 大周边), encompassing the Eurasian landmass. China needs to engage these neighbors through economic cooperation, public goods provision, institutionalization, and normative shaping efforts. The Belt and Road Initiative (BRI) is essentially such a strategy. The new type of great power relations (NTGPR) is to secure stable relations with other great powers amidst China's rise. China will also treat developing countries, especially Africa, as the key strategic support leverage whereby China has more room to cultivate its soft power and economic partnership, and to deliver its responsibilities. At the multilateral scene, China will become a proactive creator and shaper of international rules and norms. Finally, GPDCC will not be complete without realizing the dream of China as a maritime great power.

While the concept and strategy guide how China is to become a great power, it is at the responsibility level that the authors argue how China is to behave well as a great power. They argue that, on the basis of its own resources and capabilities, China should commit to greater efforts to promote economic growth and poverty alleviation in poor countries, to contribute to peace and security, to contribute to resolving global issues such as climate change, and to promote South-South cooperation and North-South dialogue. While China is not interested in exporting its own ideology, as part of the contribution to the world and delivery of responsibilities China is willing to share its own developmental lessons. Fundamentally, GPDCC is also to shape the soft power of China. As a great power, both the economic and political systems of China should be respected. "A truly Great Power should also be a Great Power in soft power" (Luo et al. 2016, 40).

Wang Fan, vice president of China Foreign Affairs University and also a prolific scholar, aptly pointed out in his work that promoting GPDCC is a "systematic project" (*xitong gongcheng* 系统工程) that requires not only comprehensive coordination, systematic planning, and institutional reforms, but importantly also the cultivation of appropriate perspectives, psychological preparation, and capacity building, among the Chinese people in general but their officials and diplomats in particular. Wang particularly emphasized four kinds of "software building" requisite of GPDCC. First, China has to cultivate great power mentality (*daguo xintai* 大国心态); it has to transition from seeing itself as a weak power to believing itself as a great power, and have the confidence to have dialogue with other great powers on the basis of equality. Second, China needs to assert great power authority (*daguo quanwei* 大国权威); it should be able to provide leadership, deliver responsibilities, and act morally. Third, China must exercise great power influence (*daguo yingxiangli* 大国影响力). China is widely recognized to be a powerful country today, but how to translate power into the kind of influence that is widely accepted is the key to the rise of great power status. To that end, China needs to enhance not only its discourse power but also its organizational capabilities in international affairs. Fourth, there needs to be sufficient theoretical and philosophical contributions coming from the great power (*daguo de xixiang jueqi* 大国的思想崛起). Echoing many Chinese scholars he judged that an important indicator of whether China has become a great power is its ability to provide and innovate on fresh and meaningful concepts that bear distinct Chinese perspectives but also have universal implications (Wang 2016, 21–22).

GPDCC is the foreign policy/diplomatic aspect of the overall Xi's transformation of China in politics, economics, military, and technology, which has been termed as China's "Third Revolution" by Elizabeth Economy. Commenting on Xi's diplomacy, Economy wrote that "more than any post-revolution leader, Xi staked the legitimacy of the Communist Party at least in part on its ability to reclaim a leadership role on the global stage" (Economy 2018, 190). The above discussions on GPDCC, by Xi Jinping himself and by leading Chinese foreign affairs specialists, show that to a large extent, China is indeed preparing and envisioning itself to "reclaim a leadership role on the global stage." (It should also be pointed out here that they continue to emphasize that China will be *a* leader but not *the* leader of the world.) But the normative and emotive assessments could not be more markedly different inside China and outside (especially in the developed world), in the sense that most Chinese scholars and officials see such leadership role as positive, natural, befitting to the status of China today, and fundamentally consistent and reflective of the way the international system has evolved and continues to evolve. Many Western scholars and officials, however, are at best ambivalent and at worse hostile to the idea of China claiming a leadership role at the global level, more so under a Communist Party state led by Xi Jinping, a very authoritarian leader.

Regardless, GPDCC was the mind-frame of the Chinese policy elite by the time Donald Trump came into power. The GPDCC narratives imbued a strong sense among both the elite and the populace at large, of a China being back to its rightful place in the world and hence deserving of some kind of deference and respect. To a large extent, a seemingly contradictory dynamic was set in motion with the full development of GPDCC. GPDCC indeed has made China's exercises in diplomacy more proactive, assertive, confident, muscular, and some might even say jingoistic, but it has also stressed the necessity for China to deliver its responsibilities to the world community, to be mindful of providing public goods to its neighboring countries, and to carefully cultivate relations with the other great powers to avoid conflicts, most importantly with the United States.

US–CHINA RELATIONS: THE FAILURE OF CHINA'S PROPOSAL OF NEW TYPE OF GREAT POWER RELATIONS

An operative component of GPDCC is the new type of great power relations (NTGPR), which lays out the guiding cooperative principles China will establish with other great powers, most importantly the United States. Before Trump, China believed that the proposal of constructing a NTGPR stood a chance to be accepted by the United States, despite the ideological differences and the many disagreements in multiple policy areas. From the

Chinese perspective, it was an immensely sensible proposal. China believed that this NTGPR, based on the principles of "no conflicts, no confrontation, mutual respect and win-win cooperation," will avoid the historical patterns of conflict dynamics between established and rising powers (widely known as the Thucydides Trap).

Xi Jinping first raised such a formulation to the Obama administration in his 2012 visit to the United States (Ruan 2015, 15–19). But throughout the Obama presidency the United States responded only cautiously. The United States felt that even if the objectives of the NTGPR were perhaps noble and agreeable, the proposal was too generic, idealistic, nonoperationalizable, and very likely would result in substantial concessions and costs once agreed upon. Furthermore, Chinese actions did not exactly match its words. Xi's China, bolstered by the more nationalistic GPDCC ethos, generated greater anxiety among both the United States and China's neighbors (many of them happen to be US allies) in the way it acted forcefully in the maritime disputes with its neighbors. American cynicism towards this proposal hence became even more profound (Li and Xu 2014).

From China's point of view, the NTGPR was not about the details. It was a "big picture" proposal, to put out a set of broad and agreeable patterns of relations that serve as the foundation for future directions in the bilateral relations. The details were to be worked out later after first achieving a grand consensus. Xi's China was also oblivious to the shifting perception of China. It interpreted its own assertive actions in its dispute with neighbors as reacting to challenges that were infringing upon the core national interests of China. With such differences, China's proposal for the new type of great power relations went nowhere with the Obama administration.

Early into the Trump administration there were some tentatively positive signs to the Chinese that the United States would perhaps be more willing to accept China's proposition. Rex Tillerson, the first secretary of state of the Trump administration, once famously agreed to the Chinese formulae of "no conflicts, no confrontation, mutual respect and win-win cooperation" in March 2017, during his first visit to China, but this proved to be an outlier incident with no significant impact at all. Instead, after an uncertain 2017, the bilateral relationship started to deteriorate significantly throughout the Trump administration, after President Trump initiated the trade war in 2018.

GREAT POWER DIPLOMACY WITH CHINESE CHARACTERISTICS AND US–CHINA TRADE WAR

Since GPDCC became the major diplomatic concept in 2014, China was immersing itself in the rhetoric of national rejuvenation and a leadership role in the world. It was under this context that China was confronted with the trade war. At least some of the complaints and charges made against China by the United States, such as limited market access, lack of intellectual property protection, and subsidies to state-owned enterprises, were not unreasonable. If China were to make reforms along these demands, these reforms would be in line with some of China's own market-oriented reform direction. But China did not interpret the trade war in purely economic and technical sense. Thomas Pauken II, a Beijing-based observer, noted that the inclusion of very hawkish anti-China personalities such as Steve Bannon, John Bolton, and Peter Navarro as high-level officials in the Trump administration alarmed Beijing significantly, and helped entrench the Chinese interpretation that the trade dispute was not just about trade matters but beyond that. Moreover, both the leadership and the public of China were also convinced that China and the United States were on equal terms and China should not easily give in to the demands from the Trump administration. "Xi would have lost more by signing a trade agreement with Trump it if had appeared that he was surrendering too soon" (Pauken 2020, 100).

The way that the trade war eventually developed, with spillovers into technological battles against Chinese major technological companies such as Huawei, ZTE, Tencent, and ByteDance, and into other policy areas such as Xinjiang and Hong Kong, reinforced the interpretation that the trade war was more about trade and investment disputes; it was a key strategic tool to slow down, if not contain, the rise of China. GPDCC, premising on a stronger China ready to defend its interests better, predictably led to firm and forceful responses from the Chinese government in the face of the trade war.

Amidst the US–China trade war, GPDCC also underpinned the more proactive diplomatic activism of China. Since the beginning of the trade war, Chinese official media often highlighted that the US trade war was targeted not only against China but also against many long-standing trade partners of the United States. Coupled with American withdrawal from various multilateral commitments, these were manifestations of the selfish, unilateralist, and protectionist "Make America Great Again" ethos of the Trump administration. American unilateralism was often contrasted with the BRI, which exemplifies continued Chinese active contribution and delivery of responsibilities to the developing world. China's participation in and support for regional and global governance institutions were reinforced, illustrating a more confident China engaging with, contributing to, and ready to lead multilateral institutions. Finally, securing stable relations with other great powers in the context of the US–China trade war was a crucial test of Chinese exercises of its diplomatic skills as a great power.

The BRI and the Developing World

The BRI has often received skeptical, if not outright negative and hostile reactions, from the mainstream media, policy makers, and think tank circles in developed countries (and in India). But the BRI vision has successfully captured the imagination of many leaders, officials, and entrepreneurs of the developing world. It successfully highlights the need to redouble the efforts to invest in basic infrastructure, which has been vastly underfunded in many parts of the developing world. As a long-term vision, the success or failure of the BRI is not defined in the short term, nor by a few notable controversial projects. By and large, most governments of the developing world understand how infrastructure connectivity opens up new venues for trade, investment, opportunities, mobility, and so forth that will be vastly beneficial to the well-being of their people. Moreover, the BRI vision was backed by substantial increase in infrastructure funding, either through the China-initiated Asian Infrastructure Investment Bank or bilaterally with Chinese developmental banks. Hence, charges of "debt trap diplomacy" notwithstanding, the BRI has continued to garner support in large parts of the developing world. The First BRI Summit, held in Beijing in 2017, gathered the attendance of 30 foreign leaders, and in the Second BRI Forum in 2019, the number increased to 39. According to Chinese official numbers, as of March 2019, the "Chinese government China had signed 173 cooperative agreements with 125 countries and 29 international organizations" (Office of the Leading Group for Promoting the Belt and Road Initiative 2019, 6), with a vast majority of these countries coming from the developing countries in Eurasia. The Second BRI Forum also saw China taking on some of the criticisms leveled against it, by promising that China will double the efforts to ensure that the BRI will be high quality, "cleaner," and "greener." China is also eager to present this international endorsement of the BRI as the demonstration of the international support that China has in the face of an increasingly hostile developed world, led by the United States, and as a testimony to China's shouldering up its responsibilities.

Other than the BRI, there are also other mechanisms where China connects with the developing world. Forum on China-Africa Cooperation (FOCAC), first initiated in 2000, has become the major avenue for Beijing to coordinate its economic relationships with the African continent. In September 2018, the Third Summit of FOCAC was held in Beijing, which issued a joint declaration titled *Toward an Even Stronger China-Africa Community with a Shared Future*, formally endorsing a major Chinese preferred rhetorical term. China agreed to undertake eight major initiatives in the areas of industrial cooperation, infrastructure connectivity, trade facilitation, green development, capacity building, health care, people-to-people exchange, and peace and security.

China also pledged $60 billion USD to fund various projects and cooperation plans. In June 2019, a follow-up meeting was held where a more detailed implementation blueprint was issued, covering a very comprehensive agenda of cooperation from economics to security.

Despite the persistent issue of the South China Sea dispute, China's economic relations with Southeast Asia have also been strongly enhanced in recent years, and the trend will likely continue after the signing of the Regional Comprehensive Economic Partnership (RCEP) in November 2020. RCEP includes almost all East Asian economies, excludes both the United States and India, and will cement a major East Asian economic trading bloc, with China as the largest economy within it. The fate of RCEP was strongly contrasted by the Trans-Pacific Partnership (TPP). The American withdrawal created an economic leadership vacuum in East Asia. Although Japan undertook a major effort to continue TPP in the form of the Comprehensive and Progressive Trans-Pacific Partnership (CPTPP), the major appeal of TPP was lost with the absence of the vast American market. For many developing countries in Southeast Asia, the economic opportunities provided by RCEP, together with the BRI, both underlie and entrench China's position in the region.

The BRI, FOCAC, and RCEP are just a few examples of where Beijing made significant inroads to mobilize and consolidate its growing appeal and support in the developing world. This is not to suggest that there are no contentious issues between China and the developing world. Nevertheless, these relations with the developing world are very useful for China to present itself as a responsible great power, exercising effective GPDCC, demonstrating Chinese leadership and commitment, and mobilizing even more support, in contrast to the unpredictable and capricious Trump administration.

Multilateralism and Global Governance

Chinese official narratives also often framed the US–China trade war as one aspect of the destabilizing foreign policy of the Trump administration. The disdain towards regional and global multilateral institutions shown by Trump and his leading officials also presented great opportunities for China to underscore its active engagement in these institutions, and to emphasize China as a constructive actor to preserve and stabilize the current order. While the Trump administration withdrew from the Paris Climate Agreement, the Iran Joint Comprehensive Plan of Action, United Nations Economic, Social and Cultural Organization (UNESCO), the World Health Organization (WHO), and the arms control treaties with Russia and significantly weakened the World Trade Organization (WTO) by blocking the appointment of judges to the WTO dispute resolution body, China steadily made advances in many multilateral bodies. More than any of the permanent members of the United Nations Security Council, Chinese nationals are now leading four of the fifteen specialized agencies of the United Nations (Food and Agriculture, International Telecommunication, Industrial Development, and International Civil Aviation).

China has also become more skillful in leveraging other multilateral platforms to advance its interests, visions, and agenda. Despite its gradual declining efficacy as a multilateral regional economic regime, China continued to emphasize the importance of the Asia-Pacific Economic Caucus (APEC). China utilized the APEC platform to portray China's commitment, contribution, and leadership in terms of regional economic integration. In 2014, Beijing used its host advantage to announce a roadmap towards the ambitious Free Trade Area for Asia Pacific (FTAAP). In the November 2020 APEC summit, Xi Jinping announced China's serious considerations to join the CPTPP, potentially upending a trade regime that was originally designed to exclude China. Although these promises may not always materialize, China was adept in using these platforms to underscore its commitment to multilateralism.

Other than APEC, the G20 is also another significant multilateral governance platform for China to exercise its leadership role. China utilized its hosting role in 2016 to change G20 from a short-term multilateral coordination mechanism to a forum focusing on more long-term changes and reforms in global economic governance. China broadened the agenda of G20 from a narrow focus on finance to a more comprehensive set of global economic issues, enhanced cooperation with other multilateral economic bodies, and increased the voices and representation from the developing world (Ren 2017). China also sees the G20 as more reflective of the developmental trend (compared to the G7) and a more balanced institution where established and emerging powers have an equal say on global economic governance matters.

He Yafei, a former deputy foreign minister of China, offered a prescient analysis of Chinese active participation in these multilateral governance bodies and institutions. He acknowledged that the existing rule-based international political-economic order has been beneficial to China. China needed to, and should, follow the rules established mostly by the developed powers in the past, and use these rules to protect and advance its interests. But from a long-term perspective, the critical question is not whether China should follow the rules but whether China has any say in the formation, shaping, and evolution of these rules and norms in the future. In future global governance, China should not be a marginal player in the setting of rules and norms but an important or leading actor (He 2015, 178–179). Seen in this light, the greater diplomatic activism of China in participating, leading, and shaping international and multilateral governance institutions is consistent with the kind of ambitions or vision the GPDCC conception implied.

Relations with Other Great Powers

GPDCC guided that China should also apply the same framework of NTGPR ("no conflicts, no confrontation, mutual respect and win-win cooperation") towards great powers other than the United States, including Russia, Europe (both as a collective European Union and individual major European powers such as France and Germany), Japan, and India. But this did not mean China would necessarily be more accommodating. In fact, as a great power more determined to protect its own national interests, China could and would harden its attitudes even more if it felt that its core interests were being challenged and undermined, especially by another great power.

Amidst the US–China strategic rivalry, China's approach to other great powers was to consolidate its relationship with Russia, prevent Japan and Europe to form a united front with the United States, and induce India to maintain its strategic autonomy.

The most successful relationship was with Russia. Although there are ample reasons for China and Russia to be suspicious of each other, both countries managed to not only stabilize their relationship but greatly expanded and improved it during the post–Cold War period. Chinese scholars often stress that there is a genuine sense of mutual respect, mutual trust, and status equality that forms the basis for China and Russia to develop their relationship (Xing 2016), while foreign observers tend to argue that the relationship is more driven by temporary convergence of strategic interests. Regardless, it counted as a diplomatic achievement for Beijing as Russia did not pivot to the United States after a relatively Russia-friendly Donald Trump entered the White House. Instead, both countries reinforced their relationship during the Trump years, exemplified by the two joint bilateral statements issued in June 2019 (*Joint Statement on the New Era of Comprehensive Strategic Partnership of Coordination* and *Joint Statement on Enhancing Global Strategic Stability*). The US–China trade war also provided opportunities for China to import more Russian agricultural produce. In 2019, bilateral trade volume hit $110 billion USD, a historic height. While the relationship is still manifested most strongly in political and strategic terms, it is increasingly being supplemented by a more substantial economic relationship in the midst of the US–China trade war (Zhongguo guoji wenti yanjiyuan 2020, 304–307).

Xi Jinping visited Brussels in April 2014 and secured a Four Partnership relationship with the European Union (EU): Peace Partnership, Growth Partnership, Reform Partnership, and Civilizational Partnership (Wang 2016,

271). Within a few years, however, China–EU relations deteriorated. Both the EU and major European countries were dismayed by the increasing authoritarian turn in Xi's China, its more assertive foreign policy, and its lack of economic reforms. No longer highlighting the Four Partnership, the EU in 2019 labeled China "an economic competitor in pursuit of technological leadership" and "a systemic rival promoting alternative models of governance," although these descriptions were balanced by statements that China could still be a "partner" in some policy areas (European Commission 2019). Various European governments also started to restrict the participation of Chinese companies in the construction of 5G telecommunications infrastructure. Some Chinese analysts attributed the hardening European attitude towards China as being caused by the domestic populism within Europe (Zhongguo guoji wenti yanjiuyuan 2020, 321).

China and the EU have common interests in climate change cooperation, preserving the Iran nuclear agreement, and preserving the multilateral trade order centered on the World Trade Organization (WTO). While there were strong reasons for the EU to be dissatisfied with China's performance under the WTO, both sides have had enough consensus to preserve the WTO in contrast to the dismissing attitude from the Trump administration. The successful conclusion of the EU–China Horizontal Aviation Agreement in May 2019, the EU–China Geographical Indications Agreement (which protects the brand names of both European and Chinese products) in November 2019, and most importantly, the Comprehensive Agreement on Investment (CAI) in December 2020 (still subject to approval by European Parliament) underscored that both the EU and China have common grounds in economic cooperation. The successful conclusion of the CAI negotiation meant China managed to prevent the EU from fully becoming an anti-China united front led by the United States, notwithstanding the growing misgivings about China in many European capitals. The structural differences in EU-China economic relations are actually similar to US–China trade disputes, and China could point to the CAI as a different way to resolve such differences in contrast to the US-launched trade war.

China-Japan relations during the Trump years, however, were better than expected. Former Japanese prime minister Abe Shinzo managed to produce an excellent relationship with the Trump administration. But Abe's Japan also maintained remarkably a relatively stable relationship with China despite the difficult geopolitical environment. Top-level political interactions between Japan and China were actually quite frequent. Xi Jinping visited Osaka in June 2019 for the G20 meeting and would have made a state visit to Japan in 2020 if not for the COVID-19 pandemic. Abe also visited Chengdu in December 2019 for the 8th China-Japan-Korea meeting. These visits built on the positive momentum created in the 2018 mutual official visits of Premier Li Keqiang and Prime Minister Abe. Japan also has not explicitly opposed the BRI. Japan and China held a Forum on Third-Party Market Cooperation to explore Japanese participation in the BRI, and some Japanese enterprises are already quietly participating in some BRI projects. Japan also played a key role in facilitating the conclusion of RCEP negotiation (Japan had insisted before that India's inclusions must be secured for RCEP). Japan even appeared reluctant to condemn Beijing's imposition of a National Security Law in Hong Kong. These developments, however, happened concurrently with the deepening of Japanese strategic and security alignment with the United States in the new strategic framework of the Indo-Pacific. Japan also acted as the major competitor of the BRI through its own infrastructure initiative called Partnership for Quality Infrastructure.

Finally, India is another great power with which China seeks to have a stable relationship. An India fully aligned with the United States and other Indo-Pacific partners in security and strategic matters will be deeply troubling to China. Up until the middle of 2020, China managed to ensure India to stay relatively neutral and continue its tradition of strategic autonomy. As an ambitious growing great power of its own, India did not seek a formal alliance that would restrict is room of diplomatic maneuver. As long as relations with China remained manageable, benefits of strategic autonomy would seem to outweigh the costs. China also fully leveraged on this strategic autonomy tradition of India. Xi Jinping and Prime Minister Narenda Modi held two informal summits in Wuhan (2018) and Chennai (2019), which secured India's relative detachment from the growing US–China strategic rivalry. Before the deadly border conflict that erupted in May 2020, China had managed well its relationship with India, with growing multisectorial cooperation and dialogue mechanisms, and many points of consensus regarding North-South division and other global issues. Both militaries also participated in bilateral joint exercises and multilateral exercises under the Shanghai Cooperation Organization (SCO) framework.

The May 2020 border conflict, however, changed the dynamics and strategic calculations of Indian political elite significantly. India signed a crucial military intelligence sharing agreement with the United States in October 2020 (*Basic Exchange and Cooperation Agreement on Geospatial Cooperation*) and expanded the 24th Exercise Malabar (held in early November 2020), which hitherto was restricted to mainly the United States, India, and Japan, to include Australia, bringing all four navies of the Quad in the Indo-Pacific for joint naval exercise together for the first time. While India has not formally abandoned its strategic autonomy, it is clear that its strategic and security alignment is increasingly tilted towards the United States. Both China and India were led by leaders who saw themselves leading the revival of great power status of their respective countries, and felt difficult to back down.

In reviewing the four sets of relations between China and the other great powers, China could count the relations with Russia as a successful case of embodiment of the NTGPR. Relations with Japan and Europe were always going to be difficult given the strategic divergence between them and China. Many Japanese and European enterprises were equally disappointed with the lack of access to the Chinese market, and could benefit greatly if the objectives of the US–China trade war in forcing China to open up more sectors, reduce subsidies, and protect intellectual property rights are realized. But due in no small part to the unpredictability and unilateralism of the Trump administration, the EU and Japan also refused to go all the way in joining the United States in confronting China. Instead, the signing of RCEP and CAI testified to their continued commitment to cooperative economic relationship with China. China could also claim that it managed relations with India relatively well, until the border issue escalated drastically in the middle of 2020. Without this incident, China could have secured almost all its major objectives in managing relations with these great powers in the midst of the US–China trade war.

CONCLUSION

This chapter examines the US–China trade war from the perspective of GP-DCC, the dominant diplomatic conception under Xi Jinping. It argues that this conception is the explicit articulation of a great power national identity that first emerged after the global financial crisis. Under GPDCC, China has been a much more proactive, confident, and assertive actor on the international scene. Chinese analysts stress that under GPDCC China is going to offer more public goods and deliver its responsibilities to the international community, but this diplomatic conception also stresses a China that will defend its interest even in a more forceful way. Chinese intransigence and nationalism could be further driven by the more muscular GPDCC narratives. Hence, GPDCC arguably results in a more contradictory China as well.

Viewed from this perspective, Chinese leaders would interpret the US–China trade war not as an attempt to deal with economic issues but an attempt to stifle the rise of China. In the face of the US–China tensions, China mobilized even greater support in the developing world, strengthened participation in the multilateral global governance institutions, and attempted to manage well its relations with other great powers, all consistent with the GPDCC conception and discourses. Through the BRI and other initiatives, China did manage to secure strong support in the developing world. The attempts by the United States and other developed countries to criticize China's human rights records at the UN General Assembly often failed exactly because of the support given to China by many countries in the developing world. China also successfully enlarged its presence and influence in many multilateral global governance institutions as the influence of the United States waned under the Trump administration. On managing relations with other great powers, China only managed partial success. Relations with Russia were well consolidated and with Japan and Europe relatively stabilized. China–India relations, however, suffered a serious breakdown due to the border dispute that erupted in May 2020.

Given that the COVID-19 pandemic first started in China and the slow responses by the local authorities contributed to the growing spread of the coronavirus, China was especially sensitive to international criticisms that negatively affect its self-portrayed image of a great power with leadership aspiration and responsibilities to the international community. Some of its diplomats reacted to foreign criticisms in a very defensive or even aggressive way, which backfired and earned China fewer friends rather than more. Whether China will adjust its diplomatic style remains to be seen, but the great power identity and the GPDCC narratives will continue to stay in the years to come. China wants to have an "order shaping" role in the world, and be recognized as such. Although China has often argued that it does not want to replace the United States as the leading great power, it does see an international order that revolves around and is sustained solely by the primacy and superiority of the United States as incompatible with China's preferred vision. These are also explicated in the GPDCC discourses. These normative differences add on to the structural dynamics that have already caused greater tensions in US–China relations.

REFERENCES

Bader, Jeffrey. 2012. *Obama and China's Rise: An Insider Account of America's Asia Strategy*. Washington, DC: Brookings Institution Press.

Christensen, Thomas. 2015. *The China Challenge: Shaping the Choices of a Rising Power*. New York: W. W. Norton.

Economy, Elizabeth. 2018. *The Third Revolution: Xi Jinping and the New Chinese State*. New York: Oxford University Press.

European Commission. 2019. *EU-China: A Strategic Outlook*. Brussels: European Commission.

He, Yafei. 2015. *Xuanze: Zhongguo yu quanqiu zhili* (China's Historic Choice in Global Governance). Beijing: Zhongguo renmin daxue chubanshe.

Hoo, Tiang Boon. 2018. *China's Global Identity: Considering the Responsibilities of Great Power*. Washington, DC: Georgetown University Press.

Hu, Weixing. 2018. "Xi Jinping's 'Major Country Diplomacy': The Role of Leadership in Foreign Policy Transformation." *Journal of Contemporary China* 25, no. 115: 1–14.

Li, Cheng and Lucy Xu. 2014. "Chinese Enthusiasm and American Cynicism: 'New Type of Great Power Relations.'" *China-US Focus*, December 4, 2014. https://www.chinausfocus.com/foreign-policy/chinese-enthusiasm-and-american-cynicism-over-the-new-type-of-great-power-relations/

Luo, Jianbo et al. 2016. *Zhongguo tese daguo waijiao yanjiu* (A Study on Great Power Diplomacy with Chinese Characteristics). Beijing: Zhongguo shehui kexue chubanshe.

Ngeow, Chow Bing. 2017. "China's Great Power National Identity and Its Impact on China-Southeast Asia Relations." In *Southeast Asia and China: A Contest in Mutual Socialization*, edited by Lowell Dittmer and Ngeow Chow Bing, 21–49. Singapore: World Scientific.

Office of the Leading Group for Promoting the Belt and Road Initiative. 2019. *The Belt and Road Initiative: Progress, Contributions and Prospects*. Beijing: Foreign Languages Press.

Pauken, Thomas II. 2020. *US vs China: From Trade War to Reciprocal Deal*. Singapore: World Scientific.

Ren, Xiao. 2017. "The G20: Emerging Chinese Leadership in Global Governance?" *Global Policy* 8, no. 4 (November): 433–442.

Ruan, Zongze. 2015. *Zhongguo meng de quanqiu jingwei* (The Global Dimensions of the China Dream). Hong Kong: Zhonghua shuju.

Wang, Fan. 2016. *Daguo waijiao* (Great Power Diplomacy). Beijing: Beijing lianhe chuban gongsi.

Wang, Jianwei. 2018. "Xi Jinping's 'Major Country Diplomacy': A Paradigm Shift?" *Journal of Contemporary China* 25, no. 115: 15–30.

Xi, Jinping. 2018. *Lun jianchi tuidong goujian renlei mingyun gongtongti* (On Promoting and Constructing a Community of Common Destiny). Beijing: Zhongyang wenxian chubanshe.

Xing, Guangcheng. 2016. "Zhong E guanxi shi xinxing daguo guanxi de dianfan (China-Russia Relationship is the Model Relationship of the New Type of Great Power Relations)" *Shijie jingji yu zhengzhi* (World Economics and Politics), no. 9 (September): 14–18.

Zheng, Bijian. 2005. "China's 'Peaceful Rise' to Great-Power Status." *Foreign Affairs* 84, no. 5 (September–October): 18–24.

Zhongguo guoji wenti yanjiuyuan. 2020. *Guoji xingshi he Zhongguo waijiao lianpishu 2020* (Blue Book on International Situation and China's Foreign Affairs 2020). Beiijng: Shijie zhishi chubanshe.

Chapter Six

Chinese Domestic Politics and the Trade War

R. Lincoln Hines

INTRODUCTION

What role did domestic politics play in shaping China's behavior during the trade war? This chapter argues that the trade war between the United States and China threatened to challenge core components of the Chinese Communist Party's (CCP) legitimacy: 1) China's economic performance and 2) the party's nationalist credentials. If China's government made substantial concessions to the United States, it risked appearing weak at home. On the other hand, if it played the nationalist card, the CCP could potentially reap domestic political benefits of nationalism. However, fomenting the flames of nationalism risked prolonging the trade war, tying Chinese hands, and increasing costs to China's economy by depressing exports. The potential challenges to the CCP's legitimacy were even more pressing, considering that the trade war occurred against the backdrop of China's largest economic slump in forty years, unrest in Hong Kong, and eventually the outbreak of COVID-19.

How did Chinese leaders manage this challenge? I argue that at the outset of the trade war, the CCP was cautious about inflaming domestic nationalist sentiment, seeking to, instead, constrain public debate. If the CCP incurred audience costs, it risked constraining its diplomatic options and prolonging what could potentially be economically costly. However, as it became apparent that the trade war would be protracted, the CCP increasingly exploited the opportunity to foment nationalism sentiment. Yet the CCP did not "tie its hands" by allowing anti-American protests or by committing itself to concrete actions. Instead, the CCP engaged in vaguer and broader appeals to nationalism or what some scholars refer to as nationalist "bluster" (Weiss & Dafoe 2019) or "diversionary cheap talk" (Baggot Carter 2019).

Consequently, the CCP maintained a degree of diplomatic flexibility while reaping the domestic benefits of nationalism. The United States also provided the CCP a useful scapegoat for blaming China's slowing economy. Moreover, the Trump administration's desire to attain a symbolic "victory" meant that it provided the CCP cover for its handling of other hot-button domestic political issues, such as its treatment of Uighurs, the political protests in Hong Kong, and the outbreak of COVID-19.

Beyond explaining China's behavior during the trade war, this case also sheds light on how China might respond to future crises or disputes with the United States. This case illustrates that the CCP may view nationalism's domestic benefits to outweigh potential economic costs. Therefore, this case suggests a degree of caution for analysts and scholars assuming that increasing costs from economic interdependence will serve as a check on Chinese foreign policy. Instead, China's behavior suggests that the CCP may believe that it can strategically draw upon nationalism to stomach the economic costs of a protracted conflict.

More broadly, this case suggests potentially worrisome consequences for future conflicts or disputes with China. If China's economic growth continues to slow, leaders may become more reliant on nationalism, viewing it as an effective strategy for explaining away China's slowing economic growth. However, this case also has some less worrisome implications. As of this writing, the government has not allowed or encouraged massive anti-foreign protests, as it did during the 2012 Senkaku/Diaoyu Island dispute. This suggests that China, under Xi Jinping's leadership, may be cautious about opening the Pandora's box of audience costs. Consequently, this means that China's leaders may have increased diplomatic maneuverability, which increases the likelihood of cooperation. More broadly, although it is too soon to take stock of the long-term consequences of this dispute for US–China relations, the conflict may have shifted Chinese elite thinking to focus more on self-reliance and "economic decoupling" from the United States and provided fodder for emergent tropes of a Cold War between the United States and China.

This chapter is organized as follows. The following section discusses the role of nationalism and economic performance as sources of legitimacy for the CCP. It then briefly reviews scholarship on how domestic pressures shape China's foreign policy. Based on this analysis, I discuss the difficult policy choices the trade war presented to Chinese leaders. Finally, I conclude with a discussion on the lessons learned from this conflict for understanding the role of domestic politics in China's bargaining behavior.

REGIME LEGITIMACY AND THE TRADE WAR

To comprehend the challenges the trade war posed to the CCP, it is necessary to describe the role of economic performance and nationalism in the CCP's domestic legitimacy. As an authoritarian regime, the CCP is comparatively more insulated from domestic public opinion than democratic countries. However, although China's government is authoritarian, the CCP does not wholly disregard public sentiment, nor does its rule depend solely on coercion.

The CCP legitimizes its rule, in part, by claiming to restore China to its rightful position. According to nationalist narratives, after millennia of Chinese dominance and dynastic rule, China fell into disarray after its encounters with Western imperialist powers. This period, roughly dating from the First Opium War to the founding of the People's Republic of China (PRC) in 1949, is often referred to as China's Century of Humiliation (Wang 2014). During this time, China suffered several foreign incursions from Western powers and "unequal" treaties, and China began to disintegrate due to large-scale rebellions (i.e., the Taiping and Boxer Rebellions). Ultimately, the Qing Dynasty collapsed, and China fell into a period of warlordism, followed by a Japanese invasion and then a civil war. It was only with the PRC's founding that China was finally unified, with Mao announcing that China had "stood up" to the world.

Owing to this history, the CCP presents itself as the heir to the nationalist May 4th Movement, and the guarantor of China's security, sovereignty, and prestige, mandated to restore China to former glory (Callahan 2010; Wang 2014). Under Mao's leadership, this nationalist myth combined with China's Marxist-Leninist ideology, served as the foundation of the CCP's legitimacy. However, after Mao's death and the ushering in of the reform era, China's market liberalization provided the CCP a new pillar of legitimacy: economic performance. Yet China's economic reforms also created several new challenges for regime legitimacy. Rapid economic modernization led to problems such as growing corruption, income inequality, and pollution. China's economic reforms, moreover, were not accompanied by political reforms. At the same time, China's market-oriented reforms undermined the ideological pillar of the regime's legitimacy. This legitimacy crisis came to a head in 1989 during the CCP's violent crackdown on Tiananmen Square protestors, an event that rattled the country. Moreover, watching the fall of communist-led countries abroad, Chinese leaders believed China had narrowly dodged a bullet (Meisels 2012).

To manage this growing legitimacy crisis, the CCP sought alternative sources of legitimacy, even attempting to revive traditional elements of Chinese culture such as Confucianism (Wu 2014). Importantly, scholars note that in the reform era, the CCP's legitimacy rests on a combination of nationalism and performance legitimacy (e.g., see Downs & Saunders 1998–1999; Wang 2014; Zhong 1996). However, the second pillar of the CCP's legitimacy, economic performance, is increasingly under threat. As China moves away from cheap, export-led growth to becoming a higher-income and skills-based economy, it must avoid stagnating or falling into what is often called the "middle-income" trap (Glawe & Wagner 2020). The pace of China's economic development has already begun to cool. After decades of breakneck economic growth between 8 and 10 percent per year, in 2018 China's GDP growth slowed to 6.8 percent, and in 2019 decelerated to 6.1 percent (Zhang & Yao 2019).

In this context, the trade war threatened to significantly challenge the CCP's domestic legitimacy. The trade war harmed China's economic interests by decreasing exports and injecting a high degree of uncertainty into global investment markets. Considering these economic costs, China's leaders had a clear interest in ending the trade war as soon as possible. However, this goal of quickly resolving the dispute was at odds with maintaining the CCP's nationalist credentials at home. If the CCP appeared to back down to the United States, it risked appearing weak to domestic audiences. Therefore, although it might quickly end the trade war, even symbolic acquiescence to the Trump administration's demands threatened to damage the CCP's image domestically.

DOMESTIC POLITICS AND FOREIGN POLICY

China's political system and its foreign policymaking system are not monolithic, and concerns over public opinion and legitimacy can potentially place real constraints on Chinese policy making. To conceptualize how domestic considerations shape Chinese behavior on the world stage, Putnam's (1988) conception of "two-level" games is worth considering. According to the "two-level" games model, when actors (or states) engage in strategic interactions or bargaining with other states, their "bargaining space" or their options for diplomatic negotiation are constrained by domestic audiences' preferences. If domestic audiences are strongly opposed to some issue, then diplomatic actors have fewer negotiating options and, therefore, may adopt a hard-line stance. On the other hand, if a problem is less salient for the public, policy makers may have greater latitude for pursuing their policy interests. Similarly, scholars argue that democracies may have a bargaining advantage over autocracies during crises because they can better signal their resolve. When democratic leaders "go public" with a dispute, they effectively "tie their hands" to domestic audiences. If, after going public with these disputes, leaders "back down," they risk being punished at the ballot box (Fearon 1994; Slantchev 2006; Tomz 2007).

Similarly, scholars argue that authoritarian regimes can also face domestic audience costs (Weeks 2008). Weiss (2013, 2014) finds evidence of audience costs in the Chinese context. In China, street-level, anti-foreign protests cannot occur without the government's permission. These protests can quickly escalate and can have a cascading effect, leading to massive demonstrations, which may threaten to topple the regime. Therefore, when China allows nationalist or anti-foreign street protests, it can incur domestic audience costs because the government can signal that it will be punished if it backs down. These audience costs can benefit the regime's foreign policy by providing a costly or credible signal of its resolve. However, these audience costs limit the regime's diplomatic options. Should the government seek an alternative means to resolve the dispute, it may risk looking weak and suffering domestically. Consequently, if the CCP fans the flames of nationalism too much, it risks being backed into a corner (Shirk 2008) and adopting a costly policy that it would not pursue otherwise.

However, although Chinese leaders may invoke nationalism, they do not always go as far as incurring domestic audience costs. For example, rather than committing to specific actions or tolerating or encouraging anti-foreign protests, the government can use vague, nationalist rhetoric or "bluster" to reap the benefits of nationalism. Weiss and Dafoe (2019: 965) define bluster as "aggressive, vague rhetoric that is not followed by tough action." Using survey experiments, Weiss and Dafoe find that Chinese citizens approve of the CCP's "bluster," even when this rhetoric is not followed by concrete action. While bluster may not provide the CCP the bargaining advantages of audience costs, it provides the CCP diplomatic leeway for pursuing its strategic interests. Similarly, Baggot Carter (2019: 1) shows that regimes engage in "diversionary cheap talk," which is defined as "hostile foreign policy rhetoric that targets other nations." This rhetoric is used when regimes are experiencing a decline in domestic popularity, such as declining economic performance (Baggot Carter 2019: 2). As this scholarship suggests, Chinese leaders can employ heated nationalist rhetoric for purposes of diversion, without tying their hands and forcing them to take concrete actions which may be at odds with their strategic interests.

Whether it chooses "diversionary cheap talk" or "bluster," this scholarship suggests that the CCP has ways to reap domestic political benefits of nationalism from an international dispute without incurring domestic audience costs. In the context of the US–China trade war, this nationalist "bluster" provided the CCP a useful means by which to look tough on the United States before

Chinese domestic audiences. This allowed the CCP to uphold its nationalist credentials while maintaining diplomatic options for pursuing its strategic interests in trade negotiations. Moreover, the trade war provided Chinese leaders an opportunity to engage in "diversionary cheap talk," allowing Chinese leaders to use the United States as a scapegoat for China's declining economic performance.

THE TRADE WAR AND BEIJING'S CAUTIOUS NATIONALISM

In past disputes, from the American bombing of China's embassy in Belgrade to the 2012 anti-Japanese protests, Chinese leaders have fomented nationalism and encouraged anti-foreign demonstrations. By tying its hands to an angry, nationalist public, the regime generated domestic audience costs. However, during China's trade war with the United States, leaders were much more cautious in fomenting nationalism. Although the CCP promoted nationalist rhetoric, it did not promote anti-foreign protests—and, therefore, generate domestic audience costs. Instead, calculations about a protracted trade conflict and the bargaining leverage and resolve of the United States drove Chinese leaders to promote nationalism, albeit cautiously.

As discussed above, the trade war presented the CCP with a difficult dilemma. First, when the trade war began, China was experiencing an economic slowdown; thus, the economic performance pillar of the CCP's legitimacy was already strained. The trade war threatened to even further exacerbate these challenges to the government's legitimacy. Therefore, from an economic standpoint, China was incentivized to make as few concessions as possible, yet to also see a quick end to the trade war. Second, the CCP also had to manage the challenge of nationalism and public opinion. If the CCP faced audience costs, it could strengthen China's bargaining strength and projection of resolve. However, tying China's hands could potentially backfire. The Trump administration's erratic behavior did not indicate that it would act as a "rational" negotiating party. For example, upon assuming office, President Donald J. Trump withdrew the United States from the Trans-Pacific Partnership (TPP), an agreement negotiated over several years, which would decrease regional trade barriers and create a regional trade bloc tied to the United States (and which excluded China) (Baker 2017). Trump's reversal of this decision that appeared to be so clearly aligned with US strategic interests signaled that his approach to China reflected domestic considerations, rather than a logic of realpolitik.

Trump had staked considerable political capital in his ability to "win" a trade war. Trump had even claimed that "trade wars are good and easy to win" (Franck 2018). Trump's path to election victory in 2016 was in winning swing states along the country's economically depressed Rust Belt—a region that had lost manufacturing jobs as a result of globalization. On the campaign trail, Trump promised to return jobs to these areas through a victorious trade war. However, such a promise was nearly impossible to keep. Decreased exports to China would shift American manufacturing to other low-cost countries in Southeast Asia. Nonetheless, Trump staked his reputation and image on being tough on China. Trump sent several signals about his intention to adopt an aggressive posture toward China. For example, Trump had appointed the hawkish trade advisor Peter Navarro, who had written a book entitled *Death by China*, outlining economic damage wrought by a strategic trade relationship with China (Beech 2016).

Therefore, Trump did not appear willing to "back down" and thus it became apparent that the trade war would be protracted. However, if China decided to "go public" with the dispute and incur audience costs, it would risk also having its hands tied. If both the United States and China had their hands tied, it could set both countries on an intractable and economically devastating collision course. As such, the CCP estimated that in its handling of the dispute, it would serve its interests to maintain diplomatic flexibility, as it seemed that the Trump administration was either unwilling or unable to back down.

At the same time, it did not appear that the United States could gain anything other than a Pyrrhic victory from the dispute. The immediate effect of the trade war, placing tariffs on Chinese goods, was that it increased costs on American consumers (Hass & Denmark 2020). Moreover, as the United States did not assemble an international coalition to wage a trade war with China, China had outside options for shipping its exports (Bloomberg 2021). As such, the costs for the United States were comparatively higher than they were for China. Therefore, although the Trump administration had a political interest in appearing tough in China, it had not enjoyed much comparative leverage vis-à-vis China; and tit-for-tat escalation did create real economic costs for the United States. Therefore, the Trump administration had a political interest in appearing to "win" and look tough on China while also avoiding large or sustained economic retaliation.

The Trump administration had demonstrated its willingness to accept symbolic "deals" that it could celebrate to domestic supporters, even if such deals did not translate to a real-material advantage. For example, the Trump administration depicted its high-level summitry with North Korean leader Kim Jung-un as a major diplomatic victory. Although President Trump claimed he deserved a Nobel Peace Prize for his efforts (Rampton 2019), most analysts viewed the outcomes of these agreements as a political nonstarter. For example, before it would consider denuclearizing, the North Koreans required "completely eliminating the US nuclear threat to Korea" (Sang-Hun 2018); and unless the United States could completely eliminate its nuclear arsenal, it could not make this assurance. Nonetheless, although the Trump administration returned empty-handed from its negotiations with North Korea, these negotiations demonstrated that the Trump administration was content with accepting symbolic, albeit hollow diplomatic victories.

Based on this information, Chinese leaders could expect that a trade dispute with the United States would likely be protracted, yet China could weather the costs by shifting its exports abroad or through engaging in import substitution. Moreover, as the economic costs were higher for the United States than for China, the United States did not have much bargaining leverage over China, and the Trump administration would likely accept a token or symbolic gesture as long as it could portray these negotiations as a victory to American audiences.

With these considerations in mind, Chinese leaders were cautious about tying their hands or incurring audience costs. Otherwise, they would lose their diplomatic options for responding to the Trump administration. However, there was a risk that even if the CCP did not seek to create domestic audience costs through state-led nationalism, grassroots nationalism might pressure the regime to tie its hands—eliminating its bargaining options. However, to prevent the emergence of a grassroots nationalism, the regime drew upon China's massive surveillance and censorship apparatus to limit discussions about the trade war on Chinese social media (Chan 2018; Jiang 2019).

Despite its initial reluctance to tolerate public debate on the trade war, as the conflict continued, Chinese leaders began to fan the flames of nationalism. Some outlets argued that American restrictions on China were only a "paper tiger" (Xinhua 2018). Another article used even stronger rhetoric, describing the trade war as a real "people's war" (Xinhua 2019). Perhaps most notably a broadcaster for China's most famous nightly news show, Xinwen Lianbo, said, "If the US wants to talk, our door is open. . . . If the US wants to fight, we'll be with them till the end" (Li 2019; Weiss 2019b). However, despite this heated rhetoric, the regime was cautious. The regime did not allow or promote anti-American protests and although it used heated rhetoric, it never committed China to any specific course of action—thus providing China leeway to justify backing down if it needed to do so (Weiss 2019b). Similarly, although Chinese media outlets increasingly referred to a "trade war," it was reported that some media outlets were forbidden from using this term (Bloomberg 2019). Similarly, another article read, "Talk—fine! Fight—we'll be there! Bully us—delusion!"(Bloomberg 2019). However, this article also opened the door for "talking" (or some sort of bargain).

Similarly, the *People's Daily*—the official mouthpiece of the CCP—ran an editorial reminding Chinese citizens of China's "Century of Humiliation," yet the article emphasized caution and sought to use nationalism to promote domestic cohesion: "We are fully aware that the great rejuvenation of the Chinese nation cannot be achieved easily and with drums and gongs. We firmly believe that as long as all Chinese people are united, no one can stop our progress (Ren Ping 2018b). Although this article emphasized unity, it also urged restraint against excessive nationalism, or using "drums and gongs." Similarly, another article referenced China's "resistance" of the United States during the Korean War, yet it also cautioned against "drums and gongs," and expressed confidence that China's public would behave calmly (Ji Fan 2018).

The CCP also sought to reassure its domestic public that it would be able to withstand economic pressure from the United States, and promoted domestic propaganda about its economic model. For example, one article assured Chinese domestic audiences that China would suffer minimal impacts because of China's high levels of domestic demand, its integration into global supply chains, and its diversified international trade—arguing that these factors served as a "stabilizer" against economic shocks (Ren Ping 2018a). Another article argued that the United States would be unable to stop Chinese innovation (Zhong Xuanli 2018).

Overall, although China sought to shape the narrative and enjoy the nationalist benefits from fighting a trade war with the United States, China's leaders were reluctant to tie their hands. Thus, China's propaganda, though nationalist, did not commit China to any sort of concrete steps, and it was used to promote China's economic model to domestic audiences. Thus, in managing its precarious situation during the trade war, the CCP cautiously used nationalist bluster to serve its domestic goals yet to provide it greater diplomatic leeway for negotiating a resolution of the conflict with the United States.

CONSEQUENCES

Considering that the trade war occurred between the world's two largest economies, it undoubtedly had significant consequences in the United States, China, and globally. It is estimated that the trade war reduced American GDP by 0.7 percent in 2019 and cost 300,000 American jobs (Haas & Denmark, 2020). More broadly, the trade war injected uncertainty into global investment markets and sank US–China relations to their lowest point in decades (Huang & Smith 2020; Shephard 2020).

Considering the relatively recent nature of the trade war, it may take years before scholars fully understand the domestic consequences of this conflict.

However, preliminary evidence suggests that the conflict likely had cross-cutting effects. The trade war strained China's economy by raising the costs of its exports. As China's economic development was already beginning to cool, this undoubtedly added political pressure on China's government. For example, anecdotal reports allege that Xi may have incurred some political costs for his handling of the trade war, as party officials criticized his management of the dispute (Blanchard 2018). However, as the CCP did not fully commit to "tying its hands" in the dispute by tolerating or promoting anti-foreign street protests, the party was largely insulated from nationalist sentiment.

The CCP may have even benefitted domestically. Anxious about China's slowing economic growth, the CCP viewed the United States as a useful target for channeling nationalist anger and blame for China's economic problems. The CCP also benefitted in some other unanticipated ways from the dispute. In its determination to win a symbolic "victory" in the trade war—however Pyrrhic the victory may be—the United States was willing to excuse and even praise China's handling over other sensitive political issues. For example, former US national security adviser John Bolton alleged in his memoir that President Trump did not criticize China's widespread and systematic abuse of its Uighur Muslim population, because he wanted to make a trade deal with China (Myers 2020). Similarly, eager to cut a deal with China, Trump turned a blind eye to China's crackdown on pro-Democracy protestors in Hong Kong (Bender and Deng, 2019). Likewise, when the outbreak of COVID-19 challenged the CCP's domestic legitimacy and global image, Trump, eager to strike a trade deal during an election year, heralded China's response to COVID-19. Trump praised China's COVID-19 response over fifteen times, lavishing praise upon China (Ward 2020); however, it is important to note that although Trump *initially* commended China's response to the pandemic, he would later peddle conspiracy theories and use racist labels for the disease, such as the "China virus" (Marlow 2020).

The US–China trade war also affected broader public and elite perceptions of China's interests and its relationship with the United States. For example, the trade war exposed the potential vulnerabilities for China if it relied too heavily on the United States. By seeking other partners and developing its domestic market, China avoided being vulnerable to American economic pressure. Drawing lessons from this dispute, Chinese elites have increasingly called for an economic decoupling from the United States (Li 2019). While it is still too soon to gauge the durability of these views, the continued possibility of Trump-style protectionism suggests that China would be wise to reduce its dependence on the American economy. The trade war may have also altered China's attitudes regarding economic cooperation and free trade. Recent scholarship suggests that the trade war may lead the public to be less supportive of free trade. Using survey experiments, some scholars find evidence that when Chinese respondents are primed to think about American protectionist actions, it leads to a decline in public support for free trade (Steinberg & Tan, working paper).

More broadly, the effects of the trade war cannot be divorced from the broader bilateral US–China relationship. During this conflict, a narrative emerged of "Cold War 2.0" between the two countries. Although scholars argue that the "Cold War" model is inappropriate for explaining US–China tensions (Weiss 2019a), growing nationalism in both countries may transform such narratives into reality. Combined with efforts toward economic decoupling, both countries may have fewer reasons to cooperate. Although it is difficult to assess the long-term effects of the trade war on the US–China relationship, the nationalist outrage unleashed suggests a turbulent road ahead.

CONCLUSION

This chapter sought to provide a preliminary examination of the logic behind the CCP's decisions during the trade war. I argued that the trade war presented a dilemma for China, as it threatened to challenge key elements of the CCP's domestic legitimacy. The trade war posed a risk to China's continued economic development and threatened the regime's domestic standing (should it be viewed as mishandling the conflict?). As such, at the outset of the trade war, the CCP was highly cautious, seeking to provide itself greater maneuverability for managing its relationship with the United States. However, as Chinese officials realized that the trade war would be protracted, they altered China's strategy and began fanning the flames of nationalism. Ironically, although the trade war initially posed a potential challenge to the CCP's domestic image, it ultimately served the CCP's domestic political goals by providing the regime a useful scapegoat for explaining away China's economic problems. China's leaders made vague nationalist appeals, yet they did not allow the emergence of nationalist or anti-foreign street protests. China, therefore, did not truly "tie its hands"—allowing the CCP to enjoy the political benefits of nationalism without necessarily backing itself into a corner.

China's behavior during this conflict also provides a glimpse into how it might behave in future disputes. For example, although China's government has tolerated street protests in the past, should Chinese leaders continue to be cautious about "going public" with disputes in the future, they may be less constrained by domestic audiences. This suggests that if China is given some face-saving compromise in future disputes, it may have a greater degree of flexibility for cooperating in future bargaining disputes.

China's behavior during the trade war also holds clues for how China might behave should the pace of its economic expansion continue to cool. As China's behavior during the trade war illustrates, the CCP viewed nationalism as a useful political strategy and a means for explaining away China's economic problems to domestic audiences. Should the regime continue fanning the flames of nationalism, it could ultimately undermine Chinese grand strategy by leading China to continue adopting a more assertive posture in its foreign policy (Weiss 2020). Increased efforts by the CCP to foment nationalist sentiment, coupled with rising American nationalism, could portend a volatile path ahead for the future of US–China relations, particularly in the domain of trade.

Should the Biden administration seek to repair the US–China relationship, it will need to understand these evolving domestic political dynamics within China, as well as the lessons drawn by China's leaders and public during this dispute. From a broader perspective, neither Chinese nor American behavior during the trade war is explained by structural imperatives of an anarchic international system. Instead, policy makers would be wise to investigate the domestic political considerations shaping China's approach to foreign policy.

REFERENCES

Baggott Carter, Erin. 2019. Diversionary Cheap Talk: Economic Conditions and US Foreign Policy Rhetoric, 1945–2010. *International Interactions*.

Baker, Peter. 2017. "Trump Abandons Trans-Pacific Partnership, Obama's Signature Trade Deal," *New York Times*, January 23.

Beech, Eric. 2016. "Trump Picks 'Death by China' Author for Trade Advisory Role," Reuters, December 21.

Bender, Michael C., and Chao Deng. 2019. "Trump Calls Hong Kong Protests 'Complicating Factor' in Trade Talks," *Wall Street Journal,* November 22.

Blanchard, Ben. 2018. "China's Xi Says His Propaganda is 'Absolutely Correct' While Facing Criticism Over Trade War," *Business Insider*, August 23.

"How China Won Trump's Trade War and Got Americans to Foot the Bill," *Bloomberg*, January 12, 2021.

Callahan, William A. 2010. China: *The Pessoptimist Nation*. Cambridge: Oxford University Press.

Chan, Taylor Francis. 2018. "China Is Trying to Downplay a Brewing Trade War with the US by Censoring Trump and US Authorities," *Business Insider*, July 3.

"China Vows 'People's War' as Trade Fight Takes a Nationalist Turn," *Bloomberg News*, May 18, 2019.

Curran, Enda, Andrew Mayeda, and Jenny Leonard. 2018. "China Strikes $60 Billion of US Goods in Growing Trade War," *Bloomberg*, September 17.

Downs, Erica Strecker, and Phillip C. Saunders. 1998–1999. "Legitimacy and the Limits of Nationalism: China and the Diaoyu Islands," *International Security* 23(3): 114–146.

Fearon, James D. 1994. "Domestic Political Audiences and the Escalation of International Disputes," *American Political Science Review* 88 (3): 577–592.

Franck, Thomas. 2018. "Trump Doubles Down: 'Trade Wars are Good, and Easy to Win,'" CNBC.

Glawe, Linda, and Helmut Wagner. 2020. "China in the Middle-Income Trap?" *China Economic Review* 60.

Haas, Ryan, and Abraham Denmark. 2020. "More Pain than Gain: How the US-China Trade War Hurt America," *The Brookings Institution.*

Huang, Yukon, and Jeremy Smith. 2020. "In US-China Trade War, New Supply Chains Rattle Markets," *Carnegie Endowment for International Peace*, June 24.

Ji Fan. 2019. "The Confidence of 'Not Afraid to Fight a Trade War'" (People's Forum) ['不怕打贸易战' 的底气（人民论坛)]," *People's Daily*, May 18.

Jiang, Steven. 2019. "China Censors Trump and Boosts Propaganda Ahead of Vital Trade Summit," CNN, May 9.

Li Wei. 2019. "Towards Economic Decoupling? Mapping Chinese Discourse on the China-US Trade War," *Chinese Journal of International Politics*, 12(4): 519–556.

Li Zhongxuan. 2018. "The Trade War Cannot Stop China from Moving Forward: International People are optimistic about China" [贸易战阻挡不了中国前进步伐——国际人士看好中国], *People's Daily,* October 15.

Li Yuan. 2019. "In China, Some Fear the End of 'Chimerica,'" *New York Times*, May 14.

Marlow, Iain. 2020. "Trump's Racially Charged Retweet of 'China Virus' Message Fuels Tensions with Beijing," *Time.*

Meisels, A. Greer. 2012. "What China Learned from the Soviet Union's Fall," *The Diplomat*, July 27.

Myers, Steven Lee. 2020. "China Lashes Out at US's Action Against Mass Incarcerations," *New York Times.*

Putnam, Robert D. 1988. "Diplomacy and Domestic Politics: The Logic of Two-Level Games," *International Organization* 42 (3), 427–460.

"Putting Pressure on Tariff Limits is Just Another Paper Tiger" [用关税极限施压只不过是又一只纸老虎], *Xinhua*, May 14, 2019.

Rampton, Roberta. 2019. "Trump Makes His Case for Nobel Peace Prize, Complains He'll Never Get It," Reuters, February 15.

Ren Ping. 2018a. "Trade War Pessimism Is Not Reliable" [贸易战悲观论调不靠谱]. *People's Daily*, October 17.

Ren Ping. 2018b. "What Is the Essence of the US Provoking a Trade War?" [美国挑起贸易战的实质是什么?]. *People's Daily*, August 10.

Reuters Staff. 2019. "Trump Says China's Xi Has Acted Responsibly on Hong Kong Protests," Reuters, July 22.

Rummler, Orion. 2020. "Bolton Alleges Trump Encouraged Xi to Continue with Uighur Detainment Camps," *Axios*, June 18.

Sang-Hun, Choe. 2018. "North Korea Says it Won't Denuclearize Until US Removes Threat," *New York Times,* December 20.

Shephard, Christian. 2020. "China Says Ties With US at Lowest Point Since 1979," *Financial Times,* July 9.

Shirk, Susan. 2008. *China: Fragile Superpower*. Oxford University Press.

Slantchev, Branislav L. 2006. "Politician, the Media, and Domestic Audience Costs," *International Studies Quarterly*, 50(1): 445–477.

Steinberg, David A., and Yeling Tan. "The Political Consequences of the US-China Trade War: Understanding the Chinese Public Reaction," working paper.

"The US Keeps Shouting to Boost Its Ego," *Xinhua*, May 13, 2019.

Tomz, Michael. 2007. "Domestic Audience Costs in International Relations: An Experimental Approach," *International Organization* 61(4): 821–840.

Wang, Zheng. 2014. *Never Forget National Humiliation: Historical Memory in Chinese Politics and Foreign Relations*. New York: Columbia University Press.

Ward, Myah. 2020. "15 Times Trump Praised China as Coronavirus was Spreading Across the Globe," *Politico* April 15.

Weeks, Jessica L. 2008. "Autocratic Audience Costs: Regime Type and Signaling Resolve," *International Organization* 62(1): 35–64.

Weiss, Jessica Chen. 2013. "Authoritarian Signaling, Mass Audiences, and Nationalist Protest in China," *International Organization* 67(1): 1–35.

Weiss, Jessica Chen. 2014. *Powerful Patriots: Nationalist Protests in China's Foreign Relations*. Cambridge: Oxford University Press.

Weiss, Jessica Chen. 2019a. "A World Safe for Autocracy? China's Rise and the Future of Global Politics," *Foreign Affairs* July/August.

Weiss, Jessica Chen. 2019b. "What's the Response in China to the Trade War?" *Washington Post*, May 15.

Weiss, Jessica Chen. 2020. "China's Self-Defeating Nationalism," *Foreign Affairs*, July 16.

Weiss, Jessica Chen, and Allan Dafoe. 2019. "Authoritarian Audiences, Rhetoric, and Propaganda in International Crises: Evidence from China," *International Studies Quarterly* 63(4): 963–973.

Wu, Shufang. 2014. "The Revival of Confucianism and the CCP's Struggle for Cultural Leadership: A Content Analysis of the People's Daily, 2000–2009," *Journal of Contemporary China* 23(89): 971–991.

Zhang, Lusha, and Kevin Yao. 2019. "China's 2019 Growth Seen Slowing to 6.2 % as Trade War Weighs," Reuters, July 10.

Zhong, Yang. 2007. "Legitimacy Crisis and Legitimation in China," *Journal of Contemporary Asia*, 26 (2): 201–220.

Chapter Seven

The Radicalization of China's Global Posture

Narratives and Strategies

Zhimin Lin and Qi Wang

INTRODUCTION

Few observers of the China affair would disagree that since Xi Jinping's ascendance in late 2012, China has accelerated its march toward global primacy at the expense mostly of the United States. The question is whether what happened under Xi is just one more step in a long and continuous path or represents a radical departure in the big scheme of things. This chapter argues that the latter is more accurate. The departure from what China has inherited from Deng Xiaoping and his course of reform anchoring on open-door policy, market-driven reform, and integrating China into the international system is of course not a one-time occurrence. It is, indeed, a process, a process of radicalization of China's global posture. This process started even before Xi took over the helm though somehow unnoticed by the West[1] and consolidated and accelerated ever since. The accumulative results of this radicalization process and its ramifications should by now be obvious to most though what it encompassed has not been fully explored. This chapter will try to help narrow this gap by examining two of the most salient features of such a process, namely, how Xi radicalizes the narratives China used to describe and justify its global posture and a series of strategies he has employed to translate these narratives into reality. It will also briefly discuss what the radicalization process meant for China's handling and approach to trade disputes with the United States at the end.

AN EXPANDING NARRATIVE AIMED AT BOTH JUSTIFYING AND SELLING CHINA'S VISION OF A NEW WORLD ORDER

The common definition of radicalization refers to a process "by which an individual or group comes to adopt increasingly radical views in opposition to a political, social, or religious status quo, the action or process of making somebody more extreme or radical in their opinions on political or social issues."[2] The radicalization of China's global posture can thus be traced first and foremost to the key narratives the Chinese leadership adopted in describing and justifying its new global role. Since 2012, four such narratives began to take shape and subsequently took over China's official expression when outlining and communicating its global agenda.

Big Change in a Hundred Years Narrative

In June 2018, Xi Jinping introduced the theme "change in a hundred years" (百年未有之巨变) for the first time at a national conference on diplomatic work. "Our country," he argued, "is at the best juncture of development in modern time while the world faces big changes not seen in a hundred years" (Xi 2020, 428). This narrative, which originally had been used to highlight the favorable international conditions conducive to China's diplomacy, has now become a standard starting point of how China perceives itself and the rest of the world for good reasons.

First, it aligns well with the two centenary goals Xi promised to accomplish in his political report to the 19th Party Congress held in 2017.[3] The first goal was to complete the building of a moderately prosperous society in all respects by 2021 (the first centennial of the founding of the Chinese Communist Party) followed by the second goal of completing the modernization of China by 2049 (the first centennial of the founding of the People's Republic). While the second centenary is still decades away, to group them together not only helps lay the groundwork of a roadmap for a nation humiliated by the West in the past one hundred years and poised to regain its destiny as a world leader in the next thirty years or so but also implies, however subtly, the need for one person as the "chosen one" to complete the job that goes far beyond 2023, the year Xi would have stepped down as the president of China had he not been able to remove the ten-year term limit from the Chinese Constitution in 2018 (more on this point in the next section). Secondly, with a broad brush that combines the past, the present, and the future, the narrative allows Xi to make macro comparisons in a historical context. The difficulties the West, especially the United States, has encountered since the election of Donald Trump in 2016 fell "conveniently" into this category. In a recent interview,

Wang Yizhou, a well-established expert on China's foreign policy, pointed out that for one hundred years, it was always about what the West could offer to China. Now, he argues, the time has come for China to impact the rest of the world (like how it handled the COVID-19 pandemic) though he at the same time counseled against overextending China's evolvement (Wang 2020). Zhu Feng, another noted Chinese scholar in the field, similarly argued that successful rising powers were few in history. Those who failed in their attempts were the ones who failed to grasp the big direction, bid adjustments, and big patterns. For China, that means in the next three decades, it must strive to be the one to fully appreciate what the historical moment of change meant and how to take advantage of it (Zhu 2019). In this sense, the "big change in a hundred years" narrative can simultaneously serve three purposes for Xi: to construct an overarching theme that addresses both China's grievance of the past and yearning for greatness in the future; to place himself right at the center of steering this rising power to its historical destiny; and to allow China and not just the West be the author of this page of world history.

The "Great Struggle" Narrative

Xi did not lose sight of reality even as he touted hefty goals for China. Another recent theme central to his narratives was his call for engaging in "great struggle" (伟大斗争). In a speech he made in January 2018, Xi reminded his followers that while "we are at a historical moment for great achievements," we must take full account of the risk we face." The more achievements we make, the more we need to be cautious to avoid making "strategic and subversive mistakes" (Xi 2020, 73). On the other hand, to be cautious was not to be equated with hesitation or avoiding risks. To the contrary, in one of the biggest departures from his predecessors,[4] Xi put a premium on taking the challenges head-on. In one of the most publicized speeches on the subject he made in September 2019, Xi outlined what he called five risk challenges that only with "great struggle" can China have a chance to win. These risks include challenges to China's aspirations, namely, challenges to China's political system, to China's sovereignty, security, and *interests associated with development* [italicized by author], to China's various core interests and basic principles, and to Chinese efforts to achieve the dual centenary goals (Li & Yan 2019). Whenever these challenges appear, according to Xi, China must take the threat head-on. China should not only be ready and possess the ability to join the struggle but more importantly have the "guts" to draw its sword when facing direct and immediate threat.

The emphasis on struggle has been particularly important in appreciating Xi's leadership style and tactics. Xi was known for his use of plain language on the international stage to push back against foreign criticism against China well before he became China's top leader.[5] Once he took full reign of the country, his preference to confronting external challenges directly and openly was increasingly put on full display. Chinese leaders including Xi himself no longer shy away from challenging the West or its positions openly on the international stage. The recent rise of the so-called wolf warrior diplomacy was just one open display of how daring to struggle has become a norm even for Chinese diplomatic corps whose members were traditionally taught to use and were known for using a soft approach in handling diplomatic issues.

This departure from traditional Chinese diplomacy deserves special attention both because of its novelty and the inner logic behind the scene. For Xi, the emphasis on struggle reflects more than a personal preference; it served him well. Nothing works more effectively in rallying public support behind his pitch for the China dream than projecting an image of a nation willing and ready to stand up to Western pressure or "bullies." The wide use of wolf warrior diplomacy by Chinese diplomats in recent years, for example, was heavily criticized in the West. However, there has been no sign of China backing off, a phenomenon that would have been impossible in a tightly controlled state without the encouragement if not explicit consent from the top leadership. The emphasis on struggle has another benefit as well. As one can see from the five risk challenges identified by Xi, the distinction between what presents a domestic or an external threat to China had virtually disappeared under Xi's rule. Under the unifying theme of struggle, Xi could more easily use external threat to help justify internal crackdown or vice versa. Finally, the concept of struggle is a very vague and elastic concept. The call for struggle in fact allows Xi to update its content and targets whenever he sees fit. For example, to elevate China's interest related to its development (which could include virtually anything) to the same category of such long-established and well-defined concepts as national sovereignty and security raised more than eyebrows among observers; it shows that China under Xi has indeed reached a point of no return when it chooses to confront rather than seek a detour if not compromise when encountering challenges from abroad. As one Chinese observer put it, "If there was a period during the early era of reform when China practiced low-profile diplomacy (based on Deng's dictum of hiding one's capability and biding one's time), that era is gone further and further away" (Sun 2020).

A Community of Shared Destiny of Mankind Narrative

This narrative was part of the original rationale behind Xi's flagship initiative—the road and belt initiative (RBI). First appearing in 2014, the narrative has since been substantially expanded. By now, it has become a catchall, not only helping China promote its global reach but also legitimizing China's behavior abroad. The question is, unlike the first two narratives, in what sense has this narrative, benign enough at first look, also become an integral part of the radicalization of China's global posture?

The answer can be seen in several key perspectives. While the narrative was introduced in 2014, it was more of an attempt for Xi to seek a clear identity in global affairs that had been dominated overwhelmingly by the West since World War II. However, as time passed by, the narrative took on broader and more strategic significance in China's efforts to compete in the liberal world order. For example, the narrative has given the role of helping China to gain higher moral ground (Xi 2020, 487). It is also increasingly used as a branding opportunity for China to distinguish itself from the norms and values of the West in handling nation-to-nation relations. Xi has made this point rather clear. Because of the emphasis on shared destiny, he argued that the rules of the community must be made by the collective body of the world community and not determined by "muscle power" only (Xi 2020, 459), a clear reference to how the United States structured the post–World War II global hierarchy. China, by contrast, is committed to providing public goods, under this narrative, to all participating nations, and indeed to the whole world (Xi 2020, 464).

Donald Trump's America-first policy and push to reduce US global commitments has provided a godsend opportunity to China to put more meat to what appears to be an abstract concept at best initially and in sharp contrast to where the United States now stands. For example, China has basically touted itself as the true defender of multilateralism as opposed to unilateralism championed by Trump. China now paints itself as the one who prefers goodwill negotiations and compromises while the United States relies on bullying and coercive diplomacy over cooperation. China now claims that it takes the interests of the world, especially that of the less developed world, to heart just as the United States has retreated from much of its global responsibilities. In doing so, China was able not only to discredit the previously prevailing norms and rules of the West but also managed to sell its values and norms with its strengthened power in global discourse. Instead of focusing on traditional concepts such as human rights, for example, China now feels more confident and outspoken in promoting its emphasis on win-win solutions, a balance between power and responsibility (a clear jab at the Western power), and the importance of sustainability of global growth, among other critical topics in international dialogues (Mardell 2017). So useful is the concept of shared destiny of the world community that it became rare that when Chinese leaders spoke at international forums they would fail to tout this narrative.

System Advantage Narrative

The final narrative Xi used to boost China's global stance is the argument that the Chinese system is far more superior than the Western system. Until recently, Chinese leaders tended to be mostly on the defense when the subject came up in international dialogue of which system, the one of the West or the one of China, worked better. Back in the late 1990s, for example, President Clinton, during his visit to China in 1998, would confidently tell the Chinese audience at Beijing University that "we want China to be successful, secure and open, working with us for a more peaceful and prosperous world."[6] He would even tell the visiting Chinese leader, Jiang Zemin, to his face, that human rights policy had put China on "the wrong side of history."[7] As China become more powerful, the United States became less sanguine about that prediction. When he visited China for the first time in 2009, President Obama had already noted that China's economic success allowed its brand of authoritarian capitalism to become "a plausible alternative to Western-style liberalism" (Obama 2020, 481).

Now a decade has passed, and what was a possible alternative in the eyes of Obama then has now become one of the newest and striking talking points among Chinese leaders and scholars. When Xi first promoted the notion of confidence in (China's political) system in 2014, it did not raise many eyebrows in the West. However, by 2019, Xi felt confident enough that he called upon his followers to "tell a good story of China's system and constantly enhance the ability (for China) to convince and attract (support) of the Chinese way of governing" (Xi 2020, 129).

Prior to 2020, if China's advocacy of the superiority of its system was primarily based on its ability and record in reducing poverty, coordinating economic development, and improving the living standard (Hu 2020), the COVID pandemic may well be a game-changer for what was once a fringe Chinese narrative. The slow and ineffective responses by the West in handling the crisis came in sharp contrast with China's ability to place the pandemic under quick and almost complete control even after the initial blunders; this will continue to fuel more debate over whether the Chinese system is better equipped to deal with at least a public health crisis. In the word of one of the leading Chinese scholars on the subject, "System advantage is the biggest advantage for a political party and a country." The Chinese system, he argued, has proved to be "the most promising, most efficient, most reliable, and most result-producing system in the world!" (Qu 2020).

New Chinese Narratives vs. the Traditional Image of China in the West

Armed with these narratives, the radicalization of China's global posture has become a lot easier and complete. These narratives have also painted a picture of China far different than the traditional image of what China was in the eyes of Western observers merely a decade ago.

Under the traditional image, China since 1978 was viewed first and foremost as a country finally unshackled from Mao's revolutionary evangelism and committed to forging a cooperative relationship with Western countries. While the efforts by the West to integrate China into the existing system played a role, Western politicians and scholars believed that it was China itself with the help of the market forces unleashed by the reform that did "more to link China to the global economy than the conscious strategies of foreign capitals" (Christensen 2015, 17). Second, China was believed to have adopted, in the words of David Lampton, a more or less "consensus grand strategy that emphasizes securing the external conditions conducive to internal economic growth and social change" (Lampton 2008, 35). Third, even as China's power grew by leaps and bounds, if one can narrow down what China wants regarding interest and power only, "the less clear material interests in overturning the existing order and less it is certain that China can grow in power to the point where it reaches parity with the United States or the West, the more it chooses—grudgingly or otherwise—a strategy of accommodation and integration" (Ikenburry 2008, 91). Finally, before Xi came to power, there were significant disagreements among Western scholars on this question: What will Beijing do with this new global power? How would China run the world or try to "internationalize the Chinese norms" given the arrival of the so-called China century (Callahan 2011, 3)? Some believed China would liberalize eventually if China were to become a more open and dangerous rival or to help anchor a true trans-pacific entente (Friedberg 2011, 2). Others believe that China would rise peacefully though more and more on China's terms (Zhu 2013, 17). In other words, if there was certainty among Chinese observers, it was the uncertainty of what China wanted and how it would get it.

Not anymore. The arrival of the most powerful leader after Mao with an undisputable trail of authoritarian rule who introduced and promoted the narratives shown above since 2013 shattered the traditional image of how the West viewed China. Together, these narratives sent the unmistaken message that China's assessment of both itself and the world had fundamentally changed. No longer satisfied to play second fiddle or be merely a student of a mighty teacher who until recently seemed to hold the keys to China's economic prosperity and modernization, China now believes the time has come to regain its rightful position as the premier and powerful leader of the world. While China is still willing to work with its competitors to a certain extent or even compromise when necessary, the underlying message embedded in Xi's new narratives is that China will never back down when it is challenged nor limit its ambition and expansion only to areas where the West traditionally confined China to being a world-class supplier of finished goods or a regional power mostly in East Asia. Instead, China seems more determined than ever to be on the offensive at its own pace and according to its agenda regardless of whether it pleases the West. In short, while narratives sometimes can be dismissed as just talking points or, worse, propaganda gimmicks, in a country where correct names were historically viewed as important as actions themselves, the set of new narratives Xi launched and continued to expand are no laughing matters. They are, collectively, the most clear and definitive indicators of how much China has broken away from the course it had inherited from Deng since the late 1970s and how radical the nature of the transformation has been.

STRATEGY AND TACTICS

To translate its newer and radical narratives into action, Xi has adopted a few strategies and tactics. These strategies and tactics include at least a political strategy that ensures his continued rule at home that will last far beyond the original ten-year term and strengthens his complete control through a top-down, one-person power structure; a geoeconomic strategy that weaponizes China's fast growing economic, financial, and supply-chain capacities to achieve its diplomatic and strategic goals far beyond what one has ever seen; a military and high-tech strategy aimed at narrowing or even closing the gap with the West as an ultimate insurance of its safety and security; a diplomatic strategy that uses novel practices such as summit diplomacy, gaining control in international institutions together with more conventional approaches such as cohesive diplomacy and money politics to establish itself as a credible and fearsome global leader; and, finally, a soft-power strategy that will help China brand itself as an alternative to the liberal world order led by the United States since World War II. Many of these strategies are still being developed or tested, and some of them inevitably will be adjusted or even replaced as the situation warrants. Still, the fact that so many of these strategies and tactics have been employed at such a large scale and in well-coordinated fashion is a further indicator of how far and how fast the radicalization of China's global posture has taken place.

The Political Strategy

Xi's political moves since 2012 are too numerous to be listed here. However, few would disagree that his decision to do away with the de facto term limit set in stone by Deng since the late 1970s, including having written it into the 1982 Chinese constitution, was among the most momentous and far-reaching decisions Xi has made in declaring the arrival of a new era (Economy 2018b). By removing the last constraint of his power, Xi managed to connect all the dots he set up since 2012. It removes one of the biggest uncertainties (at least for the short term) associated with any authoritarian rule, namely, the succession challenge. With no challengers to his power in sight, Xi put himself in a position to serve as the "chosen one" to carry out the ambitious narratives listed above he took pains to construct. It also allowed him to amass so much power that the highly touted "collective leadership" (Hu 2015) until recently had been effectively changed to a system where other members of the Standing Committee of the Politburo of CCP served merely as his lieutenants. The expansion of his personal and institutional power gave him both the space to implement his vision (unthinkable just a few years ago under the leadership of Hu Jintao) and also the time he needed to complete his stated goals. As a result, he now has the freedom to not only set up exceedingly ambitious and long-term goals but also design a timetable without being disrupted due to various limits his predecessors had to live with.

The political strategy seems to have worked, at least for now. On the one hand, the narratives along with the ambitious goals they convey helped justify the extraordinary concentration of power on Xi. On the other hand, Xi's massive power, free from traditional term and age limits, ensures that the initiatives he took would be carried out with an unprecedented degree of efficiency, consistency, and precision even by Chinese standards. It is no coincidence that many regard Xi as the second most powerful leader next only to Mao both at home and abroad (Blackwell & Campbell 2016), making him a standout even in the world that saw a growing number of autocrats beat their democratic oppositions.

The Geoeconomic Strategy

Using his uniquely powerful position, Xi has employed several strategies since 2012 to help achieve his goals. One that stood out as his signature strategy is an ever aggressive and conscious use of China's growing economic power to extract greater diplomatic and strategic gains in direct competition with rivals such as the United States without resorting to use of military might or threat as the old Soviet Union did during the Cold War. "To use purse but not gun," explained by Blackwell, as he quoted an observer, Beijing "has been playing the new economic game at a maestro level" (Blackwell and Harris 2016, 93).

China had deployed the strategy long before Xi. It has used both economic incentive and military pressure to keep Taiwan's independence impulse at bay. It used economic assistance to maintain its influence over the leaders of North Korea. It drove and kept a wedge between the United States and Japan through economic ties. It expanded its reach and influence in Southeast Asia spearheaded by trade and mega commercial projects there. It maintained close economic links with India but closer economic ties with Pakistan to keep itself in the regional triangular game (Blackwell and Harris 2016).

When Xi took over, he kept all these geoeconomic games and played them with more intensity and greater skill. However, what anchored his new version of geoeconomic strategy was no doubt the RBI initiative unveiled in 2014. Some six years later, the initiative has been transformed into a vast network of economic partnerships far beyond anything the West was able to accomplish during the heyday of the Cold War or would even dare to envision—so much so that Robert Gates, the former defense minister under George W. Bush and Barack Obama, lamented that the United States "cannot compete directly with China's Belt and Road projects development assistance." What is left for the United States, Gates argued, is to "look for ways to leverage the power of our private sector" among other possible countermeasures (Gates 2020).

To understand how RBI represents an elevated type of geoeconomic strategy that indicates the radical nature of Xi's global posture, one only need to look at three angles. The first angle is its sheer audacity. While the original concept may well be someone else's, Xi was able to see its huge potential to place it at the center of his undertaking to build a new superpower on par with the United States. Whether it was the total amount of investment or the speed with which it moved quickly from the original contour to crash into new areas such as Latin America, few outsiders would have anticipated the scope and the rhythm of expansion of the initiative back in 2014 or 2015. Another angle is the level of innovation and attention paid to details. Clearly, the initiative was big. However, big is not the same as effective. What impressed outsiders the most were the efforts to quickly institutionalize the arrangements, whether it was multilateral banks, financing instruments, or supporting mechanisms, that were set up with a clear goal of generating synergy and using the spillover effects to multiply the impact and reach of the initiative. Finally, and probably most to the fundamental arguments of this chapter, by being so involved in the initiative, Xi essentially took personal ownership of the initiative. In the past, some top Chinese leaders would let others know that only certain and specific policies were under their purview. Deng, for example, was known for his close supervision over any policies towards the

United States. By identifying so closely and personally with the RBI initiative, Xi's "heavy-handed" approach towards the initiative (Zhao 2010, 18) was very telling of the importance he attached to not only the initiative but the overall geoeconomic strategy in a clear departure from the norms and practice of the past.

Xi's major geoeconomic initiatives such as BRI were by no means a complete success (Zhao 2010). Nor was BRI likely to bypass many of the same traps that had either undercut or even doomed previous attempts by the Western powers such as the debt crisis and rising resentments against outside influence by the recipient countries as the recent developments have shown. However, the attractiveness of geoeconomic strategy is such that unless China faces concerted pushback from the recipient countries or unintentionally touches off economic backlash at home that takes away the incentive associated with RBI-type actions, Xi has perfect reason to expand rather than shrink the use of geoeconomic strategy to achieve his global ambition based on a radicalized version of the old silk road.

The Military and High-tech Strategy

China's military modernization was well underway when Xi took over. However, since 2012, the strategy Xi adopted in this area shared several features that were missing or at least not as prominent in the earlier efforts. As Taylor Fravel notes (2019, 273), most of the changes in military strategy in the past were initiated by senior military officers. However, the 2013 reform and subsequent changes in military strategies and postures, in his view, were different in that Xi's intervention played an essential role. As a result, like other major initiatives China undertook over the last eight years, Xi provided more than an approving seal; he took control of the entire process. Military modernization in terms of both strategy and capabilities became an integral part of the grand and long-term strategy Xi undertook. A fast modernizing military allowed Xi to expand China's global reach at a level or speed unapparelled in the past; the more ambitious and assertive global posture in turn fueled even greater emphasis on moving military presence to the forefront of China's global posture.

Xi's role made it possible to integrate what was traditionally compartmentalized branches of government and industries into one giant, collective machine working in sync. Another feature in Xi's military/high-tech strategy was the central role high-tech played in the overall military strategies. Various US organizations have offered sober and sometimes alarming assessments of how fast and how much the Chinese military has become a formidable fighting force capable of threatening the basic layout of the US military as well as the cohesion of the alliance system the United States led since World War II. China's new and accelerated military global reach especially its maritime power projection in the Indo-Pacific regime has become what Andrew Ericson called "a new Chinese wave" (2019, 255) on par with the heyday of Chinese maritime presence in the region in history, though it was far better equipped and trained thanks to the enormous investment China put into military-related technologies.

The concerted efforts to modernize China's military, reform its strategy, and infuse more high tech in the process have further emboldened Chinese leadership and fanned growing nationalistic or even militaristic sentiment among some segments of Chinese society. According to a communique released after a high-level meeting last month, the People's Liberation Army (PLA) will be transformed into a modern military force by 2027. Analysts say China's ultimate aim is to build an army that is on par with that of the United States.[8] The US military also concluded that while there are still major gaps and weak spots, Xi's stated goal of China becoming a world-class military by 2049 intends to strengthen and modernize the PLA in nearly every respect and is "indeed already ahead of the United States in certain areas" (Office of the Secretary of Defense, 2020, i). The US Congressional Research Service recently listed six areas of emerging military technologies. According to the report, China is closely behind the United States in at least five of the six emerging technologies (artificial intelligence, lethal autonomous weapon systems, hypersonic weapons, directed-energy weapons, biotechnology, and quantum technology) (Congressional Research Service 2020).

The only thing that has not yet happened in connection with Xi's military/high-tech strategy is a "hot" conflict face to face with the US military or its allies. Even without this step, it was clear enough that with the newly gained military/high-tech capabilities, Xi is in a far stronger position to promote more aggressive foreign policy than any of his predecessors. He may well decide that for now at least, it would be in China's best interest not to use the military power openly or in the vicinity of US military presence for fear of distracting if not torpedoing his overall global strategy and agenda. However, that was only because he chose to do so and not because he lacked the capability to do it.

The Diplomatic Strategy

If there is a strategy that Xi promotes that contradicts directly with Deng's legacy in foreign policy, it is his adoption of the so-called big power diplomacy (大国外交) strategy. The departure and its ramification associated with

Xi's diplomatic strategy were at the center of discussion in several recent publications (Hu 2019; Lin 2019; Wang 2019).

Deng's diplomacy put emphasis on integrating China with the existing international system and taking advantage of the favorable international conditions conducive to China's reform; Xi's strategy orients towards remaking the system in the context of the growing power and influence of China. Or, in the words of Ruan Zongze, former director of the influential China Institute of International Studies, to "*create* [italicized by author] favorable conditions for realizing the Chinese Dream" (Zongze 2020, 9). Deng preaches for patience and moving cautiously; Xi argues that China must be ready not only to defend and defuse risks, it also has to be able to fight a "strategically proactive war" to turn danger into opportunity (2020, 75). Deng warns China not to try to stick its neck out around the world; Xi's strategy favors doing exactly the opposite especially in areas most sensitive to US hegemonic power even before the United States and the entire Western world had been bogged down in the fight against the pandemic. Deng prefers to manage internal affairs well before taking on external responsibilities; Xi views the two as different sides of the same coin inseparable and, indeed, mutually reinforcing (2020, 428). In short, Xi's diplomatic strategy laid the foundation and benchmark for a China far more ambitious, aggressive, and assertive in global posture than anything the world had seen in recent memories.

Xi's new diplomatic strategy also serves his other strategies well—for example, his political strategy. A hallmark of Xi's big power strategy has been an unprecedented and extremely enthusiastic embracing of the so-called summit diplomacy. In 2019 alone, for example, Xi made seven overseas trips that took him to thirteen countries, hosting for global summits plus receiving numerous visits to China by foreign dignitaries.[9] By contrast, Donald Trump in 2019, one of his busier global travel years as the president of the United States, visited seven foreign countries, attended four summits (and hosted none), and received far fewer foreign visitors.[10] In 2020, even with the restraints imposed by the pandemic, Xi kept the pace of summit diplomacy at a very high level. He took part in virtual summit meetings twenty-two times and made more than eighty phone calls to foreign as well as international organization leaders.[11]

With the help of summit diplomacy and China's new, concerted efforts to staff key international institutions to ensure that it is in a position not only to play by the rules or norms of these institutions but to remake these rules and norms, Xi deftly used his diplomatic strategy to strengthen his political strategy as the former puts him in the frontline, center, and indeed, gravity, of every move China makes globally.

Xi's new diplomatic strategy is not without its share of problems. In addition to helping ring the alarm in the United States and many Western counties of China's real aim and plan louder or even "prematurely," the implementation of Xi's new and more aggressive diplomatic strategy has also produced new problems. The use of wolf warrior diplomacy with open endorsement from the top leadership of China's normally cautious or even conservative diplomatic corps and the growing push-back by other nations, for example, show the complexity and hidden traps involved in any country's attempt to transform itself from one of the key players in global affairs to the leader of the pack, let alone China (Sun 2020).

The Soft-Power Strategy

China has been paying attention to soft-power strategy since the mid-1990s (Lin 2007). As China's global reach widens and more financial and human resources pours in, soft power has become an increasingly and distinctive component of China's global strategy. By the time he took over the reign, Xi had inherited assets in the area that were growing faster than many aspects of China's diplomacy. What Xi did was to elevate soft power to a level that is both compatible with and essential to the radicalization of China's global posture. What started with an emphasis on Chinese culture and language as a way to smooth its relations with other nations and help China establish a more favorable image there, soft power has now become an essential part of China's global strategy for both defensive and offensive purposes. The recent Chinese efforts to use soft power as an essential part of China's COVID-19 diplomacy serves as a good case in point.

China was hit hard by the outbreak of the pandemic with heavy criticism of it not being fully transparent. Once the pandemic spread to the rest of the world, the accusation against China intensified. To counter the accusations and reassert China's role in the global fight against the pandemic, China quickly mobilized its apparatus abroad and at home. The efforts included creating a highly publicized campaign of showing China providing medical supplies to many parts of the world (known as mask diplomacy initially and now known as vaccine diplomacy); assembling teams of diplomats and native and foreign journalists to counter Western accusations point by point; showing China's leadership in development, trial, and distribution of COVID vaccine, especially highlighting China's commitment to treat the vaccine as public goods and supplying it to developing countries at low cost or free, in direct contrast to the practice of many Western countries serving their own citizens first; and engaging in dialogue with local media and social platforms around the world to help explain China's plans and policies (Zhao & Zhao

2020). These efforts, while not being able to completely ward off the negative impact on China's diplomacy and global standing in the wake of the worst pandemic originated again (in addition to the 2003 SARS pandemic) from China, proved to be highly effective in setting the tone of global opinion especially of nations outside the wealthy club of the West.

The soft-power strategy does not always work well or according to China's plans. For example, China has focused on expanding its ties with Europe both with Western European nations as well as Eastern European counties. However, the ties have recently encountered some headwind. China's mishandling of the COVID-19 pandemic and its aggressive wolf warrior style of diplomacy have generated heavy pushbacks and tarnished its good-will offensive and image-making efforts. A recent survey of nearly twenty thousand people from thirteen countries in Europe has found that negative views of Beijing have grown across the continent.[12] While Europeans continued to regard trade and cooperation with China on climate change in a positive light, their views of China have worsened substantially in the last three years. In the words of Richard Turcsanyi, who wrote a report based on the survey, "Such highly negative public opinion across Europe creates a pressure on European policymakers to push for more in their relations with China—be it human rights, 5G, or trade and investment negotiations."[13]

CONCLUSIONS

The four narratives and five supporting strategies Xi employed and expanded form what many called China's new grand strategy (Scobell et al. 2020). This chapter argues that calling it a new grand strategy does not capture the whole meaning and far-reaching implications of the ongoing radicalization of China's global posture. What China has experienced under Xi is not just the adoption of another strategy; it is the start of a process of reshaping China's global posture that is fundamentally different from anything the world had witnessed vis-à-vis China. It has huge impact on everything China has been doing and will do globally, including how it handles tension or conflict with the United States, such as the ongoing trade disputes.

To name just the most obvious, the presence of an extremely powerful leader in charge of a fast rising power with no institutional limits to his reign and armed with a set of carefully articulated narratives and strategies makes it highly unlikely that China will treat concrete diplomatic issues or negotiations on narrow grounds or focus on petty merits. To the contrary, it will view and treat any and every challenge it faces with the most systemic and strategic perspective while reserving its greatest attention for how the outcome will affect the political standing of Xi and carrying out of his global vision. This means that when Chinese representatives come to negotiate with their US counterparts, they will come with a very different mind-set and agenda than people usually sitting at the opposite side of the table. They will be far more patient, strategic, and, believe it or not, flexible on small details but unyielding on issues that would hurt China's overall global ambition.

To suggest that there is a radicalization going on in China's global posture does not imply that the process will inevitably lead to full-scale clash with the United States or the liberal world order; nor does it suggest that the process will succeed in the end. To the contrary, there has been plenty of evidence to suggest that even under the best scenario, Xi would have difficulty keeping the current pace of global expansion without encountering major resistance or even setbacks. There is a big question, for example, of whether the pace of China's economic reform and resultant economic growth will be able to keep up with its ambitious goals abroad and beyond. If there is one area where there was little to show off even after almost eight years of reign under Xi, it is China's economy. Most of the measures adopted during this period appeared to be of more of a patching-up nature than long-term and meaningful changes required for a sustainable and healthy Chinese economy. The recent call for moving from a one-directional integration with the international system to a so-called dual circulation (双循环) economy that puts equal emphasis on strengthening China's global reach and domestic consumption involves a recognition that the international environment favorable and conducive to China's explosive growth of the 1980s, 1990s, or the first decade of the new millennium was gone.[14] With China's economic engine somewhat in question, it is doubtful that however hard he tries, Xi would be able to fully achieve his ambitions at home and abroad.

NOTES

1. The consensus now is that the United States had misread Xi in the years leading to his ascendance, mistaking him as a globalist rather than an autocrat. https://www.wsj.com/articles/xi-jinping-globalist-autocrat-misread-11608735769

2. https://en.wikipedia.org/wiki/Radicalization

3. http://language.chinadaily.com.cn/19thcpcnationalcongress/2017-11/06/content_34188086.htm

4. Especially in comparison with Hu Jintao's call for harmony and not disturbing things for nothing.

5. During his visit to Mexico in February 2009, Xi accused foreigners of having "a full stomach and nothing better to do than trying to be the backseat drivers of our

country's own affairs." https://world.time.com/2009/02/13/a-chinese-leader-talks-tough-to-foreigners/

6. https://clintonwhitehouse4.archives.gov/textonly/WH/New/China/19980629-6683.html

7. https://www.chicagotribune.com/news/ct-xpm-1997-10-30-9710300304-story.html

8. https://www.scmp.com/news/china/military/article/3109443/chinas-military-modernisation-must-be-driven-innovation

9. http://www.gov.cn/xinwen/2020-01/18/content_5470440.htm

10. https://history.state.gov/departmenthistory/travels/president/trump-donald-j

11. http://www.xinhuanet.com/politics/leaders/2020-12/27/c_1126913476.htm

12. https://www.wsj.com/articles/pushback-xi-china-europe-germany-beyond-u-s-11609176287

13. https://www.scmp.com/news/china/diplomacy/article/3110516/china-loses-its-lustre-among-europeans-doors-remain-open

14. Read Xi's speech at the 7th Central Finance and Economic Committee Meeting on April 10, 2020. http://www.qstheory.cn/dukan/qs/2020-10/31/c_1126680390.htm

REFERENCES

Blackwell, Robert D., and Kurt M. Campbell. 2016. *Xi Jinping on the World Stage, Chinese Foreign Policy under a Powerful but Exposed Leader*. New York: Council on Foreign Relations.

Blackwell, Robert D., and Jennifer M. Harris. 2016. *War by Other Means, Geoeconomics and Statecraft*. Cambridge, MA: The Belknap Press of Harvard University.

Callahan, William A. 2011. "Conclusion: World Harmony or Harmonizing the World?" in *China Orders the World, Normative Soft Power and Foreign Policy*, edited by William A. Callahan and Elena Barabantseva, 249–268. Washington: Woodrow Wilson Center Press.

Christensen, Thomas J. 2015. *The China Challenge, Shaping the Choices of a Rising Power*. New York: W. W. Norton and Company.

Congressional Research Service. 2020. *Emerging Military Technologies: Background and Issues for Congress.*

Diresta, Renee, et al. 2020. *Telling China's Story: The Chinese Communist Party's Campaign to Shape Global Narratives*. Stanford, CA: Hoover Institute.

Economy, Elizabeth C. 2018a. *The Third Revolution, Xi Jinping and the New Chinese State*. New York: Oxford University Press.

———. 2018b. "China's New Revolution, The Reign of Xi Jinping," *Foreign Affairs* (May/June).

———. 2019. "The Problem with Xi's China Model, Why Its Successes Are Becoming Liabilities," *Foreign Affairs* (March).

Ericson, Andrew S. 2019. "China's Global Maritime Interest and Investment in the Far Seas," in *Strategic Asia 2019, China's Expanding Strategic Ambitions*, edited by Ashley J. Tellis, Alison Szalwinski, and Michael Wills, 3–48. Seattle, WA: National Research Bureau of Asian Studies, 247–248.

Fravel, M. Taylor. 2019. *Active Defense, China's Military Strategy since 1949*. Princeton, NJ: Princeton University Press.

Friedberg, Aaron L. 2011. *A Contest for Supremacy, China, America, and the Struggle for Mastery in Asia*. New York: W. W. Norton & Company

Gates, Robert. 2020. "The World Is Full of Challenges. Here's How Biden Can Meet Them," *New York Times*. https://www.nytimes.com/2020/12/18/opinion/biden-foreign-policy.html

Godement, Francois. 2019. "China's Promotion of New Global Values," in *Strategic Asia 2019, China's Expanding Strategic Ambitions*, edited by Ashley J. Tellis, Alison Szalwinski, and Michael Wills. Seattle, WA: National Research Bureau of Asian Studies, 341–366.

Hu, Angang. 2015. "Minzhu Jueche, Zhongguo Jiti Lingdao Tizhi" (Democratic Decisionmaking, China's Collective Leadership System). Beijing: Renmin Chubanshe.

———. 2020. "Chongfeng Fahui Zhongguo Zhidu Youshi" (Fully display the system advantage of China). Beijing: Xushujie (No.2), 5–26.

Hu, Weixin. 2019. "Xi Jinping's 'Major Country Diplomacy': The Role of Leadership in Foreign Policy Transformation," *Journal of Contemporary China* 28 (115): 1–14.

Ikenburry, G. John. 2008. "The Rise of China, Power, Institutions, and the Western Order," in *China's Ascent, Power, Security, and the Future of International Politics*, edited by Robert Ross and Zhu Feng, 89–114. Ithaca, NY: Cornell University Press.

Lampton, David M. 2008. *The Three Faces of Chinese Power, Might, Money, and Minds*. Berkeley: University of California Press.

Li, Yuan, and Yan Yan. 2019. "Xi Jinping's latest talk on struggle." http://cpc.people.com.cn/n1/2019/0904/c164113-31335631.html

Lin, Zhimin. 2007. "Ruanshili, Guoji Yanjiu de Tupokou huo Xianjing" (Soft power, breakthrough point or trap in China's international studies), in *International Relations*, edited by Jianwei Wang. Beijing: Renmin Chubanshe.

———. 2019. "Xi Jinping's 'Major Country Diplomacy': The Impacts of China's Growing Capacity," *Journal of Contemporary China* 28 (115): 31–46.

Mandelbaum, Michael. 2019. "The New Containment, Handling Russia, China, and Iran," *Foreign Affairs* (July–August): 92–102.

Mardell, Jacob. 2017. "The 'Community of Common Destiny' in Xi Jinping's New Era, Building a 'Community of Common Destiny' Is the Motivating Force behind China's Future Foreign Policy," *The Diplomat*, https://thediplomat.com/2017/10/the-community-of-common-destiny-in-xi-jinpings-new-era/

McGregor, Richard. 2019. "Xi Jinping's Quest to Dominate China," *Foreign Affairs* (March–April): 123–131.

Office of the Secretary of Defense. 2020. *Military and Security Developments Involving the People's Republic of China*.

Obama, Barack. 2020. *A Promised Land*. New York: Crown.

Qu, Qinshan. 2020. "Woguo Zhidu Youshi zai Kangji Yiqing zhongde Liliang Xianshi" (The powerful display of our country's system in combating the pandemic) *People's Daily*, http://theory.people.com.cn/n1/2020/0617/c40531-31749226.html

Scobell, Andrew, et al. 2020. *China's Grand Strategy, Trends, Trajectories, and Long-term Competition*. Santa Monica CA: Rand Corporation.

Sun, Haichao. 2020. "Oumei Weihe Dui Zhong 'Xinwaijiao Fengge' Gandao Jibu Shiying" (Why did European and the US feel extremely difficult to adjust to China's new diplomatic style), *Gonggong Waijiao Jikang* (Beijing) 3: 33–40.

Sun, Fei. 2020. "Zhongguo Lingdaoren Pingti 'Fazhan Liyi' de Beihou" (Behind the frequent mentioning of interest of development among Chinese leaders), *Lianhe Zaobao* (Singapore) https://www.haozaobao.com/mon/keji/20201029/80076.html

Tang, Shiping. 2008. "From Offensive to Defensive Realism: A Social Evolutionary Interpretation of China's Security Strategy," in *China's Ascent, Power, Security, and the Future of International Politics*, edited by Robert Ross and Zhu Feng, 141–162. Ithaca, NY: Cornell University Press.

Tellis, Ashley J. 2019. "An Analysis of the Progression of China's Efforts to Expand Its Global Reach in Ways That Will Challenge U. S. Primacy," in *Strategic Asia 2019, China's Expanding Strategic Ambitions*, edited by Ashley J. Tellis, Alison Szalwinski, and Michael Wills. Seattle, WA: National Research Bureau of Asian Studies, 3–48.

Tobin, Daniel. 2020. *How Xi Jinping's "New Era" Should Have Ended U.S. Debate on Beijing's Ambitions.* https://www.csis.org/analysis/how-xi-jinpings-new-era-should-have-ended-us-debate-beijings-ambitions

Vogel, Ezra. 2011. *Deng Xiaoping and the Transformation of China.* Cambridge, MA: Harvard University Press.

Wang, Jianwei. 2019. "Xi Jinping's 'Major Country Diplomacy': A Paradigm Shift?" *Journal of Contemporary China* 28(115): 15–30.

Wang, Jisi, et al. 2018. "Did America Get China Wrong?" *Foreign Affairs* (July–August): 183–195.

Wang, Yi. 2018. "Speech at the opening symposium on the international situation and China's foreign relations in 2018." https://www.fmprc.gov.cn/web/wjbzhd/t1620761.shtml

Wang, Yizhou, Wang Jin and Nian Yao. 2020. "Rehuati Yu Lengsikao—Xinquan Feiyi Yiqing Yu Guoji Guanxi Weilai Zhouxiang (Hot Topics and Cool Considerations—Covid Pandemic and the Future Direction of International Relations)." Beijing: *Dandai Shijie Yu Shehuizhuyi* (No. 3): 4–11.

Weiss, Jessica Chen. 2019. "China's Rise and the Future of Global Politics," *Foreign Affairs* (July August): 92–102.

Wise, Carol. 2020. *Dragonomics, How Latin American Is Maximizing (or Missing Out on) China's International Development Strategy.* New Haven, CT: Yale University Press.

Xi, Jinping. 2020a. *Xi Jinping Lun Zhiguo Lizheng (The Governance of China, vol. 3)*. Beijing: Waiwen Chubanshe.

———. 2020b. http://www.xinhuanet.com/politics/2020-12/12/c_1126852702.htm

Yuan, Zongze. 2020. "Thorough Grasp of Theoretical and Practical Significance of Xi Jinping Thought on Diplomacy." *China International Studies*, (March/April): 5-31.

Zakaria, Fareed. 2020. "The New China Scare, Why America Shouldn't Panic about Its Latest Challenger," *Foreign Affairs* (January–February): 52–69.

Zhao, Kejin, and Danyang Zhao. 2020. "Yingji Waijiao: Xinguan Yiqing Xiade Zhongguo Waijiao Bianhua" (Pandemic diplomacy, the COVID pandemic and changes in China's diplomacy), *Waijiao Pinglun* 4 (Beijing): 26–48.

Zhao, Suisheng. 2010. "China's Belt-Road Initiative as the Signature of President Xi Jinping Diplomacy: Easier Said Than Done," *Journal of Contemporary China* 29 (123): 319–335.

Zhu, Feng. 2019. "Bainian Dabianju de juedingxing Yinshu Fengxi" (An analysis of the decisive factors of hundred years of Chang), *Journal of Nanjing University* 5: 1–11.

Zhu, Zhiqun. 2013. *China's New Diplomacy, Rationale, Strategies and Significance* (2nd edition). Burlington, VT: Ashgate Publishing Company.

Part III

DOMESTIC FACTORS
IN THE UNITED STATES

Chapter Eight

US Domestic Politics and the US–China Trade War

Robert Sutter

The year 2018 saw the initiation by the Trump administration of US punitive tariffs targeting Chinese trade practices seen as grossly unfair and adverse to important US interests. The US tariffs soon prompted retaliatory Chinese tariffs on US exports to China, leading to a process of sometimes escalating and sometimes declining tariffs, dependent to some degree on erratic progress the two sides made in off-again, on-again negotiations focused on trade issues. The trade war was not a unique dispute. It was part of a much broader US whole of government effort begun by Trump administration leaders aligned with majorities on both sides of the aisle in Congress to counter serious challenges from China on trade and other disputes over economic, security, and political matters. The US government effort came despite acute partisanship in Washington. It was directed by three sides: senior officials of an administration; Republicans, who controlled the Senate and controlled the House of Representatives up to early 2019; and Democrats, who were in the minority until they took control of the House in January 2019. One reason for this accord was a widespread sense of urgency to take action against Chinese practices coming at US expense that had brought Beijing to a point of wealth and power that it could overtake America in the industries of the future and thereby assume global economic and military leadership with the United States subservient.

Reflecting the role of domestic politics in the US–China trade war, the work of this bipartisan, bicameral legislative-executive group of officials was essential in the creation of and in sustaining the momentum behind the broad US government pushback against various challenges coming from China, with trade being a major set of challenges. This chapter explains how this coalition emerged and its priorities and practices. It argues that the dramatic US policy shift toward toughness against China, the most important change

149

in US China policy since the depths of the Cold War, was determined by this coalition of US political forces working collaboratively in Washington D.C. It also shows that the plans in Washington were poorly understood and supported by mainstream media for over a year and by public opinion for two years. Part of the problem was that President Trump was avowedly unpredictable and appeared repeatedly to be conflicted on applying pressure to counter Chinese challenges.

The sense of urgency seen in efforts to counter China in 2018 gave way to considerable ambivalence in 2019. The January 2020 "phase one" compromise bilateral trade deal with China suggested significant thaw. But acute acrimony emerged in March as the concurrent coronavirus outbreak in China spread with devastating consequences for the United States. The Trump administration blamed China and the argument resonated strongly with Americans turning sharply against the Chinese government. China policy was the main foreign issue in the 2020 election campaign, with Republicans and Democrats promising toughness on China. Prospects for easing tensions with China under incoming President Joseph Biden were constrained by widespread congressional, media, and popular antipathy toward Beijing.

THE ORIGINS OF THE
AMERICAN TURN AGAINST CHINA'S CHALLENGES

The roots of the extraordinary change in US China policy since 2018 involved growing dissatisfaction among an increasing number of American policy makers in the administration and the Congress, and among foreign policy elites, with the negative implications of various challenges posed by China's newly assertive government under the leadership of strong man ruler Xi Jinping (2012–). The Chinese challenges came notably in massive Chinese island building and coercive expansion in the disputed South China Sea; creating international banks and major international infrastructure and development campaigns undermining US interests and US-backed international development institutions; cyber espionage and other theft of US economic knowledge annually costing Americans hundreds of billions of dollars; grossly unfair trade and investment practices; deepening internal authoritarian rule and abuse of human rights led by the Chinese Communist Party; and ever closer cooperation with the Russian government of Vladimir Putin in mutual efforts to undercut US influence (Shambaugh 2013; Harding 2015; Schell & Shirk 2017; Sutter R. 2018a).

Chinese trade, economic, and many other practices made China policy an issue during the 2016 presidential election campaign. But China policy was overshadowed by many domestic and other foreign policy priorities. Though most presidential candidates in the 2016 campaign voiced harsh criticism of Chinese policies and behavior, they generally offered limited and middling policy recommendations. The contenders' views were in line with American public opinion that, on balance, disapproved of the Chinese government but ranked China low as an economic or military threat (Sutter & Limaye 2016, p. 11).

Hillary Clinton said China maneuvered for selfish gains at the expense of US international interests and American workers. She resolved to rectify various wrongs, holding Beijing accountable for egregious Chinese military intimidation and unfair economic practices, and suppressing human rights in China. Her main Democratic Party opponent, Bernie Sanders, focused primarily on trade and how China's development had come at the cost of American workers (Sutter & Limaye 2016, pp. 19–20).

According to Republican front-runner Donald Trump, the main problem the United States had with China was that the United States wasn't using its power to influence them. The source of US power over China, according to Trump, was US economic strength. Overall, Trump was not hostile to or confrontational with China, having said, "We desire to live peacefully and in friendship with Russia and China. We have serious differences with these two nations . . . but we are not bound to be adversaries." Trump tended to avoid discussing China as a national security threat. He averred that issues with China could be dealt with through negotiations, using American strengths as leverage (Sutter & Limaye 2016, p. 21).

The main implications of the 2016 election debate over China highlighted that US policies dealing with China were seen as not working in several important areas, including the economic issues that would become the target of the Trump administration's trade war with China. However, China was not seen as a major threat by the candidates or American public opinion. Meanwhile, officials and specialists in Beijing saw negatives with both Hillary Clinton and Donald Trump. They were frustrated with the downward trend in US–China relations and judged that trend would worsen at least to some degree if Clinton were elected. They judged that China could "shape" President Trump to behave in line with its interests, as Donald Trump was seen as less ideological and more pragmatic than Hillary Clinton (Sutter & Limaye 2016, p. 21).

TRUMP ADMINISTRATION
CONGRESSIONAL ALIGNMENT TARGETS CHINA

President-elect Trump up-ended these sanguine Chinese views when he accepted a congratulatory phone call from Taiwan's president in December

2016. When China complained, Mr. Trump condemned Beijing's economic and security policies, but he eventually was persuaded to avoid offending China by challenging past American views of the one China policy. His informal summit meeting with President Xi Jinping in Florida in early April 2017 went well as did the US president's remarkable visit to Beijing in November (Sutter 2018d).

After the Florida summit, planned arms sales to Taiwan, freedom of navigation exercises in the South China Sea, and other US initiatives that might have complicated America's search for leverage with China in order to pressure North Korea to stop nuclear weapons development were temporarily put on hold. The United States and China also reached agreement on a one-hundred-day action plan to further bilateral economic cooperation (Glaser & Norkiewicz 2017). But President Trump registered dissatisfaction with China's efforts on North Korea in June, and Taiwan arms sales and freedom of navigation exercises went forward. And a July US–China economic dialogue reached no agreement (Glaser & Flaherty 2018; Sutter 2019a).

For its part, Congress remained preoccupied in 2017 with failed efforts to end the Obama administration's health care program and a successful tax cut plan. Congress approved the Trump government's strong pressure on North Korea and on China to pressure North Korea to denuclearize (Sutter 2018c).

The Trump government's national security strategy of December 2017 and its national defense strategy of January 2018 harshly criticized China in language not seen in official administration documents in fifty years. They viewed Beijing as a predatory rival and the top danger to American national security. They highlighted a new danger China posed to the United States as it carried out plans to be the leading country in various high-technology industries seen as essential for sustaining US international leadership and national security (White House 2017; Department of Defense 2018).

US trade representative Robert Lighthizer saw Chinese economic policies posing "an existential threat" to the United States. FBI director Christopher Wray highlighted another newly prominent issue, Chinese overt and covert influence operations, including espionage in the United States (Lynch 2018; Sutter 2018b). Congressional members of both parties agreed with the warnings and took action, making 2018 the most assertive period of congressional work on China in thirty years.

However, the broader impact of the policy change on American politics was diluted because 1) President Trump did not use and appeared to disagree with the anti-China language seen in the administration strategy documents; 2) senior administration officials remained seriously divided on economic issues with China; 3) public opinion stuck to its longstanding view of not liking the Chinese government but also seeking to avoid trouble with China

(Chicago Council on Global Affairs 2018); and 4) media remained largely unaware of the major shift (Sutter 2018c). Against this background, congressional members sometimes grumbled about the adverse impact of the Trump government's punitive tariffs on their constituents (Tiezzi 2018a; L. Seligman 2018).

Reflecting strong negative congressional views of China were many China-related bills calling for strengthening US support for Taiwan. A bill advocating more and higher-level US official visits to Taiwan passed with unanimous congressional approval and was signed by President Trump in March 2018. Achieving a unanimous vote on an issue strongly opposed by China indicated deep congressional antipathy (Glaser & Flaherty 2018, p. 230).

The National Defense Authorization Act FY-2019, the most important foreign policy legislation in 2018 (passed in August 2018), officially launched as a matter of US law the avowed "whole of government" hardening toward China (House Armed Services Committee 2018). Harsh language accused Beijing of using military modernization, influence operations, espionage, and predatory economic policies to undermine the United States. Despite the bill's required voluminous treatment of military matters, it made plain that economic issues with China were of top concern to the Congress and the administration. The Defense Department's annual report to Congress on Chinese military and security developments now required treatment of "malign activities" including predatory economic and lending practices. An entire section of the act focused on measures to counter Chinese "predatory" investment practices targeting US high-technology companies and strengthen US export controls of high technology to Chinese firms. It contained a detailed set of provisions to modernize, strengthen, and broaden the scope of the interagency body employed to counter Chinese high-technology investment and acquisitions, the Committee on Foreign Investment in the United States (CFIUS). It included key reforms in US export controls that would better protect emerging technology and intellectual property from Beijing and other potential adversaries. Meanwhile, the act's many provisions on Taiwan reaffirmed various aspects of longstanding American commitments to Taiwan that China opposed.

Chinese officials responsible for US–China relations remained confident into early 2018 that whatever differences President Trump had with China could be dealt with readily through negotiations and making what the US president called "deals" that perhaps would involve some economic or other comparatively minor concessions from China. Thus, they were not well prepared for President Trump's decisive use of punitive tariffs against China beginning in 2018 (Medeiros 2019; Sutter 2018b).

An administration announcement in June promised steep tariffs on $50 billion Chinese higher-technology imports seen to have benefited from China's abuse of American and international intellectual property rights. An announcement in July said planned punitive tariffs of 10 percent would be imposed on $200 billion of Chinese imports. An August 1 announcement increased the rate of those proposed tariffs to 25 percent at the end of the year. As those tariffs were implemented in September, the United States threatened tariffs on an additional $267 billion of Chinese imports if Beijing retaliated, which it promptly did with Chinese punitive tariffs covering most of China's imports of American products (US Special Trade Representative 2018).

Concurrent with the escalating trade war, throughout the fall, administration officials continued to turn up the rhetorical heat on China. In September, Trump condemned China for influence operations seeking to undermine the Republican Party in US midterm elections. US ambassador to China Terry Branstad, National Security Council (NSC) senior China official Matthew Pottinger, National Security Advisor John Bolton, and Secretary of State Michael Pompeo all registered strong opposition to Chinese government practices. Vice President Michael Pence in a speech in October 2018 explained to the American people, media, and international audiences the wide extent of the US policy shift and its purported durability. He detailed key disputes including a wide variety of Chinese trade and economic practices (Sutter 2019a; "Special Report" 2019).

Other tough measures against China, not seen in past US practice, came from various US agencies. Several involved economic issues along with the escalating punitive tariffs. Entering November, the Justice Department rolled out what was called a "New Initiative" to combat Chinese economic espionage. Standing in for absent President Trump, Vice President Pence repeatedly criticized Chinese economic and military practices, underscoring the administration's hard line for the international audiences in remarks at annual multilateral summits meeting in Asia (Glaser & Flaherty 2019b; Sutter 2019a; "Special Report" 2019).

The Trump–Xi summit on the sidelines of the G20 meeting in Argentina on December 1 resulted in a temporary halt to escalating US punitive trade tariffs against China, pending agreement involving extensive US demands by March 2019. On the same day of the summit came the arrest of the chief financial officer and daughter of the president of China's leading telecommunications firm, Huawei, by Canadian authorities in Vancouver for extradition to the United States. The US charges involved Huawei's involvement in subverting US sanctions against Iran. Beijing reacted strongly, arresting and detaining Canadians in China; but it avoided actions against the United States. More negatives followed with National Security Advisor John Bolton's strong attack on China's policies in Africa in a speech on December 13 and with President Trump's signing on December 31 of the Asia Assurance Initiative Act which provided funding to counter China in Asia in line with provisions of the National Defense Authorization Act, noted above. Congress finished the year with other legislation likely to be revived in the 116th Congress taking aim at Beijing's massive crackdown on dissent among Uighur Muslims in northwestern China, continued repression in Tibet, and proposed penalties against Chinese high-technology firms that violate US international sanctions (Sutter 2019e).

COUNTERING CHINA IN 2019—MIXED IMPLEMENTATION, UNCERTAIN RESOLVE

As trade negotiations dragged on in 2019, administration spokespersons were publicly more restrained in criticizing China. Nevertheless, the whole-of-government pushback against Chinese practices went forward. The Justice Department publicized a wide array of convictions of Chinese agents or those working for Chinese authorities engaged in egregious episodes of espionage, intellectual property theft, and influence operations. Department officials warned universities of clandestine Chinese espionage using Chinese students to seek advanced technology (Glaser & Flaherty 2019a, p. 28).

At the State Department, Secretary of State Michael Pompeo and Assistant Secretary of State David Stilwell delivered a series of speeches endeavoring to build support in the United States and abroad for the harder Trump administration approach to China. Secretary Pompeo made special efforts to persuade US allies, US high-technology companies, and US governors of the wisdom in avoiding interaction with Huawei on grounds of national security. National Security Adviser Robert O'Brien, like Vice President Pence in 2018, strongly criticized Chinese policies and practices during the multilateral meetings in Asia in 2019. Vice President Pence made another major speech explaining the hard US government approach toward China one year after his 2018 speech (Sutter 2019d; Doherty 2019).

By this time, mainstream America media were more focused on the Chinese challenges to America. Repeated news stories about China's perceived ambitions to overtake America's lead in high-technology industry, placing the US military technology leadership in jeopardy, joined trade and other disputes in having a measurable negative impact on American public opinion. In one poll in early 2019, 21 percent of Americans now considered China the country's greatest enemy, compared to 11 percent at the same time in 2018 (McCarthy 2019).

Several important groups of disgruntled Americans were now more focused on economic and other dangers posed by China. They were: 1) people
afraid of being displaced by alien immigrants and perceived pernicious
foreign influence; 2) workers concerned about being sold out to China and
angry about the complicity of US elites in the betrayal; 3) manufacturers worried about having their technology stolen and market access blocked; and 4)
Christians frustrated with obstacles to proclaiming the Gospel with China as
the largest malefactor. Meanwhile, China was "the global menace" featured
above any other international dangers at the annual Conservative Political
Action Conference (Sutter 2019d; Schreckinger 2019).

The growing tensions between the US and Chinese governments resulted
in the atrophy of the scores of official dialogues used in the past to manage
trade and other tensions and build positive interchange in Chinese–American
relations (Tiezzi 2018b). Moreover, the wide range of cooperative US–China
programs fostered by many US government departments and agencies with
Chinese counterparts, including many related to trade and economic development, atrophied. Putting aside cooperation, senior US leaders now gave
top priority to countering forthrightly China's adverse trade, investment, and
other practices. They employed punitive tariffs and related restrictions on
Chinese investment in the United States and on the US export of high technology to China.

Internationally, US officials sought to create a growing united front of
like-minded governments targeting Chinese economic and security practices
against their common interests. Notable results were closer collaboration
among the United States and its allies and partners to share intelligence and
other information, tighten export controls and investment approvals, issue
statements condemning Chinese economic espionage, and strengthen surveillance of Chinese influence operations and economic and other espionage in
a wide range of developed countries (Sutter 2019e). US efforts to mobilize
government and private sector investment in the Asia-Pacific to compete with
China enjoyed strong support from allies and partners, Australia and Japan
in particular. Complementing the above collaboration was greater military
cooperation against Chinese advances.

The collapse of the protracted US–China trade negotiations in May 2019
saw President Trump and his government move swiftly to raise the tariff rate
on $200 billion of Chinese imports from 10 percent to 25 percent, and to be-
gin consideration of tariffs on the remaining Chinese imports valued at $250
billion a year. An executive order imposed restrictions on exports to Huawei
that endeavored to undermine the controversial Chinese firm by cutting off
supplies of advanced computer chips (Bajak & Arbel 2019; Behsudi 2019).

As of September 1, approximately 67 percent of US imports from China
were subject to increased tariffs, most in the range of 15–25 percent, while

approximately 60 percent of China's imports from the United States faced additional tariffs, most in the range of 5–25 percent. On October 15, 2019, the United States was to increase many existing tariffs from 25 percent to 30 percent. On December 15, 2019, the United States was to impose an additional 15 percent tariff on most remaining imports from China and China was to both expand the coverage of its tariffs and increase certain existing tariffs (Congressional Research Service 2019, pp. 1–2). The planned tariff increases were avoided as the two sides moved toward a first phase trade agreement, concluded in January 2020.

Though Congress remained negative about China, the most important foreign policy legislation of the year, the National Defense Authorization Act of 2020, had scattered provisions dealing with China, without the priority and substance given to China in the previous year. China issues were addressed in many other proposed bills, but the vast majority of such legislation garnered little congressional support (Sutter, R. 2020b).

On the campaign trail, Democratic candidates and the American media registered little urgency over the China danger. Beijing's human rights abuses in Xinjiang and control in Hong Kong were duly criticized, usually without calling for strong US countermeasures to punish China. China received low-priority treatment in the Democratic candidates' debates. Media interviews with the candidates saw issues with China, if they came up at all, addressed toward the end of the discussion, not in the beginning (Sutter, R. 2020b; Wright 2019).

Bernie Sanders and Elizabeth Warren were critical of the US trade relationship with China, but they placed the blame on American negotiators reflecting corporate interests rather than the Chinese government. Sanders said China was not an existential threat to America; he urged stronger US efforts to establish a positive cooperative relationship with Beijing on climate change and other issues. Like Sanders, Warren also wanted to reduce the defense budget and the involvement in Afghanistan. But unlike Sanders's disavowal of such power politics, Warren sought to bolster the US position in competition with China through greater security cooperation with allies (Beinart 2019; Sutter R. 2020b; Yang 2020).

Vice President Biden backed away from his remarks earlier in the campaign about the insignificance of China's challenge, but he repeatedly emphasized Chinese weaknesses in comparison to US strengths, asserting that China was in a much worse position than and no match for America. Peter Buttigieg saw a danger in China as a dominating high-tech power, yet his remedy was not to confront China. He favored strengthening American competitive assets at home, adding that cooperation with China was needed on climate change and other issues. Senator Amy Klobuchar favored well-managed US-allied pressures to get China to stop its trade and economic practices harming America.

She graphically illustrated her limited concern about China when among the one hundred steps she proposed to take in the first hundred days of her presidency only one, against Chinese steel dumping, was about China and it came far down the list (Sutter, R. 2020b).

The Democratic Party candidates' episodic disapproval of Chinese government practices was in line with US public opinion. Using polling data, Jake Sullivan, a leading Democratic Party functionary, advised in June 2019 that the "inside the beltway" discourse about the acute danger posed by China was not shared by the American public. He judged that "the bottom line is there's a broad view that China shouldn't be our enemy, that we can work with this country, that we can trade with this country, and that we can seek investment from this country." He saw this view prevailing going into the 2020 election campaign (Episode 135, 2019).

Sullivan's views were supported by polling from the Chicago Council of Global Affairs in September. Americans were divided over imposing punitive tariffs on China with 72 percent of Republicans favoring and 71 percent of Democrats opposing raising tariffs on products imported from China. Such public ambivalence meant that substantial attention to the trade war and other elements of the China debate were unlikely in the 2020 campaign, according to assessments by prominent experts at the Brookings Institution and the Center for New American Security in late 2019 (Kafura 2019; Hass 2019; Fontaine 2019).

PANDEMIC, PUBLIC OPINION
UPEND CAMPAIGN STRATEGIES, TARGET CHINA

By January 2020, the reported campaign plans of President Trump and Vice President Biden, the prospective Democrat nominee, seemed generally clear. The president emphasized the remarkable growth of the American economy during his administration. The first phase trade deal with China signed in January fit with the campaign's narrative of the president advancing US economic interests at home and abroad.

Announced on January 15, the deal promised improved access to China's agricultural market for American producers. The United States agreed to delay tariffs scheduled to take effect December 15, 2019, that would have affected approximately $160 billion worth of imports from China, particularly consumer electronics. For US tariffs enacted on September 1, 2019, the United States, as of February 14, 2020, cut the tariff rate from 15 percent to 7.5 percent. The remaining US tariffs enacted since March 2018 remained in effect. China reciprocated with adjustments in its tariffs against US products.

Core US concerns on theft of intellectual property, forced technology transfer, industrial policies, and state subsidies remained to be addressed in purported future phase two talks (Sutter, K. 2020).

Vice President Biden's presidential campaign depicted the candidate offering a return to the steady and moderate foreign policy approach of the Obama years. China was viewed as "a special challenge," requiring a "get tough" American approach. Unlike President Trump's "reckless tariffs" alienating close US allies and partners, Biden called for building a "united front" of US allies and partners to confront China's abusive behaviors and human rights violations, even as he sought to cooperate with Beijing on issues where interests converge, such as climate change, nonproliferation, and global health security (White House 2020; Wright 2020; Biden 2020).

Though Chinese leaders now assessed Donald Trump as more unpredictable and disruptive than they had anticipated, they nonetheless were said to favor the president's reelection over a Democratic challenger. Mr. Trump's transactional approach to politics was arguably preferable to a more principle-driven president. And Chinese strategic planners welcomed President Trump's continued pressures upsetting allies and partners that weakened American ability in Asia and elsewhere to counter challenges posed by China (Fifield 2020; *Economist* 2020).

The plans of both campaigns ended with the first wave of the coronavirus pandemic hitting the United States with devastating consequences involving over two hundred thousand dead by September 2020 and the deepest dive in economic growth and employment since the Great Depression ninety years earlier. The Trump campaign plan was overtaken by events. The self-isolation required to curb the virus's lethal impact curbed the president's mobilizing electoral support through mass rallies held in key battleground states. For a time, Mr. Trump and his political advisors employed the president's personal involvement in daily White House media briefings on the "war" against the virus as a means to keep his leadership as a "wartime president" before the public. But the president's performance was erratic, showed lapses of judgment and poor knowledge, and coincided with a decline in approval ratings of the president's leadership (Olorunnifa & Parker 2020; Scherer & Dawsey 2020; Rogin 2020a).

The need for a campaign message that would help reelect the president came with an increase in leadership invective in US–China relations. With the phase one deal duly celebrated in the administration, the whole of government counters to Chinese challenges resumed with greater prominence. The attorney general and the FBI came out strongly in February against Chinese theft of US high-technology information and the enormous negative consequences of China's quest for high technology leadership at American expense. Secretary Pompeo made speeches critical of China at home and abroad; Pompeo, Defense Secretary Mark Esper, and House Speaker Nancy Pelosi pressed anti-China warnings at the annual Munich Security Conference in February. The Defense Department increased the number of freedom of navigation operations challenging Chinese hold of disputed territory in the South China Sea and for the first time deployed US warships to counter Chinese harassment using Coast Guard and maritime militia of other South China Sea claimants surveying for oil and gas in areas within China's broad territorial claim. The State Department for its part was much more public in rebuking Chinese "bullying" and supporting the other South China Sea claimants, viewing Beijing's claims as illegal. Also in February, the United States required five Chinese media organizations in the United States to register as foreign agents and China soon after required the senior American staff of three major newspapers to leave China (Department of Justice 2020; Qi 2020; Glaser & Flaherty 2020b, pp. 32–34, 39; Sutter & Huang 2020b, pp. 65–67).

Beijing in March sought the global leadership spotlight as a benefactor supplying needed protective equipment abroad and providing a model of efficient methods in checking the spread of the virus in China. The narrative ignored China as the source of the virus and the poor initial Chinese handling of the virus leading to devastating consequences for other countries including the United States. When the Chinese foreign ministry spokesman and other Chinese diplomats abroad suggested that the virus was clandestinely planted in Wuhan by visiting US military delegates, President Trump and the administration reacted strongly. Trump emphatically blamed China, calling the virus the "Chinese" virus for several days, even though American opinion leaders judged the term racist. Secretary Pompeo pressed international bodies to examine the source of what he called the "Wuhan" virus. Chinese leaders responded negatively to the "smear" campaign (Glaser & Flaherty 2020b, pp. 28–32).

The acrimonious charges and countercharges influenced American opinion of the Chinese government. A wide variety of polls showed unprecedented levels of disapproval of the Chinese government, even more than following the Tiananmen crackdown in 1989. Chinese leader Xi Jinping was viewed with no confidence by over 70 percent of Americans. China was seen as a threat by nine in ten Americans. Republicans were more supportive than Democrats in calling for tougher US measures in response to Chinese responsibility for the crisis, but all registered broad antipathy for the Chinese government and its leadership (Caputo 2020).

By April the Trump administration and associated political action committees set an agenda for the campaign that featured President Trump standing up firmly to Chinese challenges and depicting Vice President Biden as a holdover from the failed China policies of the past. Underlining this point, the president in May 2020 tweeted a picture of all the living former presidents posing with Barack Obama in the White House in January 2009 with the caption "You can thank these men for allowing Communist China to grow to the dominant dictatorship superpower that it is!" (Martin & Habberman 2020; Davis 2019).

The US president had no publicly acknowledged conversation with Xi Jinping after a phone talk on March 27. In April Trump said he was "tired of China." In May, he threatened to "cut off the whole relationship" and advised in regard to negotiations with Xi Jinping that "right now I don't want to speak to him." The president led the administration's charge against the World Health Organization, labeled a "puppet" of China, for faulty warnings about the pandemic that disguised early Chinese mismanagement of the outbreak. He cut off US funding and later formally withdrew from the WHO. He was ambivalent about the phase one trade deal with China, advising that "I feel differently about that than I did three months ago" (Martin & Habberman 2020; Lynch 2020; Rauhala, Armus & Shih 2020; Phillips 2020).

Concurrently, the administration went forward with added restrictions impeding advanced chip exports to Huawei. It blocked visas for Chinese students with affiliation with Chinese military institutes who were involved with US university research on advanced science and technology. The government was considering restrictions on Chinese firms listing in US stock markets and the possible use of the US dollar as a tool in competition with Beijing. Administration officials announced success in decoupling of the US and Chinese economies. President Trump blocked substantial US government pension funds investments in China. (Lynch & Rauhala 2020; Lighthizer 2020; Hille 2020; Panda 2020).

President Trump and his supporting campaign apparatus targeted Vice President Biden on China policy and Biden returned in kind. As Beijing moved to impose a national security law on Hong Kong, Biden said on May 23 that Trump had given China "a pass on human rights"; he added, "It's no surprise China's government believes it can act with impunity to violate its commitments. The administration's protests are too little, too late—and Donald Trump has conspicuously had little to say." In response, Trump signaled he was willing to scrap his trade progress with China in order to punish China over the coronavirus and Hong Kong, adding in a tweet on May 26 that "nobody in 50 years has been WEAKER on China than Sleepy Joe Biden. He was asleep at the wheel. He gave them EVERYTHING they wanted, including rip-off trade deals. I am getting it all back!" (Rodriguez 2020).

Mass protests of police brutality against African Americans and overall racism in America following the killing of George Floyd by police in Minneapolis on May 25 occurred along with the mounting death toll and massive economic impact of the coronavirus pandemic, reoccupying media and public concerns in the following weeks. China remained the most important foreign policy concern. Members of Congress faced an avalanche of 330 legislative proposals critical of China over the virus and many other matters; administration leaders further restricted exports of high-technology products to Huawei and other Chinese firms, and tried to curb activities of Chinese propagandists in the United States. President Trump returned to harsh and arguably racist language in criticizing Beijing's "Kung flu" during resumed mass rallies for his ardent supporters.

During the summer, the administration went forward with what one senior US official characterized as "an explosion" of measures targeting the Chinese Communist Party-State as a predatory and powerful systemic opponent of US interests and influence whose advance fundamentally endangered the American "way of life" and those of US allies and partners. Senior official speeches laid out frameworks involving Cold War–style ideological struggle with China; the administration imposed serious political and economic sanctions and economic restrictions over political and economic disputes; the respective restrictions on the other's journalists grew; consulates in Houston and Chengdu were ordered closed; military shows of force were more prominent in support of allies and partners disputing Chinese territorial claims; and stepped up engagement and support for allies and partners came with the sensitive partnership with Taiwan receiving extraordinary attention—all with a focus to push back and more effectively deter Chinese advances at others' expense and to impose serious costs when China is not deterred (Glaser & Flaherty 2020c).

In addition to showing President Trump as much tougher toward China than past policies associated with Vice President Biden seen as failures, media reports also said the various US measures were in line with plans by Trump officials to make it very difficult for a Biden government to reverse the recent course of US policy toward China in the event that President Trump was not reelected (Glaser & Flaherty 2020c, p. 32; Rogin 2020b). In countermoves, Mr. Biden went on the offensive as a tough-minded protector of American interests against Chinese challenges, though he remained open to cooperation on areas of common interest.

Beijing remained defiant in the face of US pressure. It reportedly no longer showed preference for President Trump, though on economic issues it remained cautious in response to various US affronts, seeking to avoid further deterioration. Beijing's rhetoric against advances in US relations with Taiwan was often accompanied by strong shows of military force threatening military conflict (Wang 2020).

Congress continued to stoke anti-China measures notably in the hundreds of pieces of legislation on China pending and the draft National Defense Authorization Act for FY-2021 expected to pass in late 2020. US and international commentators commonly depicted US–China relations taking on the attributes of a Cold War, with enhanced danger of a hot war conflict over Taiwan or the South China Sea where the US and Chinese military forces faced and challenged each other frequently, sometimes more than once a day.

Nevertheless, American public opinion appeared volatile on China as election day approached. Polling results by the Chicago Council of Global Affairs published in September and based on surveys in July showed wide differences among Democrats and Republicans in their attitudes toward China. Consistent with Trump administration policy, Republicans were much more focused on China as a threat to America, favoring strong US countermeasures. Democrats gave much greater attention to global threats posed by the ongoing pandemic and climate change. Democrats and Republicans shared negative views that Beijing was a rival to Washington, though most Democrats favored a strategy of engagement over containment. Six in ten Democrats said that the United States should pursue friendly engagement with China (Chicago Council on Global Affairs 2020).

SHORT-TERM OUTLOOK—PROTRACTED STRUGGLE

The impressive recent momentum of domestic forces supporting strong American opposition to the broad range of challenges posed by Xi Jinping's China will be hard to stop under a Democratic administration in January 2021. Bipartisan majorities in Congress have passed numerous laws in the past three years that exert a lasting legacy on future congressional action and keep the Congress in the forefront of American counteraction against Chinese challenges. The trade war continues, as most important trade and related economic issues remain unresolved, along with a long list of other contentious disputes. The Chinese government continues its offensive challenges with little sign of meaningful compromise, and Xi Jinping promises to stay in power for a long time to come.

Speculation that President Biden will seek compromise with China is based on Biden's avowed interest in a nuanced approach to China, seeking cooperation with China on common interests while staying firm on areas of difference. Yet, taking the initiative to move US policy toward a more moderate approach to China will face bipartisan negative views in Congress, in the American media, and among the aroused American people—all harboring deep suspicions of an untrustworthy Chinese leadership. Given the enormous domestic challenges facing US leaders in 2021, a contentious moderate direction in policy toward China may be seen as an unattractive diversion from higher domestic priorities.

Of course, circumstances influencing the recent negative dynamic in US–China relations could change. For instance, the Chinese government could see the wisdom of accommodating some to the American concerns about Chinese government policies and practices. A US–China military confrontation might cause one or both sides to seek negotiations in the interest of avoiding war. Americans' willingness to counter Chinese practices could be deemed as too costly amid economic and budget crises now facing the United States. For now, none of these possible changes seems likely.

REFERENCES

Bajak, F., & Arbel, T. (2019) "Huawei hit by US export controls, potential import ban," *AP* May 16. Available at: https://www.apnews.com/97e72ba36d814c63ad03 25688963a9d9 (accessed June 11, 2019).

Behsudi, A. (2019) "Trump planning more restrictions on tech exports to China," *Politico* May 23. Available at: https://www.politico.com/story/2019/05/23/trump -restrictions-tech-exports-china-1469467 (accessed June 11, 2019).

Beinart, P. (2019) "Elizabeth Warren illuminates the left's foreign policy divide," *The Atlantic,* November 29. Available at: https://www.theatlantic.com/ideas/ archive/2018/11/what-elizabeth-warrens-foreign-policy-speech-means/576928/ (accessed June 9, 2020).

Biden, J. (2020) "Why America must lead again," *Foreign Affairs,* January 23. Available at: https://www.foreignaffairs.com/articles/united-states/2020-01-23/why -america-must-lead-again (accessed August 1, 2020).

Caputo, M. (2020) "Anti-China sentiment is on the rise," *Politico,* May 20. Available at: https://www.politico.com/news/2020/05/20/anti-china-sentiment-coronavirus -poll-269373 (accessed August 1, 2020)

Chicago Council on Global Affairs (2018) "China Not Yet Seen as a threat by the American Public," October 19. Available at: https://www.thechicagocouncil .org/publication/lcc/china-not-yet-seen-threat-american-public (accessed August 8, 2020).

Chicago Council on Global Affairs (2020) *Divided We Stand,* September 17. Available at: https://www.thechicagocouncil.org/sites/default/files/report_2020ccs _americadivided.pdf (accessed September 20, 2020).

Congressional Research Service (2019) "U.S.-China Tariff Action by the Numbers," Washington DC: Report R45949 October 9.

Davis, W. (2019) "Trump Call Himself 'the Chosen one' to take on China," *The Daily caller. com* August 21. Available at: https://dailycaller.com/2019/08/21/donald -trump-chosen-one-china-israel/ (accessed June 9, 2020).

Department of Defense (2018) *Summary of the National Defense Strategy of the United States,* Washington DC: Department of Defense. Available at: https://dod .defense.gov/Portals/1/Documents/pubs/2018-National-Defense-Strategy-Sum mary.pdf (accessed September 11, 2020).

Department of Justice (2020) "Attorney General William Barr delivers the keynote address to the Department of Justice's China Initiative Conference," Department of Justice *News* February 6. Available at: https://www.justice.gov/opa/speech /attorney-general-william-p-barr-delivers-keynote-address-department-justices -china (accessed August 10, 2020).

Doherty, B. (2019) "Asean summit: US condemns Chinese intimidation in South China Sea," *The Guardian* November 4. Available at: https://www.theguardian .com/world/2019/nov/04/asean-summit-us-condemns-chinese-intimidation-in-the -south-china-sea (accessed September 20, 2020).

Economist (2020a) "China views Donald Trump's American with growing distrust and scorn," January 2. Available at: https://www.economist.com/china/2020/01/02/ china-views-donald-trumps-america-with-growing-distrust-and-scorn (accessed June 9, 2020)

Economist (2020b) "America Takes aim at China." July 30. Available at: https://www .economist.com/leaders/2020/07/30/us-china-relations-are-entering-a-dangerous -period (accessed September 1, 2020).

Episode 135 (2019) "How might a Democratic president deal with China?" Carnegie-Tsinghua Center for Global Policy: China in the World podcast cast transcript, June 25. Available at: https://carnegieendowment.org/files/Episode_-_How_Might_a _Democratic_President_Deal_with_China_1.pdf (accessed June 9, 2020).

Everett, B. (2018) "Republicans gobsmacked by Trump's tariffs," *Politico,* May 31. Available at: https://www.politico.com/story/2018/05/31/trump-tariffs-canada -mexico-republican-response-615479 (accessed June 10, 2020).

Fifield, A. (2020) "China hopes Trump will be reelected," *Washington Post* November 26. Available at: https://www.washingtonpost.com/world/asia-pacific/china -hopes-trump-will-be-reelected-hes-easy-to-read/2019/11/26/70538d98-00ca -11ea-8341-cc3dce52e7de_story.html (accessed June 9, 2020).

Fontaine, R. (2019) "Great-power competition is Washington's top priority—but not the public's," *Foreign Affairs,* September 9. Available at: https://www.foreignaf fairs.com/articles/china/2019-09-09/great-power-competition-washingtons-top -priority-not-publics (accessed June 9, 2020).

Glaser, B. & Flaherty, K. (2018) "US-China Relations," *Comparative Connections* 20 (1) May.

Glaser, B. & Flaherty, K. (2019a) "US-China Relations," *Comparative Connections* 21 (1) May.

Glaser, B. & Flaherty, K. (2019b) "US-China Relations," *Comparative Connections* 21 (2) September.

Glaser, B. & Flaherty, K. (2020a) "US-China Relations," *Comparative Connections* 21(3) January.

Glaser, B. and Flaherty, K. (2020b) "US-China Relations" *Comparative Connections* 22 (1) May.

Glaser, B. and Flaherty, K. (2020c) "US-China Relations" *Comparative Connections* 22 (2) September.

Glaser, B. and Norkiewicz, C. (2017) "North Korea and Trade dominate the agenda," *Comparative Connections* 19 (2) September pp. 21-34.

Harding, H. (2015) "Has U.S. China Policy Failed?" *Washington Quarterly* 38 (3), no. 3, pp. 95–122.

Hass, R. (2019) "Why has China become such a big political issue?" Washington DC: Brookings Institution, November 15. Available at: https://www.brookings.edu/policy2020/votervital/why-has-china-become-such-a-big-political-issue/ (accessed June 9, 2020).

Hille, K. (2020) "US 'surgical' attack on Huawei will reshape tech supply chain," *Financial Times,* May 18. Available at: https://www.ft.com/content/c614afc5-86f8-42b1-9b6c-90bffbd1be8b (accessed June 9, 2020).

House Armed Services Committee (2018) *Reform and Rebuild: The Next Steps— National Defense Authorization Act FY-2019* Washington DC: US Congress, July.

Kafura, C. (2019) "American favor US-China Trade, split over tariffs," The Chicago Council on Global Affairs, September 3. Available at: https://www.thechicago council.org/publication/lcc/americans-favor-us-china-trade-split-over-tariffs (accessed June 9, 2020).

Lighthizer, R. (2020) "The era of offshoring US jobs is over," *New York Times,* May 12, p. A27.

Lynch, D. (2018) "Trump's Raise the Stakes Strategy," *Washington Post,* July 21, A14.

Lynch, D. (2020) "President ties trade angst to China's virus response," *Washington Post,* May 16, A1.

Lynch, D. & Rauhala, E. (2020) "Trump lashes out at China, orders action on Hong Kong," *Washington Post,* May 30, p. A1.

Martin, J. & Habberman, M. (2020) "GOP aiming to make China the scapegoat," *New York Times,* April 19, A1.

McCarthy, J. (2019) "Americans' favorable view of China take a 12 point hit," *Gallup News,* March 11. Available at: https://news.gallup.com/poll/247559/americans-favorable-views-china-point-hit.aspx (accessed June 11, 2019).

Medeiros, E. (2019) "China Reacts: Assessing Beijing's Response to Trump's New China Strategy," *The China Leadership Monitor* March 1. Available at: https://www.prcleader.org/medeiros (accessed June 9, 2020).

Olorunnifa, T. & Parker, A. (2020) "Trump opts to stick with old message in a new time," *Washington Post,* May 24 A1.

Panda, A. (2020) "US UN ambassador pushes back against Chinese South China Sea claims," *The Diplomat,* June 4. Available at: https://thediplomat.com/2020/06/us-un-ambassador-pushes-back-on-chinese-south-china-sea-claims/ (accessed June 9, 2020).

Phillips, M. (2020) "Trump on China trade deal," *Fox News,* May 19. Available at https://www.foxnews.com/politics/trump-china-trade-deal-i-feel-differently (accessed August 1, 2020).

Qi, Ren (2020) "Anti-China stance at Munich security conference criticized," *China Daily* February 18. Available at: https://www.chinadaily.com.cn/a/202002/18/WS5e4b47b5a310128217278510.html (accessed July 15, 2020).

Rauhala, E., Armus, T. & Shih, G. (2020) "With ultimatum, Trump deepens crisis with World Health Organization," *Washington Post,* May 20, p. A29.

Rodriguez, S. (2020) "Trump increasingly cornered on China," *Politico* May 26. Available at: https://www.politico.com/newsletters/morning-trade/2020/05/26/trump-increasingly-cornered-on-china-787870 (accessed June 9, 2020).

Rogin, J. (2020a) "Covid-19 sparks unity on US China policy," *Washington Post* May 22, p. A23.

Rogin, J. (2020b) "Trump's China hawks are on the loose," *Washington Post* June 26, p. A23.

Schell, O. & Shirk, S. (2017) *US Policy toward China: Recommendations for a New Administration.* New York: Asia Society.

Scherer, M. & Dawsey, J. (2020) "Ignoring Trump's offensive, Biden battles on his own terms," *Washington Post,* May 18 p. A1.

Schreckinger, B. (2019) "CPAC's new boogeyman: China," *Politico* February 28. Available at: https://www.politico.com/story/2019/02/28/cpac-conservatives-china-1194212 (accessed June 11, 2019)

Seligman, L. (2018) "Congress caves to Trump in fight over China's ZTE," *Foreign Policy,* July 26. Available at: https://foreignpolicy.com/2018/07/25/congress-caves-to-trump-in-fight-over-chinas-zte/ (accessed January 15, 2020)

Shambaugh, D. ed. (2013) *Tangled Titans.* Lanham, MD: Roman & Littlefield.

"Special Report: China and America" (2019) *The Economist,* May 16. Available at: https://www.economist.com/special-report/2019/05/16/trade-can-no-longer-anchor-americas-relationship-with-china (accessed September 1, 2020).

Sutter, K. (2020) *US-China Trade and Economic Relations: Overview* Washington DC: Congressional Research Service Report IF11284, January 29.

Sutter, R. (2018a) *US-China Relations: Perilous Past, Uncertain Present* (third edition). Lanham, MD: Roman & Littlefield.

Sutter, R. (2018b) "Pushback: America's New China Strategy," *The Diplomat,* November 2. Available at: https://thediplomat.com/2018/11/pushback-americas-new-china-strategy/ (accessed September 1, 2020).

Sutter, R. (2018c) "Congress and Trump Administration China Policy: Overlapping Priorities, Uneasy Adjustments and Hardening toward Beijing," *Journal of Contemporary China* December 26. Available at: https://www.tandfonline.com/doi/abs/10.1080/10670564.2018.1557944?af=R&journalCode=cjcc20 (accessed June 30, 2019).

Sutter, R. (2018d) "The United States and Asia in 2017," *Asian Survey* 58 (1), pp. 10–20.

Sutter, R. (2019a) "Trump, America and the World—2017 and Beyond" *H-Diplo/ISSF POLICY Series* January 19. Available at: https://networks.h-net.org/node/28443/discussions/3569933/issf-policy-series-sutter-trump%E2%80%99s-china-policy-bi-partisan (accessed September 11, 2020).

Sutter, R. (2019b) "The US and Taiwan Embrace Despite China's Objections, But Will It Last?" *Pacnet Newsletter* No 58 Honolulu HI: Pacific Forum November 12.

Sutter, R (2019c) "Congress and Trump Administration China Policy: Overlapping Priorities, Uneasy Adjustments and Hardening toward Beijing," *Journal of Contemporary China* 28 (118) pp. 519-537.

Sutter, R. (2019d) "Washington's 'whole of government' pushback against Chinese challenges—implications and outlook," *Pacnet Newsletter* No. 26 Honolulu HI: Pacific Forum April 23.

Sutter, R. (2019e) "United States and Asia 2018," *Asian Survey* 59 (1) pp. 10-20.

Sutter, R. (2020a) *The United States and Asia: Regional Dynamics and Twenty-First Century Relations* (second edition). Lanham, MD: Rowman and Littlefield.

Sutter. R. (2020b) "Has US government angst over the China danger diminished?" East-West Center Washington, Asia-Pacific Bulletin No. 497 January 22. Available at: https://www.eastwestcenter.org/publications/has-us-government-angst-over-the-china-danger-diminished (accessed June 9, 2020).

Sutter, R. & Huang, C. (2020a) "China-Southeast Asia Relations," *Comparative Connections* 21(3) January.

Sutter, R. & Huang, C. (2020b) "China-Southeast Asia Relations," *Comparative Connections* 22 (1) May.

Sutter, R. & Huang, C. (2020c) "China-Southeast Asia Relations," *Comparative Connections* 22 (2) September.

Sutter, R. & Limaye S. (2016) *America's 2016 Election Debate on Asia Policy and Asian Reactions.* Honolulu, HI: East-West Center.

Tiezzi, S. (2018a) "Brace Yourselves: The US-China Trade War Is About to Begin," *The Diplomat* June 5. Available at: https://thediplomat.com/2018/06/brace-your selves-the-us-china-trade-war-is-about-to-begin/ (accessed June 29, 2018)

Tiezzi, S. (2018b) "Is a thaw coming in US-China relations?" *The Diplomat* November 7. Available at: https://thediplomat.com/2018/11/is-a-thaw-coming-in-us-china-relations/ (accessed June 11, 2019).

US Special Trade Representative (2018) *Update Concerning China's Acts, Policies and Practices*, November 20. Available at: https://ustr.gov/sites/default/files/enfo rcement/301Investigations/301%20Report%20Update.pdf (accessed January 10, 2019).

Wang, D. (2020) "Restraint and Retaliation," *Gavekal Dragonomics* September 3, p. 1

White House (2017) *National Security Strategy of the United States*. Washington DC: White House, December. Available at https://www.whitehouse.gov/wp-content/uploads/2017/12/NSS-Final-12-18-2017-0905.pdf (accessed September 11, 2020).

White House (2020) "Remarks by President Trump at the World Economic Forum" Office of the Press Secretary January 21. Available at: https://geneva.usmis sion.gov/2020/01/22/remarks-by-president-trump-at-the-world-economic-forum-davos-switzerland/ (accessed August 1, 2020).

Wright, T. (2019) "Democrats need to place China at the center of their foreign policy," Washington DC: Brookings Institution May 15. Available at https://www

.brookings.edu/blog/order-from-chaos/2019/05/15/democrats-need-to-place-china
-at-the-center-of-their-foreign-policy/ (accessed June 9, 2020).

Wright, T. (2020) "The quiet reformation of Biden's foreign policy," *The Atlantic,*
March 19. Available at https://www.theatlantic.com/ideas/archive/2020/03/foreign
-policy-2021-democrats/608293/ (accessed August 1, 2020).

Yang, K. (2020) "Would Bernie Sanders defend Taiwan?" *The Diplomat* March
4. Available at: https://thediplomat.com/2020/03/would-bernie-sanders-defend
-taiwan/ (accessed June 9, 2020).

Chapter Nine

Missionary Zeal, Profits, and Constituent Interests

The Politics Behind Permanent Normal Trade Relations with China and Current Reactions

Larry M. Wortzel

The question of ending the annual review of trade and investment with China and supporting China's entry into the World Trade Organization started as a human rights, political, and economic dilemma for the United States. It played itself out for almost two years, with Clinton administration officials arguing strongly for granting China Permanent Normal Trade Relations (PNTR) and major debates in Congress.

Members of Congress from both sides of the aisle were torn between what they and their constituents hoped would be the financial benefits of trade with China under WTO rules, doubts that China would ever abide by those rules, concerns over US national security, concerns over the totalitarian form of government in China, human rights repression, and worries that cheap labor would wipe out the US industrial base (US Government Printing Office 2000).

A major factor driving the way that legislators framed their arguments was that although there were serious flaws in granting PNTR to China, many reasoned that the exposure to Western liberal values, trading in an international capitalist system, and Western forms of democracy would change the Chinese Communist Party and ultimately make China more democratic. In the end, the hope for new markets and a desire to change the communist system in China prevailed and PNTR passed.

In the House of Representatives, a statement by Stenny Hoyer summed up the aspirational hopes of those members of Congress who wanted to change the economic system, value system, and even the Communist Party of China. Hoyer said, "We have a responsibility to engage China—the most populous nation in the world—and move it, if we can, toward democratic reform, open markets and respect for human rights" (Anders & Peterson 2000). There were opponents of the bill, who vigorously argued that the trade bill would not enhance US national security. Representative Charlie Norwood (R-Ga.), summed it up this way, "The vote came down to 'jobs, bombs and Bibles'— the impact on U.S. employment, the threat of Chinese nuclear weapons and the persecution of Chinese religious dissidents" outweighed any trade and economic benefits (Anders & Peterson 2000).

On the other side of the capitol a few senators argued vehemently against granting PNTR for a variety of security, economic, and human rights reasons. Senator Jesse Helms (R-NC) summed up the opposition position this way (Helms 2000):

> I express my admiration to, among others, Senator Byrd and Senator Thompson, Senators Bob Smith, John Kyl, Paul Wellstone. These Senators were Churchillian in their efforts. Sir Winston Churchill demonstrated seven or eight decades ago that there would be no stacked deck when he courageously called for a principled confrontation against the despotism of Nazi Germany. In the course of the Senate's debate, we did succeed in making an indisputable record concerning the deplorable state of human rights in China. . . . And we did succeed in exposing the heinous practice of forced abortion.
>
> The interests of various American businesses will, no doubt, be served, but to those of us who have worked in the Senate Chamber during this debate, it is highly questionable whether the national interests of either the United States or the interests of the people of China—the people of China—will be served.
>
> I would be less than honest if I did not confess my great apprehension that there will be little if any real change by the Chinese Government as a result of our passing this measure. But if real change is to take place, the United States must more aggressively support the aspirations of the hundreds of millions of Chinese people who want their homeland to become a nation that is both great and good. We must reach out to those people who are struggling for a freer, more open and more democratic China, and make clear to them that the American people stand with them. We must make clear to the Chinese Government that it will not be in their interests to continue their oppression of their own people, that in the long run totalitarian dictatorship cannot be tolerated.

Senator Fritz Hollings put it this way, "It would be foolish for the United States to extend Permanent MFN to China at this time. Currently, China profits much more from our trade relationship than we do, and granting Permanent MFN will only serve to worsen an already unfair situation" (Hollings 2000, 4).

However, in his testimony at the hearing chaired by Hollings, then secretary of commerce William M. Daley set out the position of those in the Clinton administration who were convinced that PNTR would change the economy and system in China:

The Chinese leadership has recognized the need to open its market to global competition in order to be able to build a modern, successful economy. One of the best indicators of the commitment of the Chinese leadership to a more open economy is its desire to take on the challenges and obligations of WTO membership. I am here today to discuss with you how supporting PNTR status for China can move China toward a more open economy. (Daley 2000, 11)

Labor unions opposed PNTR, arguing "it would cost hundreds of thousands of American jobs"; environmentalists and human rights activists fought PNTR saying the bill would forsake "working people and put natural resources in jeopardy"; (Anders & Peterson 2000). Predictions by the US steel industry that because of government subsidies in China and dumping, the US steel industry would be hollowed out proved true (Mintner 2016).

Complaints over practices in China continued, although most who supported the legislation were willing to give China time to implement all of the obligations it had accepted. By 2013, however, the blush was off the rose. Two US business school professors documented that government subsidies in China enabled the production of technologically advanced products, quadrupling Chinese exports between 2000 and 2010. These provincial and central government subsidies "took the form of free or low-cost loans; artificially cheap raw materials, components, energy, and land; and support for R&D and technology acquisitions," which ultimately led to "massive excess global capacity, increased exports, and depressed worldwide prices, and have hollowed out other countries' industrial bases" (Haley & Haley 2013b).

CONGRESS ESTABLISHES
MECHANISMS FOR ANNUAL OVERSIGHT

Even from the beginning, Congress recognized the concerns that an end to annual review would stop addressing concerns over US national security, the totalitarian form of government, human rights repression, and worries that cheap labor would wipe out the US industrial base. Congress therefore developed means to continue some type of annual review of these matters.

In the legislation establishing PNTR, Congress established a Congressional-Executive Commission on China (CECC) (Public Law No. 106–286, 2000, Sec. 301-309). The commission was composed of nine senators and nine representatives, appointed by the House and Senate leadership; representatives of the Departments of State, Commerce, and Labor; and two representatives appointed by the president. It had its own staff. The legislative mandate was (and remains) to monitor human rights and the development of the rule of law in China; maintain a database of political prisoners in China as well as persons detained or imprisoned by the Chinese government for exercising their internationally recognized civil and political rights; and submit an annual report to Congress and the president on these matters.

In separate legislation that was part of the Floyd D. Spence National Defense Authorization Act for Fiscal Year 2001, Congress established the United States–China Security Review Commission (Public Law 106-398, 2000, Sec. 1238). Subsequent legislation modified its charter slightly and changed the name to the United States–China Economic and Security Review Commission (USCC). This was composed of twelve commissioners, three each appointed by the majority and minority leadership of the House and Senate. USCC commissioners tended to have legislative branch, executive branch, academic, business, or policy experience on China; but they were not serving members of legislative or executive branch. The USCC legislative mandate requires it to monitor as well as investigate the national security implications of the bilateral trade and economic relationship between the United States as well as matters related to strategic competition and China's compliance with its WTO obligations. Like the CECC, the USCC prepares an annual report to Congress on these topics; however, the USCC has no reporting requirements to the executive branch. USCC reports tend to recommend legislative action.

Both commissions hold hearings to investigate subjects under their mandate. Over the years since their establishment, the two commissions have grown in influence. The commission members and staff regularly brief Congress on findings, and their recommendations often find their way into legislation. At the same time, Congress has not abandoned its oversight or investigative duties; committees in both houses still hold hearings on specific matters related to China.

Still, as years passed a variety of issues arose that affected the political climate in the United States about China's behavior in response to WTO accession. In some cases, these issues were catalysts for congressional action across both sides of the aisle in the House and Senate. Other issues tended to have more partisan support on one side of the aisle than another, depending on the way major constituent interest or trade balances affected a state or its districts. This chapter explores some of these factors.

Meanwhile, in addition to creating the two commissions, emergent leaders on China issues in the House of Representatives organized bipartisan caucuses around legislative issues related to China that they wanted to pursue. Three emerged, although one of them today is moribund.

The US–China Working Group (USCWG) was formed in 2005 and is currently cochaired by Rep. Darin LaHood (D-IL) and Rep. Rick Larsen (D-WA). With forty-three other members, the USCWG states that it "provides accurate information to Member of Congress and offers a forum for open and frank discussion with Chinese leaders" (Larsen 2020a). USCWG hosts meetings across a spectrum of bilateral issues and regularly organizes delegation travel to China, currently a total of nine trips. Both Mr. Larsen and Mr. LaHood are strong on US national security and have a variety of industries in their districts. For Larsen, according to his own office web page, his major campaign support came from Boeing Co., Microsoft Corp., American Dental Assn., McBee Strategic Consulting, and Puget Energy (Larsen 2020b). LaHood's district is primarily agricultural but has some manufacturing. Congressman LaHood's major campaign support came from Blue Cross Blue Shield, the National Association of Broadcasters, Ernst and Young, State Farm Insurance, and Exelon Corporation (LaHood 2020). In the case of both China Working Group leaders, their main contributors have some business in China. Generally speaking, the China Working Group supports the positions taken by the Business Roundtable, the American Chamber of Commerce, and the idea of engaging China.

The China Caucus was established in June 2005 by former Rep. Randy Forbes (R-VA) with nine other members of the House of Representatives (Dumbaugh 2005). It generally took a hawkish view on China. Sherrod Brown (D-OH) was cochair. According to Congressman Forbes, "The Caucus will seek factual information and does not intend to be particularly anti or pro-China" (Legislators Form Congressional China Caucus 2005). The caucus was designed to investigate the consequences of its growing international, economic, and political influence on US interests. The China Caucus had several of the same members as the China Working Group.

The China Caucus grew to dozens of members, bound together over issues like human rights, religious freedom, labor rights, and threats to US national security. Many members were drawn to issues like human rights, religious freedom, and US national security. Although the China Caucus was still listed in designations and titles for its members during the 115th Congress (2017–2018), by then Randy Forbes had lost his seat due to redistricting in Virginia and Sherrod Brown had been elected to the Senate. It is inactive at the time this book went into publication.

The Congressional Taiwan Caucus was established in April 2002 and under the 116th Congress was chaired jointly by Representatives Steve Chabot (R-Ohio), Albio Sires (D-N.J.), Mario Diaz-Balart (R-Fla.), and Gerald E. Connolly (D-Va.), with 134 members. The Senate Taiwan Caucus was founded in 2002 and is cochaired by Senators Bob Menendez (D-N.J.) and Jim Inhofe (R-Okla.) and has 24 other members. Both caucuses focus on improving relations with Taiwan and have been regularly vocal about supporting Taiwan's status in international organizations (Cheng 2020).

From the standpoint of domestic politics and the impact of issues like trade and human rights on China, the caucuses are important because they are ways that members of Congress and senators can coordinate efforts in support of their constituents' interests.

HUMAN RIGHTS ISSUES EXTEND
ACROSS THE AISLES OF CONGRESS

The CECC was part of the original legislation granting China Permanent Normal Trading Relationship status. This demonstrates how despite the wide range of positions taken by legislators on PNTR, attention to human rights issues was in 2000 and remains the issue that galvanizes or stimulates the most bipartisan political support in Congress and among broad segments of the US population.

The 1999 decision by the CCP and Chinese government to persecute and defeat the Taoist spiritual group Falun Gong was one milestone considered by Congress. Falun Gong emphasized "core teachings, respectively, of Taoism, Buddhism and Confucianism," and on April 25, 1999, around ten thousand practitioners of the group's meditation exercises assembled near the Chinese Communist Party leadership compound in central Beijing for the largest peaceful protest since the 1989 Tiananmen Square demonstrations (Lin 1999). The leadership of China was shocked and scared about having ten thousand of what was estimated to be seventy million Falun Gong practitioners in China gather at the center of its power. This may not have been a spiritual practice that had wide following in the United States but the CCP actions got a lot of attention.

The CCP decision to suppress underground Protestant house churches in China (Kessel 2013, 572–589) captured the attention of US legislators and advocates of religious freedom around the United States.

In 1999, when this author was Asian Studies director at the Heritage Foundation, a Congressman active in the National Prayer Breakfast (Winston 2017) asked to talk to me about how to handle his requests of the PRC government during an upcoming Congressional Delegation (CODEL) trip to China in which he was going to participate. The Congressman explained that he and a number of other CODEL members wanted to ask the State Department about setting up meeting with a house Protestant church. I explained that in my experience serving at the US embassy in Beijing, there would be Foreign Service officers that monitored the activities of underground house worship in China and even met with leaders and worshippers at the gatherings. In general, the PRC government tolerated these diplomatic activities. However, I opined that while the embassy might grant the CODEL's request, it would almost certainly mean that the church leaders and attendees with whom the CODEL members interacted would receive harsh treatment by local CCP and government authorities, perhaps even detention or arrest. Ultimately, CODEL members decided not to pursue attempting such a meeting. The desire by legislators active in the National Prayer Breakfast for such meetings is an example of the depth of commitment by legislators and their constituents to religious freedom.

Broadly speaking, two other issues that galvanize bipartisan support among US voters and Congress is China's suppression of free expression and freedom of the press, as well as other values embedded in the Bill of Rights.

Finally, because the CCP and PRC government suppress independent labor unions, labor rights in China get a lot of attention in Congress. In this author's experience, in the twenty-eight Right to Work States in the United States this issue gets less bipartisan support (National Right to Work Foundation 2020), but labor issues in China remain a continual source of attention in the US political domain.

LOSS OF PATIENCE WITH CHINA

Ten years into China's WTO accession, congressional leaders complained that there was a "massive shift of jobs and wealth from the United States to China" (US Government Printing Office 2011). One witness at a hearing noted that "in the 10 years since it acceded to the WTO, China has systematically engaged in a pattern of avoiding, delaying, and directly violating its WTO commitments" (Price 2011).

Yet the US Trade Representative (USTR), in its 2011 Report to Congress, noted that the terms of China's accession called for it to implement "numerous specific commitments over time," with key commitments phased in by December 11, 2006. According to the report:

> Chinese policymakers showed little appreciation of the carefully negotiated conditions for China's WTO accession that were designed to lead to significantly reduced levels of traded distorting government policies. Differences in views and approaches between China's central government and China's provincial and local governments also frustrated economic reform efforts. (US Trade Representative 2011, 2)

The USTR committed in 2011 to Congress to "energetically pursue increased benefits for US businesses, workers, farmers, ranchers and service suppliers from our trade and economic ties with China. Tools for achieving these objectives include productive, outcome-oriented dialogue at all levels of engagement and in both bilateral and multilateral settings; negotiation of new disciplines, where feasible; and vigorous use of the WTO dispute settlement mechanism, where appropriate" (US Trade Representative 2011, 9–10).

Not much changed in China's behavior by 2020. Indeed, under Xi Jinping, state controls and planning increased. In its 2020 report on China's record of compliance, the USTR stated:

> Compliance with WTO rules has been poor. China has continued to embrace a state-led, mercantilist approach to the economy and trade, despite WTO members' expectations—and China's own representations—that China would transform its economy and pursue the open, market-oriented policies endorsed by the WTO. At the same time, China's non-market approach has imposed, and continues to impose, substantial costs on WTO members. (US Trade Representative 2020, 4)

In the United States, however, the Trump administration began to impose a series of tariffs on Chinese goods and to crack down on the PRC's trade practices. While there is no widespread agreement on the effect of the tariffs, and a good deal of the money from them has gone to assist farmers hurt by lower sales to China, Congress has generally been favorable to imposing measures to seek China's compliance with its obligations. The general attitude was although many people opposed tariffs, by addressing the issue with China the United States had raised important questions about the multilateral trade system. In the future, the Biden administration can work with US major trade partners to help companies disadvantaged by China's practices.

Congress appears to be supporting efforts to bring China into compliance with its obligations (Reuters 2020). The Committee on Foreign Investment in the United States (CFIUS) (Department of the Treasury 2020) has seen reform and strengthening of its authorities with Congress's passage of the Foreign Investment Risk Review Modernization Act of 2018 (FIRRMA). This expanded CFIUS to address national security concerns over foreign exploitation of investment structures that traditionally have fallen outside of CFIUS jurisdiction (Department of the Treasury 2018). Given the current bipartisan mood in Congress on China's WTO activities and even concerns by the US Chamber of Commerce and business organizations, it is likely that the Biden administration will support these efforts (US–China Economic and Security Review Commission 2020, 220).

SOME PROBLEMS THAT PRECIPITATED
THE CHANGE IN THE POLITICAL CLIMATE
OVER CHINA IN THE UNITED STATES

This section addresses some of the major technical matters Congress and the executive branch have raised about China meeting its obligations under the WTO agreement.

Subsidies

Terrance Stewart, in a report on China's subsidies under the "Guideline for the National Medium- and Long-Term Science and Technology Development Plan (2006–2020)," notes that the Chinese government planned, over a fourteen-year period, to implement preferential policies to stimulate innovation (Stewart 2007, 8–9). Among the planned preferential policies were tax policies like a consumption-based value-added tax; preferential tax reductions designed to promote innovation and accelerate scientific and technological breakthroughs; support equipment upgrades; and tax deductions for R&D expenditure. Further, under the plan, new high-technology companies received tax relief and were given preferential tax treatment to support the purchase of advanced equipment. Additional policies in the plan were designed to facilitate the establishment of overseas research and development and support foreign exchange and financing. Finally, the Chinese government in the long-term plan promised preferential tax policies designed to nurture technological innovation in domestic small and medium-sized companies (Stewart 2007, 9).

In government procurement, the long-term plan gave preference to domestically produced high-technology equipment and products with domestic intellectual property ownership over high-technology goods from foreign companies or those produced with foreign intellectual property. Other provisions of the long-term plan included banking and financing policies such as preferential loans to key industrialization projects; encouraging venture capital investment with government funding; and creating a favorable environment for domestic companies to be listed on overseas stock exchanges.

In 2018, the Trump administration issued a report that concluded that "given the size of China's economy and the extent of its market-distorting policies, China's economic aggression now threatens not only the U.S. economy but also the global economy as a whole" (White House 2018).

Rare Earth Minerals

One of the issues that caught the United States off guard was China's dominance of the rare earth industry. Over time, the United States became dependent on a potential adversary for some of the most critical materials in high-technology production. Rare earth elements are a collection of seventeen elements that are critical to civilian and military high-technology applications. The rare earth elements include scandium, yttrium, lanthanum, cerium, praseodymium, neodymium, promethium, samarium, europium, gadolinium, terbium, dysprosium, holmium, erbium, thulium, ytterbium, and lutetium (Levkowitz & Beauchamp-Mustafaga 2010, 1–2). They are important in producing technology products such as cell telephones, computer hard drives, and medical imaging equipment, as well as green technology such as electric vehicle motors and wind turbines.

In military technology production, rare earths are part of guidance and control systems, advanced optics technologies, radar, sophisticated smart or guided weapons, and telecommunications (Levkowitz & Beauchamp-Mustaf-aga 2010, 2). Rare earth elements are present around the world; however, 36 percent of known reserves are located in China and 13 percent in the United States. Over time, as the US–China trade relationship developed, the cost of developing mining sites and processing rare earth elements into alloys and magnets drove the industry into China to take advantage of the labor costs and a more relaxed regulatory environment.

Today, the Mountain Pass mine in San Bernardino County, California, is the only operational rare earth metals mine in the United States, producing about 10 percent of all rare-earth concentrate, the material from which the metals are extracted, according to USGS data. But the mine does not process its own materials—nor does any other US firm (Kenlan 2020)." The extracted materials, however, are shipped to China for processing. Over time, US dependence on China for rare earth minerals became a major problem, as tensions with China increased and the Chinese government began to use rare earths as bargaining chips in trade disputes (Cheng, Loris, & Kitchen 2019).

The United States eventually realized it had to recapitalize domestic production, and president Trump issued an executive order in 2020 designed "to reduce the Nation's vulnerability to disruptions in the supply of critical minerals" (Executive Order 2020, The White House). The executive order used the provisions of the International Emergency Economic Powers Act (50 U.S.C. 1701 et seq.) (IEEPA), the National Emergencies Act (50 U.S.C. 1601 et seq.) (NEA), and section 301 of title 3, United States Code to develop new measures. The rare earths industry is one example of how Congress highlighted issues arising from the US dependence on China, sometimes stimulated by outside commentary, and the executive branch responded, albeit slowly, to correct the problem.

The Steel Industry

In the initial debate over PNTR, Senator Durbin noted that China was already flooding the US market with subsidized steel, and that "the US steel industry wouldn't be able to use US countervailing duty trade laws because that law doesn't apply to subsidization for developing countries" (Durbin 2000). For a while there was a positive effect. Chinese imports of US scrap metal, for instance, "surged by 916 percent over the 2000–2008 period" (Casey 2012, 1, 22). Between 2005 and 2011, US exports of iron and steel waste and scrap to China "increased from $1.6 billion to $2.6 billion" (Casey 2012, 1).

That balance shifted over time resulting in a significant hollowing out of the US steel industry and employment in the industry. According to a National Public Radio report, in 2018 China produced "about half of the world's steel. It singlehandedly churns out as much steel in one year as the entire world did in 2000" (Zarolli 2018). One foundation report noted "America's share [of steel exports] fell by half (from about 12 to 6 percent), Japan's by roughly equivalent amounts, and Europe's cratered from 22 to 10 percent. From 2008 to 2015, Chinese overseas shipments of steel doubled, to 112 million tons annually by 2015, more than America's total consumption of steel in a single year. There are now two Chinese steel producers who produce more steel than Japan does in a given year" (Ezell 2018). The report estimated that in 2018, there was already enough steel production capacity in China to meet the world's needs for twenty years, most of which was subsidized by the PRC government.

According to the US Congressional Research Service, in 2010 "steelmakers in the United States believe[d] that China's steel industry subsidization by it government (in the form of an undervalued currency; export rebates and/or quotas; subsidized financing; and relatively weak environmental, labor, and safety regulations) is one of the key issues affecting the health of [the] U.S. steel sector" (Tang 2010, 18). In this area, unfortunately, President Trump's tariffs have had little effect on bringing employment and production in the steel industry back to the United States.

Agriculture

There were some positive effects on the US agriculture industry over the first decade after PNTR. According to a 2011 report by the US–China Economic and Security Review Commission, "Agricultural exports from the United States to China have increased primarily as a result of increased soybean exports. . . . Other major exports like cotton and smaller exports like tobacco have also seen significant growth. There will likely be continued growth in U.S. agricultural exports to China, based both on U.S. productive capacity and on China's large and urbanizing population" (Casey 2012, 1, 14–20).

Scrap and Waste Exports

China was the largest foreign market for US exports of iron and steel waste and scrap in 2011, with a nearly 28 percent increase from the previous year. From 2005 to 2011, US exports of iron and steel waste and scrap to China increased from $1.6 billion to $2.6 billion. The waste trade at that time was highly reliant upon commodity prices and was driven by China's rapid development. Since that time, environmental policies in China have drastically reduced this sector of US industry.

Espionage

Entities in China, whether government controlled, Communist Party–controlled, working for state-owned enterprises, or supporting priority national research programs, regularly engage in cyber and other forms of economic espionage and traditional national security espionage (Wortzel 2013). For them, stealing intellectual property and proprietary information is much more cost-effective than investing in lengthy research and development (R&D) programs. Espionage allows China and its military to leap-frog ahead in R&D, field weapons systems more quickly, and produce industrial goods more quickly and cheaply than depending on domestic research, development, and production.

Various forms of espionage by China support national science and technology development plans that are centrally managed and directed by the PRC government:

> The Chinese government, including the PLA and the Ministry of State Security, supports these activities by providing state-owned enterprises (SOEs) information and data extracted through cyber espionage to improve their competitive edge, cut R&D timetables, and reduce costs. The strong correlation between compromised US companies and those industries designated by Beijing as "strategic" industries further indicates a degree of state sponsorship, and likely even support, direction, and execution of Chinese economic espionage. Such governmental support for Chinese companies enables them to out-compete U.S. companies, which do not have the advantage of leveraging government intelligence data for commercial gain. (Wortzel 2013)

The PRC has been one of the most egregious and active countries in the world in conducting various forms of espionage against the United States. The methods its intelligence services use draw on the use of students, intellectuals, and professional intelligence officers (Mattis & Brazil 2019). FBI director Christopher Wray in 2020 warned, "We are conducting these kinds of investigations in all 56 of our field offices, and over the past decade, we have seen economic espionage cases linked to China increase by approximately 1,300 percent, . . . the stakes could not be higher, and the potential economic harm to American businesses and the economy as a whole almost defies calculation" (Miller 2020).

The rules of evidence for traditional state espionage are more difficult to prove than economic espionage; therefore, many cases are prosecuted as violations of other federal statutes. One thing is clear, however: it is highly unlikely that China will stop its espionage efforts against the United States. Congress will continue to address this irritant with hearings and legislation, and the Biden administration will be pressed to conduct effective counterintelligence programs to protect the United States. American companies will be challenged to balance the risks they take by engaging in joint ventures or investment in China against the potential for espionage losses. And as cyber controls increase in China, companies will face greater risks to the data they collect and transmit in and out of China.

SOME MEASURES TAKEN BY CONGRESS

In the period between 2018 and October 2020, Congress acted on a number of actions recommended by the US–China Economic and Security Review Commission (USCC), on which this author serves, and also recommendations by the Congressional Executive Commission on China (CECC). In that period, there have been recommendations by the USCC reflected in twenty-eight Senate bills and nine House bills, all of which were bipartisan with bipartisan cosponsorship (Wortzel 2020; Larry M. Wortzel to Kevin McCarthy). In addition, there were two Senate resolutions, and thirteen House resolutions that reflected the commission's recommendations. The CECC recommendations from its annual report received similar bipartisan support for legislative measures on China's human rights behavior and the actions by the CCP or China's government in Hong Kong (Zengerly 2020). In major legislation designed to ensure the United States is able to compete in fifth generation technology, Senator John Cornyn introduced the Secure 5G and Beyond Act of 2019, which on March 23, 2020, became Public Law No. 116-129. This legislation requires the president to create an interagency strategy to secure fifth generation and future generation technology and infrastructure in the United States and with US strategic allies (Wortzel 2020b; personal email).

Another set of bills were introduced in 2019: S.945, the Holding Foreign Companies Accountable Act, and in the House a companion bill, H.R.7000. These two bills were designed to prohibit securities of a company from being listed on any of the US securities exchanges if the company has failed to comply with the Public Company Accounting Oversight Board's (PCAOB) audits for three years in a row. The Holding Foreign Companies Accountable Act was signed into law by President Trump on December 18, 2020. It amended the Sarbanes-Oxley Act of 2002 and requires the Securities and Exchange Commission (SEC) to identify public companies using registered public accounting firms located in a foreign country when that country prevents PCAOB from auditing the accounting firm involved and it prohibits these companies from trading in US markets if the PCAOB cannot audit and inspect for three consecutive noninspection years. It also imposed public disclosure obligations on foreign companies trading securities in the United States equivalent to the disclosure requirement on US firms. China's prevention of PCAOB audits and inspections of some of its companies was the basis for this legislation (Holding Foreign Companies Accountable Act 2020).

FUTURE INFLUENCES ON THE BIDEN ADMINISTRATION

One domestic political factor that will affect how US–China relations progress is the influence of the American aviation industry. Boeing is in a head-to-head battle with Airbus for long haul aircraft sales to China. Additionally, both Boeing and Airbus fear that as domestically manufactured Chinese airliners become certified, they will be the items bought by China's airline companies as a matter of government policy. Thus as 2021 plays out, Congress and the Biden administration can expect representatives of the airline industry, business councils and chambers of commerce, and legislators from states or districts where Boeing aircraft are manufactured or assembled, to argue against restrictions on selling aircraft and related software control systems and flight systems to China (Sindreau 2020).

In a year-end article on trade policy, former Congressman Charles Boustany sums up the attitudes of some in Congress about the tariffs imposed by the Trump administration and projects what to expect of US actions in the World Trade Organization and in broader trade policy. Trade promotion authority (TPA) and trade adjustment authority (TAA) expire at the end of June 2021. Respectively, these two laws provide "guidance for the U.S. trade Representative on negotiating agreements" and "authority for worker eligibility and benefits to help those who lost jobs related to trade." The outgoing administration has used tariff authorities granted by Congress expansively, generating controversy. Modifications or restrictions on how a future administration uses these tariffs may be discussed during debate on TPA reauthorization. The Trump administration initially used its authority under the Trade Act of 1974 to investigate Chinese intellectual property theft and then imposed Section 301 tariffs on a list of Chinese products as a remedy; however, according to Boustany "the Trump administration initially used its authority under the Trade Act of 1974 to investigate Chinese intellectual property theft and then imposed Section 301 tariffs on a list of Chinese products as a remedy" (Boustany 2020).

According to Boustany, "The expanded use of these tariffs . . . led the Trump administration into negotiating the phase-one trade deal with China that went well beyond the original enforcement measure" (Boustany 2020; National Bureau of Asian Research). Americans therefore can expect that despite the deep partisan divide in Congress, some agreement will be reached on a different approach to trade with China.

In the near future, the tariffs must be adjusted to comply with WTO rules; the United States must come up with broad measures to counter the China-dominated Regional Comprehensive Economic Partnership (RCEP), of which the United States is not part; and working with other partners in the Asia-Pacific region the United States must come up with a means to promote growth and compete with Xi Jinping's Belt and Road Initiative (Rolland 2019; National Bureau of Asian Research).

On tariffs, according to the Congressional Research Service (CRS) four broad policies or practices in China justify US action: "(1) China's forced technology transfer requirements, (2) cyber-enabled theft of U.S. IP and trade secrets, (3) discriminatory and non-market-based licensing practices, and (4) state-funded strategic acquisition of U.S. asset" (Schwarzenberg, Andres B. 2021). These are issues that will probably get bipartisan support in Congress and would also get support from US businesses.

Congress also is likely to examine and address some of the plans in China put into place by the 14th Five Year Plan. CRS reports that "Chinese President Xi Jinping is reviving a 'dual circulation' economic policy that his predecessor used during the 2009 financial crisis and the 'supply side' reforms that Xi introduced in 2015 to upgrade industry and launch Made in China 2025 industrial policies" (Sutter & Sutherland 2021). The concept of dual circulation means taking advantage of domestic and global demand by developing domestic capacity for products and at the same time seeking openings in global markets for the same products. Dual circulation is designed to increase both domestic supply and demand in periods of an uncertain global environment. The policy would look inward and localize foreign capabilities in China while maintaining access to global firms while Chinese firms expand into overseas markets.

CONCLUSIONS

The highly partisan domestic political environment in the United States had a major effect on Congress and the public through the inauguration of the Biden administration on January 20, 2021. That is not likely to change over the next few years. While some issues like national defense may bring bipartisan agreement, Congress will be subject to the same sort of pressures that originally affected the approval of PNTR. Some legislators and policy makers, in spite of the intervening decades, will continue to argue that eventually exposure to Western liberal values will change China. Others will cling to the hope that the Communist Party might collapse. There will be pressures from the various sectors of the US economy to come to some agreement with China to continue trade and investment there.

The future is going to be unpredictably muddy, subject to pressures from the public and new legislation. An example how this might play out can be found in the way that one major sector of the US economy, financial markets, can quickly change its approach to China and affect the domestic political climate. The SEC decided to follow a Trump administration executive order and stop trading China telecommunications stocks on the New York Stock Exchange in November 2020 (Lubold & Lim 2020). Then a short two months later the SEC reversed its own decision, ignored an executive order, and decided that those same telecommunications companies would stay on the NYSE (Ping & Otto 2021). One day after that, the NYSE flip-flopped a second time, again saying it would de-list Chinese telecommunications companies (Ospovich 2021). Waffling on decisions like this will probably continue to happen in various economic sectors for a few years.

In the meantime, there will be some decoupling from the dependence the United States has on China as a matter of risk prevention. Supply chains will diversify; however, the attraction of engagement and participation in one of the world's biggest economies and markets will keep companies and individuals arguing over how to deal with China and its system.

REFERENCES

Anders, Nick, and Peterson, Jonathan. 2000. "House Oks China Trade Bill." *Los Angeles Times*. May 25, 2000. https://www.latimes.com/archives/la-xpm-2000-may-25-mn-33913-story.html (accessed December 2, 2020).

Biden, Joseph R., Jr. 2000. US Government Printing Office. Congressional Record, Volume 146, Pt 13. Pages 183830–18384. To Authorize Extension of Nondiscriminatory Treatment to the People's Republic of China. https://www.govinfo.gov/content/pkg/CRECB-2000-pt13/html/CRECB-2000-pt13-Pg18331-7.htm (accessed December 20, 2020).

Boustany, Charles W. 2020. "Challenges for U.S. Trade Policy in 2021: A Brief Look Ahead." National Bureau of Asian Research. December 9, 2020. https://www.nbr.org/publication/challenges-for-u-s-trade-policy-in-2021-a-brief-look-ahead/ (accessed January 4, 2021).

Casey, Joseph. 2012. *Patterns in U.S.-China Trade Since China's Accession to the World Trade Organization*. U.S. China Economic and Security Review Commission. November 2012. https://www.uscc.gov/sites/default/files/Research/

UChina_TradePatternsSinceChinasAccessiontotheWTO.pdf (accessed December 28, 2020).

Cheng, Ching-tse. 2020. "At Least 131 pro-Taiwan Lawmakers Reelected in US," *Taiwan News,* November 12, 2020 https://www.taiwannews.com.tw/en/news/4051885 (accessed December 10, 2020).

Cheng, Dean, Loris, Nicholas, and Kitchen, Klon. 2019. *China Is a Paper Tiger on Rare Earth Minerals.* The Heritage Foundation, June 13, 2019. https://www.heritage.org/asia/report/china-paper-tiger-rare-earth-minerals (accessed December 27, 2020).

"China Caucus Reforms," (2005) *Roll Call,* May 27, 2005, https://www.rollcall.com/2005/05/27/china-caucus-forms/ (accessed December 2, 2020).

Daley, William M. 2000. Hearing Before the Committee on Commerce, Science, and Transportation, United States Senate, One Hundredth Congress, Second Session. April 11, 2000. https://www.govinfo.gov/content/pkg/CHRG-106shrg80403/html/CHRG-106shrg80403.htm (accessed December 2, 2020).

Dalio, Ray. 2020. "Don't be Blind to China's Rise in a Changing World, Financial Times, October 23, 2020 https://www.ft.com/content/8749b742-d3c9-41b4-910e-80e8693c36e6 (accessed December 1, 2020).

Department of the Treasury. 2018. Summary of the Foreign Investment Risk Review Modernization Act (FIRRMA) of 2018. https://www.treasury.gov/resource-center/international/Documents/Summary-of-FIRRMA.pdf (accessed November 29, 2020).

Department of the Treasury. 2020. The Committee on Foreign Investment in the United States (CFIUS) https://home.treasury.gov/policy-issues/international/the-committee-on-foreign-investment-in-the-united-states-cfius (accessed November 29, 2020).

Dumbaugh, Kerry. 2005. "China-U.S. Relations: Current Issues and Implications for U.S. Policy," Congressional Research Service, July 14, 2006, CRS-34, https://fas.org/sgp/crs/row/RL32804.pdf (accessed December 1, 2020).

Durbin, Richard, 2000. *Senate Permanent Normal Trade Relations Vote*, 2000, USC Annenberg USC US-China Institute, September 20, 2000 https://china.usc.edu/senate-permanent-normal-trade-relations-vote-2000 (accessed January 22, 2022)

Executive Order on Addressing the Threat to the Domestic Supply Chain from Reliance on Critical Minerals from Foreign Adversaries. 2020. The White House. September 30, 2020. https://www.whitehouse.gov/presidential-actions/executive-order-addressing-threat-domestic-supply-chain-reliance-critical-minerals-foreign-adversaries/ (accessed December 26, 2020).

Ezell, Stephen. 2018. "China-Induced Global Overcapacity an Increasing Threat to High-Tech Industries." Innovation Technology and Information Federation. February 27, 2018. https://itif.org/publications/2018/02/27/china-induced-global-overcapacity-increasing-threat-high-tech-industries (accessed January 4, 2021).

Ferguson, Tim. 2014. "Where the China Lobby Meets Closed Doors: Congress," *Forbes,* February 20, 2014. https://www.forbes.com/sites/timferguson/2014/02/20/where-the-china-lobby-meets-closed-doors-congress/?sh=5d3186893e7e (accessed November 29, 2020).

"For Your Protection." 2020. *The Economist.* November 14, 2020.

"Grading Trumponics: How to judge the president's economic record." *The Economist*. October 17, 2020, 10. https://www.economist.com/leaders/2020/10/17/how-to-judge-president-trumps-economic-record (accessed December 1, 2020).

Guevara, Marina. 2005. "China Steps Up its Lobbying Game." *Public Integrity*, September 13, 2005. https://publicintegrity.org/politics/lobby-watch/china-steps-up-its-lobbying-game/. (accessed December 1, 2020).

Haley, Usha C.V. and Haley, George. 2013a. *Subsidies to Chinese Industries: State Capitalism, Business Strategy, and Trade Policy*. New York: Oxford University Press.

Haley, Usha C.V. and Haley, George. 2013b. "How Chinese Subsidies Changed the World." *Harvard Business Review*. April 25, 2013. https://hbr.org/2013/04/how-chinese-subsidies-change (accessed December 1, 2020).

Helms, Jesse A. 2000. US Government Printing Office. Congressional Record, Volume 146, Pt 13. Pages 18350–18351. To Authorize Extension of Nondiscriminatory Treatment to the People's Republic of China. https://www.govinfo.gov/content/pkg/CRECB-2000-pt13/html/CRECB-2000-pt13-Pg18331-7.htm (accessed November 29, 2020).

Holding Foreign Companies Accountable Act Signed into Law. 2020. Miller Canfield Advertising. December 30, 2020. https://www.jdsupra.com/legalnews/holding-foreign-companies-accountable-37359/ (accessed January 8, 2021).

Hollings, Fritz. 2000. Hearing Before the Committee on Commerce, Science, and Transportation, United States Senate, One Hundredth Congress, Second Session. April 11, 2000. https://www.govinfo.gov/content/pkg/CHRG-106shrg80403/html/CHRG-106shrg80403.htm

Jennings, Ralph. 2020. "Indonesia Moving Navy Combat Squad HQ to Tiny Remote Islet." Voice of America. December 11, 2020. https://www.voanews.com/east-asia-pacific/indonesia-moving-navy-combat-squad-hq-tiny-remote-islet

Jia, Denise. "'Dual circulation': 5 things to know about China's new economic development strategy." *The Straits Times*, September 8, 2020. https://www.straitstimes.com/asia/east-asia/chinas-new-economic-development-pattern-of-dual-circulation-5-things-to-know-about-it (accessed December 10, 2020).

Kelly, Mike. 2020. Committees and Caucuses. https://kelly.house.gov/about-me/committees-and-caucuses (accessed December 10, 2020).

Kenlan, Alyk Russell. 2020. Rare Elements of Security. *Air Force Magazine*. November 1, 2020 https://www.airforcemag.com/article/rare-elements-of-security/ (accessed December 23, 2020).

Kessel, Karrie J. 2013. "The Rise of a Chinese House Church: The Organizational Weapon," *The China Quarterly*, No. 215 (September 2013), 572–589.

LaHood, Darin. 2020. Congressman Darin LaHood – Proudly Serving the 18th District of Illinois. https://lahood.house.gov/ (accessed December 12, 2020)

Larsen Rick. 2020a. "About the Working Group." https://larsen.house.gov/uscwg/ (accessed December 10, 2020).

Larsen, Rick. 2020b. U.S. Congressman Rick Larsen - Representing Washington's 2nd District. https://larsen.house.gov/ (accessed December 12, 2020).

Lee, Yen Nee. 2020. "Trump's tariffs could give Biden 'leverage' over China, former White House trade negotiator says." CNBC. November 25, 2020. https://www .cnbc.com/2020/11/25/trump-tariffs-could-give-biden-leverage-over-china-ex-us -trade-official.html (accessed December 10, 2020).

Legislators Form Congressional China Caucus. 2005. Hong Kong Trade Development Council. June 9, 2005. http://info.hktdc.com/alert/us0511d.htm (accessed January 5, 2021).

Levkowitz, Lee, and Beauchamp-Mustafaga. 2010. *China's Rare Earths Industry and its Role in the International Market*. U.S.-China Economic and Security Review Commission. November 3, 2010.https://www.uscc.gov/sites/default/files/ Research/RareEarthsBackgrounderFINAL.pdfber (accessed December 27, 2020).

Lin, Anastasia. 1999. "How I learned to Stop Hating Falungong," Wall Street Journal, July 18, 1999 https://www.wsj.com/articles/how-i-learned-to-stop-hating-falun -gong-11563490711 (accessed December 1, 2020).

Lubold, Gordon and Lim, Dawn. 2020. "Trump Bars Americans From Investing in Firms That Help China's Military." The Wall Street Journal. November 12, 2020. https://www.wsj.com/articles/trump-bars-americans-from-investing-in-firms-that -help-chinas-military-11605209431?mod=article_inline (accessed January 5, 2021).

Mattis, Peter and Brazil, Mathew. 2019. *Chinese Communist Espionage: An Intelligence Primer*. Annapolis, MD., Naval Institute Press, 2019.

Miller, Maggie. 2020. "FBI Director Wray warns of Chinese hacking, espionage threats against American companies." The Hill. July 7, 2020. https://thehill.com/ policy/cybersecurity/506250-fbi-director-wray-warns-of-chinese-hacking-espio nage-threats-against (December 3, 2020).

Mintner, Steve. 2016. "Cheap imports have US steel producers calling for tougher trade protections – and fast." *Industry Week*. January 25, 2016 https://www.indus tryweek.com/the-economy/trade/article/21971709/is-relief-on-way-for-embattled -us-steel-industry (accessed December 1, 2020).

Naughton, Barry J., Testimony before the U.S.-China Economic and Security Review Commission. "The Chinese View of Strategic Competition with the United States." June 24, 2020. https://www.uscc.gov/sites/default/files/2020-06/Naughton_Testi mony.pdf (accessed December 6, 2020).

Ospivich, Alexander. 2021. "NYSE Reverses Course Again, Will Delist Three Chinese Telecom Stocks". The Wal Street Journal. January 6, 2021. https://www.wsj .com/articles/nyse-reverses-course-again-will-delist-three-chinese-telecom-stocks -11609945817?mod=hp_lead_pos3 (accessed January 6, 2021).

Peck, Michael. "The U.S. Military's Greatest Weakness? China 'Builds' a Huge Chunk of It." National Interest. May 26, 2018. https://nationalinterest.org/blog/ the-buzz/the-us-militarys-greatest-weakness-china-builds-huge-chunk-25966 (accessed December 1, 2020).

Ping, Chong Koh and Otto, Ben. 2021. "NYSE Scraps Plans to Delist Chinese Telecom Stocks." The Wall Street Journal. January 5, 2021. https://www.wsj.com/ articles/nyse-scraps-plans-to-delist-chinese-telecom-stocks-11609819126 ?mod=hp_lead_pos1 (accessed January 5, 2021).

Price, Allen H. 2011. U.S. Government Publishing Office. 2011. House Hearing. "Hearing Before the Congressional-Executive Commission on China. One Hundred Twelfth Congress, First Session." December 13, 2011. https://www.govinfo.gov/content/pkg/CHRG-112hhrg74026/html/CHRG-112hhrg74026.htm. (accessed December 1, 2020).

Public Law 106-398 106th Congress. Floyd D. Spence National Defense Authorization Act for Fiscal Year 2001.Sec.1238. United States-China Security Review Commission. October 30, 2000. https://www.govinfo.gov/content/pkg/PLAW-106publ398/html/PLAW-106publ398.htm (accessed December 1, 2020).

Report to Congress: Annual Industrial Capabilities Fiscal Year 2018. May 13, 2019. Washington, DC: Office of the Under Secretary of Defense for Acquisition, Technology and Logistics. https://www.aiaa.org/docs/default-source/uploaded files/aiaa-defense-forum/fy18-industrial-capabilities-annual-report-to-congress -may-2019a16ccf64b9d84cf3855a564113d00fba.pdf?sfvrsn=bb5152f3_0&sfvrsn =bb5152f3_0 (accessed December 1, 2020).

"Renewed Great Power Competition: Implications for Defense—Issues for Congress." Congressional Research Service. Washington, DC: Report R43838. updated October 29, 2020, 13-13, 39-40. https://crsreports.congress.gov/product/pdf/R/R43838 (accessed December 1, 2020).

National Right to Work Foundation, Right to Work States. https://www.nrtw.org/right-to-work-states/ (Acccessed December 10, 2020).

Reuters. 2020. "Bill forcing Chinese firms to meet U.S. accounting standards passes Congress." *CNBC*. December 3, 2020. Bill forcing Chinese firms to meet U.S. accounting standards passes Congress (cnbc.com) (accessed January 2, 2021).

Rolland, Nadege. 2019. "A Concise Guide to the Belt and Road Initiative". National Bureau of Asian Research. April 11, 2019. https://www.nbr.org/publication/a -guide-to-the-belt-and-road-initiative/ (accessed January 4, 2021).

Ryan, Jake; Bucks, Jonathan; Bancroft, Holly. 2020. "Leaked files expose mass infiltration of UK firms by Chinese Communist Party including AstraZeneca, Rolls Royce, HSBC and Jaguar Land Rover." The Daily Mail. December 12 2020. https://www.dailymail.co.uk/news/article-9046783/Leaked-files-expose-mass-in filtration-UK-firms-Chinese-Communist-Party.htmlaccounting-standards-passes -congress-.html (accessed December 29, 2020).

Schwarzenberg, Andres B. 2021. Section 301: Tariff Exclusions on U.S. Imports from China.Congressional Research Service. January 8, 2021. https://crsreports .congress.gov/product/pdf/IF/IF11582 (Accesssed January 8. 2021.

"Shock of the New: Congress and Asia in 2009." 2009. *National Bureau of Asian Research*, February 2009. https://www.nbr.org/wp-content/uploads/pdfs/publications/shock_of_the_new_feb2009.pdf (accessed December 1, 2020).

Sindreu, Jon. 2020. "After Covid, Plane Makers Are Even More Dependent on China." *The Wall Street Journal*. December 31, 2020. https://www.wsj.com/articles/after-co vid-plane-makers-are-even-more-dependent-on-China-11609429997?mod+lead _feature_below_a_pos1 (accessed December 31, 2020).

Stewart, Terrance P. 2007. *China's Industrial Subsidies Study: Volume 1 Report*. Trade Lawyers Advisory Group. April 2007.

Sutter, Karen M. and Sutherland, Michael D. 2021. China's 14th Five-Year Plan: A First Look. Congressional Research Service. January 5, 2021. https://crsreports .congress.gov/product/pdf/IF/IF11684 (accessed January 8, 2021).

Tang, Rachel. 2010. *China's Steel Industry and Its Impact on the United States: Issues for Congress.* Congressional Research Service 7-5700 www.crs.gov R44707 . September 21, 2010. 18.

United States Trade Representative. 2011. 2011 Report to Congress on China's WTO Compliance. December 2011. https://ustr.gov/sites/default/files/uploads/ gsp/speeches/reports/2011/2011%20Report%20to%20Congress%20-%20Dec%20 12%20Final.pdf (accessed December 2, 2020).

United States Trade Representative. 2020. 2019 Report to Congress on China's WTO Compliance. Arch 2020. https://ustr.gov/sites/default/files/2019_Report_on _China%E2%80%99s_WTO_Compliance.pdf (accessed December 2, 2020).

U.S. Government Publishing Office. 2011. House Hearing. "Hearing Before the Congressional-Executive Commission on China. One Hundred Twelfth Congress, First Session." December 13, 2011. https://www.govinfo.gov/content/pkg/CHRG -112hhrg74026/html/CHRG-112hhrg74026.htm (Acccessed December 2, 2020).

U.S.-China Economic and Security Review Commission. 2020. 2020 Report to Congress of the U.S.-China Economic and Security Review Commission. December 2020. https://www.uscc.gov/sites/default/files/2020-12/2020_Annual_Report_to _Congress.pdf (accessed December 20, 2020).

U.S.-China Relations Act of 2000 (Public Law No. 106–286) TITLE III—ESTAB-LISHMENT OF CONGRESSIONAL-EXECUTIVE COMMISSION ON THE PEOPLE'S REPUBLIC OF CHINA. Sec. 301-309. Ay 11, 2000. https://www .congress.gov/106/plaws/publ286/PLAW-106publ286.pdf (accessed November 30, 2020).

US Government Printing Office. 2000. Congressional Record, Volume 146 (2000), Pt 13. Pages 18331-18389. To Authorize Extension of Nondiscriminatory Treatment to the People's Republic of China. https://www.govinfo.gov/content/pkg/ CRECB-2000-pt13/html/CRECB-2000-pt13-Pg18331-7.htm (accessed November 30, 2020).

US Government Printing Office. 2018. 115th Congress. https://www.govinfo.gov/ content/pkg/CDIR-2018-10-29/pdf/CDIR-2018-10-29-MO-H-4.pdf (accessed December 10, 2020).

"Watered with Liberal Tears: How the American Economy did Under Donald Trump." The Economist. October 17, 2020, 22. https://www.economist.com/ united-states/2020/10/14/how-the-american-economy-did-under-donald-trump (accessed November 30, 2020).

White House Office of Trade and Manufacturing. 2018. How China's Economic Aggression Threatens the Technologies and Intellectual Property of the United States and the World. June 19, 2018. https://www.whitehouse.gov/briefings-statements/ office-trade-manufacturing-policy-report-chinas-economic-aggression-threatens -technologies-intellectual-property-united-states-world/ (accessed January 5, 2021).

Winston, Diane. 2017. "The History of the National Prayer Breakfast," *Smithsonian Magazine*, February 2, 2017. https://www.smithsonianmag.com/history/national -prayer-breakfast-what-does-its-history-reveal-180962017/.(accessed November 30, 2020).

Wortzel, Larry M. 2013. U.S. Congress. House of Representatives. Committee on Energy and Commerce Subcommittee on Oversight and Investigations. "Cyber Espionage and the Theft of U.S. Intellectual Property and Technology." July 9, 2013.

Wortzel, Larry M. 2020a. Larry M. Wortzel to House Minority Leader Kevin McCarthy. Williamsburg, VA, October 29, 2020.

Wortzel, Larry M. 2020b. Legislative Reports Tracker in Personal email to L. Murry. November 15, 2020.

Zarroli, Jim. 2018. "China Churns Out Half The World's Steel, And Other Steelmakers Feel Pinched." National Public Radio. March 8, 2018. https://www .npr.org/2018/03/08/591637097/china-churns-out-half-the-worlds-steel-and-other -steelmakers-feel-pinched (accessed November 30, 2020).

Zengerle, Patricia. 2020. "U.S. congressional study urges sanctions on China over 'crimes against humanity'." Reuters. January 8, 2020. U.S. congressional study urges sanctions on China over 'crimes against humanity' | Reuters (accessed December 2, 2020).

Chapter Ten

The Impact of US Domestic Politics on the Trade War

Chung-Chian Teng and Yeh-Chung Lu

INTRODUCTION

Donald Trump assumed office in January 2017, with a not so smooth relationship with China but less so with President Xi Jinping. After meeting with Xi in April and paying a visit to China in November, President Trump seemed to reconcile, for a bit, from harsh criticisms against China during the 2016 presidential campaign. Nevertheless, trade deficits remained a key issue between the United States and China, which led to Trump's decision of high tariffs on China's exports destined to the United States.[1]

With negotiations for months, the Chinese government decided to compromise on US demands, and both sides reached the phase one agreement in January 2020 amidst uncertainties aroused from the presidential election in the United States. Owing to the fierce competition between Trump and Biden in the presidential election and the spread of COVID-19, the trade war between China and the United States has been behind the scenes of the international stage.

However, the recent position of US Trade Representative (USTR) Robert Lighthizer toward China attracted attention. When there were voices about signing the trade agreement between the United States and Taiwan and economic sanctions against China over the issues of Uyghurs and Hong Kong, Lighthizer adopted an opposition stance, even having a sharp quarrel with Secretary of State Pompeo. The role that USTR Lighthizer played in the process, especially how a long-time hawkish trade negotiator demonstrated a moderate position toward China, is under scrutiny.

The purpose of this chapter is to address the above-mentioned issue. To investigate Lighthizer's position vis-à-vis other "hawks" at the start of the US–China trade talks that led up to the phase one agreement, this chapter will employ the bureaucratic politics explanation as an approach. In addition to the traditional focus on the "structure"—or Miles's Law, which posits that "where you stand depends on where you sit"—this chapter will focus on the "process" in which "pulling and hauling" among actors or agencies are under further scrutiny. In so doing, we believe the question of Lighthizer's stance will be explained to a satisfactory degree. This chapter will proceed as follows: the first section highlights the research questions, the second section discusses why and the extent to which the "bureaucratic politics" approach helps us understand the domestic political impact on the decision of the US trade war against China, and the third section investigates how Lighthizer chose to defend the result of the trade talks in the Trump administration. While acknowledging that the Biden administration might adopt a different approach toward China, the fourth section of this chapter plans to evaluate whether Lighthizer's stance is in conformity with US interests.

BUREAUCRATIC POLITICS AND PRESIDENT TRUMP

President Trump is famous for his unorthodox approach to foreign policy, in which adjectives such as *transactional, unstable,* and *volatile* seem to describe best the nature of the decisions he made (Friedman 2017). The issues range from international security such as the US presence in the Middle East, relations with traditional allies in Europe, to normative issues such as climate change or threatening to withdraw from international institutions that he deemed as not in line with US interests. For analytical convenience, some scholars then focus on the idiosyncratic variables, rather than the international systemic or domestic level factors to explain US foreign policy under Trump. The idiosyncratic variables for foreign policy analysis usually include the decision maker's background, personalities, cognitive processes, motives, worldviews, and beliefs (George 1969; Hermann 1980; Rosati 1995; Walker et al. 1999).

Nevertheless, another group of analysts contends that the international systemic imperatives remain important and continue to influence state behavior, if not foreign policy (Waltz 1979; Gilpin 1981). They usually attribute the reason why states fear one another and are obliged to relentless competition for security to the structural factors characterized by international anarchy and the distribution of material capabilities among states. Given the fact that the United States has retained the position as unipole in the international system, which left room for it to choose strategic restraint over expansion, it seems fair for President Trump to put America first while conducting foreign policy decisions (Posen 2014; Porter 2018; Brands 2018).

By taking the systemic imperatives and idiosyncratic factors as complementary, still others in academia tend to bridge those two groups to suggest that a structuralist explanation for war or peace under varying polarity still hinges on competing psychological models of how leaders interpret the environment and the process of how decisions are made (Tetlock and Goldgeier 2000; Hagan 2001).

In the case under scrutiny in this chapter, the authors argue that the international systemic factors are less compelling to the US decision maker in comparison to other cases (e.g., President Obama's rebalancing to Asia), and how President Trump perceives and interprets the international environment is more important to explaining his decisions. However, due to limited experience in politics, whether and how Trump is interacting with his advisors accountable for foreign policy becomes a legitimate question for students in this field. In other words, it is suitable to bring the discussions on bureaucratic politics back in.

The traditional approach of bureaucratic politics focuses on the "structure," wherein the decisions are made by stakeholders or by decision units whose mandates result from their positions in the government. Miles's Law ("where you stand depends on where you sit") appropriately captures the essence of this approach (Allison 1971; Halperin 1974). And yet, it is important for us to look beyond this traditional focus because it might have neglected the dynamics between the top leader and his advisors and failed to explain why some advisors are more influential in policy making than other cabinet members or their own predecessors and successors. To answer this question, Preston and t' Hart (1999) investigate President Johnson's decisions on the Vietnam War between 1965 and 1968, in which President Johnson, with his minimal involvement in policy making, finally failed to reconcile the differences and confrontations within the group of his advisors. Preston and t' Hart aptly point out that the "process" in which "pulling and hauling" among actors or agencies is more relevant than explained by earlier research, and argue that the interaction between leaders and their advisor groups "may create bureaupolitical dynamics that affect (in either a positive or negative manner) how these advisors function and how the policy process is likely to evolve over time" (1999, 91). By bridging the gap between the individual level that focuses only on leaders and bureaucratic politics that deems policy stance to positions those advisors are holding, Preston and t' Hart invite us to examine the leadership style and the nature of advisory group to assess the extent to which bureaucratic politics may affect policy outcomes. They categorize the leadership styles on two main criteria: the degree of the need for information and that of the need for control. And they link this leadership style to the nature of the network of advisory groups, whether it is an open or closed network among the members.

Administrative Leadership Style	*Group Consensus Leadership Style*
(Leader actively involved in policymaking with open advisory network)	(Leader minimally involved in policymaking with open advisory network)
Bureaucratic Compromise Formation, Deliberation, and Economy:	Bureaucratic Compromise Formation & Deliberation:
• Broad range of advisers participate in policy formulation & decision (not limited to inner circle).	• Broad range of advisers participate in policy formulation & decision (not limited to inner circle).
• Emphasis on broad information- search & detailed staff work.	• Emphasis on broad information- search & detailed staff work.
• Leader active in guiding policy process, but seeks consensus among advisers.	• Leader inactive in guiding policy process, seeks consensus among advisers as non-directive participant.
• Tolerance of conflict: Multiple policy options & views debated prior to policy decisions.	• Tolerance of conflict: Multiple policy options & views debated prior to policy decisions.
	Bureaupolitical Waste:
	• Lack of directive leadership leads to overanalysis of policy problems & decision-making inefficiency.

High Need for Control   **Low Need for Control**

Predominant Leadership Style	*Laissez-faire Leadership Style*
(Leader personally dominates policymaking with closed advisory network)	(Leader absent/minimally involved in policymaking with closed advisory network)
Bureaupolitical Oversimplication, Isolation, and Haste:	*Bureaupolitical Distortion, Paralysis, and Waste:*
• Lack of broad information/advice- gathering & leadership/inner circle gathering network or policy guidance dominance results in narrow, limited analysis of policy.	• Lack of broad information/advice- gathering network or policy guidance from leader leads to superficial, distorted policy analysis.
• Leader/inner circle dominance leads to policymaking isolated from broader political environment.	• Lack of directive leadership & delegation of policy formulation/decision to lower-level subordinates encourages intense, paralyzing bureau-conflict.
• Emphasis on leader/inner circle preferences leads to quick policy consensus.	• Lack of directive leadership leads to overanalysis of policy problems, indecisiveness, & decision-making inefficiency.
Bureaupolitical Distortion, Paralysis, & Waste:	
• Over time, restrained competition policy-making results in bureaupoliticking within broader political system.	

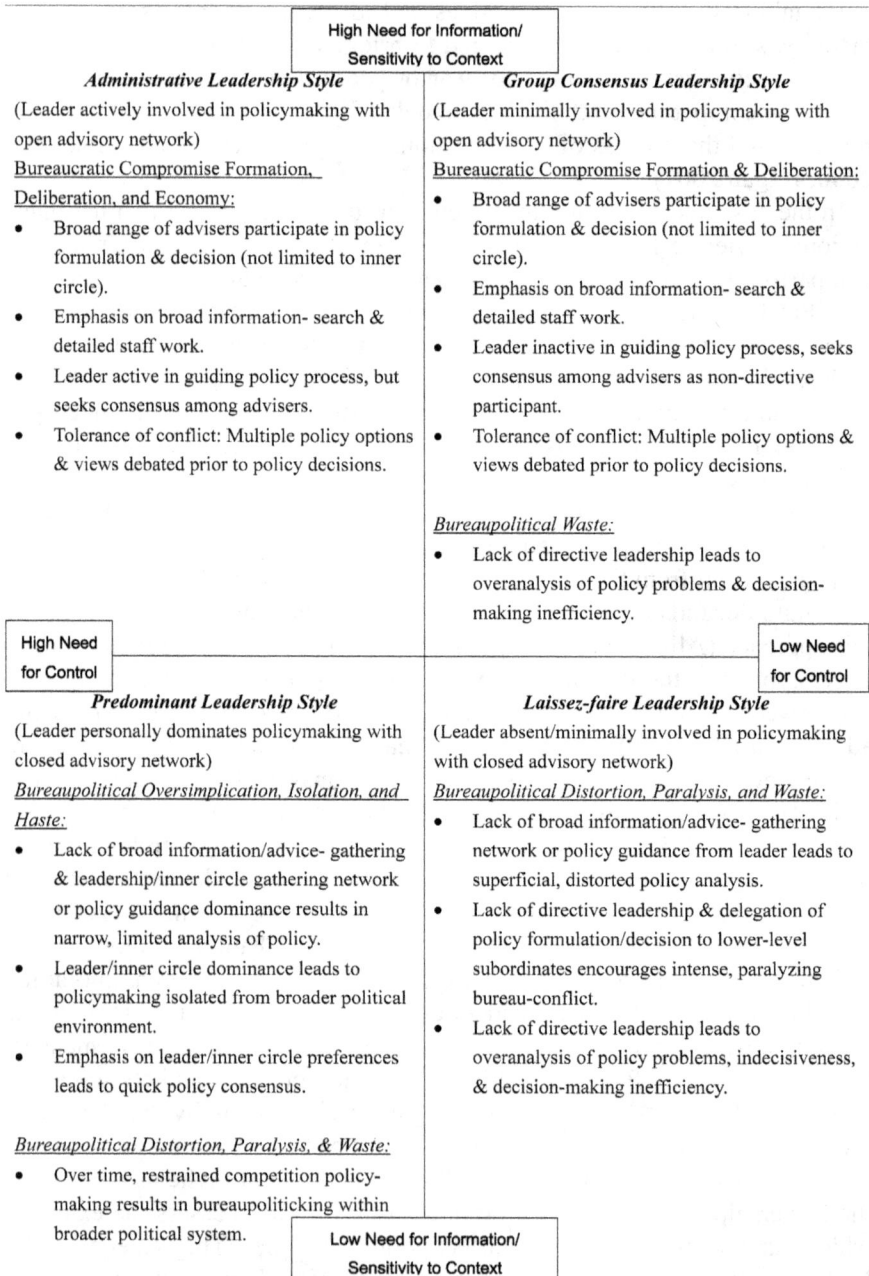

Figure 10.1. Leaders and Bureaupolitical Variation: The Normative Dimension

Source: Adapted from Thomas Preston and Paul 't Hart. 1999. "Understanding and Evaluating Bureacratic Politics: The Nexus between Political Leaders and Advisory Systems." *Political Psychology* 20, no. 1 (March): 67, Figure 4.

In this normative dimension shown as Figure 10.1, the upper-left quadrant indicates the quality decision-making process, where an active leader highly engages with a rather open network of advisors. In this ideal type labeled as "administrative leadership style," the leader guides the discussion with detailed information and staff work but seeks consensus among advisors. When multiple policy options emerge from participants, conflicts are common and most of the time compromises are reached after the debate. As for the "group consensus leadership style" in the upper-right corner, the leader's "first among the equals" minimal engagement in the process more often than not leads to over-analysis of policy problems and decision-making inefficiency, or "waste." The lower-left quadrant describes the "predominant leadership style," in which the leader highly engages, if not dominates, the policy making process with inner circle cabinet members and advisors, and pays limited attention to information gathering or the debate (if any) over policy alternatives. Oversimplication of problems and "groupthink" most times result in policy distortion and quick policy consensus, or "haste." The worst process of decision making is the "laissez-faire leadership style" as shown in the lower-right corner of the figure, in which the leader is absent from or minimally engaged with inner circle advisors with limited to no quality information. Absent-minded leaders and advisors may delegate policy formulation to lower level subordinates, leading to intense bureaucratic infighting among government agencies and "waste."

In the case of the US decision to wage a trade war with China, we find Preston and t' Hart's analysis of the nexus between political leaders and advisors useful as stated above, and the "predominant leadership style" best catches the nature of the structure and process in which the decision was made. Many observers and pundits see President Trump as a strong leader. Aubrey Immelman (2017) categorizes President Trump as an ambitious individual who is "bold, competitive, and self-assured," and "easily assumes leadership roles, expect[s] others to recognize their special qualities, and often act[s] as though entitled." Immelman further defines him as dominant in policy making style. Margret Hermann (1980) categorized political leaders as either aggressive or conciliatory to explain foreign policy behavior. Aggressive leaders are marked by certain attributes, such as a Machiavellian tendency to manipulate others in the policy-making process, a high personal need for power and authority, oftentimes leaning to suspicion and even paranoia, and a strong willingness to take action on behalf of their state. She describes conciliatory leaders as likely to display a desire for affiliation and friendship with other states with a high level of trust, and they display an ability to negotiate different policy options. Based on Hermann's account, aggressive leaders and advisors can be described as "hawks" in pursuing their own agenda without

compromising, as opposed to the "doves" who see conciliation and cooperation as mutually beneficial to their own state and others.

President Trump also demonstrates his contempt for experts, to whom an
inexperienced politician like him should listen, as well as for detailed information such as the Presidential Daily Brief (PDB), to which the president
should attend on a routine basis. He relies on close aides for advice but tends
to "echo the words of the last person with whom he spoke" (Johnson & Costa
2016), which makes it more important to know who is advising him on individual cases despite his decisions being even more unpredictable.

In comparison to his own seeing "two sets" of China, Trump held a negative view on China during the campaign since early 2016, and this is in part
due to the need for domestic political mobilization and rally and in part due
to his advisors (Trump 2015: 41–48; Woodward 2018: 6–7). Steve Bannon,
for instance, during Trump's campaign and early presidency, warned the
administration to "get China right" by equating China to Nazi Germany in
1929 to 1930 (Wolff 2018: 7–8). After stepping down as White House chief
strategist, Bannon visited Henry Kissinger to share the views that China
is the primary economic threat to America. Bannon said, "If we don't get
our situation sorted with China, we'll be destroyed economically," and the
United States would become a colony to China (Green 2017). Bannon further argued to have Kissinger's echo in seeing China as the primary threat
to the United States, though Kissinger suggested that partial cooperation
remains the optimal approach for the United States to deal with China
(Landler 2018).

President Trump also rallied against China after becoming the host of the
White House. He declared that he was the "chosen one" to take on China and
complained about his predecessors by stating: "This isn't my trade war, this is
a trade war that should have taken place a long time ago" (Breuninger 2019).
During Trump's campaign, Peter Navarro and Wilbur Ross (2016) wrote a
policy brief for the Trump economic plan. This economic plan claims that
Trump's "trade policy reforms" would generate about $1.7 trillion in gov-
ernment revenue over the next ten years (Ferguson 2018). Navarro was appointed as director of the National Trade Council at the White House, which
later on was transformed into the Office of Trade and Manufacturing Policy,
but was still charged by Navarro. With a background in economics, Navarro
was considered a loyal confidant to President Trump and a "hawk" specializing in economic affairs and strategy, who has been critical on China's
malpractices in trade and geopolitical spheres (Williamson 2017; Ball 2018;
Lowrey 2018).

Differences between the United States and China also seemed compelling
to President Trump and with China's growing economic power, it is impera-

tive for the United States to respond with the hawkish means. After meeting with Xi in April and paying a visit to China in November in the very first year in presidency, President Trump seemed to reconcile, for a bit, from harsh criticisms against China during the 2016 presidential campaign. At their first meeting in April 2017, Trump and China's president Xi Jinping agreed to a hundred-day plan for trade talks. Right before the deadline of the hundred-day plan, nevertheless, both sides reached interim arrangements but failed to reach agreement on how to reduce trade deficits in mid-July.

In August 2017, the Trump administration decided to launch a Section 301 investigation on China's trade practices under USTR, led by the trade hawk Robert Lighthizer. On December 18, 2017, President Donald Trump released his first National Security Strategy (NSS), stating that "an America that is safe, prosperous, and free at home is an America with the strength, confidence, and will to lead abroad" (White House 2017). Observers noted that the language in the national security strategy labeling China were never seen in such official documents issued by the executive branch before; even after Tiananmen, China was depicted as "the main opponent," "the main competitor," "predatory," etc. (Sutter 2019: 47). It is noteworthy that this version of the NSS did not explicitly illustrate a strategic direction for the United States to head in, but it did express dissatisfaction with the administration before President Trump for doing too little. The head of the National Security Council at that time, H. R. McMaster, a decorated lieutenant general, once expressed a pragmatic view by stating, "America first doesn't mean America alone" (McMaster and Cohn 2017).

Nevertheless, Chinese leader Xi Jinping's decision to lift the limit of terms for the position of presidency in China further alarmed Washington and the world. At the same time, President Trump replaced McMaster with the Bush-era defense hawk and former United Nations ambassador John Bolton in late March 2018. This replacement, along with other appointments in the cabinet, notably Mike Pompeo's assuming Rex Tillerson's position as the Secretary of State roughly the same time, made it more possible for the "hawks" to have a voice in the cabinet.

The US Congress has been critical of China, especially on trade and human rights issues since Tiananmen, but this is the first time that the executive branch and Congress share the same growing concern about China. For example, on a hearing in the Judiciary Committee that oversees the Department of Justice on December 12, 2018, Republican senator Chuck Grassley cautioned that China constitutes "a greater, more existential threat" to US society than Russia (Grassley 2018). Democratic senator Elizabeth Warren also agreed that the United States needs to take a hardline stance against China. During her visit to Beijing in 2018, she questioned the assumptions that economic engagement would lead to a more open China, and that US companies gave up their know-how in exchange for access to China's market (Martina 2018).

In June 2018, the White House issued a report claiming that China's spectacular economic growth was achieved "in significant part through aggressive acts, policies and practices that fall outside of global norms and rules" (White House 2018). Specifically, the report categorized Chinese economic aggressions into the following types:

1. Protect China's home market from imports and competition.
2. Expand China's share of global markets.
3. Secure and control core natural resources globally.
4. Dominate traditional manufacturing industries.
5. Acquire key technologies and intellectual property from other countries, including the United States.
6. Capture the emerging high-technology industries that will drive future economic growth and many advancements in the defense industry.

As a result, President Trump began to have a solid hawkish inner circle, as indicated in the policy direction revealed by Vice President Pence in his speech at the Hudson Institute in October 2018. In his 2019 State of the Union speech, President Trump called for China to make a "real, structural change to end unfair trade practices, reduce our chronic trade deficit, and protect American jobs" while making a trade deal (White House 2019). Nevertheless, President Trump blamed his predecessors for "allowing this travesty to happen" (Vitali 2017). To Trump, the PRC's malpractices constituted "economic aggression" (Sevastopulo & Donnan 2017).

If we follow the idiosyncratic factors and the composition of the Trump administration, it is safe to argue that President Trump himself is a predominant leader, along with inner circle advisors who basically shared similar views as treating China as a revisionist and threat to the United States. On the US side, President Trump and Vice President Pence, the head of the Office of Trade and Manufacturing Policy Navarro, Secretary of State Pompeo, Secretary of Commerce Ross, and USTR Lighthizer reached the consensus sooner than later that the United States needed to hold China responsible for inappropriate trading practices. As the timeline of the trade war shows, the failure to reach a hundred-day plan soon escalated to retaliation on tariffs. Would this hawkish view prevent the Trump administration from reaching an agreement with China? It seemed so from the above discussion, but the role of the USTR deserves more discussion because that led to the phase one agreement between the two countries in early 2020.

THE EVALUATION OF THE US–CHINA TRADE AGREEMENT

We employ Preston and t' Hart's predominant leadership style to explain the decision of the trade war against China, in which the president has a high need for control and the inner circle, composed of like-minded close aides, becomes influential in making decisions. For analytical purposes, we begin with the discussion on key persons who hold public positions in terms of structure within the Trump administration, with a special focus on the USTR as the chief negotiator in the trade talks with China.

Robert Lighthizer: A Hawkish Negotiator or a Pragmatist

It is evident that there exist two different views about trade negotiation with China in the Trump administration: hawks vs. doves (Bryan 2018; Bolton 2020). US Treasury Secretary Steven Mnuchin is classified as dovish and adopts a mild strategy of free trade, focusing on increasing China's purchase of American products and services as well as lowering China's import barriers through negotiations. This pro-trade, globalist camp also includes Cohn and Kudlow, two gentlemen who consecutively served as the chairman of the National Economic Council (Lee 2018). US Trade Representative Robert Lighthizer, on the contrary, is described as hawkish and strongly advocates taking tougher measures, focusing on China's structural economic reforms, such as cutting governmental subsidies to state enterprises through imposing extra tariffs (Davis 2018). As stated earlier, Navarro and Ross are also categorized in this hawkish camp (Bolton 2020: 290).

The role of Lighthizer is worth noting for this chapter due to the following reasons: First, the office of USTR is located right across the street to the White House and structurally has been involved in decision making and trade policy implementation since its establishment in 1962. When it comes to trade negotiations and participation in global trade policy organizations, it is definitely on USTR's turf. Second, Lighthizer is an experienced trade negotiator and has much experience in pulling and hauling with government agencies and Capitol Hill. Lighthizer was recruited into Congress in 1978 serving Bob Dole and later the Senate Finance Committee. In 1983, he was confirmed as the Deputy US Trade Representative in the Reagan administration. During the tenure as Deputy US Trade Representative, Lighthizer participated in trade negotiation with Japan that reached a "managed trade"—Japan agreed to voluntarily limit its exports of steel, cars, and other goods (Lee 2018). In May 2017, Lighthizer was confirmed to serve as the USTR and began to renegotiate KORUS and NAFTA with a hardened position to US trading partners. In November 2017, Lighthizer formally opposed China's market economy status at WTO. Lighthizer is one of the key persons in the process of decision making in the trade war.

Third, Lighthizer shares Trump's worldview of "America First" and knows how to shun the limelight in front of Trump, which helps Lighthizer win trust from Trump (Davis 2018). Lighthizer also allied with Navarro on advising the president to impose steel tariffs, which earned Trump's attention (Woodward 2018: 142–143). On Trump's second visit to Japan in May 2017, he was asking why Lighthizer was not with him when Japan's prime minister, Shinzo Abe, spoke about China (Bolton 2020: 345). In addition to his closeness to Trump, Lighthizer is also more pragmatic and skillful in comparison to his colleagues. With a background as an international trade litigator, Lighthizer is taking a rather strategic view on trade. He sees it not as only an economic or pure import-export, trade deficit issue, but in the long haul a life-or-death question for US industries. The pro-trade globalist camp aims to use tariffs and China's purchase of more US products in reducing the deficits for the short run; Lighthizer and Navarro aim to push China for more fundamental changes economically. Nevertheless, unlike Navarro's image as a nationalistic trade warrior with limited experience in public office, Lighthizer is a seasoned practitioner and actually runs a government agency with more than two hundred staff (Davis 2018).

In August 2017, Lighthizer led a heated discussion on how to deal with China on tariffs in the White House, in which he tried to bridge different factions within the Trump administration, and in the meantime to ward off too-soft propositions proposed by Terry Branstad, then US ambassador to China. Ross was expected to lead China economic policy in the administration once Trump assumed the office, but a month before the meeting, Trump withdrew his backing on Ross for the secretary's being too soft on China (Davis 2018; Landler & Swanson 2018). After the August meeting, nevertheless, Ross continued his role in advising Lighthizer on which imports from China to target for tariffs.

The August meeting at the White House set a hard line on China, which resulted in the administration's frosty welcome to the Chinese counterpart Liu He's visit in February 2018. In early May 2018, Trump sent a delegation led by Mnuchin to Beijing, but on this trip Mnuchin agreed to a private meeting with Liu without informing other members on the US side, which led to a public verbal conflict between Mnuchin and Navarro (Landler & Swanson 2018).

With his expertise as a lawyer and experience in trade negotiation, Lighthizer is a pragmatist and a political realist who, in the meantime, adheres to carry out the instructions from the superior and to protect national interests. Owing to Trump's dissatisfaction with China's response on May 22, 2018, Robert Lighthizer replaced Steven Mnuchin as the chief negotiator (Hoyama & Harada 2018; Bradsher 2018a). We can read how important the role of Lighthizer was in Trump's formulation of China economic policy.

A Juxtaposition between US Proposal and the US–China Trade Agreement: An Assessment

To understand Lighthizer's satisfaction with the economic and trade agreement with China, it is useful to look at two aspects: whether he accepted the content of the agreement and whether he was satisfied with China's implementation. For the first aspect, we can juxtapose and examine the key points of the US proposal during the trade negotiation and the main regulations in the drafted 2018 Economic and Trade Agreement of the United States and China to have a better understanding about the relative gains of both China and the United States (see table 10.1).

Table 10.1. A Juxtaposition between U.S. Proposal and the 2018 U.S.-China Trade Agreement

U.S. Proposal for Trade Deal with China	The Related Regulations in the 2018 U.S.-China Trade Agreement
Cut China's trade surplus by $100 billion in the 12 months, and by another $100 billion in the following 12 months	Chapter 6 Expanding Trade
Cut China's level of tariffs, which currently average 10 percent, to the same level as in the United States, where they average 3.5 percent for all "noncritical sectors"	NA
Strengthen intellectual property protections	Chapter 1 Intellectual Property; Chapter 2 Technology Transfer
Take "immediate, verifiable steps" to halt cyberespionage into commercial networks in the United States	Chapter 1 Intellectual Property
Halt all subsidies to advanced manufacturing industries in its so-called Made In China 2025 program. The program covers 10 sectors, including aircraft manufacturing, electric cars, robotics, computer microchips and artificial intelligence	NA
Accept that the United States may restrict imports from the industries under Made in China 2025	NA
Accept United States restrictions on Chinese investments in sensitive technologies without retaliating	NA
Open up its services and agricultural sectors to full American competition	Chapter 3 Trade in Food and Agricultural Products; Chapter 4 Financial Services

Sources: The author compiled from the text of the Economic and Trade Agreement between the Government of the United States of America and the Government of the People's Republic of China two articles and Keith Bradsher, "No Trade Deal With China As Talks End," *New York Times*, May 5, 2018.

The question central to the proposal made by the US delegation in May 2018 was on the reduction of China's trade surplus with the United States by $200 billion USD by means of increasing the purchase of American products. According a report by the *New York Times*, the US proposal consists of eight critical elements: to cut China's trade surplus by purchasing $200 billion worth of American products in two years; to reduce China's current level of tariffs; to strengthen intellectual property protection; to stop cyber espionage into US commercial networks; to stop all subsidies to China's advanced manufacturing industries; to accept possible restriction on China's imports from the industries under Made in China 2025; to allow restrictions on Chinese investments in sensitive technologies; and to open up its services and agricultural sectors (Bradsher 2018b).

Looking at the draft of the Economic and Trade Agreement between the Government of the United States of America and the Government of the People's Republic of China (hereafter the US–China Trade Agreement), there are four main parts under regulation (see table 10.1), for instance: to cut China's trade surplus by purchasing $200 billion worth of American products in two years; to strengthen intellectual property protection; to stop cyber espionage into US commercial networks; and to open up its services and agricultural sectors. The most noticeable regulation involves eleven sections dealing with intellectual property protection: Section A: General Obligations; Section B: Trade Secrets and Confidential Business Information; Section C: Pharmaceutical-Related Intellectual Property; Section D: Patents; Section E: Piracy and Counterfeiting on E-Commerce Platforms; Section F: Geographical Indications; Section G: Manufacture and Export of Pirated and Counterfeit Goods; Section H: Bad-Faith Trademarks; Section I: Judicial Enforcement and Procedure in Intellectual Property Cases; Section J: Bilateral Cooperation on Intellectual Property Protection; Section K: Implementation. The wide coverage of intellectual property protection means the other four elements (to reduce China's current level of tariffs; to stop all subsidies to China's advanced manufacturing industries; to accept possible restriction on China's imports from the industries under Made in China 2025; to allow restrictions on Chinese investments in sensitive technologies), in reality, are touched upon partially.

In the same round of negotiation of May 4, 2018, China also extended a counterproposal to include eight requests (see table 10.2): US government ends its investigation into the allegations that China forces US companies to transfer technology to Chinese partners; US government ceases its threats to impose tariffs on as much as $150 billion worth of Chinese goods; US government provides better treatment for Chinese technology companies; US government adjusts its sales ban on ZTE Corp., a large Chinese maker of telecom gears; US government allows US companies and government agen-

Table 10.2.   China's Counter Proposal of Trade Negotiation on May 4, 2018

U.S. government ends its investigation into the allegations that China forces U.S. companies to transfer technology to Chinese partners

U.S. government ceases its threats to impose tariffs on as much as $150 billion worth of Chinese goods

U.S. government provides better treatment for Chinese technology companies

U.S. government adjusts its sales ban on ZTE Corp., a large Chinese maker of telecom gears

U.S. government allows U.S. companies and government agencies to buy technology equipment from Chinese firms, which would include Huawei Technologies Co.

U.S. government allows Chinese companies to buy more American high-tech products including semiconductors

Chinese government would offer some mild concessions, for instance, China would agree to meaningfully cut levies on imported autos nationwide

Chinese government would agree to talk to the U.S. about easing the quota on imported films shown in China

Sources: The author compiled from Lingling Wei, "U.S. and China Make Scant Progress in Trade Talks," *Wall Street Journal*, May 4, 2018. https://www.wsj.com/articles/u-s-wants-200-billion-cut-in-china-trade-imbalance-by-end-of-2020-1525419253.

cies to buy technology equipment from Chinese firms, which would include Huawei Technologies Co.; US government allows Chinese companies to buy more American high-tech products including semiconductors; Chinese government would offer some mild concessions, for instance, China would agree to meaningfully cut levies on imported autos nationwide; and Chinese government would agree to talk to the United States about easing the quota on imported films shown in China. However, the drafted regulations of the US–China Trade Agreement did not have anything with the first six items. About the seventh item, China did commit to encourage and ease the levies on imported autos. In other words, the United States is the winner of the US–China Trade Agreement.

Having evaluating the US proposal, China's counterproposal, and the text during the negotiations in 2018, Lighthizer certainly felt comfortable about the possible truce of trade war and expected that China might take a long time to implement its commitments. Nevertheless, the United States launched more rounds of the tariff war against China since June 2018, and many of them were suggested by the USTR aiming at pressuring China for concession.

The 2020 US Presidential Election and Beyond: Trade War Again?

The United States and China reached a phase one trade agreement in December 2019, and Trump and Liu He jointly signed the agreement in the White House on January 15, 2020. The 2018 proposals on the trade agreement indeed served as a draft for this phase one agreement.

During the campaign leading up to the US presidential election, we did not see any ultra-active role of Lighthizer on China. While Secretary of State Pompeo attacked China from different fronts and added more sanctions against China, Lighthizer kept silent for a long time about any events related to China, including issues related to Hong Kong, Taiwan, and Xinjiang (Swanson 2020). It is reasonable that Lighthizer was observing the implementation of the 2018 trade agreement on the Chinese side.

Talking about China's implementation, the most concrete issue at this stage is the committed purchase of American products. In this regard, the US Peterson Institute for International Economics has been tracking it and its report makes a comparison between the committed target and actual purchase. In terms of total products, up to October 2020 (see table 10.3), the worth of

Table 10.3. The Implementation of Sino-U.S. Trade Agreement (Phase One): Committed Purchase Unit: 100 Million U.S. Dollar

		China's Imports from the U.S. a	U.S. Exports to China b
Total	Committed Target of Purchase (whole year of 2020)	1,731	1,590
	Committed Target of Purchase (up to October 2020)	1,373	1,254
	Actual Amount of Purchase (up to October 2020)	755	710
Product Category			
Agricultural Products	Committed Target of Purchase (whole year of 2020)	366	334
	Committed Target of Purchase (up to October 2020)	271	246
	Actual Amount of Purchase (up to October 2020)	156	175
Manufactured Products	Committed Target of Purchase (whole year of 2020)	1,112	994
	Committed Target of Purchase (up to October 2020)	907	802
	Actual Amount of Purchase (up to October 2020)	537	463
Energy Products	Committed Target of Purchase (whole year of 2020)	253	261
	Committed Target of Purchase (up to October 2020)	180	203
	Actual Amount of Purchase (up to October 2020)	62	72

Note: a. Data from Chinese customs.
   b. Data from U.S. Census Bureau
Source: Chad P. Bown, "U.S.-China phase one tracker: China's purchases of U.S. goods," Peterson Institute for International Economics, December 4, 2020. <https://www.piie.com/research/piie-charts/us-china-phase-one-tracker-chinas-urchases-us-goods>.

China's imports from the United States reached $75.5 billion USD, about 55 percent of the committed target. In terms of agricultural products, the actual purchase is about 58 percent of the committed target; in terms of manufactured products, it is about 59 percent; in terms of energy products, it is about 34 percent.

With more than a 50 percent average implementation rate, Lighthizer, of course, was satisfied with it, at least at the early stage. He did attribute the impact of COVID-19 pandemic to the low implementation rate. No less important, he would like to see the real intention of the Chinese side about the implementation of other elements. One can take China's open markets for the auto and financial industries as examples.

ASSESSMENT AND CONCLUDING REMARKS

The predominant leadership style in policy making developed by Preston and 't Hart is a valuable reference for this chapter, in which we explore how President Trump as a predominant leader interacted with his close network of advisors in the decision to wage the trade war with China. What role USTR Lighthizer played in the process, especially how a long-time hawkish trade negotiator demonstrated a moderate position toward China, is under scrutiny. Our finding suggests that Lighthizer was satisfied with the stipulation and implementation of the phase one agreement between China and the United States, at least by the end of 2020, as well as with signals of satisfaction from the domestic forces, especially related business circles in agriculture, steel, and manufacturing. The shift of Lighthizer's stance in relation to other hawks in the Trump administration demonstrates that the process of policy making is not a one-way street, and the preferences of participants are not fixed. Instead, it is a necessity for participants (especially cabinet members in democracies) to be responsive to the needs of domestic constituencies.

The success of China's open-up economic policy lies in its participation in the global market system, especially its entrance into the World Trade Organization. As the beneficiary of the market system, the best path for its climbing to the economic hegemony is adherence to the liberal market system. At the beginning of the so-called trade war, China already set the ultimate target as opening up the market continuously. When Liu He, the chief economic advisor to President Xi and vice premier, attended the Davos World Economic Forum in January 2018, he publicly expressed China's promotion of economic globalization actively and pledged to liberalizing banking, security, and insurance industries further (Xinhua 2018).

In his speech at the 2018 Boao Forum for Asia, President Xi Jinping reiterated the direction of China's economic open-up policy by identifying the liberalization and deregulation of issue areas as follows: imported vehicles; foreign ownership of automotive ventures; transportation; finance; intellectual property rights; and dispute settlement (Ren 2018).

As part of financial market deregulation and escalating tension with the United States, China in 2020 will follow the international rules to further integrate its capital markets, and continue interest rate and exchange rate reforms in a prudent way (Chow & Wang 2020). Additionally, there have been three major world financial corporations—namely J. P. Morgan of the United States, Japan's Nomura Holdings, and the Swiss UBS—obtaining formal approval from Chinses authority to establish majority-owned securities ventures in China (Sin, John, & Shen 2019).

Regarding the implementation of the agreement, both China and the United States have shown good will with each other. On the Chinese side, to express the smooth implementation of the 2020 US–China Trade Agreement, Zhao Lijian, spokesman of foreign ministry, pinpointed two critical answers in the news conference of May of 2020: first, the agreement serves the interests of China, the United States, and the world; second, the two sides should work together to implement the agreement following the principle of equality and mutual respect (heads of the Chinese and US trade consultation teams had a phone conversation on May 8, agreeing to work towards creating enabling atmosphere and conditions for the implementation of the agreement and strive for more progress) (Foreign Ministry of People's of Republic of China 2020).

On the American side, the Office of the US Trade Representative released a statement indicating that "both sides see progress and are committed to taking the steps necessary to ensure the success of the agreement." Furthermore, The USTR's brief statement also expressed that the parties discussed the following through phone conversation: China's purchase commitments related to the deal, steps the Chinese government is taking to protect American intellectual property in China, and how to create a freer business environment for American multinationals in China (McGregor 2020). Our research confirms Preston and t' Hart's proposition that a predominant leadership style usually results in "haste" in making decisions, but Lighthizer's role as an experienced negotiator in the decision-making process on the US side and with suitable means helped both the United States and China reach a temporary arrangement.

NOTES

1. The authors are grateful to the financial support of Taiwan's Ministry of Science and Technology (MOST107-2410-H004-142) on this project.

REFERENCES

Allison, G. T. 1971. *Essence of Decision*. Boston: Little and Brown.

Ball, M. 2018. "Peter Navarro Used to be a Democrat. Today He's the Architect of President Trump's Trade War." *Time* 192(issue 9/10): 52–57.

Bradsher, Keith. 2018a. "With Tariffs Postponed, China Takes Victory Lap." *New York Times.* May 22, 2018. B1.

Bradsher, Keith. 2018b. "No Trade Deal With China As Talks End." *New York Times.* May 5, 2018. B1.

Breuninger, K. 2019. "'I Am the Chosen One,' Trump Proclaims as He Defends Trade War with China." CNBC. August 21, 2019. https://www.cnbc.com/2019/08/21/i-am-the-chosen-one-trump-proclaims-as-he-defends-china-trade-war.html.

Bolton, John. 2020. *The Room Where It Happened: A White House Memoir*. New York: Simon & Schuster.

Brands, Hal. 2018. *American Grand Strategy in the Age of Trump.* Washington, DC: Brookings Institution Press.

Bryan, Bob. 2017. "Infighting among Trump's Top Advisers Led to A Negotiating Disaster on the China Trade Deal." *Business Insider.* May 22, 2018. https://www.businessinsider.com/trump-china-us-trade-deal-mnuchin-navarro-2018-5.

Chow, Emily, and Wang, Jing. 2020. "China Needs to Step up Global Financial Integration - FX Regulator." Nasdaq. September 26, 2020. https://www.nasdaq.com/articles/china-needs-to-step-up-global-financial-integration-fx-regulator-2020-09-26.

Davis, Bob. 2018. "The Man behind Trump's China Fight." *Wall Street Journal.* April 7, 2018. A1.

Ferguson, A. 2018. "The Guns of Navarro." *Commentary.* https://www.commentarymagazine.com/articles/andrew-ferguson/the-guns-of-navarro/.

Foreign Ministry of People's of Republic of China. 2020. "Foreign Ministry Spokesperson Zhao Lijian's Regular Press Conference on May 12, 2020." May 12, 2020. https://www.fmprc.gov.cn/mfa_eng/xwfw_665399/s2510_665401/t1778378.shtml.

Friedman, Uri. 2017. "What's Dangerous about Donald Trump's Foreign Policy?" *The Atlantic.* November 26, 2017. https://www.theatlantic.com/international/archive/2017/11/trump-dangerous-foreign-policy/546230/.

George, Alexander L. 1969. "The 'Operational Code': A Neglected Approach to the Study of Political Leaders and Decision-Making." *International Studies Quarterly* 13, no. 2 (June): 190–222.

Gilpin, Robert. *War and Change in World Politics.* Cambridge: Cambridge University Press.

Grassley, Chuck. 2018. "Prepared Statement by Senator Chuck Grassley of Iowa, Chairman, Senate Judiciary Committee." Hearing on China's Non-Traditional Espionage against the United States: The Threat and Potential Policy Responses. December 12, 2018. https://www.grassley.senate.gov/news/news-releases/grassley-chinese-espionage-it-s-called-cheating-and-it-s-only-getting-worse.

Green, Joshua. 2017. "Enter the Bannon." *Bloomberg Businessweek.* October 2, 2017. 40–42.

Hagan, Joe D. 2001. "Does Decision Making Matter?" *International Studies Review* 3(2 Summer): 5–46.

Halperin, M. 1974. *Bureaucratic Politics and Foreign Policy.* Washington: Brookings Institution.

Hermann, M. G. 1980. "Explaining Foreign Policy Behavior Using the Personal Characteristics of Political Leaders." *International Studies Quarterly* 24, no. 1 (March): 7–46.

Hoyama, Taisei, and Harada, Issaku. 2018. "China Hawk Lighthizer Named US Point Man for New Trade Talks." *Nikkei Asia.* December 4, 2018. https://asia.nikkei .com/Economy/Trade-war/China-hawk-Lighthizer-named-US-point-man-for-new -trade-talks.

Immelman, A. 2017. *The Leadership Style of U.S. President Donald J. Trump* (Working Paper No. 1.1). Collegeville and St. Joseph, MN: St. John's University and the College of St. Benedict, Unit for the Study of Personality in Politics. http:// digitalcommons.csbsju.edu/psychology_pubs/107/.

Johnson, Jenna, and Costa, Robert. 2016. "Trump and advisers remain split on how far to move toward the middle." *Washington Post.* August 27, 2016. https:// www.washingtonpost.com/politics/trump-and-advisers-remain-split-on-how-far -to-move-toward-the-middle/2016/08/26/e94f5eb4-6ba1-11e6-ba32-5a4bf5aad 4fa_story.html.

Kissinger, Henry A. 2014. *World Order.* New York: Penguin Press.

Landler, Mark. 2018. "The U.S. Adopts a Hard Line against China, and an Era of Engagement Recedes into the Past." *New York Times.* November 25, 2018. https:// www.nytimes.com/interactive/2018/11/25/world/asia/china-us-confrontation.html.

Landler, Mark and Swanson, Ana. 2018. "Infighting Stalls Ambitious Drive For a China Pact." *New York Times.* May 22, 2018. A1.

Lee, Don. 2018. "Trade Czar Shows Teeth." *Los Angeles Times.* November 4, 2018. A1.

Lowrey, Annie. 2018. "Trump's Trade Warrior." *The Atlantic.* December 2018. 22–24.

Martina, Michael. 2018. "Senator Warren, in Beijing, Says U.S. is Waking Up to Chinese Abuses." *Reuters.* April 1, 2018. https://uk.reuters.com/article/uk-usa -china-warren/senator-warren-in-beijing-says-u-s-is-waking-up-to-chinese-abuses -idUKKCN1H80X0.

McGregor, Grady. 2020. "The U.S.-China Trade Deal is Moving Ahead—in Spite of Everything." *Fortune.* August 25, 2020. https://fortune.com/2020/08/25/phase -1-us-china-trade-deal-progress-news-update/.

McMaster, H. R., and Cohn, G. 2017. "America First Doesn't Mean America Alone." *Wall Street Journal.* May 30, 2017. https://www.wsj.com/articles/america-first -doesnt-mean-america-alone-1496187426.

Porter, Patrick. 2018. "Why America's Grand Strategy Has Not Changed: Power, Habit, and the U.S. Foreign Policy Establishment," *International Security* 42, no. 4 (Spring): 9–46.

Posen, Barry R. 2014. *Restraint: A New Foundation for U.S. Grand Strategy*. Ithaca, NY: Cornell University Press.

Preston, T., and 't Hart, Paul. 1999. "Understanding and Evaluating Bureaucratic Politics: The Nexus between Political Leaders and Advisory Systems." *Political Psychology* 20, no. 1 (March): 49–98.

Ren, Zhong-Yuan. 2018. "The Major Points of President Xi Jinping's Speech at Boao Forum for Asia." *Economic Daily* (in Chinese). April 10, 2018. https://money.udn .com/money/story/5641/3077804.

Rosati, J. A. 1995. "A Cognitive Approach to the Study of Foreign Policy" in *Foreign Policy Analysis: Continuity and Change in Its Second Generation*, edited by L. Neack, J.A.K. Hay and P.J. Haney, 49–70. Englewood Cliffs: Prentice Hall.

Sevastopulo, Demetri, and Donnan, Shawn. 2017. "Trump to Accuse China of 'Economic Aggression'." *Financial Times*. December 16, 2017. https://www.ft.com/content/1801d4f4-e201-11e7-8f9f-de1c2175f5ce.

Sin, Noah, John, Alun, and Shen, Samuel. 2019. "JPMorgan Receives Final Approval for Majority-Owned Securities Venture in China." *The Reuters*. December 18, 2019. https://www.reuters.com/article/us-china-jpmorgan-jv-idUSKBN1YM14J.

Sutter, R. 2019. "The Trump Administration and China Policy." *Washington Journal of Modern China*. Spring 2019. Pp. 46–53.

Swanson, Ana. 2020. "China Critic Has Become Its Defender." *New York Times*. October 6, 2020. B1.

Tetlock, P. E., and Goldgeier, J. M. 2000. "Human Nature and World Politics: Cognition, Identity, and Influence." *International Journal of Psychology*, 35: 87–96.

The White House of the United States. 2017. *National Security Strategy of the United States of America*, December 2017. https://www.whitehouse.gov/wp-content/up loads/2017/12/NSS-Final-12-18-2017-0905.pdf.

The White House of the United States. 2018. *How China's Economic Aggression Threatens the Technologies and Intellectual Property of the United States and the World*. June 2018. https://www.whitehouse.gov/wp-content/uploads/2018/06/FINAL-China-Technology-Report-6.18.18-PDF.pdf.

The White house of the United States. 2019. *Remarks by President Trump in the State of the Union Address.* February 5, 2019. https://www.whitehouse.gov/briefings -statements/remarks-president-trump-state-union-address-2/.

Trump, Donald J. 2015. *Great Again: How to Fix Our Crippled America*. New Yok: Simon & Schuster.

Vitali, Ali. 2017. "Trump, Once Critical from Afar, Gives China a Pass in Trade War." *NBC News*, November 9, 2017. https://www.nbcnews.com/news/world/trump -says-he-doesn-t-blame-china-taking-advantage-u-n819221.

Walker, S., Schafer, M., and Young, M. 1999. "Presidential Operational Codes and Foreign Policy Conflicts in the Post-Cold War World." *The Journal of Conflict Resolution* 43, no. 5 (October): 610–625.

Waltz, Kenneth N. 1979. *Theory of International Politics.* Reading, Mass: Addison-Wesley Pub. Co.

Williamson, Kevin. 2017. "Professor Propaganda: Peter Navarro is positioned to give the president a lot of bad advice." *National Review*, April 3, 2017. https://www.na tionalreview.com/magazine/2017/04/03/peter-navarro-donald-trump-propaganda/.

Wolff, Michael. 2018. *Fire and Fury: Inside the Trump White House*. New York: Henry Holt and Company.
Woodward, Bob. 2018. *Fear: Trump in the White House*. New York: Simon & Schuster.
Xinhua. 2018. "A Shared Future, a Shared View in Davos." *Global Times*. January 26, 2018. http://www.globaltimes.cn/content/1086685.shtml.

Chapter Eleven

US–China Policy under Trump

The Politics of
International Economic Relations

Gordon C. K. Cheung

Acknowledgements

I would like to thank Professor Shiping Hua for inviting me to contribute a chapter to this topical book. I was on research leave during the Easter term 2019–2020 when some of the research was done for this chapter. I therefore would like to thank the School of Government & International Affairs at Durham University for granting the research leave. I would also like to thank the Universities Service Center for China Studies at The Chinese University of Hong Kong for their archival and library support for some of the research for this chapter.

INTRODUCTION

The US–China policy under Donald Trump is dramatic. Their relations were sent to the nadir on July 24, 2020, when the Chinese consulate in Houston was forced to close. Three days later, the Chinese government responded by closing the US consulate in Chengdu as a retaliation. Yet, a year ago on July 3, 2019, the *Washington Post* published an open letter to Donald Trump entitled "China is Not an Enemy," which was written by one hundred US academics, foreign policy analysts, and military and business leaders. They raised the concern of the US policy toward China and suspected it could escalate to further foreign policy derailment between the United States and China. For example, they said that "we do not believe Beijing is an economic enemy or an existential national security threat that must be confronted in every sphere; nor is China a monolith, or the views of its leaders set in stone."[1]

Such zigzagging US–China relations meandered across US–China policy as soon as Trump was sworn in as president of the United States.

During the 2016 presidential campaign, Donald Trump made a number of promises. He used "America First" as a strategy to make America great again, resulting in many hawkish policies toward China. He complained that the jobs of the American people were stolen by China. US–China policy under Trump was very clear in bringing back the politics of international economic relations to the foreign policy agenda, especially everyday encounters such as the trade war, intellectual property rights (IPR), and technological competition. International political economy (IPE) vividly captures the very nature behind the essence of the international relations between the United States and China.

Increasingly, questions have been asked about the US declining hegemonic role and its commanding power in world politics, especially in recognizing the rise of China. Yet, hegemonic succession and war do not seem to be a good explanation between the United States and China. If physical confrontation is not on the agenda and hierarchy is less important in international relations, interdependence may help redefine the current international relations (Keohane & Nye 1989). Throughout more than forty years of breakneck growth and development, China earned the status of the "factory of the world." China's economic successes, increasingly, have become the bones of contention with the United States, especially during Donald Trump's administration. To understand US–China policy under Trump, framing Chinese development along the IPE perspective may help shed some light on China's economic transformation in a changing world which may witness the United States negotiating rather than purely dominating in the world economy.

This chapter has four sections. The first section provides a theoretical exploration by questioning the US hegemonic role in explaining the current relations between the United States and China. We will also explore the connection between globalization and the various areas of IPE in determining their relations. The second section explores the changes and dynamics of the trade war between the United States and China. Empirically speaking, the US–China trade war under Trump's first administration provides strong evidence to explore the potential theoretical transformation from high politics to low politics. The politics behind the trade suggested that China may be more resilient than the United States had expected. The third section examines the political economy on IPR disputes between the United States and China. China has violated IPR for a long time, and huge counterfeiting is not uncommon. Yet, China has become more innovative and somehow is increasingly taking IPR seriously. The last section examines the technological competition between the United States and China. China is moving toward qualitative growth partly due to the slowing down of growth rate (the new normal) and partly due to regional expectation, especially in East Asia. In other words, Chinese high-tech development and some key industries are deemed to be causing troubles in US–China relations.

HEGEMONIC DECLINE AND THE SIGNIFICANCE OF THE INTERNATIONAL POLITICAL ECONOMY

After Trump became the US president, the slogan "Make America Great Again" did not fade away and he kept reminding the American people of it. Let's not take the slogan as political rhetoric alone, but instead try to understand the meaning from academic and theoretical senses. There are, at least, two major meanings. Firstly, the slogan signifies that the United States has declined and Trump wants it to make a comeback. Secondly, he wants the United States to maintain leadership and will not allow any challenger or even successor.

But the US global leadership has always been challenged. In the early 1970s, the United States already lost the international financial leadership by announcing the collapse of the Bretton Woods System in 1971. After the Asian financial crisis in 1997, the United States was heavily criticized by Joseph Stiglitz, Nobel laureate of economic sciences in 2001, who suggested it would be better to deal with its own financial problems rather than pointing fingers at other emerging economies in East Asia (Stiglitz 2002). Nevertheless, the 2008–2009 global financial crisis, which took place right at the financial center in the United States, suggested that the problem of greed on Wall Street, the burst of the financial bubble, and the United States increasingly relying on credit from emerging economies would making countries rethink the US economic model more seriously and consider whether other alternative successful economic models can be explored from the rest of the world (Bisley 2010: 71).

Using the Great Depression in the late 1920s as a case, Charles Kindleberger (1973) contended that the United State could have involved more and exercised the hegemonic stability to safeguard an open and liberal world economy. It helped set out the theoretical foundation and the philosophical support of the US overarching role. Joseph Nye in his book *The Paradox of American Power: Why the World's Only Superpower Can't Go It Alone* pointed out that the US economic scale, technological leadership, and military force collectively helped the United States facilitate the hegemonic stability for the world economy (Nye 2003: 13). But, along three levels of power structure—military, economic, and transnational—the United States can only dominate on military power. It has to negotiate with China to share the economic power context. In terms of transnational power, the United States cannot compete with the nonstate actors, bankers, and those electronic herds (Nye 2003: 39). The global system alongside with the US hegemonic role is working only because states are just "too dependent on America" (Norrlof 2010: 251). In other words, the world has been "free-riding" on the US global leadership for too long. Even when the marginal cost of having the hegemon is increasingly larger than the marginal benefit (the Asian financial crisis in 1997 and the global financial crisis in 2008–2009 were two examples), it is still very hard to find any alternative (Gilpin 1981: 156). After Donald Trump became the president, he harnessed every opportunity to reduce US global economic commitments to avoid being overstretched. For instance, he asked the alliance in Europe and East Asia to pay the United States in order to keep the military forces, a policy called "Cost plus 50."[2] Alliances should pay the full cost as well as adding 50 percent extra, according to the US government. The problem for the United States is that either the alliances may just want to spend more money on their own military or there is no such great security threat needing huge US military presence.

Again, when putting the money to the mouth, Trump was not ambiguous in the international arena and he has shown that some "break-even" foreign policy decisions should be made in order to avoid being overburdened by providing global public goods. As can be seen from table 11.1, Trump pulled the United States out from many international organizations, and such global regimes were considered by him of not fulfilling their jobs. By any measurement, the Paris Agreement, United Nations Educational, Scientific and Cultural Organisation (UNESCO), and World Health Organization (WHO) are significant in terms of global governance. But, if following his business foreign policy objective of getting break-even, those international organiza-

Table 11.1.   US Withdrawal from Major International Agreement under Trump

Month/Year	Names
January 2017	Trans-Pacific Partnership (TPP)
June 2017	Paris Agreement
October 2017	United Nations Educational, Scientific and Cultural Organisation (UNESCO)
May 2018	Iran Nuclear Deal
June 2018	UN Human Rights Council
August 2019	Intermediate-Range Nuclear Forces Treaty
May 2020	Open Skies Treaty
July 2020	World Health Organization (WHO)

Source: Compiled by the author

tions are very costly either in terms of capital input or foreign policy/strategic support. It appears that Trump tried to marginalize the United States from those organizations as much as possible. They are useful especially symbolically to the United States when Americans felt "entitled" and they deserved to succeed (Samuelson 1997: 6). But, the United States should do away with them when it needs more focus on its own political economy.

At the other end of the global economic spectrum, China is increasingly showing more economic prowess. According to the World Bank's *Purchasing Power Parities and the Size of World Economies Results from the 2017 International Comparison Program*, China's GDP was US$19,617 billion, while the US GDP was US$19,519 billion, measured in purchasing power parities (PPP) (World Bank 2020: 1), resulting in the United States losing the biggest economy status to China by a hairpin margin of US$98 billion. Yet, in terms of per capita GDP, China was even behind Brazil, Iran, Thailand, and Mexico according to Jeffrey Frankel, professor at the John F. Kennedy School of Government at Harvard University.[3] From that angle, China was winning because of its economic size. Once you take into consideration the Chinese population, there is still a long way to go for China to overtake the United States. According to Danny Quah, dean and Li Ka Shing Professor in Economics at Lee Kuan Yew School of Public Policy at the National University of Singapore, the global economy's center of gravity was around mid-Atlantic in 1980. Yet, because of the economic rise of China and the rest of East Asia, the global economy's center of gravity will move 9,300 km from the mid-Atlantic to somewhere between India and China in 2050 (Quah 2011: 3).

One may argue that international power and reputation cannot be simply measured by GDP alone. But, the United States has shown a continuous setback in global economic leadership. Fast-forwarding to the more current economic situation, inequality has become a general phenomenon of the United States, and the problem is getting worse. According to the Pew Research Center, income inequality in the United States has witnessed a 20 percent increase from 1980 to 2016. In addition, the wealth gap between its richest and poorest families has doubled from 1989 to 2016.[4] The United States, as we can see, has shown a gradual decline and more and more evidence supports that argument, particularly when the world has become more interdependent. The new global economic paradigm may suggest that a single hegemonic power may not be the most effective foreign policy model. In particular, as Xuetong Yan, professor from Tsinghua University in China, rightly pointed out, "China has chosen to prioritise its economic development; this strategy has effectively induced the Sino-American strategic rivalry to start in an economic rather than a military context" (Yan 2013: 223–224). After all, many global common economic interests can be obtained among like-minded countries that have shown similar economic growth patterns or common objectives.[5]

TRADE WAR AND US–CHINA RELATIONS

The US–China trade war began in July 2018 when the United States started imposing a 25 percent tariff on US$34 billion Chinese imports. China immediately retaliated by imposing a 25 percent tariff on 545 goods from the United States (worth US$34 billion), including agricultural products, automobiles, and aquatic products.[6] Their tit-for-tat strategies kept escalating until they signed the phase one trade deal in January 2020. According to the trade deal, China had to buy US$200 billion goods and services from the United States within two year.

The huge US deficit with China was considered as the immediate cause of the trade war. According to the US Trade Representative (USTR), the US goods and services trade deficit with China reached US$378.6 in 2018.[7] From the US perspective, the underlying cause was that since China became the member of the World Trade Organization (WTO) in 2001, China has not been fulfilling the promises of reforming its economy while still being able to tap into the global market through the WTO platform. According to Trump, the United States suffered the most partly because of the year-on-year trade deficit with China, of which it certainly benefitted from the globalization of trade.[8] As far as trade disputes are concerned, China has been adapting to make use of the WTO dispute settlement mechanism in resolving trade issues from the global platform (Cheung 2018, 62). Theoretically, globalization can help developing economies. In *The Next Great Globalization*, Frederic Mishkin, Alfred Lerner Professor of Banking and Financial Institutions at Columbia University, clearly pointed out that "only by embracing global markets can less-developed countries get rich. Trade globalization has a key role to play in economic growth by directly stimulating domestic firms to become more productive" (Mishkin 2006, 136). China is certainly a big fan of globalization. In the Davos World Economic Forum 2017, Xi Jinping, China's president, criticised excessive profit chasing as the root cause of the backlash of globalization. Yet, globalization itself is innocent.[9]

For those who believe trade war was successful, they referred to the reduction of trade deficit from 2018 to 2019. According to the US Census Bureau, in 2018, the United States exported US$120.1 billion of goods to China while importing a staggering US$539.7 billion of goods in return, resulting in US$419.5 billion in trade deficits. After a year of a trade war with China and the tariffs imposed on Chinese goods, the United States exported US$106.6 billion of goods in 2019 while importing US$452.2 billion of goods, resulting in US$345.6 billion in deficits. Although not tremendously, the trade war appeared to have some effect in trade deficit reduction with China.[10] Yet, in responding to the US–China trade war, the United Nations Conference on

Trade and Development (UNTCAD) released a report entitled *Trade and Trade Diversion Effects of United States Tariffs* on China in November 2019. By using recent data from the US Census Bureau, the report concluded that the United States did significantly decline import from China by 25 percent. As a result of the trade war, other economies, such as Taiwan, Mexico, the EU, and Vietnam, also benefitted. But the report praised China as resilient that over 75 percent of trade was still maintained with the United States. Yet, the report concluded that the trade war will be lose-lose because the tariffs will hurt US consumers as well as China because of the significant reduction of export (Nicita 2019: 13).

Economists and academics questioned the trade war and extended the argument of a lose-lose trade war scenario. John Wong, the late professorial fellow at the East Asian Institute at the National University of Singapore, argued, "But the real size of China's trade surplus has been exaggerated" because the exports from the United States, agricultural products and advanced manufacturing items, had a high degree of domestic valued added, while China's electronic goods or "Walmart type" products had low domestic value-added for China (Wong 2017, A20). Not only was the trade war wasteful, the United States actually needs China. The research from Shen and Fu indicated that they are actually complementary in terms of trade because the "US is no longer producing the goods that it imports from China" (Shen & Fu 2014: 102). Lemoine and Unal's research, additionally, found that China's foreign trade is influenced by domestic demand and indigenous capabilities. China's import is more ordinary for domestic consumption while the importing of parts and components for assembly has been declining. For instance, in 2006, 49 percent of the consumer goods imported were in the high-end segment; and it increased to 67 percent in 2014 (2017: 2 and 13). Their finding closely matched China's new normal policy, which relies less on manufacturing and assembly but more on a technologically driven and domestic consumption driven economy.

So, as much evidence points to the detrimental effects of the trade war, why is there still a trade war if both will be losers? In *Free Trade Under Fire*, Douglas Irwin, professor of economics at Dartmouth College, explained why elected representatives ignored those economic principles and still carried out trade restrictions. According to him,

> There are additional reasons to expect that the political system will be biased in favour of restricting trade in a legislative forum. Particularly when trade policy is considered at the level of a specific commodity, political influence may be skewed in favor of those seeking government assistance because those who stand to gain have more at stake than those who stand to lose. (Irwin 2002: 142)

The miners that Trump mimicked on the stage, the agricultural industries, and even some high-end sectors demanded Trump to put pressure on China. In a word, it is the broadly conceived "interests" in the United States that have helped the drum-beat of the trade war with China get louder and louder.

The United States used tariffs and sanctions for ages in trying to facilitate its economic policies when it faced economic challenges. The exercising of voluntary export restraints (VERs) on Japanese semiconductor imports to the United States in the late 1980s was not uncommon as far as US economic interest was threatened. The current trade war with China is another testimony to the usual strategies by the United States. However, William Appleman Williams, late renowned academic, did not like the weaponization of trade. He pointed out, "It is time to stop defining trade as a weapon against other people with whom we have disagreements. It is time to start thinking of trade as a means to moderate and alleviate those tensions—and to improve the life of the other people" (Williams 1972, 309). Such a noble statement (published decades ago) has been confirmed more recently by other academics. Paul Krugman, 2008 Nobel Prize laureate, argued that "having a leader who is neither trusted by our erstwhile friends nor feared by our foreign rivals reduces our global influence in ways we're just starting to see. Trump's trade war didn't achieve any of its goals, but it did succeed in making America weak again."[11]

The WTO derived a verdict on September 15, 2020, that the US tariffs on Chinese goods violated international trade rules. The experts from the WTO panel could not find the relationship between the tariffs and enhancing the public morals. Robert Lighthizer, from the USTR, immediately rebutted that the WTO was not able to hold China accountable.[12] True, the ruling of the WTO may not have much teeth or binding power to prevent the United States from imposing tariffs to many Chinese goods imported to the United States. Yet, at least, the WTO represented an independent and international voice in defending the global trading system which apparently is being shaken by the US–China trade war. On February 28, 2020, the *Financial Times* published a comprehensive report entitled "How to Navigate the US–China Trade War." The gist behind the report was that the world could be bifurcated into two spheres of influence, one servicing the United States and the other centering on China.[13] Such scenarios can be alarming if one thinks about hegemonic stability. But, a bilateral and even multilateral world may not be a totally unconceivable picture on international trade and global economic development.

According to Willy Shih, Robert and Jane Cizik Professor of Management Practice in Business Administration at Harvard Business School, the US–China trade war inevitably enabled many firms to shift to a "China plus one" strategy of diversifying production to other Southeast Asian countries. Yet,

"In the long run, though, it would be a mistake to cut China completely out of your supply picture. The country's deep supplier networks, its flexible and able workforce, and its large and efficient ports and transportation infrastructure mean that it will remain a highly competitive source for years to come" (Shih 2020: 86). They figure that leading MNCs want to hedge between US–China relations by not putting all their eggs in one basket. For instance, Apple is making its latest iPhone in both India and China.[14]

US–CHINA INTELLECTUAL PROPERTY RIGHTS DISPUTES AND CHINA'S ADAPTATION

"Taking Trump Seriously, Not Literally" was the title of one of the articles written by Salena Zito for *The Atlantic* on September 23, 2016.[15] The author was trying to point out that many reporters and media are trying to take his word literally and mostly just fact-checking, without necessarily of accepting the significance of the issues that he raised. Yet, as far as US–China IPR disputes are concerned, one may want to take him both seriously and literally! On August 14, 2017, Donald Trump signed the Presidential Memorandum for the United States Trade Representative.[16] He formally delegated the power to the government body to carry out the investigation. Robert Lighthizer responded, "After consulting with stakeholders and other government agencies, I have determined that these critical issues merit a thorough investigation. I notified the President that today I am beginning an investigation under Section 301of the Trade Act of 1974."[17] In less than a year, a 215-page report entitled *Findings of the Investigation into China's Acts, Policies, and Practices Related to Technology Transfer, Intellectual Property, and Innovation under Section 301 of the Trade Act of 1974* was released on March 22, 2018.[18] The report raised five major concerns over US–China IPR disputes, including US national security or cybersecurity, China's inadequate intellectual property (IP) protection, the using of antimonopoly law to get access to US IP, China's standardization law of transferring US IP to China, and China's talent acquisition program of recruiting top IT and other professional talent from the United States.

The report was a result of continuous US–China IPR negotiations, and their disputes endured a much longer history. They can be divided into three phases. In the 1990s, it should be called the face-off and pressing phase. When the Sino-American Memorandum of Understanding on the Protection of Intellectual Property was signed in 1992, it signified the initial encounter of US–China IPR disputes negotiation. From July 1993 to February 1995, the United States already held twelve negotiation sessions with China over

IPR infringements, leading to fifteen infringing manufacturing plants closed in 1996. The second phase in the 2000s was an independent and codevelopment phase when the US–China Joint Commission on Commerce and Trade (JCCT) carried out cooperative joint workforces to combat IPR infringement in China.[19] The 2010s denoted a phase of blurring and conflict escalation. The exhaustive and yet not entirely successful JCCT meetings between China and the United States resulted in very little concrete outcomes, leading to the USTR 2017 investigation and the release of the above-mentioned report in 2018. The National Security Strategy (NSS) in December 2017 broadly outlined future US security interests. The NSS blamed China for stealing US IP and further complained about some states using legal means of acquiring technology to undermine US leadership (NSS 2017, 19–21).

To say China did nothing to protect IPR is not entirely correct. China adopted three significant IPR laws. It adopted the patent law in 1984 (third amendment in 2008), the trademark law in 1983 (third amendment in 2013) and the copyright law in 1991 (first amendment in 2001) (Cheung 2018: 88). The repeated amendments of both patent and trademark laws suggested that China is more accustomed to using legal means to protect IPR as well as having a legal system to protect IPR, even if not perfectly. Among three legal protections, trademark infringement is the most common (trademark law amended the most!). Table 11.2 shows China's customs record of IPR infringement in 2016. More than forty-one million (98 percent) were trademark infringements.

Before the Beijing Olympic Games in August 2008, the Chinese government had already launched the Outline of the National Intellectual Property Strategy (ONIPS) on June 5, 2008. It was partly because the global mega event that would inevitably place China under the global spotlight, and IPR protection is one of the global concerns. Secondly and more importantly, China increasingly moved toward a development strategy putting lots of emphasis on innovation, which also relies on the protection of IPR. For instance, the cover page of the world edition of the *China Daily* from November 25 to December 1, 2011, was called "Brand Global." The State-owned Assets

Table 11.2: China's Custom's Record on IPR Infringement in 2016

Categorization	Numbers	Percentage
Trademark	41,456,410	98.57
Copyright	538,613	1.28
Patents	57,193	0.14
Olympic/Expo trademark	6,000	0.01

Zhongguo Zhishichanquan Nianjian 2017. Beijing: Zhishichanquan chubanshe, p. 491.

Supervision and Administration Commission began to carry out workshops to promote brands from October 2013. To put into perspective, according to *Forbes*, the one hundred most valuable brands in the world were worth \$2.54 trillion in 2020.[20] Building big brands and protecting IPR are becoming increasingly in China's own economic interest.

In addition, Lipu Tian, former commissioner of the State Intellectual Property Office (SIPO) (renamed as China National Intellectual Property Administration [CNIPA] on August 28, 2018), pointed out that "China has established, developed and constantly improved its own intellectual property system, and made it compatible with China's national conditions and needs for development and consistent with the international rules, and disseminated the intellectual property culture among its 1.3 billion people" (Tian 2011: 5). According to the 13th Five-year Plan for Economic and Social Development of the People's Republic of China (2016–2020), there were five guiding principles behind the development philosophy: innovation, coordination, green, opening up, and sharing (2016: 21–22). Innovation was a top priority as the linchpin for China's future growth and development.

As China is moving toward the new normal, striving for innovation is an imperative because there is no more break-neck growth rate to energize China's further growth and development. The new engines of growth will be high-end, high-tech, and innovative products. To illustrate the importance of IPR in China, the fifteen hundred participants and more than fifty-five hundred patent projects in the 10th China International Patent Fair (September 9–11, 2016) demonstrated the market potential of IPR in China. They strike a deal worth more than 447 million yuan (about US\$71 million).[21] Other similar examples were that on August 28, 2016, Aero-Engine Group was established in China. The group was jointly invested by China's State Council, Beijing Municipal Government, the Aviation Industry Corp of China (AVIC), and Commercial Aircraft Corp of China (CACC). According to Junxi Dong, Deputy Section Chief of SIPO, this is going to be a win-win situation in launching the Aero-Engine Group in order to pull the talent together and to "accelerate independent research, development and manufacturing of aircraft engines that will help China to achieve its goal of becoming an aviation power."[22] Similarly, mobile payment has been a consumption phenomenon in China. In 2015, more than 358 million mobile phone users accessed to mobile payment, which involved 15 trillion yuan payment. In terms of mobile payment technology, China is practically the global leader. Up to February 2016, Tencent has filed forty-six patents on mobile technology and Alibaba filed thirty-two patent applications, while Apply only applied three.[23] IPR and innovation are increasingly becoming less and less anachronistic as far as China's economic development is concerned. As a middle income economy,

China actually shows exceptional innovation capacity. It moved up to 14th in the 2020 Global Innovation Index 2020, from 25th in 2016 (Global Innovation Index 2020 2020: 14). Although not exponentially, China's innovation capacity has been recognized globally.

Before concluding this section, I want to use another example to showcase China's path of IPR protection. On September 14, 2020, the European Union (EU) and China signed a bilateral agreement to protect one hundred European geographical indications (GI) from both countries. European GI products include cava, champagne, feta, Irish whiskey, Munchener Bier, ouzo, Polska Wodka, Porto, prosciutto di parma, and queso manchego. In return, the Chinese GI products—including Pixian Dou Ban (Pixian Bean Paste), Anji Bai Cha (Anji White Tea), Panjin Da Mi (Panjin rice), and Anqiu Da Jian (Anqiu Ginger), among others—will be protected in the EU market (European Commission 2020: 1). Within the domain of IPR protection, GI is an important area to which countries are paying attention because they protect the farmers from the origin of the products as well as increase the value of the products. Since the essence of the IPR is to protect the commercial value of the goods, the agreement indicated that China did move in line with IPR protection and the bilateral agreement authenticated such development. Secondly, when the numbers of the middle class in China increase, their consumption will drive economic growth, and the importation of GI products from the EU corresponds to China's consumer demand. Finally, with the agreement, there is a potential of improving the food security in China with the protection and the enhancement of the value of the products.

For a long time, China has had a very poor track record on IPR protection. IPR infringement has been so rampant and the legal implementation was lax and weak (Dimitrov 2009). Increasingly, we have seen more significant domestic demands from different sectors in China to drive the global innovation competition, and China has become more serious about IPRs protection. Implementation of both IPR law and enforcement require further administrative support. Trump's trade war with China inevitably pushed China to accelerate innovation and, the future global competition is more about indigenous growth and technological nurturing. Previous economic development patterns on copying and producing may help the promotion of lower-end products. Moving from the "factory of the world" to "factory of knowledge and ideas" requires a more robust IPR system in China. Better IPR protection helps China to enhance foreign direct investment (FDI) and restores global confidence from its trading partners too.[24]

TECHNOLOGY, COMPETITION, AND THE GLOBAL MARKET

Donald Trump's foreign policy toward China on technology represented two major perspectives behind IPE. Firstly, knowledge (another dimension of technology) should be monopolized in the hands of the wWest and competition should be forbidden. In *States and Markets*, Susan Strange, late professor from the London School of Economics and Political Science, succinctly pointed out that "power in the knowledge structure is more easily maintained if authority can limit access to it—and, as a corollary to that, if it can exercise a jealous defence of its monopoly position against any threat of competition" (1994: 124). In other words, restricting access to knowledge and retaining monopoly power on technology are necessary to maintain the global structural power of the United States.

Secondly, technology symbolized the success of liberal democracy and paved the way for the collapse of communism after the Cold War. Jerry Weinberger, professor of political science at Michigan State University, contended that "with the exception of a few third-world stragglers, all countries now seem to be grouping toward some form of liberal democratic capitalism. It is hard to deny that technology was important if not decisive in assuring this grate revolution" (Weinberger 1993: 253). China, under the Chinese Communist Party, therefore should be following the trend and subordinate to US technological advancement. To Trump's surprise, China broke the Western monopoly of technology. In many areas, for example 5G networks, artificial intelligence, mobile payments, and electric buses, China is ahead of the United States. In addition, as a socialist market economy, China did not collapse after the end of the Cold War nor hugely suffered economically like most of the East Asian economies experienced after the 1997 Asian financial crisis. Instead, China did not depreciate its currency (renminbi), which helped China to earn genuine support from the entire East Asian region as well as accelerated regionalism in East Asia (Cheung 2017: 31–38). The political system is increasingly more consolidated, especially under the current leader, Xi Jinping.

Writing in the early period of the trade war, Lawrence Lau, Ralph and Claire Landau Professor of Economics at the Chinese University of Hong Kong, already contended that the current trade war is not about trade but has more to do with the continuous competition between the United States and China on economic and technological dominance as well as the rise of populist and protectionism, the United States in particular.[25] From the trade war to tech war, Trump's foreign policy toward China has broadened the issues to cover areas in which China is considered a threat to the United States.

Claiming that Huawei (global 5G and telecommunication giant based in Shenzhen) is a threat to the national security of the United States is a case in point. A comprehensive discussion of US–China relations and Huawei is beyond the scope of this chapter. What I am trying to point out is that even leading academics in the United States have been heavily criticizing targeting a Chinese tech firm. Jeffrey Sachs, Columbia University professor, contended that the arrest of Wanzhou Meng, Huawei's CFO, was abnormal because "the US rarely arrests senior businesspeople, US or foreign, for alleged crimes committed by their companies."[26] Later, in an interview with the BBC reporter, Sachs further contended that "targeting Huawei was never simply a security concern," and he further criticized that "the US lost its step on 5G, which is a critical part of the new digital economy. And Huawei was taking a greater and greater share of global markets."[27] Yet, Bert Hofman, director of the East Asian Institute at the National University of Singapore, expected that "in a tech war scenario, China is also likely to keep more of the new technologies it discovers to itself" (Hofman 2019: 2). One of the results is obviously a global economy losing out because of China's declining demand from high-tech goods as well as the pulling back from the global production possibility frontier. In an interview on the BBC's Talking Business Asia programme, Eric Schmidt, the chair of the US Department of Defense's innovation board (former chief executive of Google), worried that the United States may lose global technological leadership to China because of the decreasing investment on R&D as well as the stopping of the global talents coming to the United States due to immigration hurdles and general negative views on international migrants to the United States. For example, the United States revoked the visas of a thousand Chinese students to the United States because of the students' links to Chinese military.[28]

Putting aside tech war narrative, technological development in China reflects long-term changes in both social and economic aspects. To the Chinese, embracing technology and involvement in R&D have become a way of life. According to a new Chinese statistic, for the past ten years, between 2009 and 2018, the most popular subject for Chinese undergraduate science students has changed from electronics and communication (number one 2009–2012) to physics (number one 2012–2018).[29] Pure science subjects such as physics have been declining in the Western economies. But, in China, the shift toward fundamental science subjects provides some evidence of the future prospect of science knowledge resulting in more opportunities and job prospects.

Table 11.3 demonstrates the R&D population in some major Chinese districts and cities. The aggregated numbers of R&D population include those with undergraduate, masters, and PhD degrees. The table also illustrates the female population in the R&D sector. Contrary to conventional wisdom, the

Table 11.3.   Research and Development in China (no. of people) (2014)

District	R&D	Female	PhD	Master	Undergraduate
Shanghai	226,829	59,526	22,226	37,955	56,282
Beijing	334,194	109,747	60,068	76,525	81,389
Tianjin	143,667	38,256	8,598	19,475	35,045
Jiangsu	626,882	142,056	25,382	64,924	209,162
Zhejiang	416,010	95,204	25,382	64,924	106,070
Shandong	409,441	101,483	14,478	43,445	130,601
Guangdong	652,405	441,806	18,387	67,155	149,027
Whole country	5,018,218	1,250,289	287,480	661,250	1,388,171

Source: (Shan Kaiyan, Annual Report on Economic Development of Shanghai 2016: p. 36)

numbers of people involved in R&D were not necessarily concentrated in Shanghai or Beijing. In fact, Jiangsu, Zhejiang, and Guangdong have the lion's share of the R&D population in China. In addition, among the 652,405 people in the R&D sector in Guangdong, 441,806 were female. The gender balance appears to be improving gradually.

In the 2019 Government Work Report of China's State Council, China would cut the rate for broadband and mobile internet services because that will help China to nurture innovation and help the growth of emerging industries.[30] According to *Science*, China's public and private science and technology expenditure rose by 12.5 percent in 2019 to 2.21 trillion yuan (US$322 billion). It was equal to 2.23 percent of China's GDP, which was close to 2.38 percent of the OECD average spending in 2018.[31] To understand the strengths of Chinese technological catch-up (until October 2020), two of the top five unicorn companies (private companies with a valuation of more than US$1 billion and less than ten years of history) in the world were Chinese: Bytedance and Didi Chuxing. While the United States had SpaceX, Stripe, and Airbnb in the top five, the combined valuation of Bytedance and Didi Chuxing was US$202 billion, which dwarfed the combined valuation US$100 billion of three of the top five US companies.[32]

Although China's innovation and technological competition seems robust, in an article entitled "Why China Can't Innovate" from *Harvard Business Review*, the authors concluded that China did not have a good institutional framework for innovation (Abrami, Kirby, & McFarlan 2014). One of the key problems involves higher education. Yes, funding for universities in China has been enormous and keeps increasing year to year. According to the Ministry of Education, the spending on higher education in 2019 was RMB1346.4 billion (around US$201 billion), an increase of 11.99 percent from 2018.[33] But, "The governance structures of China's state-owned universities still leave too many decisions to too few, too self-important, people. Chinese universities, like state-owned enterprises, are plagued with party committees, and the university party secretary normally outranked the president. While a few extraordinary party secretaries are central to their universities' success, as rule this system of parallel governance limits its rather than enhances the flow of ideas" (Abrami, Kirby, & McFralan 2014: 111). Such assessment may not be entirely inaccurate because the political system and the constraint behind Chinese state-led development drive are undeniable.

Nevertheless, the innovation and technological demand to which China aspires may simply reflect "its stage of development" (Yip & Mckern 2016: 10). The problem is that when Trump is pushing China vehemently via trade war or tech war, the repercussions from the Chinese perspective could result in significant shifting of the conventional state-led technological approach to more bottom-up-cum-nationalistic-emancipation technological movement. Nowadays, Chinese people enjoy the benefit brought by technology, and the technologically driven growth is an unavoidable process of social change because of the new normal. Trump's tech war can backfire by bringing Chinese state and society much closer together in a more organic way because the common "enemy" of the Chinese people is clear and present from outside.

CONCLUSION

US–China relations under Trump were not in good shape. After the presidential election of 2020, Joe Biden (Democratic Party) won more than eighty million popular votes, secured 308 Electoral College votes, and was en route to be the next president of the United States.[34] Therefore Trump's administration has gone. But it does not mean that US–China relations can get back to normal. A declining United States is beyond doubt. Yet, the process and the management of the posthegemonic world appear to be very clumsy under Trump. We have demonstrated that habitually countries have been relying on US leadership. By witnessing the declining US–China relations and poor US management of the COVID-19 pandemic, the world appears to be not ready to face the very shaky image of US leadership. Even from any academic measurement, trade war with China is not a win-win strategy. But the vested interest behind the trade war is enormous. Yet, China's economic development is moving toward a high-ended and technologically driven growth pattern. The protection of IPR has become increasingly in the economic interest of China. Although the result between the United States and China on the IPR dispute has not been totally satisfactory in the past two decades, China is moving to embrace more and more the commercial interest generated from having a better IPR system. The more recent tech war between the United States and

China does not appear to be deterring China from moving toward building up a more innovative and technologically driven development policy. When Trump's tech war strategies are cutting too deep into the day-to-day livelihood among the Chinese, the repercussion may result in bringing the Chinese people closer to the state, resulting in a bigger and stronger China.

China is moving away from the catch-up phase of developmental path and looking for more lucrative if not diversified economic development pathways. From the Chinese perspective, this is sine qua non because of the new normal and of moving away from a breakneck growth rate to more qualitative growth patterns. From East Asian regional economic points of view, it is imperative for China to move up the global value chain and release some lower-end economic turfs to regional economies. Yet, moving along this pattern, China unavoidably collides with lots of the US signature economic interests: telecommunication, intellectual property, high-end technological products, AI, 5G, and even industrial robots. In the 1980s, we saw the US–Japan disputes on semiconductors, which Japan overtook the US leadership in the mid to late 1980s. Japan backed down partly because of the long established US–Japan economic and political relations and partly because of Japan's decades-long recession beginning from the late 1980s. Now, the United States is having a face-off with China on many economic fronts. But China did not appear to be backing down in terms of policy responses. Economically, China's economy is expected to increase 10 percent by the end of 2021, while the US economy will remain the same as in 2019 (*Economist*, October 10–16, 2020, 11).

Economic interdependence and globalization are still being embraced by the Chinese government and the general public. Growth, economic stability, and improvement of living standards are just as important as security and military preponderance in contemporary China. The world economy is adapting and mostly hedging if not haggling with an obvious declining United States, while also looking up to some economic as well as tangible benefits from China's increasing integration with the global political economy.

NOTES

1. *Washington Post*, July 3, 2020 [https://www.washingtonpost.com/opinions/making-china-a-us-enemy-is-counterproductive/2019/07/02/647d49d0-9bfa-11e9-b27f-ed2942f73d70_story.html?noredirect=on] (accessed August 16, 2020).

2. *Time* [https://time.com/5548013/trump-allies-pay-cost-plus-50-troops/] (accessed September 17, 2020).

3. *The Guardian* [https://www.theguardian.com/business/2020/may/29/is-china-overtaking-the-us-as-a-financial-and-economic-power] (accessed September 15, 2020).

4. Pew Research Center [https://www.pewsocialtrends.org/2020/01/09/trends -in-income-and-wealth-inequality/#the-wealth-divide-among-upper-income-families -and-middle-and-lower-income-families-is-sharp-and-rising] (accessed September 15, 2020).

5. Although this is beyond the focus of this chapter, the Belt and Road Initiative (BRI) and the Asian Infrastructure Investment Bank (AIIB) are just two major initiatives that China has been able to derive among like-minded economies (see Cheung 2018, 143–147).

6. *South China Morning Post* [https://www.scmp.com/economy/china-economy/ article/3078745/what-us-china-trade-war-how-it-started-and-what-inside-phase] (accessed September 17, 2020).

7. USTR [https://ustr.gov/countries-regions/china-mongolia-taiwan/peoples -republic-china#:~:text=The%20U.S.%20goods%20and%20services,way)%20 goods%20trade%20during%202018.&text=Services%20exports%20were%20 %2458.9%20billion%3B%20services%20imports%20were%20%2418.4%20bil- lion.] (accessed September 9, 2020).

8. Yet, when Japan was accepted to be a member of the General Agreement on Tariffs and Trade (GATT), the predecessor of WTO, in 1955, almost all the member countries were unhappy. Yet, the US just let it happened.

9. The State Council [http://www.china.org.cn/node_7247529/content_40569136. htm] (accessed 14 January 2020).

10. US Census Bureau, "Trade in Good with China" [https://www.census.gov/ foreign-trade/balance/c5700.html] (accessed 26 May 2020).

11. *The New York Times*, December 16, 2019 [https://www.nytimes.com/2019/12/16/ opinion/trump-china-trade.html] (accessed August 19, 2020).

12. *South China Morning Post* [https://www.scmp.com/news/world/united-states -canada/article/3101681/wto-rules-against-trumps-tariffs-china] (accessed September 9, 2020).

13. *The Financial Times* [https://www.ft.com/content/6124beb8-5724-11ea-abe5 -8e03987b7b20] (accessed September 1, 2020). The report was derived from the FT Think Tank meeting on January 28, 2020 in London. The meeting was attended by academics, think tanks and leading company representatives.

14. *The Financial Times*, August 17, 2020 [https://www.ft.com/content/9000d2b0 -460f-4380-b5de-cd7fdb9416c8] (accessed August 20, 2020).

15. *The Atlantic* [https://www.theatlantic.com/politics/archive/2016/09/trump -makes-his-case-in-pittsburgh/501335/] (accessed September 20, 2020).

16. The White House [https://www.whitehouse.gov/presidential-actions/presi dential-memorandum-united-states-trade-representative/] (accessed September 20, 2020).

17. *The Financial Times* [https://app.ft.com/content/a3419950-158e-38ca-9390 -343b828dfb06] (accessed September 20, 2020).

18. USTR [https://ustr.gov/sites/default/files/Section%20301%20FINAL.PDF] (accessed September 20, 2020).

19. The campaign style combating methods, however, may not be very effective in eradicateingIPRs infringement (see Dimitrov 2009).

20. *Forbes* [https://www.forbes.com/sites/martyswant/2020/07/27/apple
-microsoft-and-other-tech-giants-top-forbes-2020-most-valuable-brands-list/
#c73337a3adad] (accessed September 22, 2020).

21. *Zhongguo Zhishichanquan Bao* (*China Intellectual Property News*), 21 September 2016, p. 12.

22. *Zhongguo Caijin yu Jingji xinwen* (*China Financial and Economic News*), 14
September 2016, p. 12.

23. *Zhongguo Caijin yu Jingji xinwen* (*China Financial and Economic News*), 7
September 2016, p. 12.

24. East Asian Forum [https://www.eastasiaforum.org/2018/09/29/the-us-could
-learn-to-like-chinas-new-ip-strategy/] (accessed September 21, 2020).

25. *South China Morning Post*, August 17, 2018 [https://www.scmp.com/com
ment/insight-opinion/united-states/article/2160041/behind-us-china-trade-war-lies
-competition] (accessed May 24, 2020).

26. Project-Syndicate [https://www.project-syndicate.org/commentary/trump-war
-on-huawei-meng-wanzhou-arrest-by-jeffrey-d-sachs-2018-12?barrier=accesspaylog]
(accessed October 10, 2020).

27. "US China cold war 'bigger global threat than virus,'" BBC [https://www.bbc
.co.uk/news/business-53104730] (accessed June 22, 2020).

28. BBC News [https://www.bbc.co.uk/news/business-54100001] (accessed September 14, 2020).

29. [https://kknews.cc/zh-hk/education/9943b4l.html] (accessed September 14,
2020).

30. State Council of China [http://english.gov.cn/premier/news/2019/03/06/content
_281476551271772.htm] (accessed 6 April 2019).

31. *Science* [https://www.sciencemag.org/news/2020/08/china-again-boosts
-rd-spending-more-10#:~:text=Total%20public%20and%20private%20science,
Bureau%20of%20Statistics%20reported%20yesterday.] (accessed October 10, 2020).

32. The Global Unicorn Club [https://www.cbinsights.com/research-unicorn
-companies] (accessed October 9, 2020).

33. Ministry of Education [http://en.moe.gov.cn/news/press_releases/202006/
t20200622_467671.html] (accessed October 25, 2020).

34. By the time of this writing, Donald Trump still did not formally concede the
election to Biden. But it did not appear that his allegation of Democrats' voting fraud
has any merit.

REFERENCES

13th Five-Year Plan for Economic and Social Development of the People's Republic
   of China (2016–2020). 2016. Beijing: Central Compilation & Translation Press.
Abrami, Regina M., William C. Kirby and F. Warren McFarlan. 2014. "Why China
   Can't Innovate and What It's Doing About It." *Harvard Business Review* 92, no.
   3: 107–111.

Bisley, Nick. 2010. "Global Power Shift: The Decline of the West and the Rise of the Rest?" In *Issues in 21st Century World Politics*, edited by Mark Beeson and Nick Bisley, 66-81. Basingstoke: Palgrave.

Cheung, Gordon C K. 2017. *China Factors: Political Perspectives & Economic Interactions* (paperback) London and New York: Routledge.

Cheung, Gordon. C. K. 2018. *China in the Global Political Economy: From Developmental to Entrepreneurial*. Cheltenham: Edward Elgar Publishing.

Dimitrov, Martin K. 2009. *Piracy and the State: The Politics of Intellectual Property Rights in China*. Cambridge: Cambridge University Press.

European Commission. 2020. "EU and China sign Landmark Agreement Protecting European Geographical Indications." *European Commission-Press Release*, September 14.

Gilpin, Robert. 1981. *War & Change in World Politics*. Cambridge: Cambridge University Press.

Global Innovation Index 2020. 2020. Cornell University, INSEAD, and the World Intellectual Property Organization (WIPO).

Hofman, Bert. 2019. "Trade, Technology and Trust." *EAI Commentary* No.2 July 15. Singapore: East Asian Institute: 1–3.

Irwin, Douglas A. 2002. *Free Trade under Fire*. Princeton: Princeton University Press.

Keohane, Robert and Joseph Nye. 1989. *Power and Interdependence*, 2nd edition, New York: HarperCollins Publishers.

Kindleberger, Charles. P. (1973), *The World in Depression, 1929-1939*. Berkeley: University of California Press.

Lemoine, Francoise. and Deniz Unal. 2017. "China's Foreign Trade: A 'New Normal.'" *China & World Economy* 25, no. 2: 1–21.

Mishkin, Frederic S. 2006. *The Next Great Globalization: How Disadvantaged Nations Can Harness Their Financial Systems to Get Rich*. Princeton: Princeton University Press.

National Security Strategy (NSS) of the United States of America. 2017. [https://www.whitehouse.gov/wp-content/uploads/2017/12/NSS-Final-12-18-2017-0905.pdf] (accessed May 25, 2020)

Nicita, Alessandro. 2019. "Trade and Trade Diversion Effects of United States Tariffs on China." *UNCTAD Research Paper No. 37*. UNCTAD/SER.RP/2019/9, 1–17.

Norrlof, Carla. 2010. *America's Global Advantage: US Hegemony and International Cooperation.* Cambridge: Cambridge University Press.

Nye, Joseph. 2002. *The Paradox of American Power: Why the World only Superpower Can't Go It Alone*. New York: Oxford University Press.

Quah, Danny. 2011. "The Global Economy's Shifting Centre of Gravity." *Global Policy*, 2, issue 1 (January): 3–9.

Samuelson, Robert J. 1997. *The Good Life and Its Discontents: The American Dream in the Age of Entitlement 1945–1995*. New York: Vintage Books.

Shen, Guobing and Xiaolan Fu. 2014. "The Trade Effects of US Anti-dumping Actions Against China Post-WTO Entry." *World Economy* 37, no. 1: 86–105.

Shih, Willy C. 2020. "Global Supply Chains in a Post-Pandemic World." *Harvard Business Review* 98, no. 5: 82-89.

Stiglitz, Joseph. 2002. *Globalization and its Discontents*. London: Penguin.

Strange, Susan. 1994. *States and Market*. London: Pinter Publishers.

Tian, Lipu. 2011. "China's National Experience from Her Thirty-year Intellectual Property System." [Zhongguo zhishi chanquan zhidu 30 nian de guojia jingyan]. *China Patents and Trademarks*. [Zhongguo zuiangli yu shangbiao] 104: 3–7.

Weinberger, Jerry. 1993. "Technology and the Problem of Liberal Democracy." In *Technology in the Western Political Tradition*, edited by Melzer Arthur M., Jerry Weinberger and M. Richard Zinman. Ithaca and London: Cornell University Press.

Williams, William Appleman. 1972. *The Tragedy of American Diplomacy*. New Edition. New York: W. W. Norton and Company.

Wong, John. 2017. "A Cool Look at Trump's Looming Trade War with China." *The Straits Times* (Singapore), January 17, A20.

World Bank. 2020. *Purchasing Power Parities and the Size of World Economies Results from the 2017 International Comparison Program*. Washington D.C.: The World Bank.

Yan, Xuetong. 2013. "The Shift of the World Centre and Its Impact on the Change of the International System." *East Asia: An International Quarterly* 30, issue 3, (September): 217–235.

Yip, George S. and Bruce McKern. 2016. *China's Next Strategic Advantage: From Imitation to Innovation*. Cambridge, Mass.: The MIT Press.

Chapter Twelve

The US Congress and the Business Lobby

Jiakun Jack Zhang

In remarks at the Dole Institute in November 2020, US Trade Representative Robert Lighthizer said that the Trump administration had fundamentally changed how both Republicans and Democrats think about trade and China policy in a bipartisan way. [1]

Lighthizer's remarks come at the end of four tumultuous years where average US tariff levels on Chinese goods have increased over six-fold and covered two thirds of trade between the world's two largest economies. Prior to Trump, trade with China was seen primarily as an economic issue, justified politically by a consensus around the merits of engagement. After Trump, trade with China is increasingly seen as part of a wider national security challenge, where protectionism is justified as part of great power competition. How much credit does the Trump administration deserve for this seemingly dramatic shift in US trade policy towards China?

The answer to this question has value beyond mere academic speculation and could help predict the role trade will play in the future trajectory of US–China relations. If this shift stems from policies adopted by the Trump administration, then they can be easily reversed with different policies. If, however, the root cause of US policy reorientation can be traced to more structural forces, then present trade hostilities will prove to be much more enduring.

Most contemporary accounts of the US–China Trade War either focus on policy and rhetoric of the Trump administration and its allies in Congress or portray the conflict as the inevitable product of great power rivalry. Both types of explanation leave much to be desired. Trump-centric explanations give too much credit to an internally divided administration that lacked a coherent China policy. Systemic explanations are overly sweeping and fail to explain the decades-long period of peace between the great power that preceded the present conflict. This chapter charts a middle-range explanation that focuses on how China's integration with the global economy transformed American domestic politics. It seeks to contextualize the events of the trade war and elucidate the role that structural economic forces played in the conflict. Examining the structural context of the trade war also reveals puzzling questions that agency-centric narratives miss. Why did trade, long a source of stability in the US–China relationship, suddenly become a source of conflict? Why was the US business community, long considered champions of engagement with China, surprisingly impassive in the face of trade hostilities? Why did the Republican party, long the party of free trade, go along with the largest increase in tariffs since World War II?

This chapter argues that the answers to these questions can be found by exploring important structural shifts in the attitudes towards China in the US Congress and within the US businesses community over the past two decades. Conventional wisdom about the role of interest group politics has been shaped by the politics of engagement that enabled China's accession to the WTO. But the behavior of both interest groups and Congress seemingly deviated from established theories in the US–China trade war. Support for engagement with China proved much weaker than its advocates believed. Despite implementing costly tariffs, the Trump administration appeared to face relatively little opposition either from US interest groups or from Congress. Instead, a bipartisan consensus has emerged in Congress about the need to confront China both economically and politically.

Lighthizer and Trump, their claims to the contrary, were not the authors of this fundamental shift in US–China relations. Rather they are just the latest and most prominent politicians engaged in a practice that became especially prevalent within the Republican party since the mid-2000s: using China bashing to energize an economically distressed political base. After the global financial crisis, legislators from both parties, but particularly Republicans whose districts were threatened by Chinese import competition, blamed the economic woes of their districts on China and attacked their opponents for being "soft on China." Congressional China bashing prepared the way for Donald Trump's economic nationalist campaign. At the same time, powerful business lobbies, once unified by the goal of prying open China's markets, grew increasingly divided as more companies became disillusioned with China. Their ambivalence helps explain the inability of interest groups to resist the Section 301 tariffs.

The bipartisan consensus in Congress about the need to confront China predates Trump and will persist after his administration leaves office. However, as the economic costs of the trade war mount, the Trump administration's tariffs have realigned the political priorities of businesses and created a political dilemma for legislators. The incoming Biden administration will have to weigh the political benefits of appearing tough on China with the eco-nomic costs of maintaining tariffs. The Trump administration's tariffs have failed by nearly all its own declared metrics: the US trade deficit with China has widened, US manufacturing job growth suffered, there's no evidence of significant reshoring, supply chains have not decoupled, and Chinese efforts at indigenous innovation have accelerated. A return to the pre-Trump status quo is possible should a new alliance between the White House and business community emerge to refute the Trump administration's false narrative that China is paying the cost of the Section 301 tariffs and put pressure on Con-gress to prioritize economic welfare over political grandstanding.

THE OLD CONSENSUS: CONGRESSIONAL HOSTILITY CHECKED BY WHITE HOUSE AND BUSINESS ALLIANCE

Steps towards engaging China were made possible by an alliance of conve-nience between the White House and US business interests against a more hawkish Congress. Since the "loss of China" in 1949, Congress has consis-tently been more hawkish on China policy than the White House. As the emi-nent China watcher Michel Oksenberg noted, "While the executive branch is constitutionally charged with the management of foreign policy, on several occasions the Congress has decisively intruded into the management of China policy. When Congress has chosen to immerse itself, its impact has proven profound and long-lasting" (Xie 2008, 143). Congress passed the Formosa Resolution in 1955 to give a reluctant Eisenhower administration authority to defend Taiwan and the offshore islands with US military forces. Members of the "China lobby" in Congress lobbied vigorously against American recogni-tion of the People's Republic of China (PRC) after Nixon's 1972 visit opened the door to renewed diplomatic relations. After the Carter administration normalized relations with the PRC and terminated relations with the Repub-lic of China (Taiwan) in 1979, Congress passed the Taiwan Relations Act to maintain de facto diplomatic relations with Taiwan and commit the United States to arms sales for Taiwan's defense. In the wake of the 1989 Tianan-men Square massacre, Congress criticized the Bush administration for being too tepid in its response, passed a slew of sanctions targeting Beijing, and linked the annual extension of China's most-favored nation (MFN) trading status to China's human rights practices. The annual MFN debates became the most visible clashes between successive presidents and the Congress over China policy throughout the 1990s even as the US business community grew steadily more interested in the Chinese market. US businesses mounted a vigorous campaign to lobby Congress, particularly the Republican caucus, to

renew the MFN status and to garner congressional support for China's accession to the World Trade Organization (WTO).

Figure 12.1 shows the breakdown of China bills introduced by or referred
to the US Senate from the 101st Congress (1989–1991) to the 115th Congress
(2017–2019) by issue. The categories of issues include trade (MFN, investment, currency manipulation, etc.), human rights (Tibet, Xinjiang, Hong
Kong, Falun Gong, dissidents, prison labor, etc.), Taiwan, security (weapons
proliferation, North Korea, etc.), and other (pollution, climate, nonhostile
bills). The majority of these bills originate in the House of Representatives
and all but a few are hostile towards the PRC. The 105th Congress (1997–
1999) saw an intensification of legislative interest in China and a record number of China bills introduced. These bills, most originating from the House,
dealt with a wide range of issues from a major fight over renewing MFN
status, to prison labor exports, to forced abortions, to religious tolerance, to
China's role in missile proliferation, technology transfer, support for multilateral bank loans to China, to the US role in providing security to Taiwan.

Alliance with Business and the Emergence of the Engagement Consensus

Prior to the current nadir in US–China relations, the previous low point
for the bilateral relationship was reached in 1997. Congressional hostility

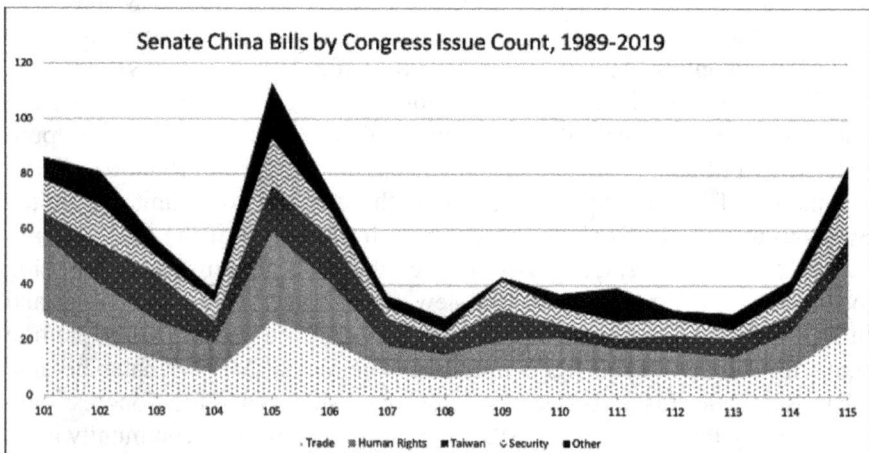

Figure 12.1. China Bills in the U.S. Senate by Issue Count (1989-2019)
Source: original figure by author

towards China was then driven by the longer-term fallout from the 1989 Tiananmen Square crackdown to more immediate tensions that resulted from the 1995–1996 Taiwan Strait Crisis. US public opinion of China in 1997 reached a historic low when only 33 percent of survey respondents reported having a favorable opinion of China. It also reflected a political struggle between a Republican controlled Congress and a Democratic White House as the 105th House of Representatives would impeach President Bill Clinton in 1998. The Clinton administration opposed many of these China measures introduced by Congress, not only for policy reasons, but also because it was planning to accept a state visit by Chinese President Jiang Zemin in late 1997 (Dumbaugh 1999, 3). Jiang would visit Washington in October 1997 and Clinton would visit Beijing in June 1998, the first exchange of state visits since the Tiananmen Square massacre in 1989.

The Clinton administration aligned itself with US business interests and congressional Republicans to push past opposition from Democrats to engage China economically. China's WTO accession, and the North American Free Trade Agreement (NAFTA), two of the largest acts of trade liberalization, were both shepherded through Congress by the Democratic Clinton administration. Clinton made the case for engagement with China on terms that seemed to promise something to everyone. To critics of China's human rights practices, engagement would bring domestic change (and eventual democratization); to security hawks wary of China's military modernization, engagement would usher in commercial peace, and to the pro-business "New Democrats," engagement would bring fabulous wealth to their corporate patrons. In doing so, Clinton was able to overcome opposition from the traditionally pro-union and anti-trade Democrats in Congress to pass the US–China Relations Act of 2000, which granted permanent normal trade relations (PNTR) status to China and made possible China's WTO accession. The US–China Relations Act of 2000 narrowly passed the House with 237 ayes and 197 noes, over the opposition of the majority of Democrats (137 noes, 78 ayes). NAFTA was ratified in 1993 with Republican support (43 noes, 153 ayes) and over Democratic opposition (156 noes, 102 ayes).

These legislative victories were possible by the vigorous lobbying by the pro-engagement business groups. According to Lingling Wei and Bob Davis, the US Chamber of Commerce targeted sixty-six districts of wavering lawmakers and the Business Roundtable focused on eighty-three others and spent more money on the lobbying campaign to grant China PNTR status than all the other trade lobbying battles through 2019 (Davis & Wei 2020, 91–92). The pro–free trade orientation of the White House and the vigorous lobbying by business overwhelmed opponents of engagement with China like Senator Jesse Helms of North Carolina, who represented declining import-competing industries with much smaller war chests. The US–China Relations Act was signed into law on Double Ten Day 2000, seemingly cementing a bipartisan consensus around engagement with China among Washington elites, but the seismic economic consequences that it would usher in at the grassroots level would transform the nature of congressional interest in China.

The Primacy of Interest Group Politics and Triumph of Structural Explanations

In light of the tumultuous US–China relationship in the 1990s, the normalization of trade relations that made possible China's WTO accession in 2001 appeared to have sealed victory for the pro-engagement business lobby and the defeat of the "China lobby." But it would, ironically, pave the way for a very broad-based and bipartisan anti-China sentiment in Congress. The mistake that many analysts made in the lead up to the outbreak of US–China trade hostilities was to assume that, after over a decade of engagement, congressional hostility towards China had dissipated and the alliance between the White House and US business had grown permanent.

Important to recall that despite candidate Trump's China bashing campaign rhetoric, many commentators felt that China could "shape" President Trump to behave in line with its interests (Sutter & Limaye 2016, 21). As late as June 2018, Chinese scholars and pundits saw little risk of a full-scale trade war between the United States and China because of: (1) a belief that the interdependent nature of the global trading system meant that both sides would avoid actions that could incur major economic losses (Zhang 2018); (2) a perceived gap between Trump's and the US business community's goals on trade as a source of leverage in US–China trade negotiations; and (3) confidence that a traditionally pro-trade Republican majority in Congress and influential special interest groups would make it difficult for the Trump administration to start a trade war with China, despite his bombastic protectionist rhetoric.

This analysis, which relied heavily on structural explanations of interest group politics, was also consistent with a consensus in the academic literature on international political economy. In "normal" trade politics, interest group lobbying constrains the president because distributive politics around trade policy are high. Milner and Tingley (2015, 65–67) explain US presidential strength across foreign policy instruments as a function of two factors: distributive politics and ideological divisions. Congress relies on interest groups to provide information about the costs and benefits of foreign policy and can thus constrain the president by voting against his legislative agenda when interest groups in their districts are harmed. Additionally, because Republicans and Democrats have historically disagreed on the merits of economic engagement, ideological divisions around this policy instrument were expected to further constrain the president. Their book predicts that trade politics is an area where the president should face the greatest constraints if interest groups are harmed by protectionism. The US–China trade war seems to contradict established theories that predict a leading role of interest groups in trade politics and a highly constrained White House (Zhang 2021).

LINKING THE CHINA SHOCK TO CHINA BASHING

Understanding the politics of Congress during the US–China trade war requires an understanding of how the structural power of pro-engagement interest groups was weaker than it appeared even before Donald Trump ran for office. Since 2001, bilateral trade between the United States and China increased nine-fold from $70 billion to $635 billion in 2017, fueled in no small part by US offshoring, and leading to a ballooning trade deficit. Economists have uncovered the effect of this "China shock" on local labor markets in recent years. They found that import competition contributed to the most dramatic period of decline in US manufacturing after 2001 and that import shocks also contributed to a loss of wages and employment outside of the manufacturing sector (Autor, Dorn, & Hanson 2013). Acemoglu et al. (2016) estimate the resulting loss of employment in the United States during 1999–2011 to be 2–2.4 million jobs. Communities with a higher concentration of lost manufacturing jobs experienced reduced lifetime earnings, higher rates of substance abuse, more broken families, falling property values, a shrinking tax base, and growing demand for government transfers.

The economic gains of engagement with China were concentrated while the societal losses were greater than anticipated and more widely felt. The business executives who lobbied to get China into the WTO reaped enormous profits; for example, Boeing's China revenue increased over six-fold between 2000 and 2015 and General Motors now sells more cars in China than in the United States (Davis & Wei 2020, 121). American consumers also benefited from trading with China, paying reduced prices for household goods at Walmart and on Amazon. But the economic costs were concentrated in industries and regions competing with cheaper Chinese imports. Manufacturing jobs in furniture and appliances fell by 42 percent and 75 percent in clothing and millions of workers, most of whom never made it beyond high school, were laid off (Davis & Wei 2020, 115). These factory closures were concentrated in the Appalachian Southeast and smaller industrial cities in the Midwest, and tended to devastate the surrounding communities, shuttering shops and restaurants that could no longer stay afloat with the loss of wage-earning customers. Contrary to abstract economic theories about creative destruction, where workers in import-competing industries would find work in the new jobs created by trade, many of those laid off were unable to make use of trade-adjustment assistance (TAA) or government assistance to attend community college. Those who had marketable skills would move out and those left behind became more dependent on government disability and, all too often, on opioids and other drugs (Davis & Wei 2020, 115). In these places, some sort of political backlash was inevitable.

The Congressional Backlash against China Predates Trump

The steady increase of China bashing in congressional communications and campaigns predates Donald Trump and can be traced back to the political responses to the economic impact of the China shock. It is important to remember that there never existed a pro-China constituency in the United States, only a pro-trade constituency which pushed through PNTR with China over the objections of a considerable anti-China sentiment in the US Congress. In the years following China's WTO accession, it gradually became clear that underlying political differences between the United States and China over human rights practices and Asia-Pacific security would not be magically resolved by economic engagement even as trade and investment with China began to create its own challenges. The War on Terror following 9/11 would temporarily distract the Washington establishment from China but a grassroots narrative was emerging, particularly in the districts most exposed to Chinese import competition, that calls into question the wisdom of engagement with China. What began as a politically convenient narrative has morphed into a full-blown case of buyer's remorse over trade liberalization with China with the election of Donald Trump.

China bashing would become a pervasive feature of congressional campaigns, especially after the global financial crisis of 2008–2009. Campaign ads criticizing candidates for being "soft on China" aired in forty-three of fifty seriously competitive House races in 2010 (Wichowsky & Weiss 2020). China made the top-ten list of issues in 2010 Democratic ads, exceeding appeals about the economy. China also made the top list of issues during the 2012 congressional elections, mentioned more frequently than social security, education, or the military in Republican ads. By 2010, trade would eclipse human rights and Taiwan as the main driver of negative congressional sentiment towards China and members representing districts more exposed to import competition were more likely to vote against China (Kuk, Seligsohn, & Zhang 2018). They find that, after 2003, members of Congress representing districts more adversely impacted by import competition more exposed to trade were more likely to vote against China, controlling for ideology and partisanship. By contrast, import competition was not a significant predictor of earlier congressional opposition to granting most-favored nation status to China (suggesting that voting on these crucial pieces of legislation was driven by noneconomic concerns such as human rights). In other words, the China shock became a motivating factor for legislators taking "tough" positions on trade as well as nontrade issues.

China Bashing to Save Free Trade

The congressional about-face on China in the 2000s was most dramatic among Republican legislators. Political scientists hold that trade liberalization creates both winners and losers, and the China shock was no exception. There were widespread welfare gains to American business and consumers from Chinese exports, but the negative impact on the manufacturing industry was acute, localized, and prolonged. A naive model of political economy would suggest that voters in the districts that experienced high import competition would punish incumbent politicians and support more protectionist economic policies. One might also expect that the China shock should favor the Democratic Party electorally and disadvantage the Republican Party, in light of the GOP's long history of free-trade advocacy (Destler 2005) in general and its support for PNTR in particular. But such a model underestimates the agency of legislators and fails to take into account the important mediating role of political communications in helping frame complex issues to voters.

Kuk, Seligsohn, and Zhang (2018) analyzed congressional press releases to demonstrate how Republican legislators engaged in more anti-China rhetoric in press releases when their districts are hit hard by Chinese imports. But import competition did not change how politicians in either party communicated about trade issues more generally. They used the China shock data from Autor et al. (2016) to map import competition per worker by congressional district. Figure 12.2 from Kuk et al. (2018) shows the uneven impact across the country—the districts affected most are concentrated in the Southeast and Midwest and represented by both Republicans and Democrats. But the ramping up of anti-Chinese rhetoric is especially pronounced among Republicans because Republican legislators are more constrained by their party platform from advocating for trade protectionism relative to Democrats.

Blaming the negative externalities of import competition on China rather than on trade policy has allowed Republican incumbents to continue to support their party's free trade platform without alienating their constituents. The concentrated job losses due to the China shock occurred during an otherwise booming economy and under the Republican administration of George W.

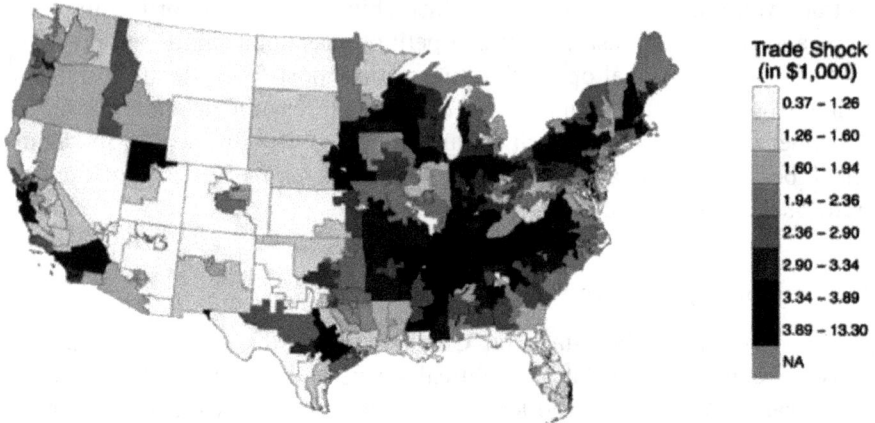

Figure 12.2.   Distribution of China Trade Shock across Congressional Districts
Source: Kuk, Seligsohn, and Zhang (2018)

Bush, which championed trade liberalization in its foreign policy. The Republican Party's 2000 platform described trade as "the force of economic freedom." But even as the Bush administration negotiated thirteen new free trade agreements (FTAs), a backlash to trade was building, unseen, at the grassroots level. Kuk et al. (2018) show that, between 2005 and 2010, legislators from districts more exposed to Chinese import competition began communicating with their constituents in fundamentally different ways from their more insulated colleagues. They found that, even though Chinese imports impacted both Republican- and Democrat-held districts, Republican politicians engage in more anti-China rhetoric in press releases when their districts are hit hard by Chinese imports. But import competition did not change how politicians in either party communicated about trade issues more generally. They attribute this partisan shift in political communication strategy to the fact that Republican legislators are more constrained by their party platform from advocating for trade protectionism relative to Democrats. The modern Republican party is an uneasy alliance of pro-business interests and rural voters united by conservative social values. These two wings of the GOP united to deliver critical votes for the extension of permanent normal trade relation (PNTR) status to China in 2000, a decision few congressional Democrats supported due to opposition of labor unions.

After the China shock, Republicans in trade exposed communities began to sound more and more like their Democratic colleagues, quietly moving away from "free trade" toward and even beyond the traditional Democratic position on "fair trade." Their congressional communications not only used more negative words when they discussed China issues but also used more words such as "currency," "imports," "steel," "prices," "manufacturing," "workers," and "trade" when discussing China topics (Kuk et al. 2018). Remarkably these same Republicans vote in large majorities for additional free trade agreements such as the Central America Free Trade Agreement (CAFTA) in 2005 where there were 202 Republican ayes to 27 noes, the South Korea–United States Free Trade Agreement (KORUS) in 2012 where there were 219 Republican ayes to 21 noes, and free trade agreements with Australia (198 to 24), Colombia (231 to 9), Panama (234 to 6), Peru (176 to 16), Chile (195 to 23), Oman (199 to 29), Bahrain (212 to 13), Morocco (203 to 18), and Singapore (197 to 27).

The Short-Term Appeal and Long-Term Consequences of China Bashing

China bashing was an appealing political narrative because it was relatively costless, at least at first. The Clinton, Bush, and Obama administrations favored engagement, tolerating congressional condemnations of the PRC but pushing back against congressional efforts to sanction China or restrict trade through legislation. The Clinton administration put pressure on legislators to ensure renewal of MFN and passage of PNTR, the Bush administration resisted bipartisan legislation favoring negotiation of a Free Trade Agreement (FTA) with Taiwan, and the Obama administration threatened to veto congressional efforts to label China a currency manipulator.

These narratives of Chinese cheating became pervasive as a result of congressional efforts even though they were not followed up by successful policy. Chinese cheating and the trade deficit are much easier to explain to voters and deal with than globalization and automation even though they are only partial truths. If American communities were devastated by trade competition with China, it must not be due to the creative destruction brought about by trade or the lack of competitiveness due to underinvestment in infrastructure, but because the devious Chinese are cheating their way to success. The fundamental cause of a trade deficit is an imbalance between a country's savings and investment rates but legislators understandably did not want to tell voters to spend less and save more. The combination of automation and globalization threatens nonmanufacturing as well as manufacturing jobs (Autor, Dorn, & Hanson 2015) but it is much easier to blame foreigners (China) and immigrants (Mexicans) than these faceless structural forces (Wu 2020). Globalization and automation are admittedly harder public policies to solve; there are no easy political targets because voters are themselves responsible for these trends and they require major investments at a time of growing budget deficits.

Narratives matter in politics. For American politicians, China became a political shorthand for the problems with globalization, particularly after the Great Recession. The story of a cheating China taking advantage of American workers proved to be an emotive and memorable one. It allowed legislators to frame anxiety about globalization and automation in nationalistic, even xenophobic, terms that were easily accessible to American voters. It is also a simplistic narrative that does not capture the costs and benefits of trade liberalization. The United States also runs high trade deficits with Germany, Japan, and South Korea and outsources jobs to India and Vietnam. But China was an easy scapegoat in part because it was the largest exporter to the United States and most associated with outsourcing. It also helped that American voters know very little about China, few have ever traveled there, and so it was a blank slate on which politicians can project their favorite political narrative. As the journalist James Palmer insightfully observed, "The people telling these tales aren't interested in complexities or, really, in China. They're making domestic arguments and expressing parochial fears. Their China isn't a real place but a rhetorical trope, less a genuine rival than a fairy-tale bogeyman" (Palmer 2015). A similar distortive process took place in the 1980s when Japan was America's favorite political bogeyman. It parallels the ongoing debate about immigration, where Mexicans, who, despite representing only 27 percent of immigrants in 2000s, became a political shorthand for the entire issue.

The fact that China became an American political scapegoat does not excuse or legitimate the many ways that Chinese trade practices stretched or broke WTO rules. There have been well documented cases of intellectual property theft, industrial espionage, dumping, and industrial subsidies involving Chinese companies (Davis & Wei 2020; Blustein 2019). Rather it is an argument about how these events are interpreted and given political meaning. Scapegoating is most evident when the narrative outlives the practice in question, as is the case with currency manipulation. US policy makers criticized China for engaging in currency manipulation—intervening in the foreign exchange market to keep exports cheap—since the mid-2000s when the dollar–renminbi exchange rate remained constant from 2002 to 2005 and leading senators Charles E. Schumer and Lindsay Graham to introduce the S.2813: Currency Manipulation Definition Bill in 2006. But the evidence is clear that the renminbi has strengthened 35 percent against the US dollar since then, meaning the price of Chinese exports to the United States rose by more than one-third (Klein 2015). This is not consistent with the charge of continued intentional underpricing. But some version of the currency manipulation bill was reintroduced in nearly every subsequent session of Congress and the US Treasury finally gave into bipartisan pressure and designated China as a currency manipulator in 2019 anyways to address a problem that has not existed for over a decade.

Reap the Whirlwind: Enter Donald Trump

Trump's unconventional campaign deviated from the norms of presidential contests in many ways, but his China bashing did not actually differ significantly from the well-established playbook from less-well-known congressional races. The anti-China campaign messages that proved effective in local races would reach a national audience with Donald Trump's 2016 presidential campaign. The Trump campaign recycled and refined the protectionist and China-bashing tropes from these local races and earlier failed presidential campaigns of Ross Perot and Pat Buchanan into potent and effective sound bites that fused economic nationalism with xenophobic appeals (Irwin 2017). Economically aggrieved voters at Trump's rallies were not hearing his message of economic nationalism for the first time. Instead, Trump's China-bashing narratives likely resonated with voters because local politicians have been expanding on similar themes for over a decade.

Trump's campaign picked up on the fact that rising import competition, specifically from China, weakened grassroots support for the Republican Party's pro-trade platform. According to Davis and Wei (2020, 142), "China became the Trump campaign's symbol for lost manufacturing jobs and the bosses and politicians who sold out blue-collar America." He emphasized trade with China to a remarkable degree in his public remarks. This topic was the subject in 1.25 percent of all paragraphs in his speeches from 2017 to 2019, both on the campaign trail and in office (Lee & Osgood 2020, 5). Many of these speeches mention offshoring, point to the trade deficit to illustrate how China is "ripping us off," and criticize the fecklessness of previous administrations and earlier trade negotiators.

As research by Kuk et al. (2018) suggests, Republican attitudes on China and trade have been evolving—long before Trump's China-bashing presidential campaign. Trump's China advisor Peter Navarro pointed to this growing "schism" between registered Republicans and the party leadership on trade in a 2016 interview with Politico. The Trump campaign went a step further to not only blame Beijing for taking advantage of America but also blame feckless American politicians who sold out their country. According to Steve Bannon, this message polled well with working-class voters who wanted to follow a leader "return America to its former greatness" (Davis & Wei 2020, 142).

Wichowsky and Weiss (2020) found that challengers who were attacked for being "soft on China" were more likely to cosponsor China-related legislation, while incumbents who were attacked for being soft on China took tougher positions on China after reelection. So, it should come as no surprise that, like legislators who ran China-bashing campaigns, President Trump would carry out many of his "tough on China" campaign messages in office. Perhaps more ominously, President Joe Biden, who was attacked in the 2020 campaign as being "soft on China" might also be pressured to adopt tougher positions on China after his election.

THE NEW EQUILIBRIUM:
UNCHECKED ECONOMIC HOSTILITY

The rise of China bashing in Congress was coupled by a decline of enthusiasm towards China within the US business community. The lack of organized opposition by the business lobby along with the bipartisan consensus in Congress towards taking a tougher stance toward China help explain why Trump faced little opposition to his trade war with China. The Trump administration was also genuinely unique in its departure from support for free trade and economic engagement with China, which has been embraced by every US president since Nixon. It leaned into rather than pushed back against the tendency of the US Congress to engage in China bashing. Without structural constraints, it is no surprise that the US–China trade war quickly escalated into one of the largest in history.

The Shifting Allegiance of the Business Lobby

Compared to their active role in lobbying on behalf of granting MFN status to China in the 1990s, American multinational corporations (MNCs) were divided over tariff policy and mostly sat on the sidelines during the onset of the US–China trade war. Zhang (2021) shows how "some [businesses] saw the trade war as a window of opportunity to address their grievances with Chinese industrial policy without realizing the costs of decoupling. Most others only acted to lobby for individual tariff exclusions while doing little to oppose the trade war as a whole. The few that opposed the trade war struggled to gain traction in Congress because of a bipartisan consensus around getting tough China." Zhang attributes the collective action failure that led to the escalation of the US–China trade war to ambivalent distributive politics among MNCs coupled with ideological convergence in Congress towards getting tough on China.

By 2016, many US businesses moved beyond the honeymoon stage of market opening and entered into a troubled relationship with the Chinese government. The idea that American businesses are friends of China mischaracterizes the complex and ambivalent relations firms of varying industries have with China. In the 1990s, a small number of large US MNCs, including Boeing, General Motors, and American International Group, worked closely with the Bush and Clinton administrations to lobby Congress for economic engagement with China (Davis & Wei 2020). These US firms organized to support China trade, both with new organizations and with what became known as the annual "door-knock," where American business groups from throughout the United States visited Washington to lobby Capitol Hill. The result appears to be a decline in the number of trade-related votes hostile to China for much of the 2000s. The reward US firms received for their troubles was the opening of the China market to American trade and investment. Some of the firms from the original group such as Boeing and GM opened from market opening but so did a range of new entrants such as Best Buy, Apple, and Qualcomm as well as countless small and medium enterprises and farmers that incorporated China into their value chains or sold their products to Chinese consumers.

In the subsequent years, many large MNCs have become increasingly pessimistic about the business climate in China and increasingly vocal critics of Chinese industrial policy. Policies like Made in China 2025 raised alarm among foreign MNCs in China because they feared that Beijing would unfairly tilt the playfield by favoring domestic Chinese companies in competition with their Western counterparts in order to reach these ambitious targets. In Donald Trump and his USTR, Robert Lighthizer, US MNCs found a pair of sympathetic ears on the need to confront China. Quietly, they fed the Trump administration the information it needed to start an offensive against Chinese economic policies. Many of their grievances are catalogued in the USTR's Section 301 report, which acted as a declaration of war and rallying cry for aggrieved US businesses when it was released in March 2018. Influential industry associations such as the US Chamber of Commerce, Business Roundtable, and US–China Business Council all testified in the USTR's public hearings on Section 301 and expressed ambivalent views critical of both China's trade practices and the Trump administration's proposed tariffs. Many US business leaders believed that China has dragged its feet on economic reforms and expected that Beijing would ultimately back down with a bit of bullying from Donald Trump.

MNC lobbying before the onset of tariffs was muddled by mixed messaging. Tariffs on Chinese imports were both a tax on domestic firms and consumers (which MNCs oppose) and a coercive instrument used to gain bargaining leverage with Beijing on a host of other issues (which MNCs support). The US–China Business Council (USCBC), which represents over two hundred MNCs that do business with China, took an ambivalent stance in the USTR hearings, supporting the Section 301 report findings but opposing the unilateral use of tariffs. Additionally, few of the members of the USCBC testified independently or submitted comments to the USTR (Liu, Vortherms, & Zhang 2020).

In China, analysts and policy makers seemingly failed to account for the ambivalence of US MNCs and continued to count on their traditional allies to put pressure on the Trump administration. Xi also miscalculated, believing "that Trump's tough talk masked a fear about the American economy . . . slowing precipitously" (Davis & Wei 2020, 16) and that China had the upper hand. The combined miscalculation would lead to the escalation of tariffs in 2019 and raise concerns that the world's two largest economies would have to "decouple."

Congress Unleashed, Lobbying Intensifies

Legislators from both parties have become as hawkish or even more hawkish than the Trump administration on China policy. Chinese foreign policy under Xi Jinping, such as the Belt and Road Initiative, have only reinforced the narrative of an increasingly assertive China in Washington. US policymakers seem to agree that being tougher on China is the only bipartisan issue that everyone in Washington can agree on. As Amy Celico, a former China director at the USTR and principal at Albright Stonebridge Group, noted that the president traditionally had more discretion on trade. But Congress has been taking the lead on stricter export controls and investment screening under the Trump administration (Celico 2020).

The 115th Congress (2017–2019) introduced seventy-six pieces of China-related legislation, nearly matching the historic high of eighty-four bills achieved by the 105th Congress. The China bills introduced by the 115th Congress are also more sweeping in scope and more tightly focused on China and the economic challenge it poses to the United States. For example, the Foreign Investment Risk Review Modernization Act of 2017 (FIRRMA) expanded the scope of "covered transaction" subject to the review of the Committee on Foreign Investment in the United States (CFIUS) review. CFIUS analyzes the national security implications of foreign investment in the United States and FIRRMA introduced additional factors that CFIUS could use in order to determine whether a proposed transaction is a national security threat: (1) whether the foreign actor is connected to a country of "special concern"; (2) whether the transaction includes critical technology or infrastructure; (3) the history of the actor in accordance with US laws; (4) the state of the relevant US industry; (5) whether sensitive information is being transacted; and (6) the likelihood of cybersecurity risks as a result of the transaction. FIRRMA gave CFIUS an annual appropriation of $20 million and created a mandatory filing requirement for foreign firms (which used to be voluntary) and to increase the resources of the committee, created a filing fee of 1 percent that is not to exceed $300,000. The expansion of CFIUS by FIRRMA was widely seen as a response to rising security concerns regarding foreign direct investment (FDI), primarily by Chinese firms, in US high-tech companies.

The 116th Congress (2019–2021), which is still in session as of the writing of this chapter, will likely shatter the record of the 115th Congress in the volume of anti-China legislation. Legislators have introduced bills like S.945: Holding Foreign Companies Accountable Act, H.R.6210: Uyghur Forced Labor Prevention Act, S.2502: American Security Drone Act of 2020, and H.R. 595: Denying Chinese Investors Access to US Small Business Aid Act that would be highly disruptive to bilateral economic relations if passed.

Tariffs Bring New Dilemmas

The persistence of the Trump administration's tariffs created an economic dilemma for businesses and a political dilemma for Congress. "Being tough on China is not a posture, not a strategy" (Celico 2020). And the Trump administration's embrace of tariffs is beginning to create economic consequences for American businesses. Evident from the USTR hearings and comments process is the number of American companies that are harmed by and oppose tariffs. Of the four thousand companies that submitted comments on tariffs (covering $260 billion in Chinese imports), 85.6 percent of participating firms are opposed to tariffs and 87.9 percent say that tariffs would disrupt their supply chains (Lee & Osgood 2020).

Most of these firms seeking to protect their sourcing from China overwhelmingly requested exclusion from tariffs. Lobbying targeting the USTR also increased dramatically as a result of the US–China trade war. According to OpenSecrets, the number of firms lobbying the USTR increased from 541 in 2017 to 697 in 2018 (29 percent increase YoY) to 719 in 2019 (3 percent increase YoY). Companies large and small affected by tariffs also began to lobby their legislators to help avert their costs. As Zhang (2021) has argued, "The exclusion process creates concentrated costs (individual firms must pay for lobbying) and diffuse benefits (removal of tariffs will benefit all firms in a product category). Faced with these incentives, individually rational firms overwhelmingly opted to hire lobbyists to voice support for the trade war while seeking individual exclusions for their own products." Normally a narrow interest group lobby for a particular piece of trade legislation, the modal number of firms lobbying on a typical trade bill is actually one (Kim 2017).

By contrast, over four thousand firms attempted to lobby the USTR on the single issue of Section 301 tariffs and countless more have tried to solicit the help of their local legislators. The channels for access in Washington remain constant, but as the number of firms trying to squeeze through these channels is increasing, to get their voices heard, they are crowding each other out. This has resulted in a classic tragedy of the commons where few have succeeded in obtaining exclusions while the majority of firms will continue to pay the cost of high tariffs.

Members of Congress have the incentive to maximize economic gains and minimize economic losses because failure to do so would render them vulnerable to electoral backlash from their constituents. Unlike the costless China bashing that many of them tolerated and indulged in, many of the trade war measures hurt their constituents. Republican legislators, in particular, face a dilemma on the current trade war because their president (who is popular with their voter base) started the trade war but many of their constituents are hurt by the tariffs. The author collected public comments, open letters, and bills sponsored by members of Congress in response to the USTR's Section 301 tariffs since 2018. This data was coded for whether they are opposed or in favor of tariffs and the constituency they are writing on behalf of. Figure 12.3 is a heatmap of the United States that demonstrates the relative participation of members of Congress and senators of each state in the USTR public comments forum. Legislators from California, Kansas, and South Carolina were among the most active. Less than 10 percent of House members took any public

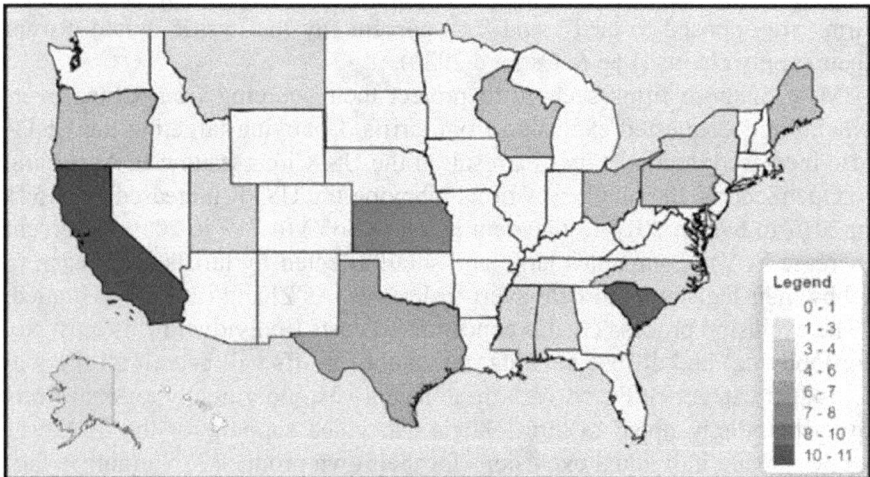

Figure 12.3. Heat Map of Congressional Participation in USTR Comments
Source: original figure by author

action compared to 30 percent of the Senate. Of the seventy-five actions by House members, 27 percent (twenty) were initiated by Democrats and 73 percent were by Republicans (fifty-five). Of the eighty-five actions by Senators, 19 percent (sixteen) were initiated by Democrats and 81 percent (sixty-nine) by Republicans. Most of the comments from legislators are written on behalf of a specific company or industry and requesting exemption of products that deal greatly with the state's/region's economy. A few pieces of legislation were introduced, such as H.R. 7665: Export Tariff Act, cosponsored by Rep. Jackie Walorski (R-IN) and Rep. Collin Peterson (D-MN) to provide American businesses another year of relief from tariffs under Section 301 of the Trade Act of 1974 by extending product exclusions currently in effect.

The bipartisan consensus in Congress around confronting China is unlikely to fade under a Biden presidency. But as the Trump administration enters its lame duck period, there are signs that more coordinated opposition to the China tariffs may emerge. Over thirty-five hundred US companies filed lawsuits in the US Court of International Trade against USTR Robert Lighthizer and the Customs and Border Protection agency for what they call the unlawful escalation of the US trade war with China through the imposition of a third and fourth round of tariffs (Shepardson 2020). Additionally, major MNCs like Apple, Coca-Cola, and Nike are stepping up their efforts to lobby Congress to alter legislation cracking down on imports of goods made with forced labor from persecuted Muslim minorities in China (Swanson 2020) while associations like the Business Roundtable have begun lobbying the incoming Biden administration for tariff relief (Schwartz 2020).

CONCLUSION

The Trump administration was not the first to link China and trade in an economic nationalist message. One of the most surprising political effects of the economic engagement with China and the subsequent China shock was the division of the Republican party, the party that had consistently supported engagement with China in the 1990s and championed PNTR. Republican representatives whose districts are adversely affected by the import shock adopted a much more critical view of trade with China than do either Republicans in less affected districts or most Democrats. The Trump campaign amplified this message that resonated with working-class voters and indulged in the same kind of China bashing that members of Congress running in competitive districts have relied on since the Great Recession.

Viewed from this perspective, the China trade war was not a flash in the pan, but rather a match dropped on a mound of kindling that has slowly been accumulating after decades of perceived economic grievance. Political opposition to the China trade war has been muted because Republicans are increasingly skeptical of trade with China and Democrats continue to be skeptical of trade. Paul Blustein summarized this growing skepticism towards engagement: "What the supporters of China's WTO accession really got wrong was correctly identified by Robert Lighthizer in 2010 when he derided their hubris for assuming that WTO membership would lead Beijing to adopt a Western economic, political, and legal model" (Blustein 2019, 219). Unlike previous presidents, Trump leaned into and fed the new bipartisan consensus in Congress that views trade and investment as part of a broader strategic competition between the United States and China. Frustration with China's post-WTO politics led its past allies in the US business community to withhold political pressure at the onset of the trade war, allowing the conflict to escalate.

The China trade war was sold as a populist response to a working-class problem but actually solved few of the issues like offshoring or creating manufacturing jobs. But unlike congressional China bashing, which scores political points without actually doing economic damage, tariffs carry real economic consequences for US businesses. By 2019, the trade war had cost the United States three hundred thousand jobs and shut down eighteen hundred factories, leaving American workers and consumers bearing the consequences of the conflict (Polaski et al. 2020, 17). Lincicome (2020) found that the conventional wisdom that protectionist policy benefits districts with large manufacturing sectors has not held through the trade war as the US manufacturing industry is highly dependent on imported intermediate goods and those districts have experienced lower GDP and employment growth due to the trade war.

The incoming Biden administration must devise a strategy to address the economic costs of maintaining tariffs without appearing to be soft on China. It will inherit a Congress brimming with legislative proposals, from banning pension funds from investing in China to sanctioning state-owned enterprises, to accelerate economic decoupling from China. Congress has historically been more involved in the details of China policy more so than any other aspect of foreign policy. It has become even more engaged on the issue as a result of both real economic grievances and convenient half truths about Chinese cheating. But congressional power is a hammer. Its constitutional power of the purse and ability to create new statutes gives it weight but it is a blunt instrument because it tends to botch the policy details. With the proper strategy, the Biden administration can harness the power of Congress as a source of leverage to negotiate a deal with Beijing that Donald Trump talked about but could not deliver. If it adopts some version of the economic engagement pursued by the Clinton administration in 1997, it will likely find allies in the

US business community who hope that Biden will roll back tariffs and pursue a more judicious foreign policy towards China.

NOTES

1. Acknowledgments: I would like to thank Spencer Shanks and Quinn Lee for their invaluable research assistance as well as my coauthors John Kuk and Deborah Selighsohn for helping develop the research agenda referenced in this chapter.

REFERENCES

Acemoglu, Daron, David Autor, David Dorn, Gordon H. Hanson, and Brendan Price. 2016. "Import Competition and the Great US Employment Sag of the 2000s," *Journal of Labor Economics* 34(S1).

Autor, David, H., David Dorn, and Gordon H. Hanson. "The China syndrome: Local labor market effects of import competition in the United States." American Economic Review 103, no. 6 (2013): 2121–68.

Autor, David H., David Dorn, and Gordon H. Hanson. 2015. "Untangling Trade and Technology: Evidence from Local Labour Markets," *Economic Journal* 125(584): 621–646.

Autor, David H., David Dorn, and Gordon H. Hanson. 2016. "The China Shock: Learning from Labor-Market Sdjustment to Large Changes in Trade," *Annual Review of Economics* 8: 205–240.

Blustein, Paul. 2019. *Schism: China, America, and the Fracturing of the Global Trading System.* CIGI.

Celico, Amy. 2020. "Remarks at CHINA Town Hall: Economics & Trade," National Committee on US-China Relations, November 17, 2020. https://www.ncuscr.org/event/CTH-2020-economics-trade

Davis, Bob, and Lingling Wei. 2020. *Superpower Showdown: How the Battle between Trump and Xi Threatens a New Cold War.* New York: Harper Business.

Destler, Irving M. *American trade politics.* Columbia University Press, 2005.

Dumbaugh, Kerry. 1999. China and the 105th Congress: Policy Issues and Legislation, 1997–1998, report. Washington, DC.

Irwin, Douglas A. 2017. "The False Promise of Protectionism: Why Trump's Trade Policy Could Backfire," *Foreign Affairs* 96: 45.

Kim, In Song. "Political cleavages within industry: Firm-level lobbying for trade liberalization." American Political Science Review 111, no. 1 (2017): 1–20.

Klein, Michael. 2015. "What You May Not Know about China and Currency Manipulation," Brookings Institution. https://www.brookings.edu/opinions/what-you-may-not-know-about-china-and-currency-manipulation/

Kuk, John Seungmin, Deborah Seligsohn, and Jiakun Jack Zhang. 2018. "From Tiananmen to Outsourcing: The Effect of Rising Import Competition on Congressional Voting towards China," *Journal of Contemporary China* 27(109): 103–119.

Lee, Jieun, and Iain Osgood. 2020. "Firms Fight Back: Production Networks and Corporate Opposition to the China Trade War." In *Geopolitics, Supply Chains, and International Relations of East Asia,* edited by Etel Solingen. New York: Cambridge University Press.

Lincicome, Scott. 2020. "Tariffs, Michigan, and the Perils of 'Political Protectionism.'" Cato Institute: Research Briefs in Economic Policy.

Liu, Rigao, Samantha Vortherms, and Jiakun Zhang. 2020. "In the Middle: American Multinationals in China and Trade War Politics*," 2020 ISA Midwest Conference Paper.*

Milner, Helen V., and Dustin Tingley. 2015. *Sailing the Water's Edge: The Domestic Politics of American Foreign Policy.* Princeton, NJ: Princeton University Press.

Palmer, James. 2015. "For American pundits, China isn't a country. It's a fantasyland," *Washington Post,* May 29, 2015. https://www.washingtonpost.com/opinions/for-american-pundits-china-isnt-a-country-its-a-fantasyland/2015/05/29/24ba60e0-0431-11e5-a428-c984eb077d4e_story.html

Polaski, Sandra, et al. 2020. "How Trade Policy Failed US Workers—And How to Fix It." Institute for Policy Studies.

Shepardson, David. 2020. "Some 3,500 U.S. companies sue over Trump-imposed Chinese tariffs." Reuters, September 25, 2020. https://www.reuters.com/article/usa-china-tariffs/some-3500-u-s-companies-sue-over-trump-imposed-chinese-tariffs-idUSKCN26H03S

Sutter, Robert, and S. Limaye. 2016. *America's 2016 Election Debate on Asia Policy and Asian Reactions.* Honolulu, HI: East-West Center.

Swanson, Anna. 2020. "Nike and Coca-Cola Lobby Against Xinjiang Forced Labor Bill," *New York Times,* November 29, 2020. https://www.nytimes.com/2020/11/29/business/economy/nike-coca-cola-xinjiang-forced-labor-bill.html

Swartz, Brian. 2020. "Lobbyists begin to prepare for a potential Joe Biden presidency." CNBC, October 19, 2020. https://www.cnbc.com/2020/10/19/lobbyists-begin-to-prepare-for-a-potential-joe-biden-presidency-.html

Wichowsky, Amber, and Jessica Chen Weiss. 2020. "Getting Tough on China: Are Campaign Ads a Signal of Future Policy or Just Cheap Talk?" *Legislative Studies Quarterly.*

Wu, Nicole. 2020. "Misattributed Blame? Attitudes Towards Globalization in the Age of Automation." PhD dissertation, University of Michigan.

Xie, Tao. 2008. *US-China Relations: China Policy on Capitol Hill,* vol. 10. New York: Routledge.

Zhang, Jiakun Jack, Deborah Seligsohn, and John Seungmin Kuk. 2018. "The Partisan Divide in US Congressional Communications after the China Shock," *21st Century China Center Research Paper* 2018-03.

Zhang, Jiakun Jack. 2018. "Chinese Perceptions of Trump's Trade Policy." European Council on Foreign Relations. https://ecfr.eu/publication/china_analysis_trump_opportunity_chinese_perceptions_us_administration262/

Zhang, Jiakun Jack. 2021. "US-China Trade War: Interest Group Politics." In *Research Handbook on Trade Wars*, edited by Ka Zeng. London: Edward Elgar Publishing.

Chapter Thirteen

Trump, Biden, and China

From a Wilsonian World Order to Jacksonian Nationalism

Dean P. Chen

INTRODUCTION

In the tumultuous four years of Donald Trump's tenure as America's forty-fifth president (2017–2021), bilateral relations between the United States and the People's Republic of China (PRC) had reached their lowest point since the two nations normalized their diplomatic ties in January 1979. The trade war between Washington and Beijing—which saw both sides using sharp-elbowed coercive tactics and ratcheting up tranches of retaliatory tariffs—came to a tentative ceasefire on January 15, 2020, when President Trump and China's vice premier Liu He signed the phase one agreement in the East Room of the White House before hundreds of politicians and American business executives (Davis & Wei 2020, 374). The deal not only committed China, over the next two years, to increase its import and purchases of American manufactured, agricultural, and energy goods and services, it also included pledges by Beijing to tighten its protections of intellectual property and eliminate any pressure for US companies to transfer technology to Chinese firms as a condition of market access, licensing, or administrative approvals (Davis & Wei, 2020, 375). In return, the United States would cut by half the tariff rate (from 15 percent to 7.5 percent) imposed on a $120 billion list of Chinese imports (while the 25 percent tariffs on $250 billion of Chinese products would remain in place). A stronger enforcement mechanism, relying on the US–China bilateral consultations instead of the World Trade Organization (WTO)'s arbitration panel, was set up to allow the aggrieved party to reimpose tariffs and other penalties if their complaints are not effectively addressed.

For Trump, the major complaint about the PRC has always been the latter's longstanding unfair economic and businesses practices in dealing with

America.[1] "Right now, unfortunately, it is a very one-sided and unfair one. But, I don't blame China. . . . I do blame past administrations for allowing this out-of-control trade deficit to take place and to grow. We have to fix this because it just doesn't work for our great American companies, and it doesn't work for our great American workers," the president remarked during his state visit to Beijing in November 2017 (Gingrich 2019, 318). He viewed himself as the first and only US leader willing to stand up and capable of standing up against China (Davis & Wei 2020, 141–142). John Bolton, the former national security advisor who worked under Trump from 2018 to 2019, agreed with the president for "appreciate[ing] the key truth that politico-military power rests on a strong economy [and] that stopping China's unfair economic growth at U.S. expense is the best way to defeat China militarily" (Bolton 2020, 289). Tariffs were the bludgeon to rectify Chinese wrongs and push the latter into negotiations that would rebalance Sino-American economic relations. Yet, the president's sole preoccupation, in the first three years of his administration, on reaching a trade deal with Beijing, took precedence over any other sticking points between the United States and China. More often than not, it even took on a transactional or ad hoc nature of quid pro quo interactions with Beijing. Regarding the Chinese Communist Party (CCP)'s crackdowns on democracy and human rights in Hong Kong and Xinjiang, Trump rejected taking firmer stances, lest any such behaviors would derail the trade talks with Beijing. "Who cares about it? I'm trying to make a deal. I don't want anything," recorded Bolton on Trump's reactions toward the thirtieth anniversary of the Tiananmen Square massacre on June 4, 2019 (Bolton 2020, 310). The president's mercurial attitude led some to question whether his hardline China policy was merely a "bumper sticker" (Bolton 2020, 290).

Notwithstanding Trump's initial questioning of the US One-China policy and taking a call from Taiwan's Tsai Ing-wen (Davis & Wei 2020, 161–162), he was "dyspeptic about Taiwan," as one of the favorite comparisons was "to point to the tip of one of his Sharpies and say, 'This is Taiwan,' then point to the Resolute desk and say, 'This is China'" (Bolton 2020, 313). The president was reportedly hesitant about selling Taiwan the F-16s, prompting speculation that he would eventually abandon American support for the democratic island (Bolton 2020, 314). Meanwhile, the US president constantly showered praises on Xi Jinping, the PRC president and CCP general secretary, touting their close friendship. Even though ZTE, a Chinese telecom company, was prosecuted by the US government for committing various criminal activities (including the violations of U.S. sanctions on Iran and North Korea), President Trump decided to relieve some of the Commerce Department's hefty penalties on the Chinese firm after having a phone conversation with Xi (Bolton 2020, 291).

Nonetheless, nationalists in the Trump administration, including Vice President Mike Pence, Secretary of State Michael Pompeo, Secretary of Commerce Wilbur Ross, Attorney General William Barr, National Security Advisor Robert O'Brien, Deputy National Security Advisor Matthew Pottinger, and White House Trade Advisor Peter Navarro took a hardline approach to push back on the PRC, calling the latter an "existential threat" to American national security interests. "In the United States, competition is not a four-letter word," Pottinger said in October 2018. "We at the Trump administration have updated our China policy to bring the concept of competition to the forefront. It's right there at the top of the president's national security strategy."[2] In spite of President Trump's capriciousness and transactional proclivities, the administration hawks have consistently commenced a whole-of-government approach to confront the PRC in the geostrategic, human rights, and high-tech realms. To name just a few instances, the United States has dispatched naval warships to the South China Sea, blocked China's tech giants like Huawei from getting advanced chips and semiconductors, bolstered relations with Taiwan through frequent arms sales (nine packages as of this writing under the Trump government) and high-ranking US official visits to Taipei, sanctioned leaders of Hong Kong and Xinjiang for their anti-democratic/human rights laws and activities, closed the PRC's Houston consulate over alleged espionage, raised alert on the CCP's misinformation and influence campaigns to affect American politics and civil society, restricted Chinese students and scholars having ties with China's military from gaining access to American universities and research institutes, and sought bans on popular Chinese apps like Wechat and TikTok from the US market.

Moreover, the global spread of the coronavirus (COVID-19) from Wuhan, China, since early 2020 further deepened animosity between the United States and China, as both Washington and Beijing exchanged accusations over the source of the pandemic. With that, Trump, to salvage his declining popularity in a presidential election year beset by a severe pandemic and steep economic downturn, labeled the contagion the "Chinese virus" and reversed his friendly attitude toward Xi Jinping, admitting he "used to like the Chinese leader but didn't feel the same way now."[3] The president ultimately closed ranks with his nationalist officials by championing their rollback on the decades-long engagement policy with China.[4]

MAIN ARGUMENTS

The Trump administration's toughening-up policy on China is doubtlessly shaped by multiple factors. There is the shifting international systemic dynamics, wherein a rising revisionist state (PRC) seeks to challenge the status-quo hegemonic power (America), as argued by Graham Allison, who called that both nations are in a "Thucydides Trap." Hence, a destined clash may be inevitable (Allison 2018). Domestic factors within the United States—heightening congressional hostility, public angst over Beijing's increasingly belligerent foreign policy behaviors and infringement on human rights, and the business interests' growing frustrations with China's statist model in undermining free and fair market competitions—have also played an important role behind the deterioration of Sino-American relations. The PRC's global reputation, according to poll numbers released by the Pew Research Center on October 6, 2020, is at its lowest in years. In fact, a massive 74 percent of Americans have negative views about China.[5]

This chapter, nonetheless, stresses the role of a set of "deeply rooted approaches" or "traditions" of American foreign policy, which "informs the democratic process and ensures that most of the time the country ends up adopting policies that advance its basic interests" (Mead 2002, 86–87). These traditions or strategic cultures essentially provide the "security imaginary" that allows US policy elites and domestic actors to interpret and assess external threats, from the standpoint of American values, socioeconomics, and political and national security interests, and come up with the most appropriate course of strategic actions to respond and address the foreign challenges (Weldes 1999). I attempt to explain how the shift from Wilsonian liberal internationalism toward the America First Jacksonian nationalism has coincided with the deterioration of Sino-American ties, and together they've accounted for a recalibration of US–China strategy, essentially switching from liberal engagement toward greater zero-sum confrontations.

The interaction between power politics and ideational factors leading to a major shift in foreign policy is built on the international relations theory of neoclassical realism (Rose 1998; Zakaria 1998; Ripsman et al. 2016). The argument states that even though international structure constrains the overarching direction of a state's strategic approach, the specific contours of that policy are shaped and filtered by its internal-level variables, which, for instance, include the central decision makers' perceptions of international balance of power and their interpretations of national interests given the material capabilities and actions of their allies and adversaries (Rose 1998, 146–147). Consequently, Washington's revised China strategy is a function of both the increasingly combative relations between the United States and China (a systemic-level factor) and the emergence of an "inward-looking nationalism" or "hegemonic retrenchment" (a domestic-level determinant), which echoes Trump's Jacksonian-Fortress America tradition (Schweller 2018, 25–26).

The Jacksonian foreign policy perspective (named after America's first populist president, Andrew Jackson, who served between 1829 and 1837) has been upheld by President Trump, who stressed defending and protecting America's folk community, which includes blue-collar workers, farmers, small-business entrepreneurs, gun enthusiasts, and religious nativists mostly from the southern and western hinterlands of the United States and their values as his top priority (Cha 2017, 83–97). This "instinctively democratic and populist" notion is manifested in the heartland America's suspicion of the elite establishment of the western and eastern seaboards, which tend to advance the Wilsonian internationalist outlook (named after President Woodrow Wilson, in office between 1913 and 1921) espousing globalization, free trade, democratic peace, multilateral cooperation with international institutions as well as collective alliances, and opening America to immigration and foreign influences (Mead 2002, 238). The Jacksonian conservative nationalists in the American west and south believe that "capitalists, financiers, and intellectuals in urban areas aim to exploit country workers economically and tarnish their authentic national (i.e., white and Christian) identities in the name of cosmopolitanism and multiculturalism" (Cha 2017, 85). While Jacksonians today are more receptive than in the past to non-White and non-Anglo cultures, they've maintained an exclusivist attitude toward "outsider" races, genders, and ethnic groups, blaming them for wasteful social-welfare spending and criminal activities that they believe ultimately contaminate the American system (Nau 2015, 42–43).

The Jacksonian and Wilsonian traditions differ in their normative orientations, and their policy proposals and priorities have "developed over time in response to historical, social, and economic changes both within the United States and beyond its border" (Mead 2002, 89). However, it is important to view these two schools of thoughts as complementing rather than being mutually exclusive of each other (Hemmer 2015, 22–23), as they both seek to effectively defend and strengthen US national interests, albeit with different means. During the Cold War, for instance, "Wilsonians linked their vision of a universal moral order on earth to the concrete needs of the American hegemony whereas Jacksonians provided forty years of broad and unwavering popular support for the bloody and dangerous [US–Soviet struggles]" (Mead 2002, 89). Yet, despite their mutual agreement that American democracy is the core foundation of US containment policy, Jacksonians (e.g., congressional Republicans like Senators William Knowland, William Jenner, and Barry Goldwater) regard that democratic experiment as unique, worthy to be emulated by other nations (if they wish to follow) but it should not by imposed upon other nations, whether through coercive or multilateral initiatives. In contrast, the Wilsonians (e.g., Presidents Harry Truman, John F. Kennedy, Ronald Reagan, and George H. W. Bush) believe it would be conducive to American security to spread republican principles and institutions abroad, even by armed interventions and regime change if necessary (Dueck 2020, 65–74). Joe Biden's election as the forty-sixth US president in the wake of a contentious and bitter 2020 race may revert to some of the Wilsonian policies of the pre-Trump era. However, the strong nationalist forces and anti-China sentiments unleashed by Trump will check against the Biden administration from returning to the liberal engagement with the PRC, even though the bilateral competitions would be managed to prevent a total break or a new Cold War between Washington and Beijing.

POST–WORLD WAR II WILSONIAN LIBERALISM

For the most part following the end of World War II, US foreign policy preferences are delimited or circumscribed to a great extent by the American national identity embedded in the so-called "liberal tradition" or "Open Door world culture" (Hartz 1955; Williams 1959; Ikenberry 2011; Smith 2017). On January 8, 1918, President Woodrow Wilson articulated the vision of a liberal, rules-based world order anchored in democracy, free trade, international institutions, and collective security, trusting that his plan would "make the world safe for democracy" and end all future wars. However, although Wilson's idealistic experiment in global governance and liberal peace foundered in the interwar years, his program was resurrected after World War II and successfully implemented in the West during the Cold War. In the wake of the Soviet Union's collapse, Washington sought to extend the liberal order globally under the auspices of the US "unipolar moment" (Kegley & Raymond 2021, 122–123). Wilsonianism, as the lodestar of a liberal internationalist grand strategy, believes that US national security "requires that other countries accept basic American values and conduct both their foreign and domestic affairs accordingly" (Mead 2002, 88). International and multilateral cooperation, through institutionalized agreements and economic exchanges, will "engender values of pluralism, tolerance, and eventually democracy" (Nau 2015, 49–50). Even authoritarian regimes will be constrained as they are "locked" into an interdependent web or networks of norms and understandings.

CONSTRUCTIVE ENGAGEMENT WITH THE PRC

The disintegration of the Soviet Union and bankruptcy of communism in the early 1990s elevated America's prestige in its ultimate triumph of economic and political liberalism. The notion of the "end of history" renewed Washington's confidence about China's future (Fukuyama 1992). Although the Tiananmen incident was viewed as a retrograde motion, many assumed that in the long run China would not be able to resist the tendency to evolve toward a more liberal, democratic form of governance (Schell & Delury 2014, 394–395). Hence, between the initial post–Cold War era and commencement of the Trump White House in 2017, US leaders from both the Democratic and Republican Parties had opted for a constructive engagement policy with China to promote its greater integration to a liberal international economic order (Friedberg 2012, 116). When China becomes more deeply vested in such an open and multilateral global system, its aggressive and negative policy tendencies would be retrained or "tied down" (Sutter 2018, 273). Skeptics and critics, however, have remained vigilant and often voiced their concerns in Washington. While acknowledging China's incredible economic achievements, they insist that the CCP leaderships still perceive the world as a zero-sum environment. Beijing, therefore, is merely biding its time to build up its economic, military, and technological capacities. Once attaining power ascendancy, China's nationalistic and expansionist impulses will be revealed. Thus, in addition to engaging China, Washington has also relied upon resolute military power as a counterweight to this potential Asian hegemon, remaining resolute in dealing with their economic and security conflicts as well as human rights issues, while working closely with traditional allies and friends in the Asia-Indo-Pacific region. This engagement + hedging approach, therefore, has allowed Washington to deepen cooperation with the PRC and reassure Beijing that the United States has no intention to stymie its power ascendancy. A prosperous and confident China, in this view, is conducive to American interests as well as global peace and stability. Yet, the United States must also back up its outreach to China with strong military and economic capabilities in order to deter Beijing from pursuing destabilizing actions. Thomas Christensen (2015) noted that the Bill Clinton, George W. Bush, and Barack Obama administrations did this to "shape the choices of a rising China" to become more responsible and integrated into the liberal international order that champions economic interdependence, democracy, and multilateralism.

JACKSONIANISM AND CHINA

Nonetheless, for the first time since the end of World War II, US foreign policy today hinges on an America First vision, predicated on commercial mercantilism, unilateralist diplomacy, and conservative nationalism (Chen 2017, 903–905).[6] Trump is unique for campaigning against the US-led

postwar liberal order, arguing that American leadership and free-trading globalism were hurting the United States (Jervis et al. 2018, 62–63). In 2016,
he ran as a furiously populist and anti-establishment nationalist. The image
offered "was of a kind of Fortress America, separated from transnational
dangers of all kinds by a series of walls—tariff walls against foreign exports, security walls against Muslim terrorists, literal walls against Hispanic
immigrants, and with the sense that somehow all these dangers might be
interrelated under the rubric of the 'false song of globalism'" (Dueck 2020,
108–109). A great driving force for the voters' support of populist-nationalist
candidates like Trump is a sense of cultural upheaval. The very same rise
of postmaterialist cosmopolitan, multicultural issues and values that inspire
liberals has also triggered a culturally conservative reaction from those segments of the public unpersuaded by the benefit of such changes. Whereas cosmopolitan liberals champion progressive values (environmental protections,
gun controls, abortion, LGBTQ rights, and same-sex marriage), populist
nationalists embrace traditional and nativist values. Over the past forty years,
the Republican Party's appeals on concerns related to religion, national sovereignty, moral tradition, commercial protectionism, and anti-immigration have
attracted strong support from the White working class—once the mainstay
of the Democratic New Deal coalition. Based in America's Rust Belt small-
town counties in Pennsylvania, Michigan, Wisconsin, and Ohio, these folks
usually are non–college educated and tend to be center-left on economics but
reactionary on cultural matters (Dueck 2020, 148–149).

Trump also lashed out at the seeming weaknesses of presidents from both
parties that allowed these foreign abuses of America's working class to en-
dure while criticizing their venturous military interventions abroad that led
to the unnecessary losses of US lives and financial resources (Brands 2017,
77–78). The conservative nationalists have found their inspirations from an
iconic populist US president, Andrew Jackson, and linked him with Trump's
Fortress America program.

Economic Nationalism and Fortress America

Ronald Inglehart and Pippa Norris (2017) indicated that voters most drawn
to populist-nationalist parties and candidates on both sides of the Atlantic are
indeed concerned by issues of economic inequality and globalization.[7] Profound structural changes transforming the workforce and society in postin-
dustrial economies—including the rise of knowledge economy, technological
automation, global flows of labor, goods, people, and capital, the relative
decline of traditional manufacturing, and migrant inflow—have encouraged
a sense of economic insecurity.

That is a reaction towards the sentiments, shared among many middle- and working-class Americans, who think that China, among other countries, has taken advantage of the US-led liberal free trade policies and international institutions, such as the WTO, as well as America's domestic deregulations of unfettered capitalistic and financial interests to take away jobs, manufacturing opportunities, intellectual property, and other socioeconomic benefits that should rightfully belong to hardworking Americans. Economic inequalities, then, caused huge dislocations and pains among these actors who are becoming more isolated and vulnerable to the global trend of integration (Schweller 2018, 43–45). These nationalist furies, fanned by years of open-ended US global commitments, long (and seemingly losing) wars in Iraq and Afghanistan, and economic fallouts from the global financial crisis of 2008, have culminated in the perception that the Washington elitist establishment (from both the Democratic and Republican administrations) has broken its post–WWII bargain on "embedded liberalism"—that is, subjecting free market globalization to institutionalized political controls at both the domestic and international levels—while allowing for an unrestrained American foreign expansionism to promote overseas democracy, human rights, and various multilateral arrangements and alliance obligations that came at the expenses of American democratic, security, and economic interests (Snyder 2019).

The engagement with China is the epitome of the US internationalist foreign policy. Trade liberalization, in particular, is perceived not just as an instrument of economic policy but also as a path for the PRC to embrace democratization and perpetual peace. However, the Trump administration has rejected that system of ideas. In the words of Robert Lighthizer, the US trade representative, China's accession to the WTO in 2001 is the "most devastating" to America's working class. The "U.S. trade deficit with China ballooned to over half a trillion dollars at its peak, and economists have calculated that the loss of at least two million jobs between 1999 and 2011 was attributable to the influx of Chinese imports. At the same time, Beijing increasingly forced companies to share their technology, a policy that resulted in the theft of billions of dollars of U.S. intellectual property and helped China become the world's top exporters of high-tech products" (Lighthizer 2020, 90).

And, instead of becoming a model global citizen after entering into the liberal international order, China has utilized its economic and technological gains for massive investments in its military capabilities and territorial expansion in the South China Sea and fostering "subversive sharp power projections" abroad to shape and manipulate policy discourse and programs in favor of the Chinese government (Lighthizer 2020, 80). So, as the PRC, under the Xi Jinping administration, steps up assertively in challenging and undermining US global and regional interests, that heightened international rivalry helps to reinforce the American domestic nationalist backlashes, which, together, have led to a disenchantment with the China engagement policy. This policy change has received increasing support from both the government and civil society, across bipartisan line (Diamond & Schell 2019, 15–16).

Thus, to rectify China's economically damaging behaviors, the nationalists have eyed using tariffs to hit on Chinese imports. In line with the nineteenth-century Jacksonian traditions, tariff symbolized what it meant to be an American. A high tariff not only represents commitment to advance domestic marketplace of production and consumption but also protects the integrity of US national identity, independence, and security (Bolt 2017, 100–101). Thus, the conservative nationalists backing Trump have viewed the protection of US sovereignty as more important than abiding to global norms and institutional requirements. Although the United States must stand for freedom internationally, it must focus primarily at defending America's own distinct national culture, society, identity, traditions, and ways of life as they constitute the "very material, human, and autonomous foundations of the American republic" (Dueck 2020, 30). Therefore, Trump, on several occasions, touted "sovereignty" and "nationalism for all," rejecting democracy and human rights promotions (Gingrich 2019, 3). Echoing Trump, David Stilwell, the assistant secretary of state for East Asia, noted that "just as our vision of pluralism at home is rooted in the sovereign rights of individuals, so our vision of pluralism abroad is rooted in the sovereign rights of states."[8] The US goal is not to impose democracy, like a Wilsonian crusader, on any country but to show the world that democracy is possible and that it could be chosen by other countries based on their own free will and cultural requirements. The struggle for freedom must be supported and carried out by those countries' own sovereign initiatives, not by Washington (Mead 2002, 245). In addition, the nationalists' instinct is to maintain strong national military defenses, punish severely any direct threat to US security and interests, shun international accommodations, and otherwise remain detached from multilateral obligations (Brands 2017, 79–80). On China, an emerging realization by US policy makers (across bipartisan line) is that Washington had, for too long, held on to a false democratic peace assumption to constructively engage China, assuming the latter's strong economic achievements would eventually lead to political opening and democratization while becoming a responsible and peaceful stakeholder of the rules-based world order (Pillsbury 2015; Campbell & Ratner 2018). Instead, the PRC "did exactly the opposite of what was predicted" (Bolton 2020, 287–288). In October 2019, Vice President Pence noted that "we must take China as it is, not as we imagine or hope it might be someday."[9]

Thus, the Trump government rejected engagement with China, calling it naïve. In July 2020, Secretary of State Pompeo contended: "President Nixon kicked off our engagement strategy. He nobly sought a freer and safer world, and he hoped that the Chinese Communist Party would return that commitment. American policymakers increasingly presumed that as China became more prosperous, it would open up, it would become freer at home, and indeed present less of a threat abroad, it'd be friendlier. . . . But that age of inevitability is over. The kind of engagement we have been pursuing has not brought the kind of change inside of China that President Nixon had hoped to induce." Rather, the CCP has sought to "exploit our free and open society" and made China into a "new tyranny." To preserve a free twenty-first century, Pompeo stressed that "the old paradigm of blind engagement with China simply won't get it done. We must not continue it and we must not return to it."[10] The secretary's address illustrated an ideational reconstitution driving America's new China policy.

LOOKING AHEAD: THE BIDEN ADMINISTRATION'S CHINA POLICY

The Donald Trump administration has significantly transformed US–China relations, effectively stating that no longer should the United States allow the PRC to free ride or abuse US goodwill, nor should Washington eschew its national interests based on an elusive Wilsonian idealism that expects the latter to reciprocate in kind and accept political liberalization and rules-based behaviors. As Xi Jinping's China turns more autocratic at home and intransigent in its foreign policy adventurism, the nationalistic forces in America are likely to become more firmly entrenched, hence going beyond the Trump presidency and consolidating the bipartisan resolve to counterbalance Beijing.[11] US–Chinese contentions over trade, geopolitics, technology, espionage, COVID-19, and human rights have exacerbated their relationship tremendously. In light of that, Washington has been less constrained to boost relations with Taiwan and reinforce the island democracy's security, autonomy, and international standing. During the old days of engagement, Beijing's displeasure and protests would have sufficed to prompt Washington to apply the brakes. Not anymore in today's strategic environment. Beyond Taiwan's democratic soft power, its technological prowess—flanked by the advanced chip-maker TSMC—also serves as a pragmatic imperative for the United States to ensure the island democracy won't fall into the PRC orbit.[12]

Consequently, under the Joe Biden administration, Washington is unlikely to return to the former constructive engagement with China even though the

Democratic president was once a staunch advocate of that approach in order to transform the PRC. Given the increasingly unfavorable views of the PRC in the United States,[13] the former vice president of the Obama administration has recognized that the United States must "get tough with China," although he would rely more on the "united front of U.S. [democratic] allies and partners to confront Beijing's abusive behaviors and human rights violations" (Biden 2020, 70–71). As a matter of fact, today's Sino-American rivalry predated Trump and started to intensify in the later years of the Obama administration. China's growing belligerence in the East China and South China Seas sharpened the Obama's "pivot" or "rebalancing" strategy to enhance Washington's commitment to the peace and stability across Asia-Pacific (Green 2017, 521–537). While pushing for more frequent US freedom of navigation operations in the South China Sea, President Obama also eagerly promoted the multilateral free-trading condominium, the Trans-Pacific Partnership (TPP) in order to sustain a rules-based international economic system to neutralize Beijing's state-driven Belt and Road Initiative (Economy 2018, 14–15). As a result, the Obama–Biden government then already incubated a counterbalancing measure to curb Beijing's increasing assertiveness.

The Biden administration acknowledged that the Obama government "underestimated the speed with which President Xi Jinping of China would crack down on dissent at home and the use of combination of 5G networks and its Belt and Road Initiatives to challenge U.S. influence."[14] President Biden, therefore, is prone to charter a China course that stresses steady coexistence, buttressed by greater colors of competition even though some modicum of cooperation will still be maintained (Campbell & Sullivan 2019, 97). Indeed, proclaiming "America is back" on the world stage, the president, on February 4, 2021, declared China as the United States's "most serious competitor." He affirmed his administration would "confront China's economic abuses, counter its aggressive, coercive action; to push back on China's attack on human rights, intellectual property, and global governance." Nonetheless, Biden also suggested that Washington would be "ready to work with Beijing when it's in America's interest to do so."[15] That pertains to imminent transnational issues like climate change, nuclear nonproliferation, and fighting against the global pandemic. In a similar vein, Secretary of State Blinken also noted, during the March 2021 Alaska meeting with his Chinese counterparts, that the US relationship with China will be "competitive where it should be, collaborative where it can be, adversarial where it must be."[16]

It's an amalgam of a "Trumpian wariness of China combined with a [Obama-type] preference for caution in handling strategic matters."[17] Although agreeing with the Trump administration's attempt to counteract China's unfair and predatory economic practices, the Biden team has viewed that its predecessor's unilateralist or go-it-alone trade offensive created more harms than benefits to American workers, farmers, industries, and high-tech development. Biden believed that the key rests on revamping America's domestic socioeconomic and educational infrastructures. That would further enhance US competitiveness with China. He posited, "I will make investment in research and development a cornerstone of my presidency, so that the United States is leading the charge in innovation. There is no reason we should be failing behind China or anyone else when it comes to clean energy, quantum computing, artificial intelligence, 5G, high-speed rail, or the race to end cancer as we know it" (Biden 2020, 68–69). Consequently, the rivalry between the United States and China, from Biden's perspective, is also a race about which governance institutions and normative values are superior at delivering tangible results and benefits for the people.[18] When the president gave his first remarks before the joint session of Congress on April 28, 2021, he urged bipartisan support for his $4 trillion government package containing proposed investments in American infrastructure, manufacturing, research, education, and child care. "[Xi Jinping] is deadly earnest about becoming the most significant, consequential nation in the world. He and others—autocrats—think that democracy can't compete in the 21st century with autocracies because it takes too long to get consensus," Biden pitched in a clarion call for immediate action from Congress. China is rapidly catching up, so the United States must be alert and continue to hold the edge by "developing and dominating the products and technologies of the future: advanced batteries, biotechnology, computer chips, clean energy." "America's adversaries—the autocrats of the world—are betting we can't. And I promise you, they're betting we can't. They believe we're too full of anger and division and rage. They look at the images of the mob that assaulted the Capitol as proof that the sun is setting on American democracy. But they are wrong. You know it; I know it. But we have to prove them wrong. We have to prove democracy still works—that our government still works and we can deliver for our people."[19]

Thus, the Trump government's trade war was deemed by the Democratic administration as counterproductive because it not only targeted its economic nationalism on China but also alienated Washington's longtime allies like the EU, Mexico, Canada, South Korea, and Japan. "The Trump administration's decision to pick trade fights with U.S. allies rather than rally them to a common position vis-à-vis China is such a waste of American leverage" (Campbell & Sullivan 2019, 106). While pursuing "competitive interdependence" with China, Brookings analyst Ryan Hass argued that Washington "holds significant advantages over China, which should give the United States confidence to concentrate more on nurturing its own sources of strength and less on defensively seeking to blunt China's progress" (Hass 2021, 7). As well, the United States should embrace "collective leverage"—that is, how the Biden government will handle the Trump tariffs on China or whether or not the United States would reenter the TPP (renamed the Comprehensive and Progressive Agreement for Trans-Pacific Partnership [CPTPP] after President Trump withdrew from it) to jointly pressure China to abide by international economic rules and norms will be decided after consulting with like-minded democratic allies and partners from Europe and Asia.[20] Similar to Trump, Biden has been frustrated with the WTO's deficiencies to effectively address China's statist and anti–free market policies. Nevertheless, he would like to reform that international organization through multilateral negotiations with other trading partners.

In other areas of widening differences between Washington and Beijing, including the Taiwan Strait tensions, South China Sea disputes, suppressions of democratic freedoms and human rights in Hong Kong and Xinjiang, and the CCP's enhanced sharp power campaigns to project authoritarianism abroad, the Biden government will focus on upgrading America's military and technological capacities to more effectively deter China's increasingly sophisticated asymmetric (the anti-access/area denial A2/AD) and cyber powers.[21] Biden, despite his friendly relationship with Xi Jinping dating back to 2011–2012, has voiced concerns about the latter's increasingly authoritarian bent and human rights violations, calling the Chinese leader a "thug," who has neither the respect nor interest for democratic governance.[22] In an interview with CBS News, the president acknowledged the fact that Xi had no "democratic, small D, bone in his body," stressing that Washington and Beijing "need not have a conflict," but there "is going to be extreme competition."[23] All in all, "competition with China is far more than a military one, and its economic, technological, political, and ideological elements cannot be neglected." Successful deterrence also relies on the clear and consistent dialogue/communication of interests and intent in order to minimize the risk of miscalculation.[24]

On the sensitive issue of the Taiwan Strait, Biden was one of the first prominent US politicians congratulating Taiwan's president Tsai Ing-wen on her successful reelection in January 2020 and inauguration in May 2020.[25] Biden's inauguration ceremony on January 20, 2021, was notable for many reasons (e.g., held in the aftermath of the January 6 Capitol riot and in the midst of a severe pandemic), one of which was the attendance by Taiwan's de facto ambassador to the United States (Hsiao Bi-Khim) for the first time since 1979 with an official invitation. The US–Taiwan ties were off to a "strong start" in the Biden era.[26] Days later, responding to the PRC's incessant warplane incursions into Taiwan's airspace, the State Department expressed US concern regarding Beijing's "ongoing attempts to intimidate" the island democracy, urging China to cease these coercive pressure campaigns. Reaffirming Washington's "rock-solid" backing for Taiwan, the Biden government pledged it would support a peaceful resolution of the Taiwan Strait differences "consistent with the wishes and best interests of the people on Taiwan." Though reciting the longstanding US commitments toward the Taiwan Relations Act and three Sino-American Joint Communiqués, it was notable that the State Department eschewed the explicit articulation of the One-China policy. Instead, in line with the former assistant secretary of state of East Asia and Pacific Affairs David Stilwell's August 2020 statement on Taiwan, the Biden government also included Reagan's Six Assurances as another key foundation of the US–China–Taiwan trilateral framework.[27] In Biden's first call with Xi after assuming the presidency, the American leader bluntly called out Beijing's domestic repressions and overseas belligerence. Biden "underscored his fundamental concerns about Beijing's coercive and unfair economic practices, crackdown in Hong Kong, human rights abuses in Xinjiang, and increasingly assertive actions in the region, including toward Taiwan."[28] On April 9, 2021, building on Mike Pompeo's initiative shortly before departing his state secretary post in early January, the Biden administration issued new guidelines to further liberalize contacts between American and Taiwanese officials to encourage both parties to more freely interact with each other going forward.[29]

Right after the loosening of US–Taiwan official meeting protocols, the Biden government made another move to bolster the confidence of Taiwan. On April 14, 2021, to commemorate the forty-second anniversary marking the passage of the Taiwan Relations Act in 1979, President Biden (who was one of the senators then voting for the act) sent a three-person "unofficial delegation" to Taipei, meeting with President Tsai Ing-wen and other Taiwanese officials. It's notable that the three envoys—former U.S. senator Chris Dodd and former deputy secretaries of state Richard Armitage and James Steinberg—were known for not only their longtime support of Taiwan but also their close friendship with Biden. Thus, a White House official described their visit as representing a "personal signal" from the president, "sending an important signal about the U.S. commitment to Taiwan and its democracy."[30]

However, despite calls for a more unequivocal commitment to Taiwan's security,[31] Biden continued to maintain some degree of strategic ambiguity to balance cross-strait interactions. Despite easing the rules on US–Taiwan official encounters and sending the president's confidants as messengers of goodwill to Taipei, the Biden government still rationalized these engagements as compatible with the One-China policy.[32] "Taiwan is not only a potential flash point; it is also the greatest unclaimed success in the history of US–Chinese relations. The island has grown, prospered, and democratized in the ambiguous space between the United States and China as a result of the flexible and nuanced approach generally adopted by both sides. In this way, the diplomacy surrounding Taiwan could serve as a model for the increasingly challenging diplomacy between Washington and Beijing on a variety of other issues, which are similarly likely to include intense engagement, mutual vigilance and a degree of distrust, and a measure of patience and necessary restraint" (Campbell & Sullivan 2019, 102).

Since Trump's America First nationalism has been around taking charge of American foreign policy over the past few years, one can reasonably posit that this policy idea has become more institutionalized and firmly entrenched in Washington's policy making circles (even though Wilsonian internationalism continues to retain many adherents). The highly contested 2020 presidential race—which saw not only the highest voter turnout rate since 1900 but also Biden and Trump each receiving the most (about eighty million) and second-most (about seventy-four million) popular votes in US electoral history—has revealed how deeply polarized American politics has remained.[33] In some battleground states (e.g., Arizona, Georgia, and Wisconsin), Trump only lost by a razor-thin margin, and his conservative (Jacksonian) nationalist base was fully mobilized and, arguably, could have propelled the Republican president to a second term if it weren't for his widely criticized mismanagement of the COVID-19 crisis and the resulting economic decline.[34] The overall political climate was not helped by Trump's (and his supporters') bitter resentment based on their unsubstantiated claims of voting irregularities and fraud, culminating in the violent storming of the US Congress on January 6, 2021. Hence, even though the American president traditionally enjoys a strong prerogative in setting foreign and national security policies, the Biden administration's freedom of actions is expected to encounter greater resistance from congressional Republicans and the overarching conservative nationalist forces that have stayed loyal to Trump and his stridently anti-China policy and rhetoric. Due to Biden's more globalist proclivities, his administration's China policy, while competitive and vigilant, would probably tone down some of the hawkish Cold War rhetoric and zero-sum logic from the Trump administration. Yet, in accordance with the neoclassical realist model discussed earlier, the international realities of US–PRC rivalry and the US domestic Jacksonian nationalism are mutually reinforcing to prevent the Biden White House from vastly changing the increasingly adversarial US–PRC trajectory. In sum, the Biden administration will pursue a multilateral nationalist approach, where competition takes greater center stage than cooperation along with rallying democratic allies and partners, to tackle challenges coming from Beijing.

NOTES

1. While the president is mostly focused on the lopsided US trade deficit relative to China's huge trade surplus, Robert Lighthizer, the US trade representative, has emphasized the greater need to put in place a more robust enforcement infrastructure to ensure China would change the fundamental structural problems of intellectual property theft, forced technology transfers, and the unequal advantages (i.e., subsidies) enjoyed by China's state-owned enterprises and banks in competitions with their American counterparts. See Greg Ip, "The WTO Couldn't Change China, so Robert Lighthizer Found Another Way," *Wall Street Journal* (October 21, 2020), accessible: https://www.wsj.com/articles/the-wto-couldnt-change-china-so-robert-lighthizer -found-another-way-11603308224.

2. Keegan Elmer, "U.S. Tells China: We Want Competition . . . but Also Cooperation," *South China Morning Post* (October 1, 2018), accessible at: https://www.scmp .com/news/china/diplomacy/article/2166476/us-tells-china-we-want-competition -not-cooperation.

3. Ben Westcott, "How China's Xi Jinping Blew a Golden Opportunity with U.S. President Donald Trump," *CNN* (October 31, 2020), accessible at: https://www.cnn .com/2020/10/30/world/trump-china-xi-election-intl-hnk/index.html.

4. Bob Davis, Kate O'Keefe, and Lingling Wei, "U.S's China Hawks Drive Hard-Line Policies after Trump Turns on Beijing," *Wall Street Journal* (October 16, 2020), accessible at: https://www.wsj.com/articles/u-s-s-china-hawks-drive-hard-line-poli cies-after-trump-turns-on-beijing-11602867030.

5. Laura Silver, Kat Devlin, and Christine Huang, "Unfavorable Views of China Reach Historic Highs in Many Countries," Pew Research Center (October 6, 2020), accessible at: https://www.pewresearch.org/global/2020/10/06/unfavorable-views-of -china-reach-historic-highs-in-many-countries/.

6. See also David Sanger, "With Echoes of the '30s, Trump Resurrects a Hardline Vision of 'America First,'" *New York Times* (January 20, 2017). Accessed September 7, 2020. https://www.nytimes.com/2017/01/20/us/politics/trump-resurrects-dark -definition-of-america-first-vision.html.

7. This section is excerpted and updated from this author's other publication. For a complete and substantive treatment of this subject, see Dean P. Chen, "The Trump Administration's One-China Policy: Tilting toward Taiwan in an Era of U.S.-PRC Rivalry?" *Asian Politics & Policy* 11, no. 2 (2019), pp. 250–278.

8. US Department of State, "Remarks by Assistant Secretary David Stilwell: The U.S., China, and Pluralism in International Relations," December 2, 2019. Accessed June 16, 2020. https://www.state.gov/the-u-s-china-and-pluralism-in-international -affairs/.

9. The White House, "Remarks by Vice President Mike Pence at the Frederic V. Malek Memorial Lecture," October 24, 2019. Accessed on October 25, 2019. https:// www.whitehouse.gov/briefings-statements/remarks-vice-president-pence-frederic-v -malek-memorial-lecture/.

10. US Department of State, "Communist China and the Free World's Future," July 23, 2020. Accessed August 1, 2020. https://www.state.gov/communist-china-and-the-free-worlds-future/.

11. Edward Wong and Steven Myers, "Officials Push U.S.-China Relations toward Point of No Return," *New York Times* (July 25, 2020). Accessed August 23, 2020. https://www.nytimes.com/2020/07/25/world/asia/us-china-trump-xi.html.

12. "Trump, Biden, and Taiwan," *Wall Street Journal* (August 14, 2020). Accessed August 20, 2020. https://www.wsj.com/articles/trump-biden-and-taiwan-11597445459.

13. Kat Devlin, Laura Silver, and Christine Huang, "U.S. Views of China Increasingly Negative amid Coronavirus Outbreak," *Pew Research Center* (April 21, 2020). Accessed July 10, 2020. https://www.pewresearch.org/global/2020/04/21/u-s-views-of-china-increasingly-negative-amid-coronavirus-outbreak/.

14. David Sanger, "The End of 'America First': How Biden Says He will Re-Engage with the World," *New York Times* (November 9, 2020), accessible at: https://www.nytimes.com/2020/11/09/us/politics/biden-foreign-policy.html?action=click&module=Top%20Stories&pgtype=Homepage.

15. The White House, "Remarks by President Biden on America's Place in the World," (February 4, 2021), accessible: https://www.whitehouse.gov/briefing-room/speeches-remarks/2021/02/04/remarks-by-president-biden-on-americas-place-in-the-world/.

16. US Department of State, "Remarks: Secretary of State Anthony J. Blinken, National Security Advisor Jake Sullivan, Director Yang and State Councilor Wang at the Top of Their Meeting," March 18, 2021. Accessed: https://www.state.gov/secretary-antony-j-blinken-national-security-advisor-jake-sullivan-chinese-director-of-the-office-of-the-central-commission-for-foreign-affairs-yang-jiechi-and-chinese-state-councilor-wang-yi-at-th/.

17. "Joe Biden's China Policy will be a Mix of Trump's and Obama's," *The Economist* (November 19, 2020), Accessible at: https://www.economist.com/china/2020/11/19/joe-bidens-china-policy-will-be-a-mix-of-trumps-and-obamas.

18. Jeremy Diamond, "Joe Biden Can't Stop Thinking about China and the Future of American Democracy," CNN (April 29, 2021), accessible: https://www.cnn.com/2021/04/29/politics/president-joe-biden-china-democracy/index.html.

19. The White House, "Remarks by President Biden in Address to a Joint Session of Congress," April 28, 2021. Accessed: https://www.whitehouse.gov/briefing-room/speeches-remarks/2021/04/29/remarks-by-president-biden-in-address-to-a-joint-session-of-congress/.

20. David Lawder, "Biden's Trade Policy will Take Aim at China, Embrace Allies," Reuters (November 7, 2020), accessible : https://www.reuters.com/article/usa-election-trade/bidens-trade-policy-will-take-aim-at-china-embrace-allies-idIN L1N2HP289.

21. Michele Flournoy, "How to Prevent a War in Asia," *Foreign Affairs* (June 18, 2020) accessible at: https://www.foreignaffairs.com/articles/united-states/2020-06-18/how-prevent-war-asia.

22. Edward Wong, Michael Crowley, and Ana Swanson, "Joe Biden's China Journey," *New York Times* (September 6, 2020), accessible: https://www.nytimes.com/2020/09/06/us/politics/biden-china.html. See also Steven Lee Myers, "Buffeted by Trump, China Has Little Hope for Warmer Relations with Biden," *New York Times* (November 9, 2020), accessible: https://www.nytimes.com/2020/11/09/world/asia/china-united-states-biden.html?action=click&module=Top%20Stories&pgtype=Homepage.

23. Cassidy McDonald, "Biden Says He Won't Lift Sanctions until Iran Halts Uranium Enrichment," CBS News (February 7, 2021), accessible: https://www.cbsnews.com/news/biden-interview-iran-sanctions-nuclear-agreement/.

24. Flournoy, "How to Prevent a War in Asia."

25. Oriana Skylar Mastro and Emily Young Carr, "Biden will Speak Softer but Act Stronger on Taiwan," *Foreign Policy* (November 20, 2020). Accessed November 22, 2020. https://foreignpolicy.com/2020/11/10/biden-taiwan-election-trump-china/.

26. Ben Blanchard, "Taiwan-Biden Ties Off to Strong Start with Invite for Top Diplomat," Reuters (January 21, 2021), accessible: https://www.reuters.com/article/us-usa-biden-taiwan/taiwan-biden-ties-off-to-strong-start-with-invite-for-top-diplomat-idUSKBN29Q01N

27. US Department of State, "Press Release by Ned Price, Department Spokesperson: PRC Military Pressure Against Taiwan Threatens Regional Peace and Stability" (January 23, 2021), accessible: https://www.state.gov/prc-military-pressure-against-taiwan-threatens-regional-peace-and-stability/.

28. The White House, "Readout of President Joseph R. Biden, Jr. Call with President Xi Jinping of China" (February 10, 2021), accessible: https://www.whitehouse.gov/briefing-room/statements-releases/2021/02/10/readout-of-president-joseph-r-biden-jr-call-with-president-xi-jinping-of-china/.

29. US Department of State, "New Guidelines for U.S. Government Interactions with Taiwan Counterparts," April 9, 2021. Accessed: https://www.state.gov/new-guidelines-for-u-s-government-interactions-with-taiwan-counterparts/.

30. David Brunnstrom and Michael Martina, "Biden Sends Unofficial Delegation to Taiwan in 'Personal Signal,'" Reuters (April 13, 2021), accessible: https://www.reuters.com/article/us-usa-taiwan-delegation-idUSKBN2C02MS.

31. Richard Haass and David Sacks, "American Support for Taiwan Must be Unambiguous," *Foreign Affairs*, September 2, 2020. Accessed September 14, 2020. https://www.foreignaffairs.com/articles/united-states/american-support-taiwan-must-be-unambiguous.

32. David Brunnstrom and Michael Martina, "Biden Sends Unofficial Delegation to Taiwan in 'Personal Signal,'" Reuters (April 13, 2021), accessible: https://www.reuters.com/article/us-usa-taiwan-delegation-idUSKBN2C02MS.

33. Claudia Deane and John Gramlich, "2020 Election Reveals Two Broad Voting Coalitions Fundamentally at Odds," Pew Research Center (November 6, 2020), accessible at: https://www.pewresearch.org/fact-tank/2020/11/06/2020-election-reveals-two-broad-voting-coalitions-fundamentally-at-odds/.

34. Jordan Fabian and Tyler Pager, "Joe Biden Wins U.S. Presidency after Bitter Contest with Trump," Bloomberg (November 7, 2020), accessible at: https://www

.bloomberg.com/news/articles/2020-11-07/joe-biden-wins-u-s-presidency-after-bitter
-contest-with-trump.

REFERENCES

Allison, Graham. 2018. *Destined for War.* New York: Mariner Books.
Biden, Joe. 2020. "Why America Must Lead Again," *Foreign Affairs* (March/April), 64–76.
Bolt, William. 2017. *Tariff Wars and the Politics of Jacksonian America.* Nashville, TN: Vanderbilt University Press.
Bolton, John. 2020. *The Room Where It Happened.* New York: Simon & Schuster.
Brands, Hal. 2017. "U.S. Grand Strategy in an Age of Nationalism: Fortress America and Its Alternatives," *Washington Quarterly* 40(1): 73–94.
Campbell, Kurt, and Ely Ratner. 2018. "The China Reckoning: How Beijing Defied American Expectations," *Foreign Affairs* 97: 60–70.
Campbell, Kurt, and Jake Sullivan. 2019. "Competition without Catastrophe," *Foreign Affairs* (September/October): 96–110.
Cha, Taesuh. 2017. "The Return of Jacksonianism: The International Implications of the Trump Phenomenon," *Washington Quarterly* 39(4): 83–97.
Chen, Dean. 2017. "Liberal Internationalism, Jacksonian Nationalism, and the U.S. One-China Policy," *Asian Survey* 57(5): 885–909.
———. 2019. "The Trump Administration's One-China Policy: Tilting toward Taiwan in an Era of U.S.-PRC Rivalry?" *Asian Politics & Policy* 11(2): 250–278.
Christensen, Thomas. 2015. *The China Challenge.* New York: W. W. Norton.
Davis, Bob, and Lingling Wei. 2020. *Superpower Showdown: How the Battle between Trump and Xi Threatens a New Cold War.* New York: Harper Business.
Diamond, Larry, and Orville Schell, eds. 2019. *China's Influence and American Interests.* Stanford, CA: Hoover Institute Press.
Dueck, Colin. 2020. *Age of Iron: On Conservative Nationalism.* New York: Oxford University Press.
Economy, Elizabeth. 2018. *The Third Revolution.* New York: Oxford University Press.
Friedberg, Aaron. 2012. *A Contest for Supremacy.* New York: W. W. Norton.
Fukuyama, Francis. 1992. *The End of History and the Last Man.* Free Press.
Gingrich, Newt. 2019. *Trump vs. China.* New York: Center Street.
Green, Michael. 2017. *By More than Providence: Grand Strategy and American Power in the Asia-Pacific since 1783.* New York: Columbia University Press.
Hartz, Louis. 1955. *The Liberal Tradition in America.* Harcourt Brace & Company.
Hass, Ryan. 2021. *Stronger: Adapting America's China Strategy in an Age of Competitive Interdependence.* New Haven, CT: Yale University Press.
Hemmer, Christopher. 2015. *American Pendulum: Recurring Debates in U.S. Grand Strategy.* Ithaca, NY: Cornell University Press.

Ikenberry, John G. 2011. *The Liberal Leviathan*. Princeton, NJ: Princeton University Press.

Inglehart, Ronald, and Pippa Norris. 2017. "Trump and the Populist Authoritarian Parties: The Silent Revolution in Reverse," *Perspectives on Politics* 15(2): 443–454.

Jervis, Robert, Francis Gavin, Joshua Rovner, and Diane Labrosse, eds. 2018. *Chaos in the Liberal Order: The Trump Presidency and International Politics in the Twenty-First Century*. New York: Columbia University Press.

Kegley, Charles, and Gregory Raymond. 2021. *Great Powers and World Order*. Thousand Oaks, CA: SAGE/CQ Press.

Lighthizer, Robert. 2020. "How to Make Trade Work for Workers," *Foreign Affairs* (July/August): 78–92.

Mead, Walter. 2002. *Special Providence*. New York: Routledge.

Nau, Henry. 2015. *Conservative Internationalism*. Princeton: Princeton University Press.

Pillsbury, Michael. 2015. *The Hundred-Year Marathon*. New York: St. Martin Griffin.

Ripsman, Norrin, Jeffrey Taliaferro, and Steven Lobell, eds. 2016. *Neoclassical Realist Theory of International Politics*. New York: Oxford University Press.

Rose, Gideon. 1998. "Neoclassical Realism and Theories of Foreign Policy," *World Politics* 51(1): 144–172.

Schell, Orville, and John Delury. 2014. *Wealth and Power*. New York: Random House.

Schweller, Randall. 2018. "Opposite but Compatible Nationalisms: A Neoclassical Realist Approach to the Future of U.S.-China Relations," *Chinese Journal of International Politics* 11(1): 23–48.

Smith, Tony. 2017. *Why Wilson Matters*. Princeton: Princeton University Press.

Snyder, Jack. 2019. "The Broken Bargain: How Nationalism Came Back," *Foreign Affairs* (March/April): 54–60.

Sutter, Robert. 2018. *US–China Relations: Perilous Past, Uncertain Present*. Lanham, MD: Rowman & Littlefield.

Weldes, Jutta. 1999. *Constructing National Interests*. Minneapolis: University of Minnesota Press.

Williams, William Appleman. 1959. *The Tragedy of American Diplomacy*. New York: W. W. Norton.

Zakaria, Fareed. 1998. *From Wealth to Power*. Princeton, NJ: Princeton University Press.

Index

Page references for figures are italicized

About the Contributors

Ngeow Chow Bing is Director of the Institute of China Studies at the University of Malaya. Dr. Ngeow received his PhD in Public and International Affairs from Northeastern University. He is the editor of Researching China in Southeast Asia (Routledge 2019). His scholarly articles have been published in journals such as China Review, Journal of Contemporary China, Asian Politics and Policy, Contemporary Southeast Asia, East Asia: An International Quarterly, Issues and Studies, and Problems of Post-Communism, and in many edited volumes. He has published in a range of topics, including China–Malaysia relations, the South China Sea dispute, the Belt and Road Initiative, the foreign policy of Taiwan, the development of the field of China Studies in Southeast Asia, grassroots politics in China, and the politics of think tanks and intellectuals in China.

Dean P. Chen is Associate Professor of Political Science at the School of Humanities and Global Studies, Ramapo College of New Jersey. He is the author *of U.S. Taiwan Strait Policy: The Origins of Strategic Ambiguity* (Lynne Rienner, 2012) and *U.S.–China Rivalry and Taiwan's Mainland Policy: Security, Nationalism, and the 1992 Consensus* (Palgrave Macmillan, 2017), and his articles have appeared in *Asian Survey, International Relations of the Asia-Pacific, Asian Security,* and *Pacific Focus.* Chen served as coordinator for the Conference Group on Taiwan Studies of the American Political Science Association (2014–2016). He was recipient of the Taiwan Fellowship in 2014 from the Ministry of Foreign Affairs, Republic of China (Taiwan). In 2017–2018, he was a US Fulbright Scholar in China. Email: dchen@ramapo.edu.

Gordon C. K. Cheung is Associate Professor and Director of the Centre for Contemporary Chinese Studies in the School of Government & International

Affairs (SGIA) at Durham University. He has been editing the journal East Asia: An International Quarterly since 2004. He previously taught and held visiting positions in the Academia Sinica, the Chinese University of Hong Kong, University of Hawaii, University of Hong Kong, Lingnan University, National University of Singapore, Oxford University, Renmin University, and University of Tubingen, and most recently was Wei Lun Distinguished Visiting Professor at Tsinghua University in 2016. He is the author of *Market Liberalism: American Foreign Policy toward China* (1998), *China Factors: Political Perspectives and Economic Interactions* (2007), *Intellectual Property Rights in China: Politics of Piracy, Trade and Protection* (2009) and *China in the Global Political Economy: From Developmental to Entrepreneurial* (2018). His research focuses on China and the global political economy, cross-strait relations, and the global Chinese.

Michael Fowler is a graduate of Dartmouth College, University of Virginia, and Harvard Law School and serves as Professor of Political Science at the University of Louisville, where he specializes in international law and organization, negotiation and conflict resolution, and international relations. A two-time Fulbright Scholar to Japan, he has also lectured at Bond University in Australia, the China Foreign Affairs University in Beijing, the Diplomatic Academy of Vietnam, and the Institute of Foreign Affairs in Laos. Professor Fowler has published seven books. Two were coauthored with Julie M. Bunck and published by Pennsylvania State University Press—*Bribes, Bullets, and Intimidation: Drug Trafficking and the Law in Central America* and *Law, Power, and the Sovereign State: The Evolution and Application of the Concept of Sovereignty*. Another was a book coedited with the former Assistant Secretary-General of the United Nations, Sumihiro Kuyama—*Envisioning Reform: Enhancing UN Accountability in the Twenty-first Century*. Formerly a practicing attorney, Professor Fowler has been admitted to practice law in Maryland, Massachusetts, and Washington, D.C.

Steve Hess is an Associate Professor at Transylvania University in Lexington, Kentucky, with degrees from Miami University (PhD in Political Science), the University of Louisville (MA in Political Science), and Hanover College (BA in International Studies). A specialist in comparative authoritarianism, he has written two books, *Authoritarian Landscapes: Popular Mobilization and the Institutional Sources of Resilience in Nondemocracies* (Springer, 2013) and *Charting the Roots of Anti-Chinese Populism in Africa* (coauthored with Richard Aidoo, Springer, 2015), and published over twenty research articles and book chapters. A returned Peace Corps Volunteer (China, 2006–2008), Dr. Hess has established Peace Corps Prep partnerships at both Transylvania

University and the University of Bridgeport. He has also served as a Taiwan Fellow (National Chengchi University) and an expert witness on the United States–China Economic and Security Review Commission, an advisory body to the US Congress.

R. Lincoln Hines is a PhD andidate in the Government Department at Cornell University. He was previously a Guggenheim predoctoral fellow at the National Air and Space Museum, a visiting researcher at Peking University's School of International Studies, and a Nonresident WSD Handa Fellow at the Pacific Forum. His research focuses on international security and Chinese foreign policy, examining the domestic motives behind China's pursuit of space capabilities. More broadly, he focuses on the relationship between international prestige, nationalism, and domestic politics in foreign policy. He received his MA from the American University School of International Service and his BA from the University of Virginia

Benjamin Tze Ern Ho is Assistant Professor at the China Programme, S. Rajaratnam School of International Studies (RSIS), Singapore. He obtained his PhD from the Department of International Relations at the London School of Economics and Political Science. His research focus includes the study of China's international relations, with an emphasis on Chinese political worldview and exceptionalism thinking. Other research interests include security multilateralism in the Asia Pacific region with a focus on regional institutions and fora, national security (intelligence), and the sociology of religion and public theology (Christianity). His research articles have been published in the *America Journal of Chinese Studies, China Quarterly, Journal of Contemporary China, East Asia: An International Quarterly, Alternatives: Global, Local, Political, Asia Policy, Australian Journal of International Affairs and the Yale Journal of International Affairs*. Since joining RSIS, Benjamin has been involved in a number of think-tank events and conferences, including the Track II Network of ASEAN Defence and Security Institutions (NADI), the Pacific Young Leaders program, and CSCAP meetings.

Shiping Hua is Calvin & Helen Lang Distinguished Chair in Asian Studies, Professor of Political Science, and Director of the Asian Studies Program at the University of Louisville. He has published fourteen books in English, edited or single-authored, including *Chinese Legal Culture and Constitutional Order, Chinese Utopianism: A Comparative Study of Reformist Thought with Japan and Russia (1898–1997),* and *Scientism and Humanism: Two Cultures in Post-Mao China (1978–1989).* He edits three book series, "Asia in the New Millennium" with University Press of Kentucky, "Comparative Asian

Politics" with Routledge, and "Contemporary World's Scholarly Classics: Political Science Series" (translations) with Renmin University Press.

Zhimin Lin received his BA from Fudan University, MPA from Princeton University, and PhD in political science from the University of Washington. He has taught at Valparaiso University and the University of Macau (2005–2008) and served as director of the Chinese and Japanese Studies Program from 1998 through 2014. He is currently Professor of Political Science in the Department of Political Science and International Relations and Adjunct Professor at the University of Macau. His publications cover China's politics, China's foreign policy, US–China relations, and US politics. His most recent research projects include a book on Sino-Latin American relations from both the elite and popular perspectives, a monograph on the radicalization of Chinese global posture under Xi, and several articles on the shifting patterns of US–China relations given the fundamental changes taking place in both countries.

Yeh-Chung Lu is Professor of the Department of Diplomacy and former director of the International Master's Program in International Studies (IMPIS) at National Cheng-chi University (NCCU), Taipei, Taiwan. He held visiting positions at the Henry L. Stimson Center (summer 2014) and the Woodrow Wilson International Center for Scholars (summer 2013), both in Washington, D.C., and at Yonsei University (summer 2012), Seoul, Korea.

Dr. Lu focuses on US–China relations, and American and Chinese foreign policy is his academic expertise. In addition, his research interests include IR theories, international security issues, and international institutions. His publications have appeared in scholarly journals such as *Issues & Studies*, *Journal of Contemporary China*, *Georgetown Journal of International Affairs*, *New Asia*, *Prospect Journal*, *Wenti yu Yanjiu*, *EurAmerica*, and *Prospect Quarterly*, and he has edited books. He has also peer reviewed articles in *Perspectives on Politics* and *Asian Politics and Policy* and other publications in Taiwan. Dr. Lu received his doctoral degree in Political Science from George Washington University, and his BA and MA in diplomacy from NCCU in Taipei, Taiwan, R.O.C. (E-mail: yclu@nccu.edu.tw)

Gregory J. Moore (PhD University of Denver) is Professor of Global Studies and Politics at Colorado Christian University. He is President of the Association of Chinese Political Studies, is a member of the (US) National Committee on United States–China Relations, and was a fellow at the Foreign Policy Institute of Johns Hopkins University's School of Advanced International Studies in Washington, 2019–2020. In addition to many articles on international relations and Chinese foreign policy, he is the author/editor of *North Korean Nuclear Operationality: Regional Security and Non-Proliferation* (Johns Hopkins University Press, 2014), author of *Niebuhrian International Relations: The Ethics of Foreign Policymaking* (Oxford University Press, 2020), and *An International Relations Research Methods Toolkit* (forthcoming, Routledge), and has another book in the works on Sino-American relations.

Robert Sutter is Professor of Practice of International Affairs at the Elliott School of George Washington University (2011–). He also served as Director of the school's main undergraduate program involving over two thousand students from 2013 to 2019. His earlier full-time position was Visiting Professor of Asian Studies at Georgetown University (2001–2011).

A PhD graduate in History and East Asian Languages from Harvard University, Sutter has published twenty-two books (four with multiple editions), over three hundred articles, and several hundred government reports dealing with contemporary East Asian and Pacific countries and their relations with the United States. His most recent book is *Chinese Foreign Relations: Power and Policy of an Emerging Global Force,* 5th edition (Rowman & Littlefield, 2021).

Sutter's government career (1968–2001) saw service as Senior Specialist and Director of the Foreign Affairs and National Defense Division of the Congressional Research Service, the National Intelligence Officer for East Asia and the Pacific at the US Government's National Intelligence Council, the China division director at the Department of State's Bureau of Intelligence and Research, and professional staff member of the Senate Foreign Relations Committee.

Chung-Chian Teng received his PhD in Political Science at Northwestern University in 1985. Currently, he is Distinguished Professor of Diplomacy, National Chengchi University (NCCU). In addition, he was the Dean of the College of International Affairs as well as the Chairperson of the Department of Diplomacy, NCCU. As major service for the academic community, Professor Teng is a member of the Academic Advisory Committee of Institute of Political Science, Academia Sinica. Furthermore, he is a member of the editorial board for both *Chinese Political Science Review* and *Global Political Review.*

His specialized focus is in international political economy, foreign policy, and Latin American studies. His recent major publications are as follows: "Taiwan and Its Latin American Allies: An Uphill Diplomatic Campaign," in *External Powers in Latin America: Geopolitics between Neo-extractivism and South-South Cooperation* (2021); "The Development of Mainland China's Economic Relations with Latin America under Xi Jinping Adminis-tration" (in Chinese), in *The Journal of International Relations* (December 2019); "America's Perspective and Policy Behavior toward China in South China Sea" (in Chinese), in *Review of Global Politics* (January 2018); and "The Pattern of China's Financial Initiative in Latin America and the Carib-bean," in *Issues & Studies* (March, 2017).

Qi Wang is a PhD candidate at the Department of Public Administration and Government, University of Macau.

Larry M. Wortzel is Senior Fellow in Asian Security at the American For-eign Policy Council. A veteran Asia scholar with extensive government and military experience, Dr. Wortzel served two tours of duty as a military attaché in the American Embassy in China, and also was assigned in Singapore, Thai-land, and on the demilitarized zone in South Korea. On the faculty of the US Army War College, Dr. Wortzel was Director of the Strategic Studies Institute and concurrently professor of Asian studies. He retired from the US Army as a colonel at the end of 1999. Then he was director of the Asian Studies Center at The Heritage Foundation and also vice president for foreign policy and defense studies at Heritage. Dr. Wortzel served as a commissioner on the U.S.–China Economic and Security Review Commission for nineteen years; he was chairman of the commission for two years. He is a member of the Council on Foreign Relations and the International Institute of Strategic Stud-ies. A graduate of the US Army War College, Dr. Wortzel earned his Doctor of Philosophy degree in Political Science from the University of Hawaii-Manoa.

Jiakun Jack Zhang is Assistant Professor of Political Science at the Uni-versity of Kansas (KU) and Director of the KU Trade War Lab (TWL). He received his PhD from the Department of Political Science at UC San Diego and holds a bachelor's degree in political science and a certificate in East Asian studies from Duke University. In 2018–2019, he was a postdoctoral research fellow in the Niehaus Center for Globalization and Governance at Princeton University. His research explores the political economy of trade and conflict in East Asia. He is currently working on a number of projects on the U.S.–China trade war as well as a book manuscript on the national secu-rity implications of economic interdependence with China.

Dr. Zhang has been the recipient of various grants and awards, includ-ing a Fulbright US Student Grant, the Minerva Research Initiative DECUR Partnership, the Smith Richardson Foundation World Politics and Statecraft Fellowship, and the University of California Institute on Global Conflict and Cooperation Herb York Dissertation Fellowship. He is an alumnus of the Mansfield-Luce Asia Scholars Network, the Bridging the Gap Scholar Network, the YPFP US–China Futures Project, CSIS Pacific Forum Young Leaders Program, and the Forum for American/Chinese Exchange at Stanford (FACES). Prior to entering academia, Dr. Zhang worked as a China researcher for the Eurasia Group and consulted for the Economist Intelligence Unit. Follow him on Twitter @HanFeiTzu.

www.ingramcontent.com/pod-product-compliance
Lightning Source LLC
Chambersburg PA
CBHW050631280326
41932CB00015B/2602